Great Britain Laws, William Leader

The Franchise

A Manual of Registration and Election Law and Practice (Parliamentary and

Municipal) - Together with the Acts of Parliament Relating Thereto

Great Britain Laws, William Leader

The Franchise
A Manual of Registration and Election Law and Practice (Parliamentary and Municipal) -
Together with the Acts of Parliament Relating Thereto

ISBN/EAN: 9783337139230

Printed in Europe, USA, Canada, Australia, Japan

Cover: Foto ©Suzi / pixelio.de

More available books at **www.hansebooks.com**

THE FRANCHISE,

A MANUAL OF

REGISTRATION AND ELECTION LAW AND PRACTICE

(PARLIAMENTARY AND MUNICIPAL),

TOGETHER WITH THE

ACTS OF PARLIAMENT

RELATING THERETO, AND

REFERENCES TO THE LEADING CASES THEREON,

Brought down to the close of the Session 42 & 43 Vic. (1879),

BEING AN INDEX

TO THE LAW AND PRACTICE OF

REGISTRATION, REVISION, ELECTION & PETITION,

BY

WILLIAM LEADER, B.A., LL.B.,

SOLICITOR OF THE SUPREME COURT, LATE REGISTRATION AND ELECTION
AGENT FOR SOUTH-WEST LANCASHIRE.

LONDON:

TO BE HAD OF THE AUTHOR,
39, EUSTON SQUARE, N.W.,
AND AT ALL BOOKSELLERS.

1879.

PREFACE.

THERE has been a long-felt and frequently expressed desire for a concise Handbook on the Laws relating to the "Franchise," which shall be convenient for ready reference, and at the same time present, in a moderate compass, to all interested, whether Voter, Party Agent, Official, or Candidate, the whole matter as it were "in a nutshell."

This the Author has endeavoured to do, by detailing in a popular manner, and in the form of a Dictionary, the Customary Rights and Statutory Laws affecting the Vote, short references to the cases which have arisen thereon, and been decided, both on Registration Appeals and Election Petitions, with the *times*, *forms*, and *rules* to be observed in the Revision Court, at the Polling Booth, and subsequently in proceedings on Election Petitions.

The principal Acts, nineteen in number, together with the Judges' Rules on Petitions, and such of the Forms as are not given in the Acts, will be found in the Appendix.

The Author has attempted to make a somewhat tedious and complex subject clear and intelligible, to the general as well as the professional reader, and trusts that this effort at simplicity may be a sufficient recommendation.

CONTENTS.

ADDENDA.

—o—

CASES DECIDED ON REGISTRATION APPEALS.

Michaelmas Term, 1879.

———

Ford v. Drew.—In the case of an articled clerk to a solicitor, claiming to be upon the list of voters for the City of Exeter, in respect of a freehold rent charge, (a qualification which requires residence within 7 miles of the borough for 6 months previous to the 15th day of July), and who had a room kept for him at the house of his father, which was situated within the 7 miles, but who, during the qualifying period, had gone to London to complete his articles, held not to be entitled, reversing the decision of the Revising Barrister.

Mr. Justice Grove was of opinion that the claim to vote had not been made out; or, in other words, that the claimant did not reside for six months previous to July within the City, or within seven statutable miles thereof. He paid no rent for the room at his father's house, and he had simply the permission that a father gave to a son who was not emancipated to reside in the paternal home. His residence there would depend upon two circumstances—the permission of his father to be there, and the permission of his master to be away from the office. This was not a residence within the meaning of the Act of Parliament.

Mortlock v. Farrer.—In the City of Westminster there are 11 Parishes, or precincts, within the Parliamentary Borough, each having its own Overseers. In one of such Parishes there was no Lodger List, but in the other 10 the Overseers of each made out such List, pursuant to 41 & 42 Vic. c. 26, s. 22. An objection was made to one Allen, a lodger, in respect of lodgings in St. James's Parish, as follows : " I object to your name being returned on the list of persons entitled to vote as lodgers." *Cases*

It was contended on the part of Allen and others, whose ~~appeals~~ were consolidated, that such notice of objection was bad, inasmuch as it did not specify upon *which List* the name of the party objected to was to be found, and the Barrister upheld the contention, deciding that the notice should have specified the particular list in which the name appeared, following the note to the form of objection given in the Schedule to the Act.

The Solicitor-General, for the Appellant, argued that under the statute there was only one list of lodger voters, and, therefore, that the notice of objection was good. In this particular case, also, there could have been no inconvenience from the form of the notice, for the person objected to had previously been upon the lodgers' list, and had sent in his claim to be retained upon that list for the ensuing year in respect of the same lodgings. The claim he made was to be retained upon the lodger list for St. James's, and he sent his claim to the overseers of that parish, so that he perfectly well knew the list upon which his name was, and could not be misled by any defect or omission from the notice in this respect. The most important point, he admitted, was what was the construction which should be placed on the word "list" in the statute. It was provided there that if there were more than one list of Parliamentary voters, the notice of objection should specify the list to which the objection referred. Did this mean the particular list made out for such particular parish, or did the list mean that particular *class* of voters of which there were separate lists, such as householders, reserved rights, freemen, lodgers? He submitted that the latter was the true meaning, and, therefore, that the notice was sufficient.—Mr. Wright, for the Respondent, said that his client was High Bailiff of Westminster, he having been made Respondent in his official capacity. He had no further wish in the matter than to obtain the decision of the Court upon that point, though he would regret that in any event 400 persons should be struck off the list of voters without the merits of their claims being enquired into. The learned counsel contended that the name of the parish should have been inserted in the notice, and he referred their Lordships to various decided cases, and to several enactments in the statutes in support of this contention. The Court held that the Barrister was wrong.—Judgment for the Appellant.

Hall v. Cropper.—This was an appeal from the Borough of Nottingham. The name of Boswell, of 2, Ivy-row, householder, was objected to, but the notice of objection did not state the parish in which the qualifying property was situate. The Parliamentary borough contained the parishes of St. Mary, St. Peter, and St. Nicholas, and Ivy-row was in the first. Each parish published separate lists of voters. The Barrister held the notice to be bad, and it was against such decision that the appeal was brought.

Lord Coleridge delivered an elaborate judgment in both the above cases in favour of the appellants, reversing the decisions of the Revising Barristers. If the contention of the Respondents was right, and the word "list" meant "parish list," the voters in both cases were entitled to succeed; for it was conceded that no such information had been conveyed in the notices in those cases. But another interpretation was found in the Act itself, for the word "division" points out that there are to be "lists" made out in "divisions," the word "division" being expressly defined to be divisions not parochial; and thirdly, there was the previous Act of 6 Vict. cap. 18. That dealt both with county registration and borough registration, and it had a variety of forms applying to both. Among these were forms of objection to overseers and parties in counties and boroughs, and if anything was clear from that Act it was that if you objected to a county vote you must specify the parish, whereas if you objected to a borough vote it was not necessary. The words and form of notice in the old Act had been adopted in the Act under consideration. The two Acts were *in pari materia*. The contention of the Respondent could not have been made under the former; and, as the same language was used substantially in both, the Legislature could not have contemplated that different interpretations should be put on the same words, and that in the latter Act they should have a meaning which they could not bear in the first. He did not think it meant parochial list, and it was somewhat difficult to say what it did mean; but the difficulty was not such as to overbear the violence that would be done to the Act if the main interpretation contended for by the Respondent was to prevail. No hardship had accrued to the parties objected to in these cases. Here, year by year, a local claim had to be made by local people, in respect of a local qualification. He was of opinion, therefore, that the appeals must be allowed.

Fowle v. Trevor.—Where the Barrister had decided against the claim of a sub-lessee, who held under a memorandum of agreement, from year to year,

and was in *possession*, on the ground that the landlord had himself no sub-
stantive rights, being tenant to his mother under a parole agreement, it was
held that claimant occupied *as tenant*, and that the title of the landlord
could not be gone into, reversing the Barrister's decision.

Trevor v. Fowle.—The claim to vote was in respect of a granary over a
barn, which was approached by a movable ladder placed outside. The
Barrister, though with some doubt, arrived at the conclusion that this
granary was not a " building " within the meaning of the statute, and therefore he disallowed the claim. The Court held that in so deciding he was
wrong. Appeal allowed.

Sargent v. Rodd.—Where an objector described himself as " on the list for
the Parish of the Borough of Liskeard," part of the Parliamentary Borough
being known as the " borough " of Liskeard, and another part as the " parish "
of Liskeard, but no part being known as the " Parish of the Borough," it
was contended that the notice was bad, but it was answered that the notice
followed the form in the Parliamentary and Municipal Registration Act, 1878,
and that the " Borough of Liskeard " was really a " parish " within the
definition in the statute. The Revising Barrister held the notice to be sufficient, and struck off the names objected to. Lord Coleridge said that the
notice was in accordance with the form in the statute; and besides, the
part of the " borough," having separate officers and separate rates, was really
a " parish " within the definition in the statute. The notice was, therefore,
good. Decision affirmed.

Hayward v. Bromley.—Where a voter had the separate occupation of one
room in a house, the remainder being similarly let out to other persons—
such room or tenement not being separately rated, but the landlord, who
did not reside in the house, being duly rated for the whole in all respects,
and had paid the rates by agreement with the tenant, the tenant paying a
higher rent in consequence—and where the Barrister, holding that the
interpretation of the term " dwelling-house " contained in 41 & 42 Vic. c.
26, s. 5, which is declared to be in substitution for the interpretation thereof
contained in 30 & 31 Vic. c. 102, s. 6, had declared the vote to be good,
his decision was affirmed. This case did not raise any point as to whether
such separate room was *rateable* (it being contended that *rateability* and not
rating was here involved), and the Court would not hear any argument
ad hoc.

James v. Howarth.—Where an objector signed as follows : " Henry James,
of 36, New King-street, on the list of voters for the Parish of Walcot," there
being 2 lists for the Parish of Walcot viz.,—list 1. division 1, and list 1.
division 3, and without stating that he was on the " Parliamentary" list, the
Barrister held such notice of objection to be bad, inasmuch as it omitted
to state in the description of the objector that he was on the " Parliamentary " list, and also because it omitted to define on which of the said several
lists his name appeared, and that he had no power to amend. Lord
Coleridge was of opinion that there was no foundation for the contention
that there should be appended to the description of the objector the particular list on which his name appeared, it being clear that a sufficient
intimation was conveyed on the face of the objection as to where the objector
lived, and what his qualification was. As to the omission of the word
" Parliamentary," inasmuch as 41 & 42 Vic. c. 26, includes both Parliamentary and Municipal lists, it was open to grave question whether that word
was not essential. The Barrister considered that he had no power to insert
such word, and he did not do so, but it was clear that he would have done
so, had he felt that he possessed the power. Clearly he had such power.
Here was a *mistake*, which might very reasonably be amended under sub-sec.
2 of sec. 28 of the Act of 1878. Giving a fair and full meaning to the effect

of that section, the Court held that a mistake had been made which ought to have been rectified, and which the Court would now make. Appeal allowed.

Hayward v. Scott.—This was a case in which the Revising Barrister at Bath had been asked to expunge the names of nine voters, on the ground that they had received parochial relief within the year, and 51 others on the ground that they had not owned or occupied premises within the same period. No notice of objection had, however, been given to the claimants, and the Revising Barrister retained their names on the register. For the appellant it was contended that under 41 & 42 Vic. c. 26, s. 28, sub.-sec. 7, as the grounds of disqualification were admitted, the fact of no notice having been given was immaterial, and the names should have been expunged, as of persons " incapacitated by any law or statute." The Court held that the word " incapacitated," in section 28, sub-section 7, meant a general incapacity to vote at all, and not such an incapacity as dispensed with the necessity of notice being given to those whose votes were objected to. The Revising Barrister, therefore, was right, and the appeal must be dismissed, with costs.

Pickard v. Baylis.—This was a consolidated appeal from the borough of Chelsea, and eight new claims to the lodger franchise were involved in it. In one case the amount of rent paid was not stated, and in the others the address of the landlord was omitted. The Barrister decided not to amend by supplying the amount of rent in the 4th column, or the landlord's address in the 5th column, and disallowed the claims. The question was whether he ought to have amended them under either sub-secs. 1 or 2 of 41 & 42 Vic. c. 26, s. 28.

Lord Coleridge, after hearing Mr. Crompton for the appellant, no one appearing for the other side, and after consulting the other Judges, said that they were not unanimous in their opinions. The question raised was an important one, and might affect the whole lodger franchise of the country, and they should, therefore, request the Attorney-General to argue the case, or appoint some one to do so, on behalf of the respondent.

On the re-hearing, the case being argued by Mr. Clark for the respondent, the Court held that the decision of the Barrister was correct, and should be affirmed; that the new lodger claims do not form part of any " List " upon which a name can be "retained," or from which a name can be " expunged," but are only the materials from which the " List of Lodgers " is eventually formed; that such claims are not a " List " within ss. 22 or 23 of 41 & 42 Vic. c. 26; that, therefore, the omission of the rent from the 4th column, and the landlord's address from the 5th column, were not " mistakes" with which the Barrister was *obliged* to deal under sub-sec. 1 of sec. 28, but matters with which he *might* deal under sub-sec. 2 ; that he had clearly exercised his discretion in not supplying the omissions, but in following the established practice; that every lodger should give full particulars in his claim, and that evidence of such particulars should not be given for the first time in court, the Barrister's duty being to *revise*, not to construct the Lists.

Porrett v. Lord and *Spencer v. Harrison* stood over for judgment.

THE FRANCHISE.

ABATEMENT.—An election Petition (Parliamentary or Municipal) is abated by the death of a sole petitioner, or of the survivor of several, but it does not appear that by the death of one, or more, of several petitioners, a petition is abated. Abatement does not release the petitioner's estate from the liability for costs previously incurred. Notice must be given by the parties interested (*semble*, the personal representatives of the deceased) in the same manner as notice of application to withdraw. A petitioner may be substituted by the Court or Judge. (Security as in the case of a new petition). 31 & 32 Vic. c. 125, s. 37, R. 50. 35 & 36 Vic. c. 60, s. 17, R. 50.

Where the rateable value of any hereditaments does not exceed, in the metropolis £20, in Liverpool £13, in Manchester or Birmingham £10, and elsewhere £8, a voluntary agreement (which requires to be stamped, when the subject matter is of the value of £5) may be made between the Overseers and the owner, to receive the rates from him, and to allow him an *abatement*, or commission, not exceeding 25 per cent., he agreeing to become liable for any term *not less than a year*, and to pay *whether the premises are occupied or not*. The occupier's liability continues, and if the owner omits to pay, and no power of distress upon the owner's goods is available, the occupier's goods may be distrained and sold. 32 & 33 Vic. c. 41, ss. 3-12. A person occupying his own property is not an "owner," within the meaning of the above definition. (*Poor Law Board Circ.*, 23rd *Nov.*, 1869.)

The word "dwelling-house" as used in s. 4 of the last mentioned Act does not bear the extended meaning given by 41 & 42 Vic. c. 26, s. 5.

The enactment contained in s. 19 of 32 & 33 Vic. c. 41, that, whether the rate is collected from the owner or occupier, or the owner is liable instead of the occupier, the occupier's name is to be entered in the rate book, and he is to be deemed "duly rated" for any qualification or franchise as therein mentioned, is not to apply exclusively to cases where an *agreement* has been made under s. 3, or an *Order* made under s. 4, but is to be of *general application*. 41 & 42 Vic. c. 26, s. 14.

Such abatement, commission, or deduction is not to defeat any qualification or franchise depending upon rating or the payment of rates, by reason of any irregularity or informality. 42 & 43 Vic. c. 10, sec. 2.

B

There appears to be therefore no longer any Franchise, actually dependent upon *rating* or the *payment of rates* on the part of the voter, *e.g.*, where the occupation is of such a value that it does not admit of the Statutory composition and the occupier's name is omitted, sec. 14 being *of general application*, he being omitted, but the rates being paid by someone, is entitled to be registered, apparently contradicting the unrepealed Statutes, 2 Will. 4, c. 45, s. 27, and 30 & 31 Vic. c. 102, ss. 3-6.

ABDUCTION (See "*Undue Influence*") may be either "by open force, or violence, or the threat thereof," or "by fraudulent contrivance," such as by giving drink, drugging, or by any false pretence, and is a misdemeanour. Any voter proved guilty is to be struck off the Register, and his name inserted in a separate list. Penalty £50, for which any person may sue within a year. 17 & 18 Vic. c. 102. (*Staleybridge, Coventry, and Northallerton Cases.*)

ABODE, place of, is to be inserted in the *second* column of the Register. It forms no part of the qualification in the *third* column. The object is to give information as to the identity of the voter, and where he may be met with. If the party has no fixed place of abode "he must give as good a description as he can of the region where he may be found." (Erle J., *Walker v. Payne.*) For officers in H.M.S., or persons travelling, "travelling abroad" or on H.M.S. would be a sufficient description. The Revising Barrister has power to correct any mistake, and to amend in cases where the place of abode is either wholly omitted or insufficiently described, but he should have proof of the facts. (*Luckett v. Knowles.*) And a point is likely to arise, if not to lead to an appeal, as to the power of a Barrister to amend in these cases. Under 41 & 42 Vic. c. 26, sec. 28 (6) some of the Revising Barristers have held that an *incorrect* is an insufficient description, and that if the correction was not forthcoming the name should be struck out.

At the Revision for the City of London, Sept., 1879,

The Revising Barrister said he desired to refer to the way in which the objection was raised in a large number of cases to the abode of the voter. The question whether the Barrister could touch the address had been very closely argued before the Court of Common Pleas, and decided under the old Act: but under the present Act, although the address was incorrect, he had the power to amend it if another address—that was to say, the proper address—could be supplied. The Act made it very clear that, in the absence of the proper address, whether the party was objected to or not, he ought to expunge the name; but, to prevent surprise, he would not do this without notice. By means of these objections notice had been given to the voter, and he thought the objector was perfectly justified in the course he had taken, because the address on the list did not enable him to find the voter, who was, therefore, bound to give his proper address.

A voter changing his place of abode, or whose place of abode is incorrectly stated, or who shall have received a notice of objection grounded thereon, and whose qualification remains the same, (on the 31st of July, in Counties, 15th of July in Parliamentary and Municipal boroughs), may, instead of attending the Court and giving proof, make a statutory declaration before a J.P., or Commissioner for Oaths, in the form given, or he may send in a *fresh claim*, attend the Revision Court, and supply the true place of abode, at the same time proving that his qualification remains the same. 28 Vic. c. 36, s. 10, Sch. B., and 41 & 42 Vic. c. 26, s. 24, Form (M.)

A County voter, whose place of abode is not in the same Polling District as his qualification, but in the same County, may make a claim to the Barrister* to be allowed to vote in the District where his place of abode is, and a voter whose place of abode is out of the County may make a claim to vote at any polling place in the County, the Barrister to insert opposite his name the place where he is registered to vote, and he cannot vote elsewhere. 6 Vic. c. 18, s. 36.

No form is given, but a claim may be made as follows :—

County of   } To   Esq
(or Riding, &c., of } the Barrister appointed to revise the Lists of
the county of)   } Voters, &c.

I   whose name appears on
the List of voters (or list of claims) for the Township of
and whose place of abode as stated in such List is within such county,
but not in the Polling District of   (*or* is not within such county),
claim to vote, at any election for the said county, at the Polling place
of   within the said county.

Dated   Signed

Service of a *notice of objection* (if not made through the post or personally), may be made by leaving it at "the place of abode as described in the List." Whether such service is good, is a question of fact for the Barrister.

A notice pushed under a door between 9 and 10 p.m., no one answering the knock, was held to be insufficient. (*Watson v. Pitt.*) And service of such a notice at *the place of business* of the person objected will not answer the requirement.

If no "place of abode" is described in the List, or if it be out of the Kingdom, notice is sufficient if given, in the case of a County Voter, to the Overseers, and to the occupying tenant in the case of a City or Borough Voter to the Overseers and Town Clerk, and in the case of a "Freeman being a Liveryman" of the City of London, to the Secondaries of the City, and Clerk of the Livery Company.

* Where not otherwise stated. "Barrister" means "Revising Barrister."

ABSENCE on H.M.S. does not permanently disqualify Voters entitled under reserved rights, but their rights revive on their return, 2 Will. 4, c. 45, s. 33, and the temporary absence of a Borough Voter does not disqualify, if the facts show that there is an "actual residence" and an "animus revertendi." (*Whithorn v. Thomas, Ford v. Hart, Beal v. Ford.*)

ABSTRACTS of the number of claims and objections are to be transmitted to the Revising Barristers by the Clerks of the Peace and Town Clerks respectively. 6 Vic. c. 18, s. 31.

ACCEPTANCE of an Office of profit under the Crown does not stay an Election Petition. 31 & 32 Vic. c. 125, s. 18.

Acceptance of an *old* Office of profit *from* the Crown vacates a seat, but the holder is eligible for re-election, and the same where the Office has devolved upon the Crown. Acceptance of an *old* Office *under* the Crown does not vacate the seat. But the acceptance of a *new* Office, either *from or under* the Crown, absolutely disqualifies. 6 Ann, c. 7, ss. 25-26.

Where a Member has been returned after accepting any of the offices mentioned in 30 & 31 Vic. c. 102, s. 52, he may accept any of those offices in lieu of, or in succession to, the first office, without vacating his seat.

'' ACTION.—Sheriffs, Clerks of the Peace, and others, wilfully contravening the Registration Act, 1843, liable to action. 6 Vic. c. 18, s. 17.

Actions to recover Penalties under the C. P. P. Acts must be brought within one year of the commission of the offence, and must be prosecuted without delay. 17 & 18 Vic. c. 102, s. 14. General allegations are sufficient in such Actions. 26 & 27 Vic. c. 29, s. 6.

ACTUAL OCCUPATION.—One of the four elements in some franchises: *tenement, value, occupation, and estate.* Freeholds for life or lives, of the annual value of 40s. but under £10, do not qualify, either for a County, or for a City or Town being a County of itself, unless the owner be in actual bonâ fide occupation for 6 months previous to July 31st in the former, and for 12 months previous to 15th July in the latter, unless they were acquired before the passing of the Reform Act *(7th June, 1832),* or since then by descent, marriage, marriage settlement, devise, or promotion. 2 Will. 4, c. 45, s. 18.

Sub-lessees, and assignees of a sub-lease, for the unexpired residue of a term of years, must be "in actual occupation." (See "*Assignees.*")

A £10 occupier in Boroughs must also be in "actual" occupation, as "*owner or tenant.*" Occupation by a servant, as manager to a Publican, Porter to a Lodge, Keeper to a Chapel, Gardener to a Park, is not a sufficient occupation. (See "*Occupation.*")

ACTUAL POSSESSION is also an ingredient. No freeholder, copy holder, customary tenant, or tenant in "ancient demesne" in Counties is entitled unless he shall have been in *actual possession*, or in receipt of the rents and profits, for six calendar months previous to 31st July in any year except in the case of property coming by descent, succession, marriage, marriage settlement, devise, or promotion.

Actual Possession means possession *in fact*, not *in law*. In the case of a rent charge under a grant at Common Law, it has been held to mean actual manual receipt of the rent, or of some part of it, or something in lieu of it, within the Statutory six months. (*Murray v. Thornley.*)

But where a rent charge is created by a conveyance *to uses* the grantee acquires a "lawful seisin, estate, and possession" immediately, under the Stat. of Uses, 27 Hen. 8, c. 10, and it has been held that such possession was "actual possession" under 2 Will. 4, c. 45, s. 20, though no part of the rent had been received. In *Heelis v. Blain*, where A in the month of January conveyed a rent charge of £   to B and his heirs, habendum to B and his heirs *to the use of* the five sons of A and their heirs, as tenants in common, the five sons were held to have been in possession for six months previous to 31st July, though there had been no receipt of rent until the following June. The foregoing cases were followed in the case of *Webster v. The Overseers of Ashton-under-Lyne, Orme's Case*, where A, by indenture dated the 13th Oct., 1871, granted "unto B, C, and D, and their heirs, a rent charge, habendum unto the said B, C, and D, their heirs and assigns, to the use of the said B, C, and D, their heirs and assigns for ever, as tenants in common." The first half yearly payment was duly made on the 5th of April, 1872. It was held that the use being specific, and not inconsistent with the rest of the habendum, the habendum must be read as specific, and that the deed operated as a grant at common law, and not under the Statute of Uses ; and therefore, upon the authority of *Murray v. Thornley*, that the grantees had not been in the "actual possession" of the rent charge for six calendar months previous to the last day of July, 1872, as required by the 2 Will. 4, c. 45, s. 26, and were not entitled to be registered in that year as county voters. And that case was held distinguishable from *Heelis v. Blain*, in which it was held that where a rent charge is created by a conveyance *to uses*, the grantee takes immediate seizin by the words of the statute, and is, after six months, entitled to be registered in respect thereof, notwithstanding he may not have received any part of the rent, the Statute of Uses having no application except to a case where *one* person stands seized to the use of *another*.

In a grant, "Unto, to the use of, in trust for," the word "*unto*" gives an estate at Common Law, the words "*to the use of*," the use, executed by the Statute, *i.e.*, clothed with the legal estate, and

the words "*in trust for*," a trust estate not executed by the Statute.

Persons seized of estates for life or lives, in lands or tenements of any tenure, of the clear yearly value of £5, must be in "actual possession" for six months, and lessees and assignees for the unexpired residues of any terms originally created for not less than 60 years of the clear yearly value of £5, must be in "actual possession" for six months previous to 31st of July, to qualify them for a County vote. 30 & 31 Vic. c. 102, s. 5.

Freeholders and Burgage owners in Cities and Towns being Counties of themselves, having estates of inheritance, and freeholders and Burgage owners in Cities and towns being Counties, having estates for life or lives of the value of £10, must be in possession for 12 months previous to 15th July, unless they shall have acquired by descent, &c. (See "*Franchise.*")

Mortgagors in actual possession, or in receipt of the rents and profits, are entitled, notwithstanding the mortgage, but the property must be of the qualifying value above all charges, including the interest payable under the mortgage.

A *cestui que trust* in "actual possession," though he may receive the rents, &c., through the trustee, is entitled (See "*Agreement*," "*Beneficiaries.*")

ADDITIONAL JUDGE, An, for trial of Election Petitions, was appointed by 42 & 43 Vic., c. 75.

Additional lodgings in any year or two successive years not to be deemed different lodgings. (See "*Lodgings.*") 41 & 42 Vic. c. 26, s. 6 (1).

ADDRESS.—A Commission of Enquiry into the existence of corrupt practices may be issued by the Crown, upon a joint address of both Houses, on a Petition signed by two or more electors within 21 days after the return, or within 14 days after the meeting of Parliament. 15 & 16 Vic. c. 57; 31 & 32 Vic. c. 25, s. 56.

Any Member may, when returned, send a notice to the office of the Master, appointing an Agent or stating that he intends to act for himself, and in either case giving an address within 3 miles of the G.P.O. In default, notices and proceedings may be stuck up at the Master's Office. Parly. Rule 10.

Candidates are required to give the name and address of their agent to the Returning Officer. 26 Vic. c. 29, s. 2.

On presenting a Petition, an address must be left for service.

ADJOURNMENT.—The Barrister may adjourn his Court from time to time, and from one place to another, but not after the 31st October. 36 & 37 Vic. c. 70, s. 5.

The Judges may, by Order, postpone the trial of an Election Petition on the application of a party. Rule 34.

If the Judge does not arrive at the time appointed, the trial stands adjourned, *de die in diem*. Rule 35.

No formal adjournment necessary, and if the Judge be disabled from illness, &c., the trial may be recommenced and concluded before another Judge. Rule 36.

ADMINISTRATION of Oaths.—The Barrister may administer Oaths or Affirmations, and all persons who shall swear or affirm falsely are guilty of perjury. 6 Vic., c. 18, s. 41.

Returning Officers may administer Oaths or Affirmations at the Polling Booths. ib. s. 81. (See "*Oath*")

ADMISSIBILITY.—On the trial of an Election Petition, questions as to the admissibility of evidence may be reserved. 31 & 32 Vic., c. 125, s. 12.

ADMISSIONS of Freemen should be enrolled. No stamp duty is chargeable upon the admission of any person entitled by birth or servitude.

Where the name appears on the Freeman's Roll, legal admission will be presumed. (*Thacker's Case.*)

In England entry on the roll is sufficient evidence. In Ireland the certificate of admission signed by the Town Clerk is primâ facie evidence. (15 Ir. C. L. 382.)

Admission of Freemen being Liverymen of the City of London is proved by the original record in the Chamberlain's Court, or a sealed copy.

ADVOWSON, or the right of presentation to a Benefice.—The owner is called the Patron. In no case has he a sufficient Freehold interest to qualify him for the franchise.

AFFIDAVIT.—Immediately after notice of the presentation of an Election Petition (Parl. or Mun.), and the nature of the proposed security shall have been served, the Petitioner or his agent shall file an affidavit of the time and manner of service. (Rule 70.)

The hearing upon an objection to security may be upon affidavit, or by personal examination. Rule 24.

On making the acknowledgment of the recognizance entered into by sureties, there must be an affidavit by each surety, that he is seized or possessed of real or personal estate, or both, above what will satisfy the amount of his recognizance. Rule 28.

AGE.—Full age is completed on the day preceding the 21st anniversary of a person's birth; a fraction of a day not being noticed.

To entitle a claimant to be registered under 30 & 31 Vic. c. 102, s. 6, he must have been of full age on the last day of the qualifying year, *i.e.* the 31st July in Counties, the 15th July in

Boroughs, 2 Will. 4, c. 45, s. 27 meaning that there shall be no legal incapacity on the last day of qualification for Registration. (*Hargreaves v. Hopper.*)

So there is this anomaly, that of twin brothers born between the 15th and 31st July, claiming to be registered, one for a County, and the other for a Borough, the former would be qualified under 41 & 42 Vic., c. 26, twelve months before the latter.

AGENCY.—In Election matters "there is more of the principle of Master and Servant than Principal and Agent" (Martin B., *Norwich, Wigan.*)

"Where any person is allowed by a Candidate, or has the Candidate's sanction, to try to carry on his election, and to act for him, there is some evidence to shew that he is an agent." (Blackburn J., *Taunton.*)

An ordinary agent cannot delegate his authority—"Delegatus non potest delegare,"—but an agent at an election can do so, to almost any extent, except of course agents for election expenses, agents to detect personation, and agents to be present at the counting of votes. Instances of disqualification through the acts of an agent are innumerable. Primâ facie agency terminates with the Election, and any act done *subsequently* must be proved to have been done with the privity, express or implied, of the Respondent. (*Salford.*)

On the trial of an Election Petition, agency need not be proved unless the Judge direct, before giving evidence of Bribery. 31 & 32 Vic., c. 125, s. 17.

AGENT. —It seems a moot point whether an Agent, who objects on behalf of another, can be made Appellant in a Consolidated Appeal, or whether the Appellant must be the party actually interested. (*Wanklyn v. Woollett.*)

In Parliamentary elections, a person employed either 6 months previously to, or during, or within 14 days after any Election, and paid, is disqualified from voting. 7 & 8 Geo. 4, c. 37.

The vote of any person retained or employed by or on behalf of any Candidate for the purposes of election *as agent* shall be struck off on a scrutiny. 35 & 36 Vic. c. 33 s. 25.

Payment to *one* of two partners does not disqualify the other.

An election is void if bribery be brought home to the Candidate, or his *agent, though unauthorised by him.* It was reported by the *Newcastle-under-Lyme* Committee that the bribery was *not proved* to have been committed with the member's cognizance, and by the *Derby* Committee that it was proved *not to have been done* with his cognizance. Both elections were declared void.

But in does not follow that the Candidate is liable to be sued for the Penalties; the illegal acts must have been done *by himself, or some person on his behalf*; so that if an agent (or sub-agent, acting under his authority) is guilty of illegal acts, *with* or *without* the sanction of the Candidate, and even against express orders, (unless the agent has acted treacherously, as by collusion with the other side), it will void the Election, and the candidate is to that extent liable, but not to be sued.

It has, however, been held that where the sitting member *honestly intended* to comply with the Law, and countenance no illegal act, stronger evidence was required of the agency. (*Wigan, Sligo, Taunton.*)

So that to a great extent each case will stand on its own merits, or demerits. "No one yet has been able to go farther than to say, as to some cases enough has been established; as to others enough has not been established." (Blackburn J., *Bridgewater Case.*)

An agent (or canvasser), who is employed, shall not vote, and if he does he is guilty of an offence against the Act, and is liable, on summary conviction before two Justices, to a penalty not exceeding £10.

The principles of Parliamentary Agency apply also to agency in Municipal Elections, both by the Judge's decision, and by statute. 35 & 36 Vic. c. 60, s. 21 (4).

In Municipal Elections, notice in writing must be given to the Returning Officer of the appointment of an agent. 35 & 36 Vic. c. 33, s. 20 (6).

A Candidate at a Municipal Election has a right to appoint an Agent to attend Poll and the Counting of Votes. The Candidate and one other person appointed by him, and no other persons, except for the purpose of assisting the Mayor, have a right to attend. One agent may be appointed to both duties, but previous notice is required in the one case, and not in the other. And in the case of death or incapacity, fresh agents may be appointed.

AGREEMENT by Overseers with owners for the payment of Rates should be in writing. (See "*Abatement.*")

Agreements by owners with Occupiers (or "constructive rating") under sec. 19 of 32 & 33 Vic. c. 41. (Sec. 14 of 41 & 42 Vic. c. 26 enacting that such agreements shall be of general application,) have reduced the rateable inhabitant householder Borough franchise, to a "registered residential" franchise, any part of a house, no matter how small its value, say 1s. a week, if used as a separate dwelling, and so that the landlord be *non-resident* (or what is called an "out door" landlord) and if the rates are paid by him is now entitled to appear on the Rate Book, and, as a consequence, on the Overseers' lists, and to be registered as an inhabitant householder.

Agreements for Sale and Purchase. Many questions have arisen on claims to vote in respect of lands, &c., agreed to be sold, the 8 Hen. 6, c. 7., requiring voters to have freehold of the value of 40s., being strictly limited to persons having the *legal* estate.

To remedy this, and to give beneficiaries the franchise, the 7 & 8 Will. 3, c. 26, was passed, taking the right from Trustees, and Mortgagees, unless in actual possession and receipt of the rents and profits. (See *"Beneficiaries."*) But it sometimes happened that a person who had agreed to purchase became entitled to vote until the purchase was completed the vendor (not being in receipt of the *rents* and *profits*) being held to be a trustee for the purchaser. In all such cases the question turned upon the point, who was to receive the rents, &c., by virtue of the agreement until the conveyance of the land was completed. If they belonged to the purchaser under such circumstances that he could compel a specific performance, the vendor was trustee of the legal estate for him, he took an *equitable* freehold and had a right to vote, but if they belonged to the vendor, though the purchaser was in possession, he was not entitled to vote.

Then came 2 Will. IV. c. 45, s. 23, in nearly the same words as 7 & 8 Will. 3, c. 26, s. 26, requiring 6 months' *actual possession* or *receipt of the rents "to their own use,"* to qualify freeholders and others to be registered.

Doubts having arisen as to the equitable interests involved, it was enacted by 6 Vic. c. 18, s. 74,

> "That no trustee of any lands or tenements shall *in any case* have a right to vote in any such election for or by reason of any trust estate therein, but that the cestui que trust in actual possession or in the receipt of the rents and profits thereof, though he may receive the same through the lands of the trustee, shall and may vote for the same, notwithstanding such trust."

Abolishing the right of a trustee to vote, *whether in actual possession or not.*

In consequence of this enactment there are cases in which neither vendor nor purchaser can be registered, as in the case of *Allday v. Lewis,* where it was held that a purchaser of freehold land (sufficient in value to confer a qualification to vote), to whom no conveyance had been made, and who had not been let into possession, did not acquire a right to be registered under 6 Vic. c. 18, s. 74, although he had paid the whole purchase money.

As regards agreements for Leases, it was resolved by the committee in *Brohan's Case,* "That no person be entitled to be registered as a £10 leaseholder unless the lease has been duly executed, and delivered to the applicant 6 months before he comes to be registered." This, however, was a case of a verbal contract, *not performed in part,* and there seems to be no reason, in principle, why a tenant *let into possession,* under a verbal agreement for a lease, should not be considered an equitable lessee, after unequivocal acts of part performance. (*Vance's Case.*)

AIDING and ABETTING, counselling or procuring, Personation, is a *felony*, punishment on conviction not exceeding 2 years, with hard labour.   35 & 36 Vic. c. 33, s. 24.

ALDERMEN.—The Alderman for each ward of a Municipal Borough is the Returning Officer thereof; when not divided into wards the Mayor is. Aldermen are elected openly by voting papers. No notice of election is necessary, further than the three days' notice of the Council meeting at which such election takes place. The qualification for aldermen is not to be increased in a Borough of less than 4 Wards, where it shall afterwards be divided into a greater number. Aldermen and Councillors may reside within 15 miles of the Borough, although by reason of residing beyond 7 miles they are not entitled, though otherwise qualified, to be on the Burgess List. The 15 miles is to be measured as the crow flies, according to 6 Vic., c. 18, s. 76, and not by the nearest road as provided by the Mun. Corp. Act.

In mixed Boroughs separate Lists are to be made of Burgesses entitled to be elected Aldermen and Councillors, though not entitled to be inserted in the Burgess List, and such separate List. is to be revised.   32 & 33 Vic. c. 55, s. 3, and 41 & 42 Vic. c. 26, s. 19.

ALIENS, at Common Law, are such as are born out of the dominion of the Crown.   Aliens, retaining the state of civilians, are disqualified; but if naturalized by Act of Parliament, or made denizens by Letters Patent, aliens are entitled to be registered. So, too, aliens who have obtained certificates under 7 & 8 Vic. c. 66, and 33 & 34 Vic. c. 14.

From some cases decided before Committees of the House of Commons it would appear that the objector was bound to prove, not merely that the person objected to was born *hors de allegience*, but that the incapacity had not been removed. (*Bedford, Reading.*)

This, however, would probably not be held to be law now, and on proof that the person objected to was born *hors de allegience*, the onus would be thrown on him of showing when and how the incapacity had been removed.

Children born *hors de allegience*, whose fathers (or grandfathers on the father's side) were natural born subjects, are now deemed natural born subjects.

Aliens are not entitled to Parliamentary, Municipal, or other Franchise, and are ineligible to Parliament.

ALLOTMENT.—A freehold allotment for life under a Private Enclosure Act belonging to the Freemen of the Borough of Leicester, and held so long as the allottee should pay the rent and conform to the regulations to be made by the deputies, but *not at the will* of the deputies, confers a vote. (*Beeson v. Burton.*)

ALMS, from the French "Aumône," anciently written "Aumosnes," derived from the Greek " Eleemosyne," comprises every species of relief bestowed upon the poor, including all "charities." It is seldom used in the resolutions of the House of Commons. Its widest and most popular use is in reference to Parochial relief, from the "Alms' Chests" and Sunday collections pointed out by 27 Hen. 3, c. 25, and 1 Ed. 6, c. 3, as the best means for the relief of the poor.

Recipients of alms are disqualified by *Common Law*, as well as by *Statute*, but there are some nice distinctions to be drawn, and from the earliest times until now it has been an invidious task to draw the line at which eleemosynary aid ceases, and charity begins. It was resolved by the Gloucestershire Committee, *nem. con.* that the receipt of Sacrament money did not disqualify. (25 *Journ:* 275.)

It was decided by the same Committee that one Vigo, having received, within 12 months of an Election, part of a sum given by Will to the parish, *to those not on the Parish books*, was not thereby disqualified.

In the case of Harpur's Charity, Bedford, founded 1566, by which certain surplus rents were to be distributed "in alms" to the poor, for the relief of the town, and of poor decayed housekeepers, it was resolved that the recipients were not thereby disqualified. So of Howe's Charity, and Coles' Charity.

Later, it was decided that the brethren of an Hospital, each entitled to a house for his own occupation, and a share in the rents, &c., of the Hospital, were not disqualified. (*Smith v. Hall.*)

On the other hand it was held that agricultural labourers with large families, who had received 12s. 6d. each (though without solicitation, and at the discretion of the trustee, and though they had not received parochial relief) out of a surplus fund set apart from certain rents to be distributed among the "poorest inhabitants" were disqualified (*Harrison v. Carter*); so that much will depend upon the circumstances of the individual case.

" A point of some importance arose on Thursday in the revision of the voting lists for the City. An objection was formally taken to a certain name, because the voter had during the course of the year received a certain sum from one of the innumerable small City charities 'for the purchase of groceries.' The objection does not appear to have been made for a party purpose, and with the bonâ fide object of settling the point. The Revising Barrister stated that the decision was within his individual discretion, and allowed the vote on the ground that the gift was 'not likely to destroy the independence of the voter.' This, in the case cited, was probably true enough, the dole being apparently one to which mere residence for a certain time entitled the recipient, without its being in the option of any person to give or refuse it. Unless, however, we mistake, the receipt of similar doles has in some former instances been held to disqualify, and has resulted in the striking of large numbers of names off the register. We give no opinion as to the disqualifying effect which the receipt of such charity ought or ought not to exercise. Indeed, in a country possessing so many eccentric and anomalous eleemosynary institutions as England, it would be very difficult to give a general or off-hand decision. But it is obvious that individual Revising Barristers are likely to take very different views in very similar cases as to what is, and what is not, likely to interfere with a voter's independence. In one sense it might be maintained that no necessary loss of that quality need follow the receipt of parish relief. It would seem advisable therefore that, as in this so in other cases of doles, the effect upon the political status of their recipients should be decided generally by the Legislature or the superior courts, not piecemeal by different subordinate authorities."—*Daily News, September 20th, 1879.*

By 2 Will. 4, c. 45, s. 36, it was enacted that no person should be entitled to be registered as a voter in the election of a member or members to serve in any future Parliament for any city or borough, who should within 12 calendar months next previous to the last day of July have received parochial relief *or other alms which by the law of Parliament* disqualify from voting.

Alms, "which by the law of Parliament disqualify" would appear to be such as form part, or go to the relief, of the parochial funds for the relief of the poor, though in *Mashiter v. Town Clerk of Lancaster,* excuse from the payment of poor rates on account of poverty was held not to disqualify; a distinction being made between *giving and receiving* relief, and it was laid down that the words of the Act were not to be strained against the necessity of the case.

Sec. 33 of that Act reserved the "ancient rights" to the franchise, subject to their being lost by an omission from the register for 2 successive years, except cases where such omission has been caused by the receipt of parochial relief.

ALMSHOUSES are hospitals, built by persons in a private capacity, and endowed with a revenue from land, &c., for the maintenance of poor, aged, or disabled persons.

It was clearly not the intention of the Legislature, under the 8 Hen. 6, c. 7, or the Reform Acts, to confer the franchise upon eleemosynary recipients, and it will be found, as a rule, that the receipt of a certain yearly income of this nature, whether from land or otherwise, is of itself an insufficient qualification.

The inmates of Jesus Hospital, Rothwell, incorporated 38 Eliz., who were removable *as often as it should seem convenient to the Governors* were held to have no freehold interest. (*Davis v. Waddington.*)

So the inmates of Shrewsbury Hospital, Sheffield, receiving an income of 10s. a week out of rents and profits arising from land, but where they could exercise no act of independent ownership, were held to have no sufficient interest. (*Ashmore v. Lees—Freeman v. Gainsford.*)

But in the case of Burghley Hospital, a freehold building divided into several rooms, each of the annual value of £4, and each separately inhabited by a *bedesman,* appointed under certain ordinances made in 1597 (when feoffments were allowed to be made in fee simple to the use of the poor, without incorporati on), and no bedesman had ever been removed, though there was a power of removal in the ordinances for certain infirmities and vices, it was held that each bedesman had a freehold interest in his own room and was entitled. (*Simpson v. Wilkinson.*)

In the case of Borough voters, it appears more clearly that eleemosynary occupiers are not entitled to the franchise. The Military and Naval Knights of Windsor have been held to be disqualified, the character of their body and the terms and mode of their appointment showing that they did not occupy either as *owners or tenants*; but on the other hand Pensioners of Greenwich and Chelsea Hospitals are entitled. (*Heartley v. Banks*).

And it has been held that the brethren of a Hospital, each entitled to a house for his own occupation, and to a share in the profits, though required to be above the age of 56 (except those who were lame, blind, or unfit for husbandry), and inhabitants having no competent means to live are entitled. (*St. John's Hospital.—Smith v. Hall.*)

And the occupiers Lord Coningsby's Hospital, Hereford, for six soldiers and five domestic servants (called " servitors"), nominated by the owner of the Coningsby Estates, from which fixed payments are made to the servitors, who pay no rent, and who, once appointed, hold the house they occupy for life, and cannot be removed except for murder or felony, were held to have freehold interests, and to occupy *as owners* under 30 & 31 Vic. c. 102, s. 3, and, therefore, entitled to be registered. (*Fryer v. Bodenham.*)

AMENDMENTS may be made by the Barrister in the 3rd Column, where the general nature of the qualification is embodied in the description, or can be fairly gathered from it (and when the qualification is not in fact varied), for the purpose of more clearly and accurately defining the same, and so that a *new* qualification be not imported.

The words " one undivided fifty-first part of and in" have been allowed to be prefixed to the words " Freehold Farm Rent."

The words "farm as occupier" have been substituted for the words " £50 occupier."

Where a voter claimed for a "dwelling-house," and on objection proved joint occupation of a dwelling-house under 2 Will. 4, c. 45, ss. 27-29, it was held that the word "dwelling" was rightly struck out. (*Townshend v. Marylebone.*)

Under 6 Vic., c. 18, s. 40, the Barrister was held to have power to transfer the name of a voter from a list, in which it was *wrongly* inserted, to the list in which it should have been properly inserted. (*Ballard v. Robins.*)

In the 3rd Column of the Register the qualification was given as "freehold land," the 4th column contained 15 plots of land. The appellant had sold the first 14 plots, but the 15th was freehold of sufficient value. Held that the Barrister had power to amend the 4th Column by striking out the surplus plots. (*Smith v. Woolston—Sherwin v. Whyman.*)

The Barrister may also add the number of a house in the 4th Column. (*Barlow v. Mumford.*)

But where land had been let on a long lease, and the description was "Freehold rent charge," it was held to be a *misdescription*, not an *insufficient*, or *inaccurate*, description, and that it could not be amended. (*Nicholls v. Bulwer.*)

In Borough lists large powers of amendment are now given to the Barrister in dealing with the 3rd Column of the Register or Claims, and a voter need not now be disqualified by the fact that through any technical or clerical error or mistake there has been a misdescription in his qualification, for so long as he has a *true qualification in law* sufficient to constitute a qualification of some description, though insufficient *per se* to constitute a qualification of the nature or description of that claimed, the Barrister will amend it. 41 & 42 Vic. c. 26, s. 28 (12).

At the revision for Marylebone, Sept., 1879, Mr. Bathurst announced, after deliberation, that he should supply the word " weekly " in all cases where the lodgers had not themselves inserted it in their claims, subject to being asked to grant a case. At the close of the revision the Revising Barrister was asked to grant a case on that point, there being some 208 cases of the kind in the borough, and that the case might be made a consolidated one, so as to apply to the three divisions of the borough. The case was granted, the revising Barrister supplying the word " weekly " where it was not inserted in the claim, and the agents supplying other information where necessary. Where such information was not forthcoming the name was struck off the list.

A misdescription may also be cured by a declaration (ib. s. 24), but not an insufficient description, the power of making such declarations being intended to correct errors, not to add a qualification. Where no claim has been made "in succession," by a person who has removed from one house to another during the qualifying year, on or before the 25th August, as provided by the Act, a declaration will not remedy the omission, not having the same effect as a claim.

Objection having been made to such a declaration at the Revision for the Borough of Leicester, Sept., 1879, the Barrister upheld the objection, saying that he had no power to accept such declarations, and that if he made the amendment he would be conferring a qualification. So at the same Revision for the Borough of Wigan, Sept., 1879, a woman claimed a municipal vote for a house No. 13, in one of the streets in the borough, but it was ascertained that she had resided only at that house for eleven months, having previously lived in the same street at a house No. 11. It was contended that the Revising Barrister could amend the claim by adding "houses in succession," but this was opposed. The Revising Barrister held that the rules with reference to the parliamentary list applied also to the municipal list. If he amended the claim he should be adding another qualification, and that he had no power to do. He therefore disallowed the vote.

ANCIENT DEMESNE.—Lands held " in ancient demesne " were so called from the particular feudal tenure by which they were held. Manors were reserved to the King for the support of his household and garrisons. The names, number, &c., were entered by William the Conqueror in Domesday Book.

All lands which appear by this Book to have belonged to him, or to Edward the Confessor, are of this tenure, though they afterwards came into the hands of subjects.

Each Manor had a Court where the Tenants, or *Soc-men* (or ploughmen) did suit and service, their lands passing by surrender and admission at the Court.

"Ancient demesne " is therefore a species of " Copyhold " (vide), the lands passing by *surrender according to the custom of the Manor*, but differing from Common Copyholds in some details. Tenants were either those who held freely, by the King's Grant (called " Charter Tenants "), Customary Freeholders, holding *by the Custom of the Manor*, but not at the will of the Lord (including some " Burgage Tenures "), and tenants holding *by copy of Court Roll at the Will of the Lord* (called " Bond Tenants.")

Persons holding lands of this tenure are entitled to vote for the county, but by 2 & 3 Will. 4, c. 45, s. 25, no person can vote for a County in respect of Copyholds and Leaseholds situate in a Borough.

ANCIENT RIGHTS reserved. (See *"Franchise."*)—Boroughs, with ancient rights reserved, are noticed in the Appendix.

ANNUITY, charged upon Freehold lands, or a " rent charge," as it is sometimes called, is a good qualification, if of sufficient value to satisfy the requirements of 2 Will. 4, c. 45.

ANNUAL VALUE.—(See " *Value*.")

APARTMENTS.—Lodgings include apartments, or place of residence, furnished or unfurnished. 41 & 42 Vic. c. 26, s. 5. (See " *Lodgings*."

APPEAL—The revision of the list of burgesses being now transferred to the Revising Barristers, as regards municipal boroughs within (either wholly or in part) the area of the Parliamentary Borough, for which such Barrister is appointed, the power of appeal given to Parliamentary voters is extended to burgesses (male or female). 41 & 42 Vic. c. 26, ss. 35-37.

By the same Act, in *all* cases of Appeal, whether in Counties or Boroughs, the Court of Appeal may in future order the costs of a successful Appellant to be paid by the Clerk of the Peace, or Town Clerk, as the case may be, if named as Respondent, whether he appears or not; but to enable an appellant to obtain such order, he must require the Barrister to name such Clerk of the Peace, or Town Clerk, to be Respondent before making his declaration of appeal. This the Barrister is required to do.

naming such Respondent either alone or in addition to any of the persons referred to in 6 Vic. c. 18, s. 43; viz., the interested party, Overseer, or Town Clerk.

The costs properly incurred by such Respondent, including any costs he may be ordered to pay to the Appellant, are to be allowed him as part of the expenses incurred by him in respect of the revision.

The costs of the Appeal are still in the discretion of the Court hearing the Appeal. s. 38.

At the hearing of any Appeal, the qualification in dispute may be supported by any other qualification for which the voter is entered on the register, or burgess roll, as the case may be, except in the case of a borough divided into wards, where a right to vote in one ward cannot be supported by a right to vote in another. s. 28 (14).

Any person aggrieved or dissatisfied with any decision of any Barrister may, on the refusal of such Barrister to state a case in accordance with the provisions of 6 Vic. c. 18, s. 42, within one month apply to the Court to grant a rule to compel such Barrister to show cause why he should not do so—such rule to be made absolute or discharged, with or without costs. If the rule be made absolute the Barrister must state a case, and such case will be as effectual as if originally stated in accordance with 6 Vic. c. 18—41 & 42 Vic. c. 26, s. 37. (See "*Special Case*.")

The Appeal must be on some "point of law" necessary to the decision of the case, and no Appeal, or notice of Appeal, is to be received or allowed upon any question of fact only, or upon the admissibility or effect of any evidence or admission, adduced or made in any case to establish any "matter of fact only," and the Court may remit a case to a Barrister to be more fully stated. 6 Vic. c. 18, s. 65.

There is no Appeal on a question of *costs*. s. 64.

Persons who may appeal are those—

1. Who have made a claim to be inserted in any List.
2. Who have made an objection to any other person.
3. Whose names have been expunged from any list.

The party aggrieved, or some one on his behalf, must, the same day, before the Barrister rises, give notice in writing that he is desirous to appeal, and must state therein the particular decision against which he appeals. (*Scott v. Durant.*)

The Barrister then states a case, signs it, and reads it to the appellant, who, or some person on his behalf, writes thereon, "I appeal from this decision," at the same time requiring the Barrister to name the Clerk of the Peace or Town Clerk as Respondent.

The Appellant must give notice of his intention to prosecute the Appeal within the first four days of Michaelmas Term, and also transmit to them the case signed by the Barrister; he must also give a similar notice to the Respondent. All such

Appeals are to be entered in a book kept for the purpose, and public notice is to be given of the hearing of the Appeals, and the order in which they will be heard. 6 Vic. c. 18, s. 63.

The practice is the same as in special cases, and only one Counsel is heard on each side.

The procedure in the case of *Consolidated* Appeals is the same as in single Appeals, and the judgment equally binding; but if a Consolidated Appeal is not duly prosecuted or defended, the Court may give the conduct of the case to any interested party, or name additional parties.

The Common Pleas Division of the High Court of Justice has exclusive cognizance of all matters relating hereto. 36 & 37 Vic. c. 66.

The Rule Office is in Room No. 83, Royal Courts of Justice. Mr. E. C. Cooke is the officer who has conduct of the proceedings.

APPLICATION may be made to the Court of Common Pleas for a rule to compel a Revising Barrister to show cause why he should not state a case. 41 & 42 Vic. c. 26, s. 27. (*Ante.*)

Application may be made to take an Election Petition off the file on any of the following grounds :—

1. That it was not presented in the time and manner prescribed by the Act.
2. That it was not duly signed by the Petitioner, or that interlineations were subsequently introduced.
3. That it is not in accordance with the Rules, as to statements, &c.
4. That the petitioner had no right of petition.
5. That the petition was not duly served, and notice given to the Respondent.
6. That security has not been given as required by the Rules.
7. That the matter is *res judicata*. (*Taunton.*)

Application for leave to withdraw an Election Petition (Parliamentary or Municipal) must be *special*, and be preceded by notice, and with the consent of all the Petitioners, and any person who might have been a Petitioner may apply to be substituted for the withdrawing Petitioner. 31 & 32 Vic. c. 125, s. 35, and 35 & 36 Vic. c. 60, s. 17.

Application may be made to strike irrelevant matter out of a Petition, or to amend.

Application may be made to postpone the trial of an Election Petition, or to change the venue, or for a commission to examine witnesses.

APPOINTMENT, The, of Revising Barristers, rests with the Lord Chief Justice and Judges of Assize. 6. Vic. c. 18, s. 28.

As to the appointment of Barristers to revise the Municipal registers, under 41 & 42 Vic. c. 26, it would appear to be by *implication*, not positive enactment.

Appointment of Expense Agent at a Parliamentary Election must be made and notice given to the Returning Officer on or before the day of nomination. 26 Vic. c. 29, s. 2.

Appointment of agents to detect personation and to be present at the counting of votes must be made before the time fixed for taking the Poll, and notice given to the Returning Officer or his deputy.

APPORTIONMENT of expenses of Overseers in mixed boroughs between the Parish and the Borough, to be made by the Barrister according to the rules given in 41 & 42 Vic. c. 26, s. 30.

In case of the apportionment of rents arising from lands in different Counties, in order to confer the County Franchise, the proportion arising from any one County must exceed 40s. (*West v. Robson.*)

ARCHDEACON.—It has been held that the office of an Archdeacon is a freehold, and qualifies. (*Ballard v. Gerrard.*)

ARMY or **NAVY** contractor, an, is disqualified by 2 Geo. 3, c. 45 and so of any persons entering into contracts on account of the public service.

And any Member of Parliament entering into such a Contract or continuing to hold it after the next session loses his seat.   s. 2.

Contracts executed before the Election do not disqualify, nor does the acceptance of orders where the contractor is unaware that he is dealing with the Government, and has no means of learning. (*Royse v. Birley.*)

An uncle transferred all his contracts to his nephews, and agreed to sell them his ships a few days before an Election— giving notice to his Broker to pay them all future earnings. Held that he was not disqualified, though the transfers, &c., were not registered and completed until after the election. (*Dartmouth Case.*)

In Rothschild's case, it was held that, though one of the Public Loan Contractors for 1855, he was not disqualified, there being no privity of contract between him and the Treasury.   110 *Comm. Journ.* 325.

The Lessee of a Railway is not disqualified by reason of being Lessee, or by reason of his conveying H.M. Mails on the Railway (*Londonderry Case.*)

ASSESSED TAXES.—Payment of all poor rates and assessed taxes, payable previously to the previous 5th January, a "*sine qua non.*" See Notice to Pay, 41 & 42 Vic. c. 26.   Form (B).

Overseers have power to inspect the assessments and to extract particulars any day during July, except Sunday, between 10 a.m. and 4 p.m.

Assessors or Collectors of Taxes are to deliver to the Overseers between 20th to 22nd July every year, a list of all persons who are in arrear with taxes payable on the previous 5th January, and the Overseers are to keep such list for inspection for 14 days after the publication of the List of Voters. 6 Vic. c. 18, s. 12.—

11 & 12 Vic. c. 10—41 & 42 Vic. c. 26, ss 10—18. (See *"Times to be observed."*)

Assessors of Taxes are to attend the Revision Court, and produce their books if required. 6 Vic. c. 18, s. 35.

ASSESSORS are abolished in Municipal Boroughs, which, as regards the whole or part of their area, are included in the area of a Parliamentary Borough. 41 & 42 Vic. c. 26, s. 20.

Assessors appointed by 6 & 7 Will. 4, c. 76, s. 37, amended by 7 Will. 4, c. 78, still hold office in Municipal Boroughs other than these, and the provisions of these statutes still apply there.

As to the election of Assessors, see 38 & 39 Vic. c. 40, s. 1, and Extraordinary Vacancies, 16 & 17 Vic. c. 79, and 38 & 39 Vic. c. 40, s. 9.

ASSIGNEES of an Underlease (and Sub-lessees) in Counties are required by 2 Will 4. c. 45, s. 20, to be in *actual occupation* of the premises.

This requirement is omitted in 30 & 31 Vic. c. 102, s. 5, as to Leaseholders of £5, and an opening left for the creation of faggot votes of £5 by the oversight; but Brett, J., said in the case of *Chorlton v. Overseers of Stretford* that the provision in the older Act as to "actual occupation" ought to be *read into* the Act of 1867, having regard to ss. 57 & 59 of the later Act. (See *"Lease."*)

ASSIGNMENT, The, by a landlord of the reversion of a *part* of a Lease under which an occupying tenant has taken *all* the premises, does not destroy his qualification as being "under the same Landlord," 2 Will. 4, c. 45, s. 27, so long as he continues to occupy under his original take. (*French v. Tucker.*)

ASSISTANT OVERSEERS may join in making the Poor Rates, &c. Claims to be rated may be made to them. (*Baker v. Locke, Caunter v. Adams.*)

ATTENDANCE at the Revision Court (See "*Overseer*," "*Assessor of Taxes*," "*Objector*.")

The attendance upon a Judge on the trial of an Election Petition is to be the same as at Nisi Prius. 31 & 32 Vic. c. 125, s. 30.

BALLOT ACT.—Since the passing of the 35 & 36 Vic. c. 33, all Parliamentary votes are given by *ballot papers*, except at the three Universities of Oxford, Cambridge, and London, where votes may be given by means of *open voting papers*. 24 & 25 Vic. c. 53, and 30 & 31 Vic. c. 102, s. 45.

The provisions of the Ballot Act with respect to the voting of a Returning Officer, the use of rooms for polling, and the right of voting of persons whose names are on the register, do not apply to Municipal Elections; but sec. 41 of the 41 & 42 Vic. c. 26, enacts that s. 13 of the Ballot Act shall, with respect to any Municipal Election, apply, and that no election shall be declared invalid by reason of any non-compliance with the rules, or mistake in the use of any of the forms prescribed by the Municipal Election Act, 38 & 39 Vic. c. 40, if the election was conducted in accordance with the principles laid down in that Act.

The offences relating to ballot boxes, ballot papers, &c., are stated in 35 & 36 Vic. c. 33, s. 3, and any person attempting to commit any of such offences is guilty of misdemeanour, and liable, if a returning officer, officer, or clerk, to two years', and any other person, to six months' imprisonment, with or without hard labour.

BANK.—All money by way of security for costs payable by a Petitioner on an Election Petition is to be paid into the Bank of England to an account to be called " The Parliamentary Election Act, 1868, Security Fund," vested in and drawn upon from time to time by the Chief Justice of the Common Pleas Division. *Rule* 16.

All claims to such money, at law or in equity, are to be disposed of by the Court, and the money disposed of, or returned by Rule or Order. *Rules* 63, 64.

BANKRUPT.—If a Member of the House of Commons is adjudged bankrupt, he shall be incapable of sitting or voting for one year from the date of adjudication, unless within that time either the order is annulled or the Creditors are fully paid and satisfied. 32 & 33 Vic. c. 71, s. 121.

If within the year the bankruptcy is not annulled or the debts paid or satisfied, a Certificate of Bankruptcy shall be given by the Court of Bankruptcy to the Speaker of the House of Commons, and thereupon the seat of such Member shall be vacant. (*ex parte Pooley re Russell.*)

If a Peer becomes Bankrupt, he is disqualified from sitting or voting in the House of Lords, bankruptcy including liquidation; a certificate of the Bankruptcy is to be given by the Court to the Speaker of the House of Lords and to the Clerk of the Crown in Chancery. 34 & 35 Vic. c. 50, s. 2.

If a voter becomes bankrupt, &c., he loses his qualification, *unless* he retains a sufficient estate to qualify. A borough voter who still continued to occupy his house, the assignee not having taken over his term, retained his vote as tenant. (*Worcester Case.*) But the possession by a trustee under a petition for liquidation will put an end to the possesion by the debtor.

Occupation by a Bankrupt continues until the Trustee takes possession. (*Worcester Case.*)

In a case which occurred at the Birmingham Revision Court, 1879,
    A point was raised whether a person, whose place of business was temporarily closed by creditors, consequent upon his filing a petition for liquidation during the qualifying period, was entitled to vote in respect of those premises, the debtor retaining the key and having access to the premises, where some of his goods still remained. The question was whether he lost control between the period of filing his petition

and the acceptance of the composition by the creditors. The trustee would be there against the will of the debtor, but simply in order to see that the goods were not sold to the disadvantage of the creditors. The debtor had not given up the business, and would be liable for the rent. The Revising Barrister said he did not think that anything had taken place to deprive the debtor of his character of occupier as tenant. Taking the view of the Committee of the House of Commons, he was inclined to think that the vote was good, and should therefore allow it to stand.

A scot and lot voter was objected to as an uncertificated bankrupt, but he had always paid his rates, the vote was held good. (*Taunton Case.*)

In Ireland the leasehold estates of a Bankrupt remain vested in him until the Assignee elects to take them.

BARRISTER.—See (*"Revising Barrister."*)

BEDESMAN.—The term Bedesman does not imply the holding of an *office* or *benefice* under 2 Will. 4, c. 45, s. 18, so as to qualify for a County Vote. Where the Bedesmen of Daventry, who held for life, and had for 20 years received 50s. a year, but who neither under deed nor by virtue of their appointment had any duties to perform, it was held that they did not acquire any estate to qualify them under the above Act. (*Faulkner v. Overseers of Boddington.* (See "*Almshouse.*")

BELLRINGER, appointed to a Cathedral for life, though paid out of funds derived from land, held not to have a freehold office, and not entitled to vote. (*Hall v. Lewis.*)

BENEFICIARIES, or *cestuis que trust*, being in actual possession, are entitled to vote, if the equitable fee is of sufficient value. (See "*Actual Possession.*") Before the Statute of Uses, 27 Hen. 8. c, 10 was passed, uses had become very common, and the greater part of the land in England was held *by one to the use* of another. The one was called the *feoffee to uses*, the other, enjoying the beneficial right, the *cestui a que use*, or *cestui que trust*. This was especially so after the Wars of the Roses, and inasmuch as the Statute 8 Hen. 6, c. 7, required the voter to have the *legal estate* and the *cestui que use* had no legal estate or seisin, most of the landowners were, strictly speaking, disqualified—but the contests for Counties becoming more frequent and of greater importance, an Act was passed—

"That no person be allowed to have any vote in the election of members to serve in Parliament for or by reason of any trust estate or mortgage, *unless such Trustee* or mortgagee shall be in actual possession or receipt of the rents and profits of the same, but that the mortgagor, or *cestui que trust, in possession* shall and may vote for the same notwithstanding such mortgage or trust." 2 Will. 4, c 45, s. 23.

(See "*Actual Possession.*")

The Statute of Uses made no difference in this respect, inasmuch as, while purporting to transfer the equitable *use* into the *legal* estate, it gave rise to the modern trust, the old order of things reviving again under another garb. Where land is conveyed to A, to the use or in trust for C, to the use or in trust for B, C has the legal estate, but B is the beneficiary, and having the Equitable Estate, has also, if in possession, the right to the franchise. And it is immaterial that there is a power of sale, so long as the beneficiaries are not entitled to retain the proceeds. (*Ashworth v. Hopper.*)

Freemen of the town of Berwick, who are entitled, under various charters, to certain meadow lands, or the income arising therefrom, for life, so long as they remain on those lands, or within the borough, were held to be entitled to the franchise, where the equitable interest was sufficient—viz., £5 per annum—the lands being vested in the corporation upon trust to divide the income among the resident freemen and widows of freemen.   (Revision 1879.)

> The Barrister, Mr. Trevelyan, said that the freemen, it was true, were not in actual possession of the land, but if any one considered the character of the meadow holdings and the character of stints in lieu of meadows, it was plain that the management of these should be under trustees. There were two classes of trusts which everybody acquainted with conveyancing was aware of—viz., one where persons were appointed to hold property in trust for a particular person, who was put in possession; and another where there was not sufficient confidence in the person who should receive the property, and therefore only received an equitable interest for life in it; that is, he had a beneficial enjoyment of the property, but not the actual possession of it.

BENEFICE.—It has been held that the Fellows of a College, who were entitled to a yearly payment under a Will, do not acquire an estate by *devise*, nor was their appointment *a promotion to a benefice or office* within the meaning of 2 Will. 4, c. 45, s. 18. (*West v. Robson.*)

BIRTH.—The 2 Will. 4, c. 45, s. 32 (fully set out under the head "*Liverymen*"), preserves the ancient franchise of Freemen not only to those whose fathers were entitled to claim their freedom prior to 1st March, 1831, but to lineal descendants of all who were entitled to be so admitted *before that date,* so, where A's grandfather was a freeman on that date, his father being at the time under age and not entitled to be admitted until after that date, it was held that A was entitled to make out his claim through his grandfather. (*Gaydon v. Bancroft.*)

BOOKS.—The printed books signed by the Clerks of the Peace and Town Clerks, &c., and given into the custody of the Sheriff, or Returning Officer, as the case may be, to be the Register of Voters for the year commencing the following 1st January, do not become the Register until actually signed and delivered. (*Brumfitt v. Bremner.*)

BOROUGH, from *burg—beorgan*—supposed in its original signification to mean a place of safety. *(Somn. Sax. Dict.)*

Thus the term *friburgh* was anciently applied to tythings, or communities of freemen, combined together for mutual safety. As a rule they were walled Towns; rights of markets were extended to them, and so they became the harbours of commerce. The houses erected therein were called *burgages*, and the tenants or resident householders, presented, sworn, and enrolled, and doing suit and service at the Court held therein, paying scot and bearing lot, were called *Burgwaremen*, or *burgesses.*

This class has never directly changed, though innovations have been made upon it from the Saxon times until now.

All burgesses were of necessity householders, but all householders were not burgesses. Peers, ecclesiastics, females, minors, villeins (or bondmen), and those who, from poverty or other cause, did not pay the charges, or serve the public offices of the borough, were not burgesses.

All the boroughs in the Kingdom were originally the property of the King, or some of his Barons, or of the Clergy, or Dignitaries, by whom they were put out to *farm*, to the lesser Barons, or to the burgesses themselves, or to the bailiffs or superior tenants, either in fee, for a term, or at will, and for such purposes the inhabitant householders became, in a primitive sense, *incorporated*, though there were no Municipal corporations, *quâ corporations*, prior to Richard I. the period of "time immemorial."

When a town was put out to fee farm, the town itself, as well as the burgage, was said to be held *by burgage tenure:* burgess-ship did not, however, so much depend upon tenure as upon *residence*, as a burgess of one town might be tenant of a manor elsewhere; but *non-residents* were in no case burgesses. By a Statute of Hen. 5, burgesses are defined to be "*resident, dwelling, and free, in their boroughs.*"

Many towns freed themselves from the payment of all dues by purchasing *the farm of the borough*, by, in fact, *commuting*. There are 78 boroughs mentioned in Domesday Book, but they were not all boroughs *by burgage tenure*. Heywood says that there were 29 "burgage tenure boroughs" in 1775.

All Cities were Boroughs, but all Boroughs were not Cities. See "*Cities and Towns being Counties*" of themselves.

Some ancient boroughs, like Newton-le-Willows, never had a Charter, and were never incorporated.

Boroughs were first represented in Parliament in 1265, when Simon, Earl of Leicester, summoned two burgesses from each town. In 1295, two burgesses from every leading town sat in the Great Council, with the Knights of the Shires, Nobles, and Barons.

The selection of Boroughs to be represented remained in the King's hands, their choice being for the most part left to the Sheriff. The Sheriff of Wilts, for instance, reduced the number of boroughs in that County from eleven to three. The cost of maintaining their representatives (namely, 2s. a day for borough, 4s. a day for County, members), who, indeed, were originally summoned *for their own taxation*, became a burden, and not only was no anxiety shown to be represented, but efforts were made to shirk the liability. Some boroughs made no returns to the Sheriff, while some bought charters of exemption. From Edward 3 to Richard 3 the Sheriff of Lancashire made no returns of any boroughs in his county, *on account of their poverty*.

But the importance of the Commons House of Parliament increased greatly during the reigns of Henry 6, Edward 6, Richard 3, and Henry 8, owing to the necessity of the Crown *for supplies*. The King and Courtiers bringing influences to bear upon the Members, efforts were made to control the Elections.

It was suggested that there were many *decayed boroughs* which ought to return members, and did not.

This was acted upon by Henry 8 and Queens Mary and Elizabeth to so great an extent that Parliament itself interfered to stay the power of the Crown. The last exercise of the prerogative was in the case of the borough of Newark.

By the Reform Act the words *City* or *Borough* are to include all towns corporate, cinque ports, districts or places within England and Wales, which should be entitled after that Act to return a member or members to serve in Parliament, other than counties at large, and ridings, parts and divisions of counties at large, and also the town of Berwick-upon-Tweed, and by the 6 Vic. c. 18, sec. 101, the words city or borough extend to any city, borough, or town corporate, cinque port, district, or place within England and Wales returning a member or members to serve in Parliament, other than counties at large, and ridings, &c., and to every place sharing in the election of a member for any city or borough, and the town of Berwick-upon-Tweed.

The definition of Parliamentary Boroughs will be found in 30 & 31 Vic. c. 102, s. 61, and 41 & 42 Vic. c 26, s. 4. As to Borough Voters,—(See *"Franchise," "Borough Voters."*)

BRIBERY.—A *"corrupt practice"* (*vide*), recognized by the Common Law, and defined by Act of Parliament. Bribery at common law is defined as when a person, in a judicial capacity, takes a gift or reward of any person who has business before him, for doing his office, or by colour of his office. In a larger sense bribery denotes the receiving or offering of an *undue* reward, as an inducement for acting contrary to duty, or the giving or taking a reward for a public office. Bribery was a misdemeanour at common law open to indictment or information, and punishable by fine or imprisonment.

Disqualification by bribery also existed at common law.

By a Resolution of the House, in 1677, any breach of the prohibitions contained therein against the giving of *money* or *treating* were deemed to be *bribery*.

Many Acts have been passed against bribery and treating. Among the earlier penalties, we find that where a candidate bribed parliamentary electors *after the date or teste* of the Writ, or after the Vacancy, he was disabled from sitting in Parliament, and he that took, as well as he that received, a bribe, forfeited £500, and was disabled from voting, or holding any office in a Corporation.

All the statutes which have been passed from time to time was intended to give effect to the penalties incurred at common law.

By 17 & 18 Vic. c. 102, s. 2—

Every person who shall

Give, lend, agree to give, agree to lend, offer, promise, promise to procure, or promise to endeavour to procure, any money or valuable consideration to or for any voter, or to or for any person on behalf of any voter, or to or for any other person,

To induce any voter to vote, or refrain from voting,

Or shall corruptly do any such acts on account of such voter having voted or refrained from voting, is guilty of BRIBERY.

And every person who shall *give, procure, agree to give, agree to procure, offer, promise, promise to procure, or promise to endeavour to procure any office, place, or employment* to or for any voter, or to or for any other person on behalf of any votes, or to or for any other person to induce any voter

To vote or refrain from voting,

Or shall corruptly do any such acts on account of any voter having voted, or refrained from voting, is guilty of BRIBERY. s. 2 (1, 2).

Every person who shall

Give, lend, agree to give, offer, promise, promise to procure, promise to endeavour to procure, any money, valuable consideration, office, place, or employment, to or for any person, in order to induce such person to procure or endeavour to procure the return of any person, or vote of any voter, is guilty of BRIBERY.

And every person who shall in consequence of any such gift, loan, offer, promise, procurement, or agreement, *procure, engage, promise to procure, or promise to endeavour to procure, the return of any person, or vote of any voter,* is guilty of BRIBERY. s. 2 (3, 4).

Every voter who shall *before* or *during* any Election *receive, agree,* or *contract for*

Any money, gift, loan, valuable consideration, office, place, or employment, for himself, or for any other person for voting, agreeing to vote, refraining or agreeing to refrain from voting, is guilty of BRIBERY. s. 3 (1).

Every person who shall receive

Any money or valuable consideration on account of any person *having voted*, or on account of having induced any other person to vote, or refrain from voting, is guilty of BRIBERY.

Their names were to be expunged from the register of voters of such place for ever, *ib. s. 6.* The election committees (now the Judges) were to report to the House, and prosecutions to be instituted by the Attorney-General on a report that persons had been guilty of bribery, and disfranchisement followed.

A Commission of Enquiry might be issued on a joint address of both Houses. 15 & 16 Vic. c. 57.

By the 31 & 32 Vic. c. 125, the disabilities entailed by bribery have been increased by sections 43 and 45 ; section 43 providing that a candidate guilty of *personal bribery*, and section 45 providing that any person, other than a candidate guilty of bribery, shall respectively be incapable of sitting in the House of Commons *for seeen years*, and incapable *for seven years* of voting for members of Parliament, holding any municipal or judicial office, or being appointed, or acting, as a justice of the peace.

Section 44 is a new provision. It avoids the election of a candidate who personally engages as an agent any person whom he knows to have been convicted of having been guilty of any corrupt practice.

The law in other respects remains unaltered, with the exception, first, that the presentation of petitions under 5 & 6 Vic. c. 102, complaining of general and extensive bribery, are put an end to, and secondly, that the Judges perform the functions of a select committee.

On the trial of a petition, charging corrupt practices, the duty of the Judge does not end with the mere determination of the Candidate who is entitled to the seat, or with a declaration that the electon is void; but he is required, for public purposes, to certify the following facts :

1. Whether any corrupt practice has or has not been proved to have been committed by or with the knowledge and consent of any Candidate at such election, and the nature of such corrupt practices. *If a Candidate is reported guilty of personal bribery he will be subject to all the disqualifications imposed by sec.* 43.

(2.) The names of all persons (if any) who have been proved at the trial to have been guilty of any corrupt practice. *These persons, if found guilty of bribery in any proceeding in which after notice of the charge, they have had an opportunity of being heard, will be subject to the disabilities imposed by sec.* 43.

(3.) Whether corrupt practices have, or whether there is reason to believe that corrupt practices have, extensively prevailed at the election to which the petition relates.

This is directed against the constituencies themselves, and may be followed by a Commission of Enquiry under 15 & 16 Vic. c. 57, and probably by disfranchisement.

The Judge may also make a special Report.

The duties of the Revising Barrister in regard to Voters convicted of Bribery are as follows :—

Whenever it shall be proved before the Barrister that any person who is on the register for any county, city, or borough, has been convicted of *bribery, treating, or undue influence* at an election, or that judgment has been obtained against him in respect of the offence of bribery, treating, or undue influence, the Revising Barrister shall expunge his name therefrom, or shall, in case such person claims to have his name inserted therein, disallow such claim, and the names of all persons whose names shall be so expunged, or disallowed, shall be inserted in a separate list, to be entitled "The List of Persons Disqualified for Bribery, Treating, or Undue Influence," to be appended to the list of voters. 17 & 18 Vic. c. 102, s. 6.

In order to disqualify a Candidate from being registered as a Voter by reason of *personal* bribery, or bribery by an Agent with his knowledge and consent under 31 & 32 Vict. c. 125, s. 43, he must be found by the report of the Election Judge, under ss. 11 and 14, to have been so guilty; it is not enough that the Judge states facts from which personal bribery or other corrupt practice might be inferred. (*Grant v. Overseers of Pagham*).

BRIDGE, A, is not a *building* within 2 Will. 4., c. 45.

BUILDING, or "*other building.*" For the purposes of that Act, and of the Mun. Corp. Acts, the terms "*House, Warehouse, Counting House, Shop or other building,*" shall include any part of a house where that part is *separately occupied* for the purposes of any *trade, business*, or *profession*, and any such part may, for the purpose of describing the qualification, be described as Office, Chambers, Studio, or by any like term applicable to the case. 41 & 42 Vic. c. 26, s. 5.

What is a "*building*"? has always been a question of *fact* rather than *law*. Once the fact that a certain thing is a building is decided, the only question remaining is to what uses it may be put. It ought to be capable of being adapted by man either for *residence* or for *industry*, and also to have that degree of *durability* which is included in the idea of a building. (*Powell v. Boraston.*)

The purpose for which a "*building*" is used is immaterial, it may be either agricultural, commercial, or professional, and the value may be infinitesimal if it be "bonâ fide," and add to the real value of the land occupied therewith. (*Norrish v. Harris*, and *Collins v. Tewkesbury.*)

But a pigstye is not a sufficient building. And two separate buildings cannot be joined so as to make one qualification. (*Dewhurst v. Fielden.*)

BUILDING SOCIETY, periodical payments to a, are to be deducted from the gross amount of the rent received, to ascertain the clear yearly value above all charges (*Copland v. Bartlett*, and

(*Beamish v. Overseers of Stoke*), where the payments reduced the annual value to less than 20s.

BURGAGE TENURE is the oldest existing Borough Franchise, having been so from time immemorial. Sir Richard Temple, in a debate upon a Bill to regulate the election of members, 12th Nov., 1675 said, "Anciently there was no vote in a Borough but by Burgage tenure, burgage houses. We come now to Freemen, Salesmen, Scotters and Lotters," all of which were superadded franchises, the right of voting not being in the course of time regulated by any fixed rule.

Burgage tenants were a class whose rights were reserved by the Reform Act (See "*Franchise*"—"*Borough Voters*"), some permanently, some temporarily.

There are many customs affecting these; each town having some ancient usage of its own, of which the custom of *Borough English* was one, but *registration* and *residence* are now the two great essentials.

Burgage tenure was either "free" or "base" burgage tenure —(See "*Ancient Demesne*"—"*Copyhold*.") Burgage owners have in many instances been registered as freeholders, where there has been no evidence of a Manor, or Court, and the tenements have passed without surrender, admission, or fine.

Cricklade is the only borough where copyholders, or burgage owners, holding by Copy of Court Roll, are admitted to vote, it having been decided in 1689 that freeholders and copyholders of burgage houses have the right—a usurpation sanctioned by long enjoyment.

Freehold and Burgage qualification in cities and towns "being counties" may be acquired since 2 Will. 4, c. 45, by *purchase* (See "*Cities*"), but the owner must be in possession for 12 months to entitle him to be registered, and such acquisition must be within the *new* limits of the City. s. 31. No assessment to the land tax is necessary. s. 22. The qualifying value varies in the seven cities and towns being counties; 40s. has been fixed by last determinations of the House in the cases of Lichfield and Nottingham, but Freeholders being mentioned in the cases of the other cities and towns, as being distinct from "burgage tenants," it would seem that any value will qualify when the amount has not been fixed by statute at 40s.

BURGESS, in old times, was the inhabitant and householder of a burgage town. The word also meant the member representing such town, as where the inhabitants were said "*to pay the charges of their burgesses*," meaning their representatives. (See "*Boroughs*.")

A Burgess in more modern times is an inhabitant and ratepayer. By the Mun. Corp. Act, 1835, no person may be enrolled as a burgess in respect of any other title than by *occupation* and *payment of rates*. (See "*Abatement*.")

BURGESS LISTS.—The preparation of burgess lists in boroughs, *parliamentary as well as municipal,* is provided for by 41 & 42 Vic. c. 26. (See " *Times to be observed.")*

But in regard to Boroughs *Municipal only,* the procedure is still governed by the Mun. Corp. Act, 1835, and 32 & 33 Vic. c. 55 (the Mun. Franchise Act, 1869,), supplemented by 41 & 42 Vic. c. 26.

Section 22 of the former enacts—

> That the burgess lists revised and signed shall be delivered by the Mayor to the Town Clerk, who shall cause the said burgess list to be fairly and truly copied into one general alphabetical list in a book with every name therein, and numbered, beginning the numbers from the first name and continuing them in a regular series to the last name, and shall cause such books to be completed on or before the 22nd day of *October* in every year, and shall deliver such books, together with the lists, at the expiration of his office to the person succeeding him in such office : such book to be the burgess roll of the burgesses entitled to vote in the choice of the councillors, assessors, and auditors of such boroughs at any election which may take place in such borough between the first day of *November* inclusive in the year, and wherein such burgess roll shall have been made, and the first day of *November* in the succeeding year.

And the 7 Will. 4, and 1 Vic. c. 78, enact that when such burgess list is not made out or revised the previous roll shall continue in force.

In the case of *The Queen v. Mayor of Bolton,* it was held that a notice of objection under sec. 17, and Schedule (D), to a person on the burgess list of a Borough, need not specify the Parish in which the objector's qualifying property is situate, nor the nature of the property in respect of which the person objected to is rated.

Section 37 of the same Act provides for the election of two burgesses, who shall be " assessors " of such borough.

And section 24 of 5 & 6 Will. 4, c. 76, enacts in regard to the expenses—

> That the Council of every Borough should take an account of the reasonable expenses incurred by the Overseers in carrying into effect the provisions of the Act so far as relates to such lists, and direct the Treasurer of the Borough to pay the same.

Separate lists are to be made of Burgesses who are entitled to be elected Aldermen and Councillors, if resident within 15 miles, though by reason of living beyond 7 miles they are not entitled to be on the burgess list. 32 & 33 Vic. c. 55, s. 3.

CALCULATION.—In reckoning time under 31 & 32 Vic. c. 125, Sunday, Christmas Day, Good Friday, and any day set apart for a Public Fast, or Thanksgiving day, shall be excluded. s. 49.

CAMBRIDGE.—Chambers or Rooms in a College or Hall at Oxford or Cambridge are a Dwelling-House within 30 & 31 Vic. c. 102, and therefore the Occupier is not entitled to vote as a Lodger, and s. 78 of 2 & 3 Will. 4, c. 45, forbids any person to vote for the Boroughs of Oxford or Cambridge in respect of the occupation of such Chambers. (*Barnes v Peters.*) Further than that, by the Cambridge (Local) Act, 19 Vic. c. 17, s. 35, no Member of the University or College shall be entitled to be registered or enrolled by reason of any rate on property occupied by such University or College.

CANDIDATE.—A Candidate is defined to be " any person elected to serve in Parliament at an Election, and any person who has been nominated, or declared himself a Candidate at an Election " (whether successful or not). 31 & 32 Vic. c. 125, s. 3.   A Candidate at a Municipal Election means a "person elected, or who has been nominated or has declared himself a Candidate for election to an office." 35 & 36 Vic. c. 60, s. 2.

A Candidate *who goes to the Poll* is liable for the erection of Polling Booths. *(Muntz v. Sturge.)*

A Candidate, or his proposer if the former be out of the kingdom, may withdraw from his candidature by giving written notice during the time appointed for the election, but not afterwards. 35 & 36 Vic. c. 33, s. 1.

No liability is incurred by a person *nominated without his consent.*

A Candidate is deemed to be withdrawn if he neglects to find security for the Returning Officer's charges within one hour of the two hours fixed for the election. 38 & 39 Vic. c. 84, s. 3.

A Candidate need not reside in the place for which he stands, nor is it necessary that he should have any qualification.

Two or more Candidates may be made respondents to the same Petition. 31 & 32 Vic. c. 125, s. 22. (See "*Agent.*")

CANVASSER.—A " Canvasser," by 35 & 36 Vic., c. 60, is a person who solicits, or persuades, or attempts to persuade any person to vote, or abstain from voting at an election, or to vote or abstain from voting for any candidate at any election. A paid Canvasser may not vote. If he does it is an offence against the Act.

And by 7 & 8 Geo. 4, c. 37, a canvasser may not vote. The penalty for engaging a corrupt canvasser or agent is that the election shall be void. 31 & 32 Vic. c. 125, s. 44.

The employment and payment of paid Canvassers, although on an extensive scale, is not *in itself* bribery. (*Lambeth case*—See "*Disqualification.*")

CASE, Statement of—(See "*Appeal*"—"*Special case.*")

CATHEDRAL preachers, and it is presumed Choristers (See "*Bellringers*"), who are paid out of funds which arise from land, have not a freehold interest, but are servants only, hired under an arrangement that their salary shall be paid in a particular way. (*Bushell v. Eastes.*)

CERTIFICATE, The, given by a Barrister to the Overseers for their expenses is *final.* 31 & 32 Vic. c. 58, s. 32.

A Certificate of indemnity shall be given to Witnesses by the Judge at an Election Petition Trial. 31 & 32 Vic. c. 125, s. 33.

The Judge at such trial shall give a certificate as to the result, which shall be entered in the Journal of the House of Commons. *Ib.* s. 13.

CESTUIS QUE TRUST.—(See *"Beneficiaries."*)

CHAMBERS, in Inns of Court, and flats in Mansions, separately occupied as *dwellings* (and that notwithstanding the joint occupation of other parts of the building), are now a good qualification for the Borough franchise. 32 & 33 Vic. c. 55, s. 1, and 41 & 42 Vic. c. 26, s. 5.

Qualifications in respect of separate tenements or parts of houses, which were held good *before* the passing of the Act of 1878, as in the cases of *Cook v. Humber*, are therefore confirmed by it. (See *"Occupation."*)

But there must still be an occupation, *as Owner or Tenant*.

CHANGE OF ABODE does not disqualify. If a voter on the Register change his place of abode he may send in a fresh claim (See *"Claim"*), or he may make a Declaration under 28 Vic. c. 36, s. 10, of his true place of abode, according to the form given in the Schedule (B) to that Act. If no fresh claim be sent in, and no declaration be made, he may attend and prove that he retained the same qualification, on the last day of July in a County, or the 15th July in a Borough, and supply the true place of abode, 6 Vic. c. 18, s. 40. Borough Voters whose places of abode are incorrectly described may make Declarations before a J. P., or a Commissioner to administer Oaths. 41 & 42 Vic. c. 26, Schedule Form M. (See *" Forms."*)

CHARGE, A, of a corrupt practice may be gone into, and evidence taken, before proof of agency has been given. 31 & 32 Vic. c. 125, s. 17.

No public tax is to be considered *a charge in respect of lands* and tenements, in calculating *the clear yearly value above all charges.* 2 Will. 4, c. 45, s. 21. (See *"Value."*)

CHARITIES.—Bonâ fide subscriptions to any public or charitable purpose are not election expenses.

CHRISTMAS DAY, excluded in calculating " Times," (*vide.*)

CITIES and TOWNS being COUNTIES of themselves. The greater Cities and Towns were in old times convenient barriers for the King against the growing power of the Barons. To conciliate such Towns, the King gave up his rights to tallage, or tax them, and dignified many with the privilege of being *separate Counties,* some with more, some with less, territory annexed, and to be governed by their own Sheriffs and Magistrates.

There are now only 7 Boroughs which are Counties of themselves; all other Cities and Towns being Counties having been incorporated in their respective Counties by 2 Will. 4, c. 45, s. 17, Sch. G. These are—

1. BERWICK-ON-TWEED, made a free town by treaty between Edw. and Mary, Queen of Scots. James 1 confirmed the ancient charters. The right of Election is vested in the freemen, resident and non-resident.
2. BRISTOL, made by Edw. 3, 1373, a County of itself, under the designation "*The County of Bristol.*" The franchise is in the 40s. freeholders, freemen, freemen's sons, and the husbands of freemen's daughters, a compliment paid to the last by a Charter of Elizabeth.
3. EXETER, constituted by Hen. 8 into the *City and County of the City of Exeter.* The franchise is in the freemen and resident freeholders.
4. HAVERFORDWEST (called in Welsh "Hwlford"), ordained by James 1 to be a distinct County; the only city or town in the Kingdom which has its own Lord Lieutenant. The franchise is in the freeholders, and was before the Reform Act in the burgesses, and inhabitants paying scot and lot.
5. LICHFIELD, made, with a district of 16 miles in circuit, by Queen Mary, into a County of itself. The franchise is in the 40s. freeholders, burgage tenants, and resident freemen.
6. NOTTINGHAM, constituted (with the exception of the Castle and County Gaol) the "*Town and County of the Town of Nottingham,*" 27 Hen. 6. The franchise is in the 40s. freeholders and freemen.
7. NORWICH, constituted a County of itself by Hen. 4, in 1403. The franchise is in the 40s. freeholders, and freemen generally not receiving alms.

CITY OF LONDON. —(See "*Liveryman*"—"*London.*")

CLAIMS.—Overseers are to give notice annually, requiring county voters to send in their claims. (See "*Times to be observed.*")

County claimants omitted by the Overseers shall be inserted by the Barrister, on proof of due notice of the claim, and that they were entitled on the preceding 31st July.

£12 occupiers omitted from the Overseers' Lists may send in their claims before 25th August. 31 & 32 Vic. c. 58, s. 17.

£12 occupiers may also claim to be rated, if necessary. 30 & 31 Vic. c. 102, s. 30.

County voters residing out of the polling district to which the parish or township in which their qualifying property is situate belongs, but within the same County, may claim to vote at the polling district of the place where they reside, and voters not residing in the same County may claim to vote at the polling place of *any* district in the same County, before the Barrister. 6 Vic. c. 18, s. 36. (See "*Abode.*")

D

Vexatious claims are liable to costs. *Ib.* s. 46. Persons omitted from the lists of Parliamentary Voters in Boroughs must give notice to the Overseers. 41 & 42 Vic. c. 26, Form H.

Lodgers claim in Form H 2, and if otherwise than for continuous occupation, in the same form, *adapted to the case.*

The Declaration annexed to Form H 2 is to be primâ facie evidence of the qualification, and a false declaration is liable to a penalty.

Claims by burgesses and freemen are to be made and published at the same time as those by Parliamentary Voters. Form H 3. No form is given for freemen, but a notice given to the Town Clerk is sufficient. 41 & 42 Vic. c. 26.

The 5 & 6 Will. 4, c. 76, s. 17, provides, in regard to claims and objections in the Burgess lists, that—

> Every person whose name shall have been omitted in any list, and who shall claim to have his name inserted therein, shall on or before the 15th day of September in every year give Notice thereof to the Town Clerk in writing, according to the Form Number 2 in Schedule (D), or to the like effect, and every person whose name shall have been inserted in any list may object to any other person, and every person so objecting shall on or before the *15th day of September* in every year give to the Town Clerk of such Borough, and also give to the person objected to, or leave at the premises for which he shall appear to be rated, notice in writing according to the *Form Number 4*, Schedule (D), or to the like effect, and the Town Clerk shall include the names of all persons so claiming in a list according to the *Form Number 4*, Schedule (D), and shall include the names of all persons objected to in a list according to the *Form Number 5*, Schedue (D), and shall cause copies of such lists to be fixed on or near the outer door of the Town Hall, or in some public and conspicuous situation, during the eight days next preceding the first day of October, and he shall likewise keep a copy of the names of all persons claiming, and a copy of all the names of persons objected to, to be perused by any person, without payment of any fee, at all reasonable hours during the eight days, Sundays excepted, next preceding the *first day of October* in every year, and shall deliver copy of such lists to any person on payment of a sum not exceeding one shilling for each copy.

The notice of claim required under this section must state the Parish in which the Property is situate, in respect of which the claim is made (*Reg. v. Mayor of Kidderminster*). The initials only of the Christian names in the claimant's signature are sufficient. (*Reg. v. Mayor of Hartlepool.*)

CLEAR YEARLY VALUE.—(See "*Value.*")

CLERGY, The, had no votes for knights of the Shire in former times. By a resolution of the Cambridgeshire Committee, "Parsons and Vicars having no other freehold but glebe lands ought not to have a voice in Elections," but afterwards, this resolution notwithstanding, they assumed, and without objection, enjoyed the franchise by virtue of their ecclesiastical freeholds. It is said to have been in consequence of the saving of the rights of the clergy, and for granting a subsidy to the King. 16 & 17 Car. 2, c. 3.

But their rights are recognized by several modern statutes. 10 Ann, c. 23, assumed that a parson, by presentation to a benefice, obtained the franchise, and 12 Ann, c. 5, confirms this, enacting that parsons, vicars, and others having lands, &c., *are not restrained from voting* in respect thereof.

A Benefice, or office, held for life, and whether it be *quamdiu se bene gesserit* or not, (as the law will not presume a forfeit for misconduct), with an income arising from land, is a freehold, and gives the franchise. But if there be any clause, or condition, in the deed of appointment, or in the manner of holding the benefice or office, or in the circumstances, from which it would appear to be held *at the will of another*, and not for life, or if there be a power of removal for any reason other than misconduct, it is no longer a freehold.

A perpetual curate, with a benefice for life or stipend charged upon land, of sufficient value, is entitled, but not if paid out of funds which arise from land out of the *same parish*, fees for burials *out of the parish*, or customary fees not arising from land at all. (*Kirton v. Dear.*)

CLERK OF THE HOUSE OF COMMONS, The, is to receive the reports of the Judges on a Parly. Elect. Pet. when there is no Speaker or Deputy-Speaker. 31 & 32 Vic. c. 125, s. 4.

CLERKS OF THE PEACE are to issue their precepts to the Overseers, with forms of notices, list and copies of Register. 28 Vic. c. 36, Form 1, Sch. A: to receive statutory declarations of changes of abode: to give notice of holding, and attend the first Revision Court, and deliver lists to the Revising Barrister. 6 Vic. c. 18, s. 34: to receive the County Register from the Barrister, copy the same into books, and deliver the books to the Sheriff: and to keep printed copies, and deliver copies on payment, if required. *Ib.* s. 47. (See "*Times to be observed.*")

For enabling a successful appellant to obtain an order for the payment of his costs, he must, on making his declaration of appeal, require the Barrister to name the Clerk of the Peace as respondent. 41 & 42 Vic. c. 26, s. 37.

The expenses properly incurred by the Clerk of the Peace as such respondent, including any costs he may be ordered to pay to the appellant, shall be allowed him as part of the costs of the Revision.

CLERKS OF COMPANIES.—(See "*Liverymen.*")

COACH HOUSE AND STABLE, under the same roof, but with only a window communicating, jointly of the annual value of £10, separately of less, held to be a building within 2 Will. 4, c. 45, s. 17.

COLLEGE, The fellowship of a, not a freehold office within s. 18 of that Act. (*West v. Robson.*—See "*Benefice.*")

COMMENCEMENT, the, of the Register, is to be the 1st January after the Registration. 30 & 31 Vic. c. 102, s. 38.

D 2

The Burgess List comes into operation on the 1st November in every year.

COMMISSION, A, of enquiry into corrupt practices may be issued on a Judge's Report, and has the same effect as if it were a report of a committee of the House appointed to try an Election Petition, and the expenses of any such commission are to be defrayed as if they were Registration expenses of the County or Borough. 31 & 32 Vic. c. 125, s. 15.

Agents' Commission for collecting rents is to be deducted from the gross annual value of the qualifying property to ascertain the "clear annual value." (*Sherlock v. Steward.*)

Commission may be allowed to owners on payment of Rates in respect of property whether occupied or not. (See " *Abatement.*")

COMPANIES.—Shareholders in Companies, even when unincorporated, are held to have no interest, legal or equitable, to entitle them to the franchise as freeholders, for under their deeds of Association they have only a right to their share of the profits, which is personal property. (*Bennett v. Blain.*)

The Shareholders in the Sheffield Music Hall, having by deed vested the freehold in Trustees, were held not entitled. (*Freeman v. Gainsford.*)

A Member of a Mutual Benefit Society, entitled to an annuity from funds which sprang partly from land, was held not to be entitled. (*Robinson v. Ainge.*)

Where shares in Navigations, Bridges, &c., are declared by Act of Parliament to be *personal property*, they can be no qualification for the franchise, but when they are declared to be Real property, or in cases where the shareholders are the actual proprietors, they are freeholders, and all other requirements being satisfied, are entitled.

In the case of *Baxter v. Newman,* where land was bought, and a Mill fitted up thereon, out of moneys contributed by a large number of persons (36), who by a general partnership deed conveyed the land to Trustees, the Company being managed by a Committee, who were in occupation of and worked the Mill, and when the partnership deed declared that the land, Mill, &c., were to be deemed *personal* and *not* real estate, it was held that the partners had such an Equitable Estate as to entitle them to the franchise, the land and Mill being the basis of the trade from which the profits arose. The case of *Bennett v. Blain* militates against this older case, but Erle, J., in that case stated that " it *might be* supported."

COMPOSITION for Poor Rates, by Owners, was abolished by 30 & 31 Vic. c. 102, s. 7, by which the Occupiers of all tenements in Boroughs were required to be rated except in cases of houses let out *wholly in lodgings*, in which case the owner was rateable. But two years afterwards, 32 & 33 Vic. c. 41, s. 19, revived the power of rating owners, and overseers may now enter into voluntary agreements in writing with owners for an "abatement" without disfranchisement, and by 41 & 42 Vic. c. 26, s. 14, the application of this enactment is not to be confined to cases where an agreement has been made under s. 3 of 32 & 33 Vic. c. 41, s. 19, or where an order has been made under s. 4, but is to be of *general application*.

The importance of the latter enactment cannot be overrated, inasmuch as, notwithstanding the spirit of the law and the intention of the Legislature, that no inhabitant householder shall have the franchise unless he be also a ratepayer, the letter of the law as it now stands virtually abolishes rating, or the payment of rates, as a personal obligation, and therefore an ingredient of the franchise. Irrespective of either *value* or *payment*, any Occupier may now claim to be upon the Register. (See *"Abatement"—"Occupation."*)

Cross v. Alsop, Smith v. Seghill, and *Barton v. Overs, of Birmingham* should be read in connection with s. 19 of 32 & 33 Vic. c. 41, and s. 14 of 41 & 42 Vic. c. 26.

CONSENT, The, of all the petitioners is necessary to the withdrawal of an Election Petition. 31 & 32 Vic. c. 125, s. 35.

CONSTABLES, Police (except Special Constables), are incapacitated for both the Parliamentary and Municipal franchise. 19 & 20 Vic. c. 69, s. 9, and 22 & 23 Vic. c. 32.

CONSOLIDATED APPEAL.—Barristers may consolidate appeals when a number of claims and objections determined by them depend upon the same point of law. Such appeals are to be conducted as a single appeal, and any agreement to contribute to the costs may be made a Rule of Court. If not duly prosecuted, the Court may give the conduct of it to any of the persons interested. 6 & 7 Vic. c. 18, s. 44.

CONTEMPT OF COURT.—AAny witness not attending the trial of an Election petition, when summoned by a Judge to do so, is guilty of contempt, and may be committed. 31 & 32 Vic. c. 125, s. 32. Rules 42-43.

CONTRACT.—(See *"Agreement."*)

CONTRACTOR.—A clause is inserted in all public contracts, that no member of the House shall be allowed to participate therein, under a penalty of £500. (See *"Army."*)

CONVEYANCE OF VOTERS.—A Candidate, or his Agent *for Election expenses*, duly appointed under 26 & 27 Vic. c. 29, s. 2, may provide for the conveyance of Voters to the poll, but may not pay any money or give any valuable consideration to a Voter for or in respect of such travelling expenses. 21 & 22 Vic. c. 87.

The above applies to Counties only. In all Boroughs, except East Retford, Shoreham, Cricklade, Much Wenlock, and Aylesbury, it is illegal for the Candidate, or any one on his behalf, to pay any money for the conveyance of any Voter to the poll, either to the Voter or any person on his behalf. 30 & 31 Vic., c 102, s. 36. Such payment would void the Election (*Bolton, Stroud*), but it has been held that payment of travelling expenses after the poll without any proof of previous promise was not bribery. (*Northallerton.*)

By the 35 & 36 Vic. c. 60, s. 8, if a Candidate or an Agent for a Candidate pays or agrees to pay any money on account of the conveyance of a Voter to or from the poll, he is guilty of an offence against the Act and is liable on conviction to a penalty of £5.

CONVICT, A, for treason or felony cannot vote until pardoned. The conviction must be proved, as it might have been quashed. 33 & 34 Vic. c. 23, s. 2.

COPARCENERS are the female heirs of a person seised in fee, dying without male heirs. Being females, they cannot vote, but their husbands may, if otherwise qualified.

COPIES of the Register (County and Borough) are to be printed for sale, and also to be transmitted to one of H. M. Principal Secretaries of State within 21 days after the 1st February in every year.

In Municipal Boroughs the Burgess Roll, after Revision, is to be delivered by the Mayor to the Town Clerk, who is to copy the same, in an alphabetical list, into a Book. (See *"Times to be observed."*)

Copies may be had by all persons applying for the same on payment of a reasonable price for each copy. (See *"Rates of Payment."*)

Copies of decisions on appeals are admissible in evidence in all cases. 6 Vic. c. 18, c. 68.

COPYHOLD.—By the feudal system all the lands in the kingdom were held from the king. The tenures by which they were held were either *free* or *servile*. The former were by *knights service*, or in *free socage*, the latter were *villenage*, or *privileged villenage*. (Lands reserved to the king were held in *"ancient demesne,"*) Both before and after the Conquest a great number of persons held small portions of land, which had been granted to the Barons, Clergy, and other Dignitaries, to hold at the will of the Barons, &c., upon the performance of abject services. These were the villeins, and so they remained, unless freed by their Lords, until the 12 Car. 1, c. 24, abolished villenage.

These villeins, and their descendants, having enjoyed their lands in a long course of descent, the law gave them, though mere *tenants at will*, a prescriptive right to their lands, and *under evidence of a custom*, to hold the same notwithstanding the determination of the Lord's will.

Thus are derived the modern Copyholders, who are said to hold *at the will of the Lord according to the custom of the Manor*, and are called *tenants by Copy of Court Roll*, the only evidence of their title being their Surrenders and Admissions on the Court Rolls. If they hold, not at the will of the Lord, but according to the Custom of the Manor, they are called *Customary Freeholders.*

The 12 Car. 1, c. 24, which converted all feudal tenures into *free and common socage,* excepted the tenures "in *frankalmoigne*" (or by Divine service), tenures "*by copy of Court Roll,*" and the honorary services of "*Serjeanty,*" and so these tenures exist at the present day. "Knights of the Shires being elected by those that had "frank tenement" only, and "in pleno comitatu," at the County Court, those who did no suit there, i.e., *Copyholders,* were excluded.

In 1755, it was proposed in the House that "all copyholders holding their estates by copy of Court Roll," and not having the words "at the will of the Lord" inserted in the copies by which they held, should have a right to vote for Knights of the Shire, but it was lost by 242 to 107. 27 *Journ.,* 291.

A copyholder of the Manor of Woodstock, having voted at an election for Oxfordshire, and it being proved that the customary tenants of that Manor were reputed to have a right to vote, the 31 Geo. 2, c.14, was passed, enacting that such had no right to vote.

Copyholders were let in to vote by 30 & 31 Vic. c. 102. (See "*Ancient Demesne*"—"*Franchise.*")

CORPORATION.—"Artificial persons established for preserving in perpetual succession rights, which, conferred on natural persons, would fail in process of time;" a body politic. Corporations are either *aggregate,* or *sole;* of the former class are the Mayor, Aldermen, and Burgesses of a Corporate town, the Head and Fellows of a College, the Dean and Chapter of a Cathedral. The freehold property of an aggregate Corporation, being vested in itself, and not in its individual members, such members have no right to vote in respect thereof, but *sole* corporations, such as the King, Deans, and Prebendaries, distinct from their Chapters, Parsons and Vicars, can hold lands in their corporate capacity, i.e., to them and their successors, not to them and their heirs, and vote in respect thereof.

CORRUPT WITHDRAWAL.—Formerly a petitioner might, at anytime, withdraw his petition by giving notice to the Speaker, to the sitting member and his agent, and to any party admitted to oppose. 11 & 12 Vic. c. 98, s. 8. But an Election Committee might enquire into the circumstance of the withdrawal, and whether there had been any compromise. Now no Parliamentary Election Petition can be withdrawn except by leave of the Court, and notice of the application must be given in the County or Borough to which it relates, and the Court may substitute another Petitioner, and forfeit the security of the withdrawing Petitioner, if it considers such withdrawal to have been corrupt. 31 & 32 Vic. c. 125, s. 35.

And the same with regard to the withdrawal of Municipal Election Petition. 35 & 36 Vic. c. 60, s. 17.

COSTS ON OBJECTIONS.—The Barrister may give costs, in cases of groundless or frivolous and vexatious claims, or objections.

In the case of an objection to a county voter, the Revising Barrister (who is to treat each ground of objection separately) must award costs, if applied for, to the amount of 2s. 6d. at the least, although another ground of objection may have been sustained. 28 & 29 Vic. c. 36, s. 8.

The order for costs must be in writing, and may be delivered either to the person to whom the costs are to be paid or to some other person on his behalf (such costs not to exceed in the case of any one vote the sum of £5), and must be made before proceeding to hear any other notice of objection.

This power extends to persons opposing the claims of persons who have been omitted, and who have not given notice in writing to the Barrister of intention to oppose such claims. *Ib.*, s. 39.

Costs may be recovered by distress and sale of goods. 6 Vic. c. 18, s. 71.

In Boroughs where the objection is made otherwise than by an Overseer, and the name is retained by the Barrister, unless he is of opinion that it was reasonably made, *because of a defect or error in the entry, or (2) because of a difficulty in verifying or identifying the particulars of it, or (3) it is duly withdrawn, or (4) unless for some special reason he otherwise determines,* he shall order costs not exceeding *Forty shillings* on each specified head of objection contained in the notice. 41 & 42 Vic. c. 26, s. 27.

The Court may make any order respecting the Costs of an Appeal from a decision of the Barrister. 6 Vic. c. 18, s. 70.

The costs of an appeal may, if the Appellant is successful, be ordered to be paid by the Clerk of the Peace or Town Clerk, named as Respondent. 41 & 42 Vic. c. 26, s. 38.

As to Costs and taxation on Parliamentary Election Petitions —see 31 & 32 Vic. c. 125, s. 41. Rule 55.

And on Municipal Election Petitions—35 & 36 Vic. c. 60, s. 19. *Rule* 55.

COUNCILLORS.—Separate lists of Aldermen and Councillors qualified as such, but not as Burgesses, to be made in mixed Boroughs. 41 & 42 Vic. c. 26, s. 19. For residence see "*Aldermen,*" and 32 & 33 Vic. c. 35, s. 3.

COUNTY defined to be "any County, Riding, part or division of a County, returning a Knight or Knights of the Shire to serve in Parliament." 6 Vic. c. 18, s. 101. (6.)

County shall not include for Election Petition purposes any County of a City or Town. 31 & 32 Vic. c. 125, s. 3.

COUNTY COURT AND COUNTY VOTERS.—The ancient Court, where the Freeholders did suit and service and chose the knights of the Shire (*in pleno comitatu*), &c., was the County Court.

The Kingdom was originally divided into Counties, Counties into Hundreds, Hundreds into Townships (or Manors). Each Township had its Reeve and "four good men," and its local Court, subordinated to the Hundred Court, which, represented by its twelve men, was held monthly, and attended by the four men and the Reeve of each Township. This again was subordinate to the Shire Moot, or County Court, held twice a year, and presided over by the Shire Reeve, or Sheriff.

The Freeholders (thanes), the four men and Reeve of each Township, and the twelve men of each Hundred, attended this Court and so became County Voters. The 1 Hen. 5, C. 1, A.D. 1413, makes mention of the Knights, Esquires, and others "who shall be choosers," and the 7 Hen. 4, c. 15, confirmed the election of Knights of the Shire at the County Courts, to the persons who did suit and service there.

The Freeholders becoming numerous, a restriction was put upon the qualification for this franchise in the reign of Hen. 6, speaking of it as an innovation, or rather abuse of the franchise, and limiting the franchise to 40s.

" Whereas the Elections of Knights of Shires chosen to come to the Parliaments of our Lord, the King, in many Counties of England, have now of late been made by very great (outrageous) and excessive number of people dwelling within the same Counties, of the which most part was by people of small substance, or of no value, whereof every one of them pretended to have a voice equivalent as to making such elections, with the most worthy Knights and Esquires, whereby manslaughters, riots, batteries, and divisions among the gentlemen, and other people of the same Counties shall very likely rise and be, unless convenient and due remedy be provided in this behalf. Our Lord the King, considering the premises, hath provided, ordained, and established, by authority of this present Parliament, that the Knights of the Shires to be chosen to come to the Parliaments of our Lord the King hereafter to be holden shall be chosen in every County of the Realm of England, by people in the same Counties ; whereof every one of them shall have frank Tenement to the value of Forty Shillings by the year at the least above all charges, and that they which shall be so chosen shall be dwelling and resident within the same Counties ; and such as have the greatest number of them that may expend Forty shillings by the year and above, as afore is said, shall be returned by the Sheriffs of every County, Knights for the Parliament, by Indentures sealed betwixt the said Sheriffs and the said choosers thereof to be made. And every Sheriff of England shall have power, by the said authority, to examine upon the Holy Evangelists every such chooser, how much he may expend by the year, provided always, that he which cannot expend Forty Shillings by year, as afore is said, shall in no wise be chooser of the Knights for the Parliament, and that in every writ that shall hereafter go forth to the Sheriffs to choose Knights for the Parliament, mention be made of the said Ordinances." 8 Hen. 6, c. 7

The next restraint was the 10 Hen. 6, c. 2, requiring residence in the county where the vote was given, confirming and extending the 1 Hen. 5, c. 1, requiring Knights, Esquires, and others, who should be choosers, to be resident within the Shire on the day of the date of the Writ of Summons.

> "Whereas at the Parliament holden at Westminster the morowe of Saint Matthew the Apostle, the VIII. year of the King that now is, it was ordeined by authoritie of the same Parliament, that the Knights of all Counties within the realm of England to be chosen to come to the Parliaments hereafter to be holden, should be chosen in everie countie by people dwelling and resiant in the same, whereof everie one shall have freeholde to the valure of fortie shillings by yeere at the least above all charges, upon a certaine paine contained in the same statute, not making expresse mention in the same that everie man that shall be choser of any such Knights shall have freehold to the valure of fortie shillings at the least above all charges within the same countie, where such choser with other like shall make such election or elsewhere and for so much our Soveraigne Lord the King, by the advise and assent aforesaid and at the special request of the said Commons, hath ordained that the Knights of all the Counties within the said realme to be chosen to come to the Parliaments hereafter to be holden, shall be chosen in everie countie by people dwelling and resiant in the same, whereof everie man shall have freehold to the valure of fortie shillings by yeere at the least above all charges within the same Countie where anie such choser will medle with anie such election."

(See "*Franchise.*")

COURT, Tho.—This expression for the purposes of the Parliamentary Elections Act, 1868, shall mean the Court of Common Pleas, 31 & 32 Vic. c. 125, s. 2, and "Superior Court," for the purposes of 35 & 36 Vic. c. 60, means the Court of Common Pleas at Westminster (Now the Common Pleas Division of the H.C. of Justice.)

Rules of the Court.—See Parliamentary Rules, Appendix.

The Court is to certify to the speaker its decision on a special case, which shall be final, and in every case of withdrawal is to report the circumstances to the speaker—s. 36, also whenever the Respondent declines to oppose, s. 39.

All Petitions are filed and proceedings commenced in the Rule Office, Court of Common Pleas, Room No. 83, Royal Courts of Justice.

CURATE.—(See "*Clergy.*")

CURTESY, or the " Curtesy of England," the estate or interest which a husband has for his life in his wife's freehold estates, *after her death.* There must be a legal marriage, a seisin of the wife, the birth of issue, and the death of the wife.

By the custom of *gravelkind,* a husband may be tenant by the curtesy, without having had any issue, of a moiety of the wife's lands, but if the husband marries again he loses his estate.

This estate differs from the estate which a husband takes in lands of which the wife is seised for life or lives, of the value of 40s., but under £5, and marries after the 7th June, 1832. For this the husband has a qualification "*jure mariti.*"

DATE.—It is not essential that a notice of objection should bear the exact date upon which it was signed. It is sufficient if it is dated on any day upon which the objector is qualified to object, and within the period for making objections. (*Jones v. Jones.*)

DEAD MEN.—The Overseers are to write the word "Dead" before the name of any person on the Register whom they shall have reasonable cause to believe to be dead. 6 Vic. c. 18, s. 5. The Overseers are to omit from any List made by them the name of any person who shall appear from the Registrar's Return to be dead. 41 & 42 Vic. c. 20, s. 11. (See "*Registrar of Deaths*"—"*Times to be observed.*")

DEAF AND DUMB.—Whether a deaf and dumb man is incapacitated from voting is a point which has never been expressly decided, but from the cases of persons temporarily out of their mind, it is clear that *all* who can show or express a knowledge of what they are doing, and for whom they desire to vote by signs or otherwise, and can also comprehend the nature of an oath, are entitled to vote, and their vote should be received. A deaf and dumb person shall be questioned in writing as to his or her name, and whether he (or she) understands the purport of what he (or she) is about to do, and the form of oath or affirmation should be given to him (or her) to read, and the officer administering the same should point to the words as he proceeds, after which the Deponent should kiss the book.

If sworn through an interpreter, the Deponent should be sworn to depose the truth, and the interpreter " well and truly to interpret " the questions put by the officer, and the answers thereto.

DEANS AND CHAPTERS, Prebendaries and Canons.—The first, being a Body Corporate, cannot vote individually in respect of Corporate property; but when a Dean, Prebendary, or Canon can show that they hold as a *Corporation sole*, that neither the Chapter nor other person can interfere with them, or the house they possess, it appears they are entitled to vote. (*Ford v. Harington.*)

DEATH.—The Death of a Petitioner abates an Election Petition. 31 & 32 Vic. c. 125, s. 37. (See "*Abatement.*") On the death of a Respondent any number of persons, not exceeding 3, may be admitted to oppose.

DECISION.—The question for the Barrister as to the designation of the objector's place of abode as described on the Notice of Objection *being sufficient*, is a question of *fact*, and is without appeal. (*Sheldon v. Flatcher—Jones v. Pritchard.*)

The decision of the Barrister is affirmed on appeal with costs, when the Respondent appears to support it and the Appellant does not; but if it appear that the same point occurs in other cases, the Court may suspend its judgment. (*White v. Pring.*)

The decision of the Court of Appeal is conclusive, but the Court may review its decisions and over-rule them if shown to be erroneous. (*Hadfield's Case.*)

The decision of the Court of Appeal is to be notified to the Sheriff or Returning Officer, who shall alter the Register accordingly.

"Whenever by any judgment or order of the said Court any decision or order of any Revising Barrister shall be reversed or altered, so as to require any alteration or correction of the Register of Voters for any County, or any City or Borough, notice of the said judgment or Order of the said Court shall be forthwith given by the said Court to the Sheriff or Returning Officer, as the case may be, having the custody of such Register, and the said notice shall be in writing under the hand of one of the Masters of the said Court, and shall specify exactly every alteration or correction to be made, in pursuance of the said Judgment or Order, in the said Register, and such Sheriff or Returning Officer respectively shall upon the receipt of the said notice, alter or correct the said Register accordingly, and shall sign his name against any such alteration or correction in the said Register, and shall safely keep and hand over to his successors every such notice received by him from the said Court as aforesaid, together with the said register. 6 Vic. c. 18, s. 67.

DECLARATION.—In case of a change of abode or misdescription in the second column of the Register, County Voters may make a Declaration before a J.P. or Commissioner for Oaths, instead of making fresh Claims. (See "*Abode*.")

Any person guilty of making such a Declaration falsely is guilty of a misdemeanour, punishable by fine or imprisonment, for a term not exceeding one year, and the Barrister may impound the Declaration. 28 & 29 Vic. c. 36, ss. 10-11.

The Declaration is now extended to Borough Voters and Lodgers, and it would appear to go much further than in the case of a Declaration for a County Voter. In the case of the former, " to any person entered on any list of voters for a parliamentary borough, or any borough list, subject to revision for a municipal borough, whose name or place of abode, *or* the nature of whose qualification, *or* the name or situation of whose qualifying property, is not correctly stated in such list, *or* in respect of whom *there is any other error or omission* in the said list, whether he has received notice of objection or not." 41 & 42 Vic. c. 26, s. 24. It is a nice question how this is to be read in connection with sub-sec. 13 of Sec. 28, and one upon which, in all probability, conflicting decisions will be given. (See "*Abode*"—"*Succession*.")

These Declarations are to be sent to the Town Clerk on or before the 12th September, and, as in the case of a County Voter, are to be primâ facie evidence of the facts stated therein. Declarations are to be open for inspection, free of charge, until the 15th September.

In case of a Lodger, the Declaration annexed to his notice of claim is to be primâ facie of his qualification.

False Declarations in Boroughs are punishable as in Counties. s. 25.

DECLARATION OF ELECTION, The, is to be made forthwith, after the opening of the Ballot Boxes, and counting the Votes, to the

Clerk of the Crown in Chancery. 35 & 36 Vic. c. 33, s. 2. If the votes are equal, and the Returning Officer does not vote, all the candidates who have equal votes are to be declared duly elected. *Ib.*, s. 2

DELIVERY OF LETTERS BY POST.—Notices of Objection may be sent through the post. 6 Vic. c. 18, sec. 101. (See *"Duplicate."*)

Where the Voter resided 2 miles from a Post Town, at a place where there was no delivery except by some accidental conveyance, it was held that a notice posted in time to reach the post town on the 19th of August, in the ordinary course of post, was *not evidence* that the notice had been given to the Voter at his place of residence *on or before the 20th August*, in accordance with the statute. *(Lewis v. Evans.)*

DEMAND NOTE.—The want of notice does not excuse the payment of rates, though the form of a Demand Note is provided by an Order of the Local Government Board, 1875, to be left with every Ratepayer, and in default of a Demand Note notice is to be given. 32 & 33 Vic. c. 1, and see 41 & 42 Vic. c. 26, s. 10.

DENIZEN.—Is an alien born, who has obtained "ex donatione regis," Letters Patent to make him a British subject.

DEPOSIT.—(See *"Petition"—"Security."*)

Deposit of *money* may be made in case securities offered are deemed insufficient. 31 & 32 Vic. c. 25, s. 96, and 35 & 36 Vic. c. 60, s. 13.

DEPUTY RETURNING OFFICER, a person appointed to represent the R. O. in the several places when his presence is required, to keep order, regulate the number of electors to be admitted at one time, to exclude all other persons except the Candidates, the Clerks, the Agents of the Candidates, and the Constable on duty. Such may not act as Agents (30 & 31 Vic. c. 102, s. 50), and must make the Statutory Declaration of Secrecy before opening the Poll. 35 & 36 Vic. c. 33, s. 4.

DESCENT.—When property comes by descent, possession for the stated period is not required, in the cases of 40s. Freeholders, Freeholders in cities being counties, Burgage Tenants, Copyholders, Leaseholders, or Burgesses.

DESCRIPTION.—An inaccurate description or misnomer *of any person, place, or thing*, in any List or Register of Voters, is immaterial, if denominated so as to be *commonly understood*. 6 Vic. c. 18, s. 101. But no change may be made in the qualification. (See *"Amendment."*)

At the Birmingham Revision, Sept. 1879, an objection was made to the claim of S., described as of 225, Summer Lane, the correct description being 325. As a matter of fact, the mistake was made by the person who took his statement and wrote the address 225 instead of 325. The Revising Barrister said he thought by the 13th sub-section of section 27, he had not the power to change the description of qualification. The sub-section stated, "and whether any person is objected to or not, no evidence shall be given of any other qualification than that which is described in the list or claim, as the case may be, nor shall the revising barrister be at liberty to change the description of the qualification as it appears in the list, except for the purpose of more clearly and accurately defining the same." If he acceded, should he not be doing something more than "clearly and accurately defining the same?" Should he not be giving the man a qualification other than that which was described in the list?

It was submitted that if Mr. Saint admitted the claim he would not be giving the man a qualification which he did not possess, and that in acceding, the revising barrister would only be "more clearly and accurately defining the description of the qualification." The Revising Barrister held that the claim was bad on the ground that it misdescribed the qualification in respect of which S. claimed, and he had no power to make the amendment proposed, because were he to do so, he would be giving the man a qualification in respect of which he had not claimed. The claim was accordingly disallowed.

On the other hand, at the Greenwich Revision, on an objection being made to the name of M., of No 87, Hughes-fields, on the ground that he was described in the claim as of No. 88, his Honour said he had consulted two or three friends whose opinions he highly valued, and he found they were going to exercise very largely their powers of amending where the number was wrong. He should follow the same course. (See " *Successive Occupation*.")

DISQUALIFICATION.—(See " *Incapacity*.")

DISSENTING MINISTERS, removable *at the will* of their Congregations, are, in regard to County Franchise, much on the same footing as temporary Curates, having no Freehold in their office; but there is no reason why they should not have such a freehold, legal or equitable, in their houses or lands, as would give the franchise.

In an early case, before the Gloucestershire Committee, a motion that R. Phillips, a Minister at Tewkesbury, being in possession of a house, left by the will of Mary Workman to the minister for the time being of the Congregation of Dissenters there, had thereby a right to vote, was lost by 8 to 2. (*Luders*, 430.)

One W. Dickins had been Minister of a Congregation at Keysoe upwards of 20 years, in right of which he enjoyed 2 houses and an orchard, of greater value than 40s. On the one hand it was contended that he had not a freehold estate for life, but a *place*, with perquisites annexed, at the will of the Congregation; on the other hand that he held, not during pleasure, but "*quamdiu se bene gesserit*," and therefore had a freehold interest. Two Members of the Congregation proved that they did not understand that the Congregation had power to remove their Minister, nor had any ever been removed. He was held not entitled.

But in later cases, when an equitable freehold life interest has been shown, the Vote has been allowed. Where a house and garden worth more than 40s. per annum were granted to Trustees, upon trust, to permit the Minister for the time being to dwell therein, without paying any rent, the evidence of the Minister's appointment being his own statement that it was *general, and for life*, it was held that the appointment must be taken to be *for life*, that he had an equitable estate of freehold, and was entitled accordingly. (*Burton v. Brooks.*)

Where the Trust Deed was silent as to the duration of the appointment, but no power was contained in it for the Minister's removal, and the only evidence was the opinion of the Minister and Deacons that the appointment was *for life*, the Barrister held that the appointment was not one for life in law, and the Court refused to reverse his decision. (*Collier v. King.*)

The question in such cases appears to turn upon the point whether, if the Chapel Trustees bring ejectment against their Ministers, without any legal cause for removal, a Court of Equity would grant an injunction to stay the action. (*Ibid.*)

> At the Nuneaton Revision, 1879, in the case of a Nonconformist minister claiming for freehold houses, &c., the rents of which he received as Pastor, the Barrister said, on hearing an objection to the claim, that one of the conditions was that the claimant should teach according to the tenets of his denomination; and although his departing from such teaching might subject him to dismissal, such liability was not inconsistent with his tenure, which was a freehold, and he allowed the vote.

DISTANCES.—Borough Voters, Freeholders, Voters for Cities and Town, being Counties, and Voters for New Shoreham, Cricklade, Aylesbury, and East Retford, and Burgesses, must reside within 7 miles of the Borough, in a straight line from the nearest part of the Borough, measured on a horizontal plane, or on the Ordnance Map, if there be any, showing the limits. 6 Vic. c. 18, s. 76.

"Freemen being Liverymen" of the City of London, within 25 miles, measured in the same way. 30 & 31 Vic. c. 102, s. 46.

Voters whose rights have been reserved, within 7 miles, measured "from the place where the Poll shall heretofore have been taken." (See "*Aldermen.*")

DOWER.—

> "Where any woman, the widow of any person tenant in fee or in tail, shall be entitled to dower or thirds by the common law, out of the freehold estate which her husband died seised or possessed of, and shall intermarry with a second husband, such second husband shall be entitled to vote in respect to such dower or thirds, if such dower or thirds shall be of the clear yearly value of 40s. and upwards, although the same has not been assigned or set out by metes or bounds, if such second husband shall be in the actual receipt of the profits of such dower, &c." 20 Geo. 3, c. 17, s. 12.

DRUNKENNESS.—If a Voter presents himself in such a state of drunkenness as to be unable to repeat the Oath, it is clear that the Relieving Officer would not be at liberty to record the Vote.

DUMB.—(See "*Deaf.*")

DUPLICATE.—The Notice of Objection to any person on any List of Voters, or on the Livery List of the City of London (and in Counties to the occupying Tenant), may be sent by post, prepaid delivered to the Postmaster open, and in Duplicate. After being compared with the original, the Duplicate is returned to the sender stamped. 6 Vic. c. 18, s. 100.

To be a *Duplicate* the Notice must be addressed *outside and inside* the same as the original. (*Birch v. Edwards.*)

The production of the stamped Duplicate is proof of service in ordinary course of post. (*Hornsby v. Robson.*) See "*Delivery.*" It is also, if duly signed by the Objector, evidence that the *original* was signed by the Objector. (*Lewis v. Roberts.*)

It is not absolutely necessary that the County or Borough should be mentioned in the address, although required by the Act. If the Notice reaches its destination in due course of post it is evidence that the address is commonly understood so as to bring it within the provision as to *misnomers.* (*Jones v. Innons.*)

DUTIES.—(See " *Times to be observed.*")

DWELLING-HOUSE is the proper description of the In-habitant Occupier's qualification under 30 & 31 Vic. c. 102, s. 3, and is distinct from that created by 2 Will. 4, c. 45, s. 27, as well as from that of a Burgess created by 5 & 6 Will. 4, c. 76, s. 9.

Several cases have been heard as to what constituted a Dwelling-house, the two principal cases, *Thompson v. Ward* and *Brown v. Howard*, turning on the question whether a room (or two or more rooms on the same floor, *or on different* floors, of the house) occupied by a tenant, and used by him for all purposes as a separate dwelling-house, with the sole control thereof by locking the door and otherwise, such rooms being separately rated to the relief of the poor, *would* be such *a part of a house* as was contemplated by the Legislature, even though the passage, staircase, and outer door, &c., were used in common with the other tenants, provided that neither the owner, nor landlord, nor any person representing him, occupied any part of the house, and had no control whatever over the outer door. The judges were *equally divided in numbers*, and it has never been conclusively settled until it was enacted by 41 & 42 Vic. c. 26, that—

" In and for the purposes of the Representation of the People Act, 1867, the term ' dwelling-house' shall include any part of a house where that part is separately occupied as a dwelling."

(See "*Occupation.*")

The occupier must be on the 15th July, and must have been for the whole of the preceding twelve calendar months, an *inhabitant occupier as owner or tenant*, and must not during the qualifying year have let the house furnished, or allowed any one to occupy it, for more than four months in the whole.

EASEMENTS, or privileges, such as ways and water-courses, do not confer the franchise.

EFFACEMENT.—If any list, notice, &c., shall be destroyed, mutilated, effaced, or removed, before the expiration of the period during which it should continue, it must be renewed. 6 Vic. c. 18, s. 24.

ELECTION is the legal means of supplying a vacant seat in Parliament.

In COUNTIES the Sheriffs are to give public notice within two days after the receipt of the Writ of the day and place at which they will proceed to the Election, and of the time appointed, and of the day on which the Poll (if any) will be taken, and duplicates of such notices are to be posted to the Postmasters of each Polling place in the County endorsed, "Notice of Election." To this Notice is to be added a notice that all claims against the Returning Officer must be sent to him in writing within 14 days of the return. 38 & 39 Vic. c. 84.

In Counties the place of Election shall be in a convenient room in the town in which the Election would have been held if such Act had not passed, or when the Election would not have been held in a Town then in a room situate in such Town in the County as the Returning Officer may determine. 35 & 36 Vic. c. 33, Sch. 1, Rule 3.

The place of Election shall not be in a Church or Chapel. 2 Will. 4, c. 45, s. 68, and 16 & 17 Vic. c. 68, s. 6.

In BOROUGHS the Returning Officer must give notice on the day he receives the Writ or the day after; he must proceed to the Election within 4 days after the receipt of the Writ, giving 2 clear days' notice of the day of election. 35 & 36 Vic. c 35, Sch. 1, Pt. 1, and Sch. 2.

All persons having any bills, charges, or claims, upon any Candidate, in respect of an election, shall send them in to the appointed Agents within one Calendar month from the day of the declaration of the election. 26 & 27 Vic. c. 29, s. 3.

In case of death or legal incapacity of the appointed Agent then to the Candidate.

And a detailed statement thereof shall within 2 months after the election (or one month after bills delivered by a deceased Creditor) be delivered to the Returning Officer, signed, and he shall publish the same.

£5 a day is the penalty for noncompliance by any Candidate or Agent.

In MUNICIPAL BOROUGHS "Election" means election to an office. 35 & 36 Vic. c. 60.

The Election of Town Councillors in Boroughs under 5 & 6 Will. 4, c. 76, is to take place on 1st November in every year, the Burgesses then on the list having a vote for the full number of

Councillors to be elected, but if the Borough be divided into Wards the election is to be by the Burgesses of each Ward. s. 29, 30.

One-third of the Councillors are to go out of office every year, the number being supplied by a fresh election. s. 31.

Every such election is to be held before the Mayor and Assessors for the time being, the voting to commence at 9 a.m. and close at 4 p.m. s. 32.

The nomination of Candidates is regulated by 35 & 36 Vic. c. 33.

The Poll is to be conducted as in contested Parliamentary Elections.

On an equality of votes the Returning Officer may give a casting vote, and shall as soon as possible give public notice of the names of the Candidates elected, and in the case of a contested election of the total number of votes given for each Candidate, whether elected or not. 45th Rule, 5 & 6 Will. 4, c. 76. (See *"Petition."*)

In the UNIVERSITIES, 3 polling places may be provided and the members divided between them, with Pro. Vice-Chancellors to decide all questions, and Poll Clerks to take the poll. 16 & 17 Vic. c. 68, s. 5, and 30 & 31 Vic. c. 102, s. 44.

ELECTORS.—Two or more may present a Petition to the House of Commons complaining of corrupt practices.

EMPLOYMENT.—(See " *Corrupt Practices.*")

ENCLOSURE COMMISSIONER, eligible to Parliament. 25 & 26 Vic. c. 73.

ENGLAND includes Wales and Berwick-upon-Tweed. 20 Geo. 2, c. 42, s. 3.

ENTRY, Double, the Barrister is to correct, and his power is extended to all Lists. 41 & 42 Vic. c. 26, s. 28.

ERROR.—(See *"Amendment."*)

EQUITABLE INTERESTS.—(See " *Beneficiaries.* ")

EQUITABLE TITLE.—(See *"Agreement."*)

EVASION.—In case of evasion of service of Parliamentary Election Petition, Notice may be stuck up in the office of the Master stating the Petitioner, the prayer, and the nature of proposed security, which shall be deemed equivalent to personal service if so ordered by a Judge. Rule 15.

EVIDENCE (in support of right to vote) shall only be required in respect of such right as shall be called in question, each ground of objection being taken separately. 28 Vic. c. 36, s. 7-8, applied to Boroughs by 41 & 42 Vic. c. 26, s. 26. Evidence, in support of the qualification, may be given either by the claimant, or by any person acquainted with the facts, as by the solicitor, steward, trustee; by the landlord or tenant, on his behalf if required upon oath: or by the production of probates of wills, title deeds, receipts, permits, or other necessary documents.

No evidence shall be given or any other qualification than that described in List of Voters or Claim. 6 Vic. c. 18, s. 40.

There is no appeal on the admissibility of Evidence. 6 Vic. c. 18, s. 65.

Copies of Decisions on Appeal to be admitted in Evidence. *Ib.* s. 68.

Lodgers' Declaration of qualification is primâ facie evidence. 41 & 42 Vic. c. 26, s. 23.

The burden of proof will be thrown on the *objector*, who will be liable to cost as in cases of objection to any other voter. *Ib.* s. 28.

The admissibility of evidence in Election Petition is a question of *law*, which may be reserved. 30 & 31 Vic. c. 125, s. 12.

Evidence need not be stated in a Petition, but the Court may order particulars to prevent surprise and unnecessary expense *Rule* 6.

Evidence of corrupt practices may be gone into without first proving Agency. (See *"Agency."*)

Recriminating Evidence may be given by a Respondent. 31 & 32 Vic. c. 125, ss. 24–53.

Evidence is to be taken down by a Shorthand Writer, and is to accompany the Judge's Certificate.

Evidence is not to be received against a vote on any head of objection not specified without leave. Rule 7.

EXCHEQUER, The Chancellor of the, is eligible to sit, and so is his *Secretary.* Comptroller of the Exchequer, Auditor-General, and Clerks, are ineligible.

EXCISE.—Commissioners and other officers may vote, but are ineligible for a seat. 37 & 38 Vic. c. 22.

The Clerks in the Excise Office are *ineligible, and must not interfere at Elections.* 7 & 8 Geo. c. 53, s. 9.

EXPENSES of Clerks of the Peace, as provided for by 6 Vic. c. 18, s. 54, including expenses under 30 & 31 Vic. c. 102.

Expenses of Town Clerks and Returning Officrs by 6 Vic. c. 18, s. 58, and 38 & 39 Vic. c. 84.

Expenses of Overseers and Relieving Officers by 6 Vic. c. 18, s' 57, and 31 & 32 Vic. o. 58-31.

EXPULSION from House of Commons, a disqualification. (*King's Lynn Case.*)

FACT, Questions of, to be decided by Barrister. (*Wood v. Overseers of Willesden.*)

FACTORIES.—Workrooms in factories let off to different persons for Spinning are " buildings " under 2 Will. 4, c. 45, s. 27, each tenant having exclusive use of his room with the key of his door which be approached by a common staircase, the Landlord finding steam power. (*Wright v. Town Clerk of Stockport.*)

Doubts as to necessity for " actual severance " are set at rest by 41 & 42 Vic. c. 26, s. 5.

FAST DAY.—(See " *Christmas Day.*")

FAVOURS.—The giving of favours at Election is prohibited, but the seat is not affected thereby, though the payment for such is illegal. 17 & 18 Vic. c. 102, s. 7.

FELLOWS.—(See "*College.*")

FELONS.—Persons convicted of Treason or Felony are incapacitated from voting until pardoned, or sentence expired. But judgment must be proved, as the conviction may have been quashed. 32 & 34 Vic. c. 23, s. 2.

After pardon, Felons may be elected. (*Bullock v. Dodds.*)

FEMALES, unmarried. are eligible for the Municipal Franchise. The Act says "*every person,*" but though the disability to vote at Municipal Elections has been removed for *the sex,* there remains the disability relating to *coverture.*

It has been decided that a married woman, though otherwise qualified, cannot vote at an election of Town Councillors. And a woman otherwise qualified loses her right of voting if married before an Election. (*The Queen v. Harrald.*)

FINAL.—Every judgment and decision of the Court of Appeal is final. 6 Vic. c. 18, s. 66. But the Court may review its own decisions.

FINE.—The Revising Barrister may fine—

" Any Assessor, Collector, Overseer, Assistant Overseer, or Relieving Officer, who wilfully neglects or refuses to attend any Court, or the Barrister when summoned, not more than £5 and not less than 40s., and any Overseer wilfully or neglecting to make out any list, or insert the name of any claimant, omitting, without reasonable cause, the name of any person duly qualified, or inserting it if not duly qualified, or neglecting or refusing to publish any notice, or list, or copy of the register, or to deliver the same to the Clerk of the Peace as required, or to deliver to the Barrister the several lists, or who shall be wilfully guilty of any other breach of duty in the execution of the Act," 6 Vic. c. 18, s. 50.

Fines shall be paid to the Clerk of the Peace, or Town Clerk, or secondary. s. 52.

Such fine does not take away any right of action.

FISHERY.—A several Fishery is a sufficient Freehold Interest to qualify for the County Franchise.

FIRE, Destruction of qualifying property by, will not deprive the Occupier of houses and yard, he still continuing to hold the site on which they stood. And so when a house is being pulled down and rebuilt.

FLAGS AND BANNERS.—Payment for such at Elections is illegal, and persons employed as flag bearers disfranchised. 7 & 8 Geo. 4, c. 37.

FLATS.—(See "*Chambers.*" "*Lodgings.*")

FOREIGNERS not entitled to the franchise. (See "*Alien.*")

FOREIGN SERVICE. Officers in the Army and Navy while on H.M.S. do not lose their votes. (*Walker v. Payne.*)

FORMS used in Registration:

IN COUNTIES:

1. Precept to Overseers. 28 Vic. c. 36, Sch. A., No. 1. 30 & 31 Vic. c. 102, s. 58. 31 & 32 Vic. c. 58, s. 34.
2. Notice by Overseers to Claimants. 6 Vic. c. 18, Sch. A., No. 2. 31 & 32. Vic. c. 58, s. 17. Appendix., p. 183.
3. Notice of property claim to be given to the Overseers. 6 Vic. c. 18, Sch. 2. Appendix, p. 183.
4. Notice of Claim by £12 occupiers to be given to the Overseers on or before Aug. 25. 30 & 32 Vic. c. 58, s. 17. Appendix, p. 184.
5. Declaration as to change of abode. 28 Vic. c. 36, Sch. B.
6. List of property Claimants. 6 Vic. c. 18, Sch. A., No. 3. Appendix, p. 185.
7. List of Occupiers rated at £12 and upwards. 6. Vic. c. 18, Sch. B. 3. 30 & 31 Vic. c. 102. Appendix, p. 185.
8. Notice of Objection to be given to Overseer. 6 Vic. c. 18, Sch. A. 3. Appendix, p. 186.
9. Notice of Objection to be given to parties on Register and to occupying tenants. 28 Vic. c. 36, Sch. A.
10. List of Persons objected to, to be published by the Overseers Appendix, p. 186.

IN BOROUGHS : 41 & 42 Vic. c. 26.

A. Precept of Town Clerk.
B. Notice by Overseers of a Parliamentary borough of rates in arrear.
C. Notice to party in arrear of rates.
D. List of Parliamentary voters and burgesses in " mixed Boroughs."
 (1) Under R. Act, 1832, R. P. Act, 1867, and Municipal Corporation Acts, in divisions.
 (2) Parliamentary, under any other right except freemen or lodgers
 (3) Parliamentary, lodgers, continuous occupation.
E. List of Parliamentary voters (Parliamentary boroughs).
F. List of Burgesses (Municipal boroughs).
G. List of persons qualified to be Aldermen or Councillors but not as burgesses.
H. Notices of Claim.
 (1) Parliamentary (general).
 (2) Continuous occupation of lodgings.
 (3) Municipal.
I. Notice of objection—
 (1) Parliamentary—to overseer.
 (2) Parliamentary—to party.
 (3) Municipal—to overseer.
 (4) Municipal—to party.

See Additional Forms p. 54.

K. Lists of Claimants to be published by overseers.
 (1) General—Parliamentary.
 (2) Lodger claimants—(Parliamentary).
 (3) Municipal only.
L. List of objections to be published by overseers.
 (1) Parliamentary.
 (2) Lodgers (continuous occupation).
 (3) Municipal.
M. Declaration for correcting misdescription in list.
N. Notice of withdrawal of objection,
 (1) To party objected to.
 (2) To Town Clerk.

O. Notice of revival of objection.
  (1) To party objected to.
  (2) To Town Clerk.
P. Direction for guidance of overseers in making out the lists.
Q. Directions for guidance in the formation of the Parliamentary register and burgess roll.

Additional Forms, to be used in Parliamentary and Municipal Boroughs whose boundaries are coextensive.

11. Notice of Claim—Parliamentary. Appendix, p. 187.
12. Notice of Claim—Municipal. Appendix, p. 188.
13. Notice of Objection—Parliamentary. Appendix, p. 188.
14. Notice of Objection—Municipal. Appendix. p. 189.
15. Notice of Objection—Parliamentary. Appendix, p. 189.
16. Notice of Objection—Municipal. Appendix, p. 190.

Forms used in the City of London as regards Freemen being Liverymen.

17. Notice of Objection to parties inserted in the List of the Livery. Appendix, p. 190.
18. Notice of Objection, to be given to the Secondaries of the City of London, and to the Clerks of the respective Livery Companies. Appendix, p. 191.
19. List of Freemen, being Liverymen, objected to, to be published by the Secondaries. Appendix, p 191.

FORTY SHILLINGS.—Bishop Fleetwood in his "Chronicum Pretiosum" shows that 40s. in the reign of Hen. 6 was equal to £12 in the Reign of Queen Anne, and Sir William Blackstone writes that £12 was equal in his time to £20.

FRANCHISE.—COUNTY VOTERS.

Under 8 Hen. 6, c. 7, s. 40. 40s. FREEHOLDERS. (See "County.")
Under 2 W. 4, c. 45, s. 18. FREEHOLDERS.

Persons seised of Freehold lands or tenements *for life or lives*, of the annual value of 40s., provided (*a.*) they actually and "bona fide" occupy the premises, (*b.*) or were seised on the passing of the Reform Act, 7th June, 1832, *or* have acquired the same subsequently by marriage, marriage settlement, devises, or promotion to some benifice or office. Possession of the same for 6 months previous to the 31st July unless acquired by descent, &c., and *then* possession.

Under 30 & 31 Vic. c. 102, s. 5. FREEHOLDERS.

Persons of full age, not subject to any legal incapacity, seised at law or in equity, of lands or tenements of any tenure whatever, whether for life or lives, or any larger estate, of the clear yearly value of £5 above all charges. Possessed of the same for 6 months previous to 31st July, unless acquired by descent, &c.

Under 2 Will. 4, c. 45 s. 20. LEASEHOLDERS.

Persons entitled, as lessees, or as assignees, to lands or tenements of any tenure, for the residue of a term originally created for not less than 20 years, of the clear yearly value of £50 above all charges, 12 months' possession as above, &c. Also sub-lessees and their assignees if in *actual occupation.*

Under 30 & 31 Vic. c. 102, s. 5. LEASEHOLDERS.

Persons entitled, as lessees or assignees to lands or tenements of any tenure, held for the residue of a term originally created for not less than 60 years, whether determinable on a life or lives or not, *and whether in occupation or not,* of the clear yearly value of £5 above all charges.

It has been a question whether sub-lessees and their assignees are required to be in occupation.

Under 2 Will. 4, c. 45. s. 20. £50 TENANTS. (*Chandos Clause.*)

OCCUPIERS at a yearly rent of not less than £50, of premises under the same landlord, who have not been rated at £12 per annum, and have occupied for 12 months previous to 31st July.

Under 30 & 31 Vic. c. 102, s. 6. £12 OCCUPIERS.

Every man of full age, not subject to any legal incapacity, who has on 31st July, and for the preceding twelve months, occupied lands or tenements of the rateable value of £12 and upwards, has been rated to all rates made for the relief of the poor in respect of the premises, and has on or before 20th July paid all such rates due on the previous 5th January.

BOROUGH VOTERS.

Under 2 Will. 4, c. 45, s. 3, and 30 & 31 Vic. c. 102, s. 56. FREEHOLDERS AND BURGAGE OWNERS—

Customary Freeholders, in Cities and Towns being Counties of themselves (*vide*) having estates of inheritance of the annual value of 40s., or according to the usage of the particular city or borough, possessed of the same for 12 months previous to 15th July, unless acquired by descent, &c., resident for 6 calendar months previous to 15th July within such city or borough, or within 7 miles thereof.

Under 2 Will. 4, c. 45, ss. 18 and 31. FREEHOLDERS AND BURGAGE OWNERS, as above—

Having Estates for life or lives of the annual value of £10, and possessed for 12 months, as above, and resident as above,

FREEHOLDERS AND BURGAGE OWNERS having Estates for life or lived *under* the annual value of £10, provided:

  (a.) They actually and " bona fide " occupy the premises;
  (b.) or were seised of the same on 7th June, 1832;
  (c.) or have acquired the same since by descent, &c.

Under 2 Will. 4, c. 45, s. 32. FREEMEN,

by birth or servitude, and those claiming by birth through them[*] in places other than London, who have served the required time to a freeman in some trade and been admitted and enrolled according to the charter, usage, or bye-law of the city or borough for which they claim, and have been resident, and registered.

Under 2 Will. 4, c. 45, s. 32, and 30 and 31 Vic. c. 102, s. 46, FREEMEN,

being Liverymen of the City of London, who have become entitled by presentment, election, or purchase, and have been admitted and enrolled, and also resident within 25 miles.

Under 2 Will. 4, c. 45, s. 34, temporarily reserved, continued by 30 & 31 Vic., c. 102, s. 56. FREEMEN,

who were admitted or entitled to be admitted for any cause on 31st March, 1831, and those claiming through them.

Under 2 Will. 4, c. 45, s. 34. FREEHOLDERS, OR BURGAGE OWNERS:

Customary freeholders in ordinary borough towns, who were entitled to vote on 31st March, 1831, or acquired their right between that date and 7th June, 1832, by descent, &c. If burgage tenure it must be undivided, not created within legal memory, and held of a superior lord at a fixed rent. If acquired by purchase, 12 months' possession or receipts of the rents. Residence for 6 months previous to 15th July.

Under 2 Will. 4, c. 45, s. 38. INHABITANTS AT LARGE,

occupying a tenement, and residing in the borough, though the residence need not be continuous there must be the " animus revertendi."
SCOT AND LOT voters, who must be rated to and pay the poor rates.
POT WALLERS, who must furnish and cook their own diet at their own fireside.

N.B.—Omission from the Register in any of the foregoing classes for 2 successive years (unless on account of having received parochial relief within 12 months or absence on H.M. Service) absolutely disqualifies.

Under 2 Will. 4, c. 45, 30 & 31 Vic. c. 102, and 41 & 42 Vic. c. 26. £10 OCCUPIERS:

EVERY MALE PERSON of full age, not subject to any legal incapacity, occupying within any city or borough, or any place sharing in the election therefore, *as owner or tenant,* any house, warehouse, counting house, shop, or other building, or any part of a house where that part is separately occupied for the purpose of any trade, business,or profession, (which may be described as office, chambers, or studio, or by any like term applicable to the case), either separately or jointly with any land within such city or Borough, occupied therewith by him as owner, or occupied by him as tenant under the *same landlord,* of the clear yearly value of not less than £10.

Under 30 and 31 Vic. c. 102.   41 & 42 Vic. c. 26.   INHABITANT OCCUPIERS:

Every man of full age, and not subject to any legal incapacity, who is on the 15th July in any year, and has been during the preceding 12 calendar months, the occupier, as owner or tenant, of any *dwelling-house* within the borough, and has not during such 12 calendar months let the house furnished or allowed anyone to occupy it for more than 4 months in the whole, and has during such occupation being rated as an ordinary occupier to all poor rates, and has on or before the 20th July paid an equal amount in the pound to that payable by ordinary occupiers in respect of all poor rates payable by him up to previous 5th January. But no man shall be entitled by reason of his being a *joint occupier* of any dwelling-house. (See "*Occupation.*")

Under 30 & 31 Vic. c. 102, s. 4, and 41 &42 Vic. c. 26, s. 5. LODGERS :

Every man of full age, and not subject to any legal incapacity, who as a lodger has occupied in the same borough, separately and as sole tenant, for 12 months preceding the 15th July, lodgings of the clear yearly value, let unfurnished, of £10; such lodgings *to include* any apartments or place of residence, whether unfurnished or furnished, in the same dwelling-house, and not to be deemed to be occupied otherwise than separately by reason only that the occupier is entitled to the joint use of some other part of the same house. (See "*Lodger.*")

MUNICIPAL.

Under 32 & 33 Vic. c. 55, and 41 & 42 Vic. c. 26:

Every person of full age, who, on the 15th day of July in any year, shall have occupied any house, warehouse, counting-house, shop, or other building within any Borough, during the whole of the preceding 12 calendar months, and also shall, during the time of such occupation, have resided within the said Borough, or within 7 miles thereof. Rated and enrolled.

FREEHOLD.—The 8 Hen. 6, c. 7, first requiring qualification of a certain value, forms the basis of the modern county franchise.

The words "frank tenement" in that Statute, as opposed to "villein tenure" (see "*Copyhold*"), is descriptive as well of the tenancy as the interest which the owner should have in the land, viz., Freehold. The word "Tenement" is sufficiently large to comprise not only *land*, but every profit issuing out of land, as *offices*, *rents*, *tithes*, *rent charges*, *tolls*, *several fisheries*, *free warrens*, *common of mines*, and *turbaries appendant*.

Freehold Estates are,
1. Estates of Inheritance, which are
    (a.) Fee simple, to hold to A and his heirs, for ever,
    (b.) Base or qualified fee, to A and his heirs, tenants of the manor of D,
    (c.) Conditional fee, to A and his heirs *male*,
    (d.) Fee tail, to A and the heirs of his body begotten, &c.,
2. Estates not of Inheritance, as
    (e.) Tenant in tail after possibility of issue extinct,
    (f.) Tenant by the courtesy of England,
    (g.) Tenant in dower,
    (h.) Tenant for life, or lives.

A freehold tenement sufficient to give a county vote may be made up of *two separate* rent-charges in fee, issuing out of 2 several pieces of freehold land in the same county, though neither of them alone amounts to 40s. (*Wood v. Hopper.*)

The occupier of waste land, under a lease from the lord of the manor for three lives, with a covenant for renewal, has such a freehold as will entitle him to be registered. (*Phillips v. Salman.*)

No person is entitled to vote for the county as a freeholder, in respect of any house or land in his own occupation, if such premises *would confer* a borough vote, and whether such borough vote is registered or not, but it is possible to be on the County and Borough Registers for properties within the same Parliamentary Borough, as where a person owns and occupies freehold land of sufficient value, viz. 40s., in the one case, and also occupies a house of sufficient value, viz. £10, in the other.

And some freeholders and burgage owners, whose rights were reserved, may also be upon both registers, their borough rights being expressly reserved, and their county rights not affected, as they do not occupy. 2 Will. 4, c. 45, ss. 24, 35, 131. (See "*Bedesmen*"—"*Beneficiaries*"—"*Borough*.")

FREEMAN.—The Freeman as well as the Liveryman has his origin in the early gild or trading company, called in the old charters "gilda mercatoria," or, as afterwards used, "*gilda mercatorum*," the word "*gild*" being applied to those payments made to the King, or Superior Lord, for rents, taxes, &c., in lieu of services.

Thus, in Domesday Book,
> "Stafford. Probi de burgo habent 14 (mansuras). Hi omnes habent socham et socham. Rex habet de omnibus *geldum* per annum."

Hence persons liable to the same payment to a Lord was said to be *in his gild*.

The members of trading gilds, having the right to admit strangers, new comers were introduced into the gilds, without forming any connection with the superior lord, or doing him any services. So the number of inhabitants was increased, the number of burgage owners was not. Wages being paid to their representatives in Parliament, some of the burden was thrown upon the new comers, and this led to many strangers being admitted.

In time the distinction became less marked, and all were known as "freemen of the gild," originating the right of "freemen."

Freemen are either by birth, servitude, or marriage. The right of freemen by servitude is obtained by articles of apprenticeship to a "freeman." A freeman by taking an apprentice who serves him confers upon him the franchise. But if the apprentice serves another master who is not a freeman, during a portion of his articles, he acquires no right. (*Lucas's case.*)

There are a variety of rights, which are recognized as such. Almost every city and borough has this franchise peculiar to itself, and where there is no act, charter, or last determination of the House to do so, the ancient local usage regulates it. In the words of 2 Will. 4, c. 45, s. 33, "So long as he shall be qualified as an elector according to the usages and customs of such city or borough." In Peterborough there are, or were, 2 districts, the inhabitants of which vote in different rights, in one householders *not receiving alms*; in the other inhabitants *paying scot and lot*. Some must pay church rates, some must be in possession a year, others only 40 days. (See "*Cities and Towns.*")

In Bristol persons are admitted freemen who marry freemen's daughters. In Dublin and Youghal admissions to freedom in respect of marriage are applied for *by petition*, and granted by *special grace*, but a right to vote is conferred. Other freemen claim *by birth* through those who were admitted, or entitled to be admitted, on March 1st, 1831. (See "*Birth.*")

Freemen must reside for six calendar months previous to the 15th July within the city or borough for which they claim, or within seven miles thereof. (See "*Distances.*")

Freemen are entitled to vote immediately after registration; their admissions are enrolled in the books of the Corporation. The appearance of the name upon such roll is presumptive evidence of admission, and is the only evidence of their right to be registered. 12 Geo. 3, c. 21. (See "*Liverymen.*")

No stamp duty is chargeable on the admission of any person entitled to his freedom by birth or servitude.

Claims of freemen are to be made out at the same time as other Parliamentary voters.

The Town Clerk is to make out the Freeman's Roll at the same time as the other lists, 41 & 42 Vic. c. 26, s. 16, Form D 2. The Roll may be inspected and copies taken.

In Municipal Boroughs, which are also Parliamentary Boroughs, freemen who are also Parliamentary Electors ought still to be on the freeman's roll. (See *"Liverymen."*)

FREE WARREN, a freehold qualification. "A Royal franchise granted by the Crown to a subject for the preservation or custody of beasts and fowls of Warren." (*Whart. Law. Lex.*)

FUNERAL EXPENSES, Payment of, is parochial relief. *(Oldham.)*

GREENWICH and **CHELSEA** Hospital. Pensioners are not disqualified as being in receipt of alms.

The Governor is ineligible, being a Military Governor, and so is the Surgeon. (*Dobson v. Jones.*)

GROUNDS of objection. (See *"Objection."*)

HEADS of objection to each vote, (on an Election Petition), and a list of voters intended to be objected to, are to be delivered by the Petitioner to the Master. Rule 7.

HEARING of objection to security given by the Petitioner (on Election Petition) may be heard before the Master, vivâ voce, or by Affidavit. Rule 28.

HEREDITAMENTS is a more comprehensive word than "lands" or "tenements," for it applies not only to lands and tenements, but to some subjects of personal property, and to mere rights which imply a privation of property.

HOUSE.—The 41 & 42 Vic. c. 26, s. 5, enacts that "house, warehouse, counting-house, shop, or other building," shall include *part* of a house where that part is *separately* occupied for the purpose of any trade, business, or profession; and any such part may, for the purpose of describing the qualification, be described as "Office," "Chambers," " Studio," or by any like term applicable to the case, and goes on to say that for the purposes of any of the Acts referred to in this section where an occupier is entitled to the sole and exclusive right of any part of a house, that part shall not be deemed to be occupied otherwise than separately, by reason only that the occupier is entitled to the joint use of some other part.

The interpretation contained in this section of "dwelling-house" shall be in substitution for the interpretation thereof contained in Section 61 of the Representation of the People Act, 1867.

Before this enactment, it was held that it was never intended to create part of a house used for residence, and not for commerce, a sufficient qualification, but that still, by what was called "actual severance," *a part of a house might become a house,* but that, notwithstanding, no part of that which is so used as a dwelling-house might be used *in common* with the other occupants, but the occupation must be similar to that of Chambers in Inns of Court. (*Cook v. Humber—Boon v. Howard.)*

Where, therefore, a sufficient separation, occupation, and tenancy was found *before the Act* of 1878 was passed, to meet the requirements of 2 Will. 4, c. 45, s. 27, there is now ample confirmation.

Under 2 Will. 4, c. 45, s. 27-29, house is a good description; there is nothing requiring it to be a " dwelling-house."

Where a party occupied a house and shop jointly with another person: Held that it was not necessary to state the fact of the joint occupation in the list of voters, and that the words "house and shop" were a sufficient description of his qualification. (*Daniel v. Camplin.*)

And the word "house" in the third column is sufficient although the qualification is by the occuption of two houses occupied in immediate succession, provided the fourth column gives a proper description of both houses. (*Hitchins v. Brown.*)

A claimant in a borough in which freeholders have the franchise as well as occupiers, in his notice of claim described his qualification as "house :" Held a sufficient description of a qualification as occupier of a house under 2 Will. 4, c. 45, s. 27. Held, also, that the Barrister had power to amend the inaccuracy of description under s. 40 of 6 Vic. c. 18, by adding "Occupier of." (*Ford v. Boon.*)

But the omission of such proper description of both houses in the fourth column, even though the third colunm stated "house in succession," would be fatal. (*Onions v. Bowdler.*)

HOUSE OF COMMONS.—From the earliest times there has been a General Assembly or Parliament in this Kingdom. During the Saxon times it was called the "Wittenagemote," or Assembly of Wise Men. It was continued under various names, but from the reign of Henry 3rd it has been called a "Parliament."

The House of Commons is summoned by *Warrant* or order, from the Queen in Council, to the Lord Chancellor, Lord Keeper, or Lord Commissioner of the Great Seal, commanding Writs to be issued for the Election of Knights, Citizens, and Burgesses to serve in Parliament (for old forms of Writ *see* "*Writ*"). The form now in use is prescribed by 35 & 36 Vic. c. 33, s. 2.

When a new Parliament is summoned there are to be 35 days at least between the Proclamation and the day appointed for the Meeting. 15 & 16 Vic. c. 23.

On a vacancy by death, removal to the House of Lords, acceptance of office, by bankruptcy, or otherwise, the Speaker, on motion made, issues a Warrant to the Clerk of the Crown in Chancery (the officer who immediately after Parliament meets receives all returns and issues all writs), to issue a Writ for the election of a new member.

HUSBAND.—If a woman seised of an estate for life or lives, of the yearly value of 40s. but under £5, married after the passing of the Reform Act (June 7, 1832), the husband is entitled to vote for it during her life, jure mariti, unless it be settled to her separate use under marriage settlement or goes away by devise after her death, without his occupying the premises.

A husband, excluded by marriage settlement from all interest in his wife's estate, cannot vote. *(Darley v. Darley—Tyrrell v. Hope.)*

HUSTINGS.—(See *"Polling booth."*)

IDIOTS and IMBECILES.—A person who has been "non compos" from birth or infancy, vote not allowed. *Bedfordshire.* (See *" Lunacy."*)

IMPERFECT PUBLICATION not to invalidate lists, but persons charged thereunder not exempt. 6 Vic. c. 18, s. 26.

INACCURATE DESCRIPTION.—(See *"Misnomer."*)

INCAPACITY AND DISQUALIFICATION.—Persons incapacitated for the Parliamentary franchise :—

PERSONS NOT ON THE REGISTER, this being necessary in all cases.

FEMALES.—*(Chorlton v. Lings; same v. Kessler.)*

ALIENS, not certificated. *Middlesex case.* (See *"Aliens."*)

INFANTS. 7 & 8 Vic. 3 cap. 25, 38. Full age is completed on the day preceding the 21st anniversary of birth.

IDIOTS and LUNATICS. ("See *Lunatic."*)

DRUNKEN MEN. A question of fact for the Returning Officer.

DEAF AND DUMB not disqualified if intelligent, and understanding what is nature of an Oath, and the purpose of the Poll, &c. (See *"Deaf and Dumb."*)

MEMBERS OF THE METROPOLITAN POLICE FORCE, or any City or Borough in the Metropolitan District, or Thames Police, Essex, Hereford, Surrey, or Kent. 10 Geo. 4, c. 44, s. 18.

POLICE Magistrates, Clerks, Ushers, Doorkeepers, and Messengers, in the 8 Metropolitan Districts are not entitled to vote in Middlesex, Surrey, London, and Westminster, the Tower Hamlets, Finsbury, Marylebone, Southwark, Lambeth, or Greenwich. No Commissioner, or Members of City of London Police, entitled to vote in Middlesex, Surrey, Hertford, Essex, Kent, City of London, or any Borough in the Metropolitan Police District. These three last mentioned Classes liable to a penalty of £100.

CHIEF CONSTABLES OF COUNTIES. 2 & 3 Vic. c. 96, s. 9 (except Special Constables.)

BOROUGH POLICE not entitled. 19 & 20 Vic. c. 69, s. 9.

EMPLOYES at Elections, such as paid Agents, Check Clerks, Messengers, and Door-keepers. 30 & 13 Vic. c. 102, s. 11; 35 & 36 Vic. c. 33, s. 25.

FELONS, until conviction quashed or pardoned.

TICKET-OF-LEAVE MEN, until expiration of term. 16 & 17 Vic. c. 99, & 28 Vic. c. 47.

CORRUPT PRACTICES, Persons guilty of. 17 & 18 Vic. c. 102., s. 6.

BANKRUPTS AND INSOLVENTS depend upon whether or not they retain a qualification.—(*Taunton Case—Worcester Case—Carlow Case.*)

PEERS, by Resolution of House, 13 Feb. 1700.

IRISH PEERS.

RETURNING OFFICER in England may give a casting vote, but he shall not in any other case be entitled to vote at an Election where he is Returning Officer.   35 & 36 Vic. c. 33, s. 2.

DEPUTY RETURNING OFFICER, if retained for and on behalf of the Candidate.

RECEIPT OF PAROCHIAL RELIEF AND ALMS.   30 & 31 Vic. c. 102, s. 40.

NON-PAYMENT OF RATES OR TAXES.

MANUFACTURED OR FAGGOT VOTES.

The Returning Officer can make no enquiries when the Vote is tendered except as to identity.

Persons disqualified for the MUNICIPAL FRANCHISE are aliens, and persons who have received parochial relief or other alms which disqualify, within the 12 months preceding 15th July, 41 & 42 Vic. c. 6, s. 7, but although the Act provides that 6 Vic. c. 18, s. 11, and 30 & 31 Vic. c. 102, s. 28, shall extend to municipal rates, the precept and forms in the Schedule give the old dates, in consequence of which it seems that payment may be made on the 20th July, although the qualifying year ends on the 15th. It depends upon the construction of s. 7, which must be strained to give a meaning either way.   Also Borough and County Constables, and persons convicted of corrupt practices, are disqualified.   35 & 36 Vic. c. 60, s. 3.

INHABITANT OCCUPIER.—There is a distinction between a resident Occupier of a dwelling-house and the Occupier of a " *House, Counting-house, Shop, etc.,* which need not be inhabited, but the residence may be within 7 statute miles. The simplest description of an Inhabitant is that of Lord Coke, that "a man can only be said to be conversant where his bed is." Being a *personal* franchise, it entails a *personal* duty.

But the residence need not be continuous, or without any break whatever; so that there be an *animus revertendi,* a man may have more than one dwelling-house; when he leaves his family away from home, if he still continues to inhabit and sleep at the house, for which he qualifies, it is sufficient.—(*Monmouth, Milborne Port.*)

The condition contained in the words of 30 & 31 Vic. c. 102, s. 3, "and has during the whole of the preceding 12 calendar months been an inhabitant occupier," has been the means of disqualifying numerous persons who have underlet their houses during a portion only of the preceding 12 calendar months.   This disqualification will henceforth be removed by the "House Occupiers' Disqualification Removal Act, 1878." From and after the passing of this Act every man shall be entitled to be registered and to vote notwithstanding that during a part of the qualifying period, not exceeding 4 months in the whole, he shall by letting or otherwise have permitted the premises to be occupied as a furnished house by some other person. 41 Vic. c. 3, s. 2.

INFANT is not eligible for Parliament, and cannot vote. (See *"Incapacity."*)

INSURANCE, not a charge to be deducted in calculating the annual value. (*Colvill v. Wood.*)

INTERFERENCE at Elections, by Peers, Ministers, Military, Employés of the Crown, and police forbidden. (See *"Corrupt Practice."* *" Undue influence."*) 17 & 18 Vic. c. 102.

May be by open force or violence, or a threat of it, by the infliction of any injury, damage, harm, or loss, or the threat thereof.

Practice of intimidation in any manner by abduction, duress, fraudulent contrivance, &c.

Prosecution must be commenced within one year. 26 & 27 Vic. c. 29, s. 5.

Action for Penalties must be prosecuted without delay, s. 6, and in Superior Courts; as to Security, &c., s. 9.

INTERLOCUTORY questions on Election Petitions, may be heard before a Judge. Rule 44.

INTERLINEATION of Voter's name on Rate book, sufficient rating. (*Pariente v. Luckett.*)

INFLUENCE, Undue, is a corrupt practice, and a perpetual disqualification as an Elector. By 17 & 18. Vic. c. 102, s. 5, any person committing this offence at a Parliamentary Election is guilty of a misdemeanor, and is also liable to a penalty of £50 to any person who may sue for the same. Further, any person found guilty is by s. 6 to be struck off the Register, and his name inserted by the Barrister, at the following Revision, in a separate list. In addition, such offender is incapable of being elected to or sitting in Parliament, of being registered as a voter or voting, of holding any office under 5 & 6 Will. 4, c. 76, or 3 & 4 Vic. c. 108, or any municipal or judicial office, or of acting as a Justice, for the next 7 years.

As to Candidates, 17 & 18 Vic. c. 102, s. 36 (as altered by 35 & 36 Vic. c. 33, s. 46) enacts, "If any candidate at any election for any county, city, or borough, shall be *reported by a Judge on the trial of an election petition*, guilty, by himself or his agents, of bribery, treating, or undue influence at such election, such candidate shall be incapable of being elected or sitting in Parliament for such county, city, or borough during the Parliament then in existence."

Persons committing the offence at a Municipal Election are to be liable to the like actions, prosecutions, penalties, forfeitures, and punishments, as if the corrupt practice had been committed at a

Parliamentary election. For disqualifications, 35 & 36 Vic. c. 60, s. 4.

Such disqualification may, however, be removed by the conviction for perjury of the Witnesses, upon whose testimony the conviction was obtained. 31 & 32 Vic. c 125, s. 47, 35 & 36 Vic. c. 60, s. 4.

INFRINGEMENT of secrecy on the part of officers, clerks, and agents, in attendance at a Polling Station, Parliamentary or Municipal, is punishable, on summary conviction before two justices, by imprisonment not exceeding 6 months, with or without hard labour. 35 & 36 Vic. c. 33, s. 4.

INSPECTION of Rate Books is to be permitted by Overseers. 6 Vic. c 18, s. 16; 41 & 42 Vic. c. 26, s. 13. Also the returns made to them by the Registrars of Births and Deaths. *Ib.*, s. 11.

INSPECTION of rejected ballot papers may be had by an Order of the County Court. 35 & 36 Vic. c. 60, Rule 64, sub rule (b).

INSURANCE against Fire is not to be deducted in ascertaining the "clear yearly value." (*Colvill v. Wood.*)

IRISH PEER, An, when a Candidate, may be described by his title as if it were his surname.

He cannot vote at an election, but if at the time of the Revision he is elected a Member of the House of Commons, he may be placed on the Register. (*Lord Rendlesham v. Howard.*)

JEWS are not disqualified from being elected. As to the form of Oath for a Jew, see 29 & 30 Vic. s. 19.

In Municipal Elections, it is provided by 35 & 36 Vic. c. 33, Rule 26, that if the Election takes place on a Saturday, and a person of the Jewish persuasion objects on religious ground to vote in the manner prescribed, his vote may be taken by the Returning Officer in the manner directed.

JOINT OCCUPATION.—Joint Tenants, and Tenants in common, of Freehold Estates in a County, held for *freehold interests*, have a right to vote *as owners*, the former being seised individually, *per my et per tout*, the latter having each a separate interest in their respective shares. When lands are in joint occupation, and the aggregate rateable value is such as would, if divided, give each a vote, then each is entitled to be registered, if otherwise qualified; but not more than two shall be so registered; unless they derive the premises by descent, succession, marriage, marriage settlement, or devise, or occupy as "bonâ fide" partners. 30 & 31 Vic. c. 102, s. 27 (*See " Partner.*") There is no provision in the Act for deciding which two shall be registered where there are more than two; therefore it appears to be a matter in the discretion of the Overseers; and in the event of all being omitted by the Overseers it would be open for any two to make their claims. An occupier of land under £50, who is also one of two *joint* occupiers of land, which does not give a qualification as a £50 occupier to each, is not entitled, although both tenancies are under the same Landlord; 6 Vic. c. 18, s. 73, not permitting two rents to be joined. But it is not necessary, in order to entitle a £12 occupier of lands to a vote under 30 & 31 Vic. c 102, s. 6, that he should have occupied such lands *in one holding*, or *under the same landlord*, or that there should have been *one entire rating* of the whole of the qualifying property. It is sufficient if the aggregate rateable value of lands occupied under different landlords amounts to £12, and the occupier has been rated to all rates made during his occupation in respect of the several pieces of land so occupied by him. (*Huckle v. Piper.*)

Apart from the " separate dwellings " clause under 41 & 42 Vic. c. 26, s. 5, and the cases previously decided, which were confirmed thereby, including Chambers in Inns of Court, flats, and houses let out to tenants by an "out-door landlord," there cannot be a Joint Inhabitant Occupier under 30 & 31 Vic. c. 102, s. 3. If, therefore, there be several joint and bonâ fide occupiers, none of them will be entitled to be registered. Should the house, however, be of sufficient value to give them each a £10 qualification under 2 Will. 4, c. 4, s. 27, they may all claim.

An inhabitant occupier (owner or tenant), otherwise qualified, does not lose his qualification by *letting* the exclusive use of a bedroom with the joint use of a sitting room. (*Brewer v. McGowan.*) Joint Lodgings are Lodgings *taken jointly:* there must be a *joint taking*, and a *joint liability*, without which a joint occupation is insufficient. (See "*Lodgings.*")

JOINT STOCK COMPANIES ACTS.—No freehold estate, legal or equitable, is vested in Shareholders in Companies incorporated under these Acts, in any lands held by the Company, their rights being confined to a share in the profits. (*Acland v. Lewis.*)

JUDGES.—PARLIAMENTARY ELECTION PETITIONS, and the hearing of applications for the withdrawal thereof, are to be conducted before two Judges instead of one, and the 31 & 32 Vic. c. 125, is to be construed as if two Judges were mentioned.

Every Certificate and Report sent to the Speaker in pursuance of that Act is to be under the hands of both Judges; but with that exception, and with reference to differences between the Judges as to the Election of a Member, or the subject of a Report to the Speaker, all orders, acts, and applications may be made as hitherto before one Judge. 42 & 43 Vic. c. 75, s. 2.

The Judges for the time being on the *rota* for the trial of Petitions in England may make, revoke, and alter, the General Rules and Orders. 31 & 32 Vic. c. 125, s. 25. (See *Appendix.*)

The Judges are to try Petitions according to their seniority on the *rota*, unless they otherwise agree amongst themselves.

F

The Judges are to fix the time and place of trial of each petition. R. 31.

The Judges are to be received at the places where they are about to try a Petition, as Judges of Assize at an Assize Town (s. 28)—

In the case of a Petition relating to a County, by the Sheriff;

In the case of a Parliamentary Borough which is also a Municipal Borough, by the Mayor;

In the case of a Borough not having a Mayor, by the Sheriff, or some person named by the Sheriff.

A List of Boroughs will be found in the Appendix. Those marked M are under the Mun. Corp. Act, and have Mayors.

The Judges shall be attended on the Trial as Judges sitting at Nisi Prius. A Registrar is to be appointed for each Court; the Court is to be a Court of Record: and the expenses of providing the Court are to be paid by the Treasury. ss. 28, 29, 30.

The Judges may, by order made upon the application of a party, or by notice in such form as they may direct to be sent to the Sheriff or Mayor, postpone the beginning of the trial, and may also adjourn the trial from time to time, and from one place to another, within the County or Borough. s. 11 (12), Rule 34.

The Judges may, by an order, compel the attendance of any person as a Witness, and may examine any such Witness in Court, although not called by a Party to the Petition. The expenses of the Witnesses so called and examined by the Judge are to be included in the expenses of providing a Court, and to be paid by the Treasury. ss. 31 and 34. For form of Order see Rule 41.

The Judges may reserve *questions of law* as to the admissibility of evidence, or otherwise, for further consideration by the Court, s. 12; or if it appears that the case raised by the Petition can be conveniently stated as a special case, the Court may direct the same to be so stated. s. 11 (16).

The Judge may substitute a fresh Petitioner, either on the *abatement* or on the *withdrawal* of a Petition.

The Judges are to determine whether the member whose return, or election, is complained of, or any and what other person, was returned, or whether the election was *void*, and certify in writing such determination (which is to be final) to the Speaker. ss. 11, 13, 14. The certificate is to be accompanied by a copy of the evidence taken by the shorthand writer, s. 24; but pending the decision of a question of law, they may postpone the granting of such certificate. s. 11 (12).

In addition to such certificate, when charges have been made of corrupt practices, the Judge may, in addition, report to the Speaker—

(a) Whether any corrupt practice has or has not been proved to have been committed by *or with the knowledge and consent of any candidate* at such election and the nature of such corrupt practice. (See s. 43.)

(*b*) *The names of all persons* (if any) who *have been proved* at the trial to have *been guilty of any corrupt practice.* (See s. 45.)

(*c*) Whether corrupt practices have, or whether there is reason to believe that corrupt practices have, extensively prevailed at the election to which the petition relates.

MUNICIPAL ELECTION PETITIONS are to be tried by a Barrister of not less than 15 years' standing. The Judges for the time being on the *rota*, having had the Municipal Election List sent to them, are to determine the number of Barristers, not exceeding 5, necessary to be appointed, and to assign the Petitions to be heard by them. 35 & 36 Vic. c. 60, s.14.

The Judges are also to make General Rules for the regulation, practice, procedure, and costs of Municipal Petitions, also to fix the remuneration and allowances to be paid to Barristers. s. 22.

JUDGMENTS operate as a charge on Real Property, and carry interest at 4 p.c. They must be deducted in estimating the " clear yearly value." 1 & 2 Vic. c. 110, ss. 13, 17.

A payment under a Judgment of any part of Election expenses should be sent by the Candidate or his Agent to the Returning Officer. (*Richardson v Chasen.*)

JURISDICTION.—Where the boundary of any county or borough is altered in pursuance of any Act passed during the present session of Parliament, any Clerk of the Peace, Town Clerk, Returning Officer, or other officer who would have jurisdiction in relation to the registration of the voters, or in relation to the election of members to serve in Parliament within such county or borough, if it had remained unaltered, shall have jurisdiction over the area constituting such county or borough as altered by the said Act. 31 & 32 Vic. c. 58, s. 35.

JUSTICES of the PEACE at Quarter Sessions are empowered to create polling districts, and assign polling places, at which Barristers are to hold their Courts. 31 & 32 Vic. c. 102, s. 34.

For the duties of Justices in cases of personation, see "*Personation.*"

LAND.—The primary qualification in the County Franchise "Lands or Tenements," embraces every sort of interest arising out of the land (but not easements merely), such as *tithes, rents, annuities, tolls, shares* in navigable rivers, &c., which are "incorporeal hereditaments," and do not give a *rateable* qualification or franchise, as they are incapable of being either occupied or rated to the poor.

A freeholder seised in fee, or for life or lives, of property in a Borough consisting of *land only*, of the required annual value, and even if it be in his own occupation (land alone, *without any building upon it*, not conferring the Borough Franchise), is entitled to be registered *as a County Voter.*

F 2

Where, *in a Borough*, land and buildings, together, make up the required qualification, and where the building is not of a £10 yearly value, the land is a secondary consideration. It was intended that the building should be the *primary* qualification, and the lands would only be resorted to to make *up the qualification* if the building were not worth £10. (*Powell v. Boraston.*)

Where the Revising Barrister had found that the building leased with the land was of a permanent nature, and useful for the occupation of the land upon which it stood, and further found, on the case being returned to him for amendment, that "the building was worth about 5s. a year to the tenant," it was held that, inasmuch as the building added to the real annual value of the land, though in a small degree only, the qualification was sufficient. (*Morish v Harris.*)

LAND TAX not to be deemed a charge in ascertaining the clear yearly value. County voters need not be assessed to the land tax.

No public or parliamentary tax, nor any church rate, county rate, or parochial rate, shall be deemed to be any charge payable out of or in respect of any lands or tenements within the meaning of this Act (b). In order to entitle any person to vote in any election of a knight of the shire or other member to serve in any future Parliament, in respect of any messuages, lands, or tenements, whether freehold or otherwise, it shall not be necessary that the same shall be assessed to the land tax; any statute to the contrary notwithstanding. 2 Will. 4, c. 45, ss. 21, 22.

LANDLORD, "same."—Different premises will qualify, if held under the same landlord, provided the separate premises were originally taken from the same Landlord, so long as the tenant continues to hold under that taking.

A Landlord does not deprive such tenant of his qualification by parting with the reversion of one of such tenements during the term. (*Smerdon v. Tucker.*) (See *"Joint Occupation."*)

LAY CLERKS have no interest in land to entitle them to vote. (See *Bell-ringers.*) Lay Clerks of Cathedrals and Vicars Choral, with an assignment of a house which they may occupy *or not*, do not qualify as "Occupying tenants." (*Bridgewater v. Durant.*)

LEASE—To understand the existing Leasehold Franchises for Counties, as they exist in Counties and Boroughs respectively, reference must be had to the Stat. 2 Will. 4, c. 45, and to those portions of them, printed in italics, which have been repealed.

Every male person of full age, and not subject to any legal incapacity, who shall be seised at law or in equity of any lands or tenements of copyhold or any other tenure whatever, except freehold, for his own life, or for the life of another, or for any lives whatsoever, or for any larger estate, of the clear yearly value of not less than £10, over and above all rents and charges payable out of or in respect of the same, shall be entitled to vote in the election of a knight or knights of the shire to serve in any future Parliament for the county, or for the riding, part, or division of the county in which such lands or tenements shall be respectively situate. s. 19.

Every male person of full age, and not subject to any legal incapacity, who shall be entitled, either as lessee or assignee, to any lands
or tenements, whether of freehold or of any other tenure whatever,
*for the unexpired residue, whatever it may be, of any term originally created
for a period of not less than sixty years (whether determinable on a life or
lives, or not), of the clear yearly value of not less than £10 over and
above all rents and charges payable out of or in respect of the same,*
or for the unexpired residue, whatever it may be, of any term
originally created for a period of not less than twenty years (whether
determinable on a life or lives, or not) of the clear yearly value
of not less than £50 over and above all rents and charges payable out
of or in respect of the same, or who shall occupy as tenant any lands or
tenements for which he shall be bonâ fide liable to a yearly rent of not less
than £50, shall be entitled to vote in the election of a knight or knights
of the shire to serve in any future Parliament for the county, or for the
riding, parts, or division of the county in which such lands or tenements shall be respectively situate : Provided always, that no person
being only a sub-lessee, or the assignee of any under-lease, shall have a
right to vote in such election in respect of any such term of " sixty
years " or twenty years as aforesaid, unless he shall be in the actual
occupation of the premises.   s. 20.

The words " sixty years " being the only portion relating to the
former franchise remaining unrepealed, and Leaseholds originally
created for not less than twenty years, and at not less than £50
a year, still giving a County Franchise.

The 30 & 31 Vic. c. 102, s. 5, reproduced the repealed franchise
(s. 19 above) with certain modifications, namely, leaseholds originally
created for not less than 60 years and at not less than £5 a year,
reducing the clear yearly value of £10 to £5, embodying the proviso
from 2 Will 4, c. 45, s. 26, as to possession previous to registration,
but omitting the proviso as to "actual occupation " by sub-lessees
and their assignees in s. 20.

The effect of this omission would appear to be that a sub-lessee
(a lease including a sub-lease) and his assignees are within the
provisions of the 30 & 31 Vic. c. 102, s. 5, which gives the right
of voting to the lessee or assignee of lands or tenements for the
unexpired residue of any term ; but, contra, that the effect of ss. 56
and 59 of that Act is, that the proviso in 2 Will. 4, c. 45, s. 20
(and although there is no term of 60 years, but only a term of 20
years in the section to which the proviso is thus held to apply),
must be read into sec. 5, and therefore that to be entitled to a vote
under that section the sub-lessees must be in actual occupation of
the premises.   (Brett, J. *Chorlton v. Stretford.*)

And a sub-lessee of a sub-lessee, and a sub-lessee of a portion of
the original lease, is also entitled, if otherwise qualified, *i.e.,* who has
been in the actual possession, or receipt of the rents and profits
thereof for his own use, for 12 calendar months next previous to the
last day of July, unless the property be acquired within six months
by descent, succession, marriage, marriage settlement, devise, or
promotion to any benefice or office.   And an original lessee does

not lose his qualification by conveying to a sub-lessee, provided he parts with an interest *less than his own;* in such cases both would be entitled, if both held the requisite value, and the latter be in actual occupation.

If the original lessee assigns his term, his whole interest will be gone; but an assignment, if it leaves any interest in the lessor, even a day, operates as a lease. An original lessee and his assignee are not required to actually occupy. It is, however, necessary that the residue of the term originally created, however short it may be, should be continued to the last day of the qualifying year.

Where a testator devised a term of 999 years to trustees to pay the rents, and annual produce, to the claimant for life, and the residue, after his decease, to the children of the claimant, it was held that the claimant was not possessed of the residue of the term originally created, and was not entitled to be registered. (*Gainsford v. Free-man—infra.*)

A Lease may be made of an incorporeal hereditament, as of an office, so that it does not concern the ministration of Justice; but a person, to be entitled to vote under 30 & 31 Vic. c. 102, s. 5, must be lessee of a corporeal hereditament which can be the subject of occupation, or assignee of a lease of such an hereditament; and a chattel rent-charge, though originally created for more than sixty years, does not confer a vote. (*Warburton v. Denton.*)

Leaseholders, and £50 occupying tenants, in Boroughs are not entitled to vote for a County, in respect of any estate or interest in premises which would confer on them, *or any other person,* the borough franchise, 2 Will. 4, c. 45, s. 76. And it makes no difference whether such *other person* be actually entitled or not. (*Procter v. Annison— Chorlton v. Johnson.*)

Differing from a Freeholder in a borough, who is entitled to vote in respect of any qualifying property, if he does not *himself occupy.* (*Webb v. Overseers of Ashton.*)

But, inasmuch as under 2 Will. 4, c. 45, the franchise in boroughs is not limited to a *house only,* but extends to a *warehouse, counting-house, shop, or other building, with or without land,* and 30 & 31 Vic. c. 102, limits the borough qualification *under £10* to a " dwelling-house," and as the occupation of any kind of building, with or without land, of a less yearly value than £10, *other than a dwelling-house,* will not confer upon any person, either the owner or the occupier, the borough franchise, *leaseholders* will be entitled to vote for counties, in respect of any premises *other than a dwelling-house,* of the yearly value of £5 and under £10, in boroughs, though *not* in cities and towns being counties of themselves. It appears also that a Leaseholder, or £50 occupier, in a borough may vote for a county, if the qualifying property is *land only* (in cities and towns being counties, not at all), or if the qualifying property consists of separate holdings, each of a less annual value than £10, but together of not less than £10.

By the omission of the words at "law or in equity," from s. 20 of 2 Will 4, c. 45, it seemed to be doubtful whether *equitable interests in leaseholds* would qualify, and whether an agreement for a lease would qualify, but it has been held in several cases that part performance of an agreement for a lease will give a qualification. (See "*Agreement.*")

In the case of A, who, being possessed of the residue of a lease of 999 years, bequeathed it to Trustees, in trust as to one-sixth of the rents to pay them to B for life, and after his death to his children, it was held that B was not the assignee of the residue of the term (he having only an equitable interest which would not endure to the end of the term, being determinable at his death) within the meaning of s. 20, amended by 6 Vic. c. 18, s. 74, and was not entitled to a County vote. (*Gainsford v. Freeman.*)

LISTS.—Publication of notices and Lists in *Parliamentary* and *Mixed* Boroughs shall be made, not only in the manner directed by the Parliamentary Registration Acts, but also by being affixed in or near every Post Office and Telegraph Office occupied by or on behalf of Her Majesty's Postmaster-General (but not including Receiving Houses), and every Public Office in the Parish (Municipal Parochial), including Gaols, Assize Courts, County Courts, Police Stations, Baths and Wash-houses, to which such List relates. 41 & 42 Vic. c. 26, s. 9.

Lists and Registers in Parliamentary and mixed boroughs may be arranged according to *Streets*. *Ib.*, s. 26.

Lists if effaced to be replaced. (See "*Effacement.*")

Penalty for effacing, not more than 40s. or less than 10s. 6 Vic. c. 18, s. 4.

The form of the Lists for the preceding year cannot be objected to, as, for instance, that they have *not been signed* by the Overseers. (*Morgan v. Parry.*)

If no Lists have been made, or if made, unaffixed, then the *old Register* shall be the Register in force. 6 Vic. c. 18, s. 22.

Lists of Voters (in Counties) to be kept by Clerks of the Peace. 6 Vic. c. 18, s. 47. Lists of Voters (in Boroughs) to be kept by Town Clerks. 6 Vic. c. 18, s. 35.

In Counties, Overseers are to publish copies of List of Claimants, and of that part of Register relating to their own parish, to *object* to any name, if they have reasonable ground to believe that any person is not entitled, adding word "*objected*," also adding word "*Dead*" to the name of any person they believe to be dead, and to keep copies for inspection. 6. Vic. c. 18, s. 5. Such Publication of Claims is conclusive of such claim having been made. (*Davies v. Hopkins.*) (See "*Times to be observed.*")

The Municipal Corporations Acts do not apply to any List made out under the Act of 1878, but the Parliamentary Registration Acts, as modified by 41 & 42 Vic. c. 26, are to supersede the *Municipal Corporations Acts* for all purposes of Registration in *Mixed Boroughs;* and though the List henceforth to be prepared is theoretically only *one List,* divided for purposes of convenience, the right of objection is strictly limited *to the division* in which the voter is included. 41 & 42 Vic. c. 26 requires that when an objection is taken to a voter it shall specify the list on which the voter's name appears.

The lists prepared in the City of Exeter were numbered one, two, and three—the first composed of the names of occupiers, the second of freeholders, and the third of lodgers. There were issued a great number of party objections. An objection was taken to the voter's name appearing in a certain division of what was termed " the general list." These objections were met by the other side pointing out that there was no list in existence which was legally defined as the *general list.* It was contended by the objectors that as the first list was the only one in which the names appeared in divisions, it was well known that that was the list referred to. The Revising Barrister, Mr. Speke, pointed out that the Act of Parliament was imperative, and did not allow any inference to be drawn. The notice served must be unobjectionable, but in this case the requirement of the Act had not been complied with, with that strictness which was necessary, and he, therefore, ruled that the objection against the voter could not be proceeded with. Exeter Revision, Sept. 1879.

LIVERY COMPANIES.—The Livery Companies of the City of London, of which there are upwards of 70 (the 12 *Great Livery Companies* being the Mercers, Grocers, Drapers, Fishmongers, Goldsmiths, Skinners, Merchant Tailors, Haberdashers, Salters, Ironmongers, Vintners, and Clothworkers), derive their origin from the early associations called Guilds, which were either *Ecclesiastical or Secular,* the former founded for *devotion and alms deeds,* the latter for *trade and alms deeds.* Freemen of the City of London, *being also Liverymen* of one of the Companies, are a class whose right to the Parliamentary franchise was reserved permanently by 2 Will. 4, c. 45 :—

Every person who would have been entitled to vote in the election of a member or members to serve in any future Parliament for any City or Borough, not included in the Schedule to this Act annexed, either as a burgess *or* freeman, or in the City of London as a *freeman and liveryman,* if this Act had not been passed, shall be entitled to vote in such election provided such person shall be duly registered according to the provisions hereinafter contained ; but no such person shall be so registered in any year unless he shall on the last day of July in each year be qualified in such manner as would entitle him then to vote if such day were the day of election and this Act had not been passed ; nor unless, where he shall be a burgess or freeman, or *freeman and liveryman* of any City or borough, he shall have resided for six calendar months next previous to the last day of July in such year within such city or borough, or within seven statute miles from the place where the poll for such city or borough shall heretofore have been taken: Provided always, that no person who shall have been elected, made, or admitted a burgess or freeman since the 1st day of March, 1831, otherwise than in respect of birth or servitude, or who shall hereafter be elected, made, or admitted a burgess, or freeman, otherwise than in respect of birth or servitude, shall be entitled to vote as such in any such election for any city or borough as aforesaid or to be so registered as aforesaid. Provided also, that no such person shall be so entitled as a *burgess or freeman* in respect of birth unless his right be originally derived from or through some person who was a burgess or freeman or entitled to be admitted a burgess or freeman previously to the 1st day of March, 1831, or from or through some person who since that time shall have become, or shall hereafter become, a burgess or freeman in respect of servitude. s. 32.

There is a distinction between the freedom of the Company, the freedom of the City, and the Livery, although *all three* are necessary ingredients to the Franchise.

The freedom of a Company is obtained by birth, servitude, or purchase.

The freedom of the City is obtained by birth, servitude, gift, or purchase.

1. By birth, *i.e.* being the son of a Freeman, born after the father's admission, on attaining 21.
2. By servitude to a Freeman, according to the custom of the City, for a term of 7 years; but apprentices are now frequently bound for terms of less than 7 years. In such cases it is opined that there would not be the necessary servitude.
3. By gift of the City, or honorary freedom.
4. By purchase. Persons on the Register of voters are admitted upon application to the Chamberlain, with or without the interference of a Livery Company. Persons not on the Register, but who are otherwise qualified, are admitted upon application to the Chamberlain, and producing a certificate from the constituted authority of their Ward that they have paid all Rates, &c., the Chamberlain presenting their names to the Court, and obtaining an order for their admission, subject to the payment of a small fee to the Freemen's Orphan School.

Persons occupying premises, or carrying on a business, but not qualified as above, are admitted, with or without the interference of a Company, upon the payment of an additional fine.

Persons not occupying premises or carrying on a business, but wishing to become Freemen, are admitted, with or without the interference of a Company, on the Chamberlain obtaining an Order from the Court. The fine in this case is much larger.

But the Livery has never been inheritable. It is obtained by purchase only.

By 2 Will. c. 45, s. 32, all persons admitted to be freemen *by purchase* since March 1, 1831, are excluded from the franchise, but that sec. of the Act dealt in most uncertain terms with the freemen and liverymen, *i.e.*, *freemen being liverymen* of the City of London, leading to constant litigation and appeals, and the question was not finally set at rest until the decision in the case of *Croucher v. Browne*, in which case the Lord Chief Justice said—

"The question in this case turns upon the proper construction of 2 Will. 4, c. 45, s. 32, and upon reference to it a marked distinction is observable in the use of the words '*burgess or freeman*' in an ordinary city or borough and the words '*freeman and liveryman*' in the City of London. In the first case the Act used the words '*burgess or freeman*' in the alternative, but when referring to the City of London the words are freeman and liveryman; in the commencement of the clause liveryman and freeman were coupled together, thus intending that the right of vote should depend upon the union of both characters, and this distinctive feature was observable throughout the Act itself and the schedules of forms given in it. In fact, whenever the Legislature had occasion to speak of voting for the City of London, it always used the terms as freemen *and* liverymen. Upon reference to the proviso contained in sec. 32, the same distinction was kept up throughout the Reform Act and Registration of Voters Act, the distinction of burgess or freeman in ordinary cities and boroughs and freeman and liveryman in London was clearly kept up. The objection urged upon the general scope and intention of the statute to prevent corruption and an improper swamping (if such a term might be used) of the constituency by a Corporation would not apply here, for the Corporation of the City of London had not power of itself to make voters. The parties at the time of taking their freedom must be liverymen ; this would be a reason why the disfranchising part of the clause would not apply to the City. The Barrister had come to a sound determination in applying the clause as referring to burgesses and freemen of other cities and boroughs, *excepting the City of London.* The judgment would be affirmed."

The three requisites to the reserved right spoken of as existing before the Reform Act are therefore requisites still. It is not sufficient to have the *freedom of the City* alone, or the *freedom of a Company* alone, or in conjunction with the Livery, but *all three are necessary:* neither is any Liveryman, *as such*, entitled to vote in municipal elections.

The sons of Aliens born in England are admitted as naturalized subjects.

IN MUNICIPAL ELECTIONS (in Common Hall), a freeman of London, duly admitted and recorded in the Chamberlain's Court at the Guildhall, in the Company to which he belonged at the time of his admission, and who subsequently takes the livery of that Company, is, after the expiration of 12 months, entitled to vote.

IN PARLIAMENTARY ELECTIONS, a freeman of London, duly admitted and recorded as above, and taking his livery as above, is, provided he resides within 25 miles of the City of London, and has been 12 months admitted as aforesaid, entitled to be placed on the list of voters, and, if allowed by the Revising ¡Barrister, is entitled to vote.

If a freeman of London, either through negligence, ignorance, or design, is admitted and recorded without the intervention of or presentation by a Company, it is the practice of the Court of Aldermen upon application to remedy his disability by directing the Chamberlain to alter the record so as to insert the Company in the books of the Chamberlain's Court, thus enabling him to be registered and to vote.

The following are the steps to be taken and forms to be followed to acquire this franchise :—

1. Admission to the Freedom of a Company, by birth, servitude, or purchase
2. Presentation to the Chamberlain, of the Freeman, by the Company.

3. Admission to the Freedom of the City in such Company (*i.e.*, as a freeman of such Company), and record of the same in the Chamberlain's Court. These two steps are practically an exchange of the admissions, or documents.

4. Admission of the freeman (so admitted) to the livery of his Company.

5. Entry of the name of the Freeman in the list of the Livery of the company, by the Clerk of the company, for *municipal* purposes, and entry of the name in the Parliamentary lists (when entitled) for Parliamentary purposes.

6. In some companies it is necessary to make an annual return of the Livery to the Town Clerk's office, in accordance with the terms of the grant of the Livery from the Court of Aldermen.

According to the "Custom of London," the only legal and valid proof of a person's freedom is the original record in the Chamberlain's Court, or a sealed copy of such record. If that record is in anyway defective, a vote may be called into question.

No stamps are required on admission by birth or servitude. 1 & 2 Vic. c. 35.

If within 2 years of an election any freeman "being a Liveryman" has received alms, or been discharged from the payment of rates, he loses his qualification. 2 Geo. 1, c. 18, s. 14.

For the purpose of preparing their Lists the secondaries of the City issue their precepts to the Clerks of the several Companies on or before the 20th July in every year, to make out List of "Freemen being Liverymen" and entitled to vote, and transmit the same, on or before the 31st July, signed, with 2 printed copies, to the secondaries, who are to fix one copy in the Guildhall and one in the Royal Exchange, there to remain 14 days. 6 Vic. c. 18, s. 20.

The Clerks of the Companies are to allow inspection and perusal by any person, without fee, between 10 a.m. and 4 p.m. every day, except Sunday, for 4 days after publication, and to deliver copies on payment.

Claims and objections sent to the secondaries are to be printed in two Lists, and affixed in the Guildhall and Royal Exchange on or before Sept. 1st.

The secondaries are to attend the first Court of Revision, and deliver such List to the Barrister with the original notices of claim and objections, and to answer all questions and produce all documents.

Liverymen entitled to vote at the Guildhall, and Liverymen voting as Occupiers, may vote in the district in which their property is situate, and such vote may be entered as Liveryman or Occupier, as he may direct. 5 & 6 Will. 4, c. 36, s. 7.

The Returning Officer shall take the votes of such freemen being liverymen as are entitled to vote at the Guildhall, taking one poll of the whole number, without polling booths. 6 Vic. c. 1, s. 92.

LODGERS AND LODGINGS.—Lodgers first obtained the franchise under 30 & 31 Vic. c. 102, s. 4. No definition of the term

"Lodger" was given in the Act, but a proviso was inserted "that the occupier should hold separately, and as sole tenant," which was thereupon held to exclude him from the joint use of any other portion of the house, and great trouble was experienced in drawing the line between a *tenant* and a *lodger*, especially in regard to the payment of rates.

41 & 42 Vic. c. 26, s. 5, however, enacts, that for the purposes of 30 & 31 Vic. c. 102, the term "Lodgings" shall include any apartments or place of residence, "whether furnished or unfurnished, in a dwelling-house," and provides for "additional lodgings," "successive lodgings in the same house," and the "joint occupation of lodgings."

As regards the distinction between "apartments in a dwelling-house" and rooms forming "separate part of a dwelling-house," a separate part of a house (as rooms in a College at Oxford or Cambridge) is a *dwelling-house* within the meaning of 30 & 31 Vic. c. 102, and the occupier is not entitled to vote as a lodger in respect of such rooms. *Barnes v. Peters, Perown v. Peters*, and *Bakewell v. Peters*, were claims by a Scholar, a Fellow, and an Undergraduate of Cambridge, in respect of rooms, each set having a door on a common staircase, leading into a "quad," approached by an outer gate, of which the Master and Fellows, described and rated as landlords, had control. Byles, J., said: "I think, clearly, occupiers and lodgers, within the meaning of the Acts, are distinct, and that no one can be both. The term 'lodger' has not been defined, but the term 'occupier' has, to some extent, and it is admitted that the appellants are occupiers of dwelling-houses within the definition already given by this Court, and they therefore cannot be lodgers."

Lodgers are required to reside for 12 months preceding the 15th July in any year. In the case of a servant employed to attend upon a gentleman, lodgings were taken for him in the same house, in which he might, and did, usually sleep, but he was not bound by his agreement to do so. He had also a lodgings in the Borough, where his wife and children resided, and in which he could sleep at any time, and did, in fact, sleep, at least once a week. It was held that he resided in the lodgings in the Borough, within the meaning of 30 & 31 Vic. c. 102, s. 4, sub-sect. 3, and was entitled to vote as a lodger for the Borough. (*Taylor v. St. Mary Abbotts, Kensington.*)

And where A had occupied the same Lodgings for 12 months, as sole tenant under a yearly tenancy, such lodgings being part of one and the same dwelling-house, and of a yearly value, if let unfurnished, of more than £10, and had also during the whole of this period occupied a house in the country, where he had resided during such portions of the year as he was not in London, but when in London had actually resided at the said Lodgings on six different occasions, amounting in the aggregate to nine weeks, it was held that he had resided at these Lodgings during the whole of the 12

months. (*Bond v. St. George's, Hanover Square.*) Lodgings may
consist of one room, or any number of rooms, and "clear yearly
value" means, not *rental*, but *clear yearly value* as construed in the
case of the £10 franchise under 2 Will. 4, c. 45, s. 27. That Act
contains no definition of the term "clear yearly value," but in *Coogan
v. Luckett* it was held that the proper criterion of value is the price
which the premises would fetch if let bonâ fide.

Additional Lodgings. A person may now retain two or more
sets of lodgings, going from one to the other, but he cannot qualify in
several boroughs for different lodgings in each, during the same year.

The occupation of different Lodgings in the same house, *in succession*, will also qualify.

And *joint* takers of lodgings (for joint lodgings must be *taken
jointly*) are also entitled, a provision analogous to 2 Will. 4, c. 45,
s. 29, but as only *two* joint takers of lodgings can be registered, a
difficulty may arise, as in the case of "joint occupiers," where there
are *more than two*. Probably the overseers, by omitting them all,
may oblige those two who desire the franchise to send in their claims.

Lodgers' claims must be renewed *yearly*. 41 & 42 Vic. c. 26, s.
26. (See "*Precept*," "*Schedule*," *and* "*Forms*.")

The form of declaration provided by that Act is to be primâ
facie evidence of the qualification, and claimants are not obliged
to attend the Revision Courts to support their claims, unless
objected to. Care should be taken that the description is carefully
made out, and that the rental be fully inserted, whether quarterly,
monthly, or weekly; if weekly, it must exceed 4s. a week.

LONDON.—41 & 42 Vic. c. 26, applies to the Parliamentary
franchise in the city of London, and to its registration and revision,
but not to the Municipal franchise, the City of London not being
under the Municipal Corporation Acts. (See "*Liverymen*.")

LONDON UNIVERSITY Graduates on the register are entitled
to vote if of full age, and not subject to any legal incapacity.
30 & 31 Vic. c. 102, s. 25.

LUNATIC, A, is a person " who is some time of good and sound
memory and understanding, and sometimes not ; he may be seised
of freehold estates, but incapable of governing himself or his affairs.
He has not understanding sufficient to direct him how he should
vote, and therefore, by common law, he is excluded from that
privilege." (Heyw., 165.)

In the case of *Bishop's Castle*, 4 Feb. 1699, the vote of H. W. was
objected to as a Lunatic. It was proved that he had been in
Bedlam some years before, had lost his benefice by not taking
the oaths, and had acted like a madman, *but was not so at the time of
the election*, and answered rationally.

Also in the *Wendover Case*, 22 Nov. 1702, one Benning was
objected to "as a melancholy man, and scarce 'compos mentis,'
and that his vote was carried by others to the polling place."

In neither of these cases was it held that the Sheriff would be justified in rejecting the vote ; and in the latter, the objection was not that the voter was *wholly lunatic,* but scarce " compos mentis," which admitted that he was in a situation to give his vote ; while in the former case the voter presented himself to the Sheriff in a sane mind, whatever he was before. (13 Journ. H. of C. 42—172.)

The Committee of a Lunatic, being a *quasi-Trustee,* cannot vote. He is not entitled as *owner,* and neither the Master in Lunacy nor any act of his own can make him a *tenant.* 2 Will. 4, c. 45, s. 20. (*Burton v. Langham.*)

MANAGER—Managers of businesses, stores, public-houses, &c., living upon, and having a key, and the command of the premises, but not rated thereto, have no right to a vote either Parliamentary or Municipal, in respect of the premises where they are engaged, being servants merely, and not occupiers, as either *owners or tenants.*

MANDAMUS.—By 1 Vic. c. 78, s. 24, any person whose claim shall be rejected, or name expunged, at the Revision of any Burgess roll, may apply before the end of the term following to the Court of Queen's Bench for a Mandamus to the Mayor for the time being to insert his name, and thereupon for the Court to enquire into his title to be enrolled.

The decision of the Mayor was conclusive on all moot points until the 7 Will. 4, and 1 Vic. c. 78, s. 24, enacting, in regard to remedies for persons whose names had been rejected, &c.,

> That it should be lawful for any person, whose claim has been rejected or name expunged, to apply to the Court of King's Bench for a mandamus to the Mayor to insert his name upon the burgess roll, and for the Court to inquire into the title of the applicant, and if the Court should award such mandamus, the Mayor is to insert the name, and to add the words, " By order of the Court of King's Bench," and to subscribe his name to such words ; and the person whose name shall be so added should be deemed a burgess in all respects as if his name had been put upon the burgess roll by the Mayor and Assessors, and the Court should have power to make an order as to costs.

Where the Mayor erroneously determined that certain notices of objection were invalid, and refused to inquire into the qualifications of the persons objected to, it was held that they had declined jurisdiction, the Court granted a mandamus commanding him to hold a Court to revise the list, although the time had elapsed ; and it was laid down that only very special circumstances would induce the Court to interfere with decisions on matters of fact, *secus* on matters of law, and that when persons exercising an inferior jurisdiction on a mistaken view of the law refuse to hear a case they are in error, and the Court will compel them *by mandamus.* (*Reg. v. Mayor of Rochester.*)

MARRIAGE.—Possession for twelve months previous to the period of qualification is not required in the case of Freehold property coming by marriage, marriage settlement, &c. 2 Will. 4 c. 45, s. 26.

Freeholds for life or lives in "Cities and Towns being Counties of themselves," coming by marriage, &c., confer the franchise. *Ib.* s. 18.

If more than 2 are joint occupiers of land, in Counties, coming by marriage, exception is made to the Member who may qualify. 30 & 31 Vic. c. 26, s. 27.

Since 1st March, 1831, no burgage tenement in any city or town (other than "Counties of themselves") qualify for the franchise, unless acquired by marriage, &c. (See "*Courtesy*"—"*Dower.*")

MARRIED WOMEN are not entitled to the Parliamentary or Municipal Franchise. (*Reg. v. Harrald.*)

MASTER, The, of the Court of Common Pleas, who is to perform the duties of *prescribed officer*, under 31 & 32 Vic. c. 125, is to be selected by the Chief Justice of the Common Pleas, s. 27. The prescribed officer is now J. Talbot Airey, Esq., Room No. 101, Royal Courts of Justice.

The Master is to keep a book at his office in which he is to enter the names and addresses of Petitioners' and members' agents ; such book to be open to inspection by any person during office hours. (G. R., 10-12.)

Also a roll of persons entitled to practise as Attorneys or Agents in Election Petitions. (G. R., 56.)

The Master, or his Clerk, is to give a receipt, if required, on the Presentation of Petition.

He is to send a copy to the Returning Officer, together with the name of the Petitioner's Agent (if any), and the address given as prescribed.

He is to keep a List of Election Petitions hung up in his office, with the names, &c. (G. R., 30.)

He is to receive notices of application for leave to withdraw, or of intention to be substituted as a Petitioner. (G. R., 45-48.)

He is to give Notice to the Speaker of the withdrawal of a Petition, or when the Respondent, on a double return, declines to defend. 31 & 32 Vic. c. 125, s. 40.

He is to receive Bank receipts for all money deposited as security. (G. R., 16.)

He is to allow inspection, and office copies, of the lists of votes intended to be objected to, and of the heads of objection to each vote. (G. R., 7.)

He is to send the copy of any notice by a Respondent that he does not oppose to the petitioner or his Agent, and to the Returning Officer. (G. R., 52.)

He is to stick up notice of the time and place of trial of every Election Petition in his office, sending copies by post to the petitioner, the respondent, and the returning officer. (G. R., 31.)

He is to ackowledge Recognizances. (G. R., 18.)

MAYOR.—The Mayor is the Returning Officer in all Municipal Boroughs and in all Parliamentary Boroughs which may become *Municipal.* 31 & 32 Vic. c. 58, s. 33; 41 & 42 Vic. c. 26.

MEASUREMENT.—(See *"Distances."*)

MEETING HOUSE.—(See *"Dissenting Minister."*)

MEMBERS (of Parliament) may appoint an Agent as soon as returned. Rule 9.

Revising Barrister cannot be a Member for the place to which he was appointed, for 18 months afterwards.

Persons elected members for one place, but disqualified, are ineligible for another, except at a General Election, but a Candidate petitioning for one place may be elected and returned for another, pending such petition.

Members cannot be arrested or imprisoned, except for felony, or misdemeanor under the Bankruptcy Consolidation Acts.

METROPOLITAN POLICE are disqualified from voting. —(See *" Incapacity."*)

MILITIA.—A Militiaman may go to vote *without leave,* and is not liable to punishment for doing so. 52 Geo. 3, c. 38, s. 196.

The acceptance of a Militia Commission by a Member does not vacate the seat. *Ib.* s. 195.

The Agent of a Militia regiment is ineligible to Parliament.

MILITARY SERVICE, Absence on, does not disqualify. 6 Vic. c. 18, s. 33.

MILITARY KNIGHTS of Windsor.—(See *" Hospitals."*)

MINISTERS.—(See *"Dissenting Ministers."*)

MINOR, A, is disqualified.—(See *"Incapacity"—" Full Age."*)

MISNOMER, or an inaccurate or insufficient description in any Rate, is not to prevent a ratepayer from being registered. (6 Vic. c. 18, s. 75. (*Mossv. St. Michael's, Lichfield.*)

But an *omission* does not come under above head. (*Rogers v. Lewis.*)

The Rule applies to £12 occupiers in Counties. 30 & 31 Vic. c. 102, s. 30.

The Barrister shall correct any such misnomer. 6 Vic. c. 18, s. 40. Also in Parliamentary Boroughs and Mixed Boroughs. 41 & 42 Vic. c. 26, s. 28.

A Misnomer in the address of a Notice to the Overseers does not invalidate, if the Overseers are designated. (*Elliott v. Ov. of St. Mary.*)

And "no misnomer or inaccurate description of *any person*, place, or thing, named or described in any Schedule, or in any rate, list, or copy of Register of Voters, *or in any notice*, shall in any wise abridge the operation of the Act, provided the person, place, or thing shall be *so denominated as to be commonly understood.*"

MISCARRIAGE of Notices of Trial of Election Petition does not vitiate, the sticking up in the Master's Office being deemed good notice. (G. R. 32.)

MISDEMEANOR, A, does not disqualify from voting, unless expressly mentioned by statute. 2 Will. 4, c. 45, s. 27.

MISTAKES are to be corrected by Barrister. 41 & 42 Vic. c. 26, s. 28.
There is no provision for a Voter making a mistake at the poll, and it would appear that it cannot be rectified except at the trial of an Election Petition, as where a voter voted twice under different names one will be struck off. (*Oldham.*)

MORTGAGE, A, whether legal or equitable, is a charge on the estate, and the interest payable is, *pro tanto*, a diminution of the yearly value of the freehold; but if the mortgage comprises distinct premises, it may be apportioned according to their value. (*Moore v. The Overseers of Carisbrooke.*)

MORTGAGEE, A, is not entitled unless in "Actual possession" (*Vide.*)

"No mortgagee of any lands or tenements shall have any vote in the election of a Knight or Knights of the shire, or in the election of a member or members to serve in any future Parliament for any city or borough, in which freeholders now have a right to vote, for or by reason of any mortgage estate therein, unless he be in the actual possession or receipt of the rents and profits thereof, but that the mortgagor in actual possession, or in receipt of the rents and profits thereof, shall and may vote for the same notwithstanding such mortgage."

MUNICIPAL BOROUGH, "any place for the time being subject to the Municipal Corporations Acts."
The "area" of a Municipal Borough is defined by statute, or by Order of Queen in Council.

MUNICIPAL FRANCHISE.—(See "*Franchise*"—"*Burgesses.*")
Occupation for the Municipal Franchise is 12 calendar months previous to 15th day of July in any Borough, or within *seven* miles thereof.

The Municipal Franchise is not confined to males. 32 & 33 Vic c. 55, s. 9. But married women are disqualified. (See "*Married Women.*")

The title to the Municipal Franchise may be acquired by descent, marriage, &c.

Disqualifications for the Municipal Franchise are being *Aliens*, *receipt of parochial relief, and being in the Police.*

MUNICIPAL REGISTRATION.—(See "*Times to be observed.*")

a

NAMES.—The Overseers are to be guided in making out the lists
of names, and objections, by the directions given in 41 & 42 Vic. c..
26, Sch. Note P.

The Barrister is to insert in the list of County Voters the names
of Claimants, omitted by the Overseers, on proof of qualification. 6
Vic. c. 18, s. 40.—(See "*Omissions.*")

Names and addresses of Election Agents are to be left with
Master, Common Pleas Office.   (G. R. 9, 10, 30, 56.)

NEEDLESS EXPENSES to be thrown upon the party causing the
same.

NOMINATION.—In Counties and District Boroughs, the day of
election is to be fixed not later than the ninth day after the receipt
of the writ by the Returning Officer, with 3 clear days between the
day on which notice is given and the day of election. In other
Boroughs not later than the 4th day after receipt of the Writ, with
an interval of not less than 2 clear days, as above. 35 & 36 Vic. c.
33, 1st Sch R. 2) The order would be, supposing the writ to be
received on 1st January—

Jan. 1. Receipt of Writ.
    2. Last possible day for notice of election.
    4. First possible day for nomination of candidates.
    5. Last possible day for nomination of candidates.
    6. First possible day for the Poll in ordinary Boroughs.
    7. First possible day for the Poll in Counties, and District
        Boroughs.
    9. Last possible day for the Poll in ordinary Boroughs.
    12. First possible day for the Poll in Counties, and District
        Boroughs.

The time appointed for the election is to be such two hours
between 10 a.m. and 3 p.m. as the Returning Officer may appoint,
and he is to attend during those two hours. Rule 4.

The nomination for the University of London is to be held within
6 days after receipt of the Writ.   30 & 31 Vic.c.102, s. (42.)

The places for holding Nominations in a County are provided for
by 35 & 36 Vic. c 33. 1st Sch. R. 3.

No express provision is made as to the places for holding nominations in Boroughs generally. In some Boroughs they are specified
by the local Acts But they may not be held in any Church, Chapel,
or other place of Public Worship, 2 Will. 4. c. 45, s. 6, which does
not, however, apply to the Universities of Oxford and Cambridge.

On the day of Nomination or Polling, no soldier within 2 miles is
to be allowed to go out of Barracks, except to mount or relieve
guard, or give his vote at an Election, when he is to return with all
convenient speed; and when a new Writ is issued, the Clerk of the
Crown in Chancery, or other officer, is to give Notice to the Secretary for War, who is to give like notice to the General commanding
the district, to see that this is done.   10 & 11 Vic. c. 21, s. 3.

Candidates are nominated by the delivery, within the appointed time, of the nomination paper, duly filled up and subscribed, to the Returning Officer (who is to attend at the time and place appointed in his notice), *by the Candidate himself,* or his proposer, *or* seconder.

The delivery by an *agent* is insufficient, and invalid in all cases.

The Returning Officer is to attend for *one hour* after the time appointed (35 & 36 Vic. c. 33, s. 1), to enable objections to be made, ou grounds other than the sufficiency of the Candidate's description, as well as for the purpose of declaring the candidates elected, if, at the expiration of the hour, no more Candidates are nominated than there are vacancies, and not for the receipt of further nominations. 1st Sch. R. 4.

Each Candidate is to be nominated by a *separate* nomination paper, and each nomination paper is to be subscribed by two registered electors as proposer and seconder, and by eight other registered electors as assenting to the nomination; but the same electors, or any of them, may subscribe as many nomination paper as there are Candidates, and diffierent sets of Voters·may nominate the same Candidate in separate nomination papers. (*Barnstaple Case.*) As to Objections to nomination papers, see "*Objections.*"

The persons who may attend nominations are the Candidate, his proposer and seconder, and any person selected by him. Immediately a nomination paper is delivered to the Returning Officer, he is to forthwith publish the names of the person nominated, and of his proposer and seconder, by placarding them in a conspicuous place outside the building.

A Candidate, who is nominated, may *withdraw* during the time appointed for the nomination, but not afterwards, by giving a notice to that effect, signed, to the Returning Officer, who shall publish a notice thereof during the 2 hours appointed. *1st Sched. R. 10, par. 3.*

A Nomination may be adjourned, in case of riot, *de die in diem,* until the obstruction ceases, and the day on which the nomination is concluded is to be deemed to be the day fixed for the election. 5 & 6 Will. 4, c. 36, s. 8.

If, at the end of an hour from the time appointed for the nomination, no more canddiates are nominated than there vacancies, the Returning Officer is to declare the Candidates elected; but if more Candidates are nominated than there are vacancies, the Returning Officer shall adjourn the election for the purpose of taking a poll. (*Ib. s. 1. par, 2.*)

In Muncipal boroughs the Election of Town Councillors is fixed by 5 & 6 Will. 4, c. 76, to take place on the 1st Nov. every year.

The Election of Councillors, Assessors, and Auditors, is to be preceded by a notice stating the day on which the election will be held, how candidates are to be nominated, and when objection to nominations may be made. 38 & 39 Vic. c. 40.

As to the number of persons to be Elected, see 22 Vic. c. 35, s. 8.

Formerly a burgess might nominate himself, and several candidates might be nominated in the same document (22 Vic. c 35 ss. 5-7), but those sections have been repealed, as well as the form of nomination, given in the Sched. to that Act, the form given in the Sched. to 38 & 39 Vic. being substituted.

The delivery of a nomination paper to an Agent will invalidate the Election. The latest instance of this occurred at Maidstone, October, 1879.

NOTICE.—Notices to Overseers are governed by 6 Vic. c 18.

" Wherever any Notice is by this Act required to be given or sent to the Overseers of any parish or township, it shall be sufficient if such notice shall be delivered to any one of such Overseers, or shall be left at his place of abode, or at his office or other place for transacting parochial business, or shall be sent by the post, free of postage, or the postage thereof being first paid, addressed to the Overseers of the particular parish or township, naming the parish or township, and the county, city, or borough respectively, to which the notice to be so sent may relate, without adding any place of abode, of such Overseers; and wherever by this Act any notice is required to be given or sent to any person or persons whatsoever, or public officer, it shall be sufficient if such notice be sent by the post in the manner and subject to the regulations hereinbefore provided with respect to sending notices of objection by the post. s. 101. (See "*Notice of Objection.*")

Printed forms of Notice are to be sent with the precepts by Clerks of the Peace and Town Clerks.

Notices of holding *Revision Courts* and the times and places, for Counties between the 20th September and the 31st October, for Boroughs between the 15th September and the 31st October, and for Burgess Lists before the 12th October, are to be given by the Revising barristers to the Clerks of the Peace, Town Clerks, &c., who are to give notice to the Overseers, and also by Advertisement.

Notices to pay all *Rates*, &c., before the 20th July are to be published by the Overseers, and in Boroughs they are to give notice to occupiers *in arrear* in default of a demand note, the 32 & 33 Vic. c. 41, applying to the occupiers of premises which qualify for the Parliamentary Franchise, although the owners thereof have made themselves liable under that Act (30 & 31 Vic. c. 102, s. 28, Sch. E.). For *Penalties* on Overseers for withholding such notices, see the Act.

Notices are also to be given under 6 Vic. c. 18, s 11.

"The Overseers of every such parish or township shall on or before the 20th day of June in every year publish a notice in writing according to form numbered (2) in the said Schedule (B), stating that no person will be entitled to have his name inserted in any list of voters for the City or Borough then next to be made in respect of the occupation of premises, of the clear yearly value of *not less than* £10, situate wholly or in part within such parish or township, unless he shall pay on or before the 20th day of July then next ensuing all the poor's rates and assessed taxes which shall have become payable from him in respect of such premises during the twelve calendar months next before the 5th day of January then last past."

Notices are to be given by the Overseers of rates in arrear where the whole or part of the area of a Municipal Borough is co-extensive with or included in the area of a Parliamentary Borough, and by 40 & 41 Vic. c. 26, s 10, 30 & 31 Vic. c. 102, s. 28, shall extend with the necessary modifications to the rates, the payment of which is required as a condition of enrolment on the burgess roll, and the provisions of those sections so amended shall apply to the Overseers of parishes situate wholly or partly in a Municipal Borough accordingly.

Any notice required to be given under s. 10 shall be deemed to be duly given, if delivered to the occupier, or left at his last or usual place of abode, or with some person on the premises in respect of which the rate is payable.

In case no such person can be found, then the notice required to be given under this section, or under 30 & 31 Vic. c. 102, s. 28, shall be deemed to be duly given if affixed upon some conspicuous part of the premises.

Any overseer who with intent to keep an occupier off the list or register of voters for a Parliamentary Borough or off the burgess lists or burgess roll of a Municipal Borough shall wilfully withhold any notice required to be given to such occupier, shall be deemed guilty of a breach of duty in the execution of this Act.

Notices should be given to the Overseers of additions and corrections in the list of householders under 32 & 33 Vic. c. 44, s. 19.

For the purposes of *Registration*, notices are to be given by the Overseers in Counties requiring claims to vote to be sent.

The Overseers of the Poor of every parish and township shall, on or before the 20th day of June in every year, publish a notice according to the form numbered (2), Schedule (A), having first signed the same, requiring all persons entitled to vote in the election of a knight or knights of the shire to serve in Parliament in respect of any property situate wholly or in part within such parish or township who shall not be upon the register of voters then in force; and also all persons so entitled as aforesaid who, being upon such register, shall not return the same qualification or continue in the same place of abode, as described in such register, and who are desirous to have their names inserted in the register about to be made, to give or send to the said Overseers, on or before the 20th day of July then next ensuing, a notice in writing by them, signed, of their claim to vote as aforesaid, and every such person and any person who being upon such register may be desirous to make a new claim shall, on or before the said 20th day of July, deliver or send to the said Overseers a notice signed by him of his claim according to the form of notice set forth in that behalf in the said form or to the like effect. 6 Vic. c. 18, s. 4.

The delivery of such notices on the 20th July is sufficient even on a Sunday, and delivery by post on that day is sufficient. (*Rawlins v. Overseers of West Derby.*)

These notices do not apply to £12 occupiers, who may claim if *omitted* by the Overseers, whose duty It is to put them on the list in the first instance.

> Every person whose name shall have been omitted in any such list of voters for any city or borough so to be made out as aforesaid, and who shall claim as having been entitled on the last day of July (now the 15th July) then next preceding to have his name inserted therein, and every person desirous of being registered for a different qualification than that for which his name appears in the said list, shall, on or before the *25th day of August* in that year, give or cause to be given a notice according to the form numbered 6 in the said Schedule B, or to the like effect, to the Overseers of that parish or township in the list whereof he shall claim to have his name inserted, or if he shall claim as a freeman of any city or borough or place sharing in the election therewith, then he shall in like manner give or cause to be given to the Town Clerk of such city, borough, or place a notice according to the form numbered (7) in the said Schedule (B), or to the like effect, and the overseers and town clerks respectively shall include the names of all persons so claiming as aforesaid in lists according to the forms numbered (8) and (9) respectively in the said Schedule (B). 6 Vic. c. 18, s. 15.

> Where a party agent had delivered a number of claims at the house of the Assistant Overseer, on the evening of August 25, about 9 p.m., the Overseer at the time and until the 29th was from home, and the claims —12 in number—had been put under the door, and were not published in the list of claimants for the borough, it was contended that the services of the notices at the " place of abode" of the Assistant Overseer was a service required by the Act. The Revising Barrister said he considered that as the claims were put under the door, and were not served personally on the Overseer, or some person at his house, in his absence, the service was not made properly. He considered that the term employed in the Act—viz., " left at his place of abode," was intended to be understood as a delivery to some person on the premises. A case was not asked for, otherwise the Barrister was prepared to grant one.

NOTICES OF ELECTION.—(See "*Nomination.*")

NOTICE OF OBJECTION.—Overseers (in Counties) may object to the names of any person whom they believe to be not entitled, or dead, and any person on the County Register for the time being may object to the name of any other person, either on the Register or list of Claims, as not having been entitled on the last day of July.

> It shall be lawful for any person whose name shall be on any list of voters for any county, city, or borough, to oppose the claim of any person so omitted as aforesaid to have his name inserted in any list of voters for the same County, City, or Borough, and such person intending to oppose any such claim shall in the court to be holden as aforesaid for the revision of such list, and before the hearing of the said Claim, give notice in writing to the Revising Barrister of his intention to oppose the said claim, and shall thereupon be admitted to oppose the

same by evidence or otherwise, without any previous or other notice, and shall have the same rights, powers, and liabilities as to costs, appeal, and other matters relating to the hearing and determination of the said claim as any person who shall have duly objected to the name of any other person being retained on any list of voters, and who shall appear and prove the requisite notices as hereinafter mentioned. s. 39.

But a person on the list of claims can make objection to none but Claimants. Notices are to be given to the Overseers on or before the 20th August, in form No. 4, Sch. A, and to the person objected to in form No. 5, Sch. A, or to the like effect.

In every year every person who shall be upon the register for the time being for any county may object to any other person upon any list of voters for such county, as not having been entitled on the last day of July then next preceding to have his name inserted in any list of voters for such county; and every person so objecting (save and except overseers objecting in the manner hereinbefore mentioned) shall on or before the 20th August (*substituted for 25th August by 28 Vic. c. 36, s. 4*) in such year give or cause to be given to the overseers of the poor of the parish or township to which the list of voters containing the name of the person so objected to may relate, a notice according to the form numbered (4) in the said Schedule (A), or "to the like effect;" and the person so objecting shall also, on or before the said 25th day of August, give or cause to be given to the person so objected to, or leave or cause to be left at his place of abode, as described in such list, a notice according to the form numbered (5) in the said Schedule (A), or to the like effect, and every such notice of objection shall be signed by the party so objecting as aforesaid; and wherever the place of abode of the person objected to, as described in the said list, shall not be in the parish or township to which such list may relate, and the name of the occupying tenant of the whole or any part of the qualifying property, together with his place of abode, shall appear in such, list the person so objecting shall also on or before the same day give to or leave or cause to be given or left at the place of abode of any such occupying tenant a duplicate notice signed as aforesaid. 6 Vic. c. 18, s. 7.

There will be a sufficient signature within the statute if the objector affixes his name on the notice of objection by means of a stamp, in which is engraved a fac-simile of his ordinary signature (*Bennett v. Brumfitt*), and his address must be subscribed.

The sufficiency of the description of an objector's place of abode in a notice of objection to a county voter is a question of fact for the Revising Barrister. (*Jones v. Pritchard.*) In the case of *Nosworthy v. The Overseers of Buckland-in-the-Moor*, it was held, as regards County voters, that "the said list" means the exact copy of the register sent to the overseers by the Clerk of the Peace, together with the list of the Claimants as defined in 6 Vic. c. 18. Where, therefore, an address in the copy of the register was altered, by substituting the true address of the voter, it was held that a notice of objection sent by post to such new address was not a compliance with sec. 100, and the service of the notice was insufficient.

A notice of objection to a county voter served upon overseers under 6 Vic. c. 18, s. 7, was in the following form :—" I hereby give

you notice that I object to the names of the persons mentioned
and described below being retained in the list of voters, &c., the
several names and descriptions of the parties objected to being contained in a schedule at the foot of the notice." *Held* a sufficient
compliance with the statute. (*Smith v. Holloway.*)

If there be more than one list of voters (in all places except
London, when only one List is made by the Overseers, all the other
Lists being made by the Companies) the Notice served upon the
Overseers should specify the list to which the objection refers. 6
Vic. c. 18.

And if there be two or more persons of the same name the objections should point to the one intended. (*Huggett v. Lewis—Barton v.
Ashley.*) 6. Vic. c. 18, Sch. B. (Form 10).

The Notice must specify the ground of objection. 28 Vic. c.
36, s 6.

A notice of objection sent to a voter on the list of £12 occupiers
for a county must specify the ground of objection according to the
provisions of 28 Vic. c. 36, s. 6. (*Bennett v. Brumfit—Alderson's Case.*)

A notice of objection to a voter on the register of county voters
stated that the objection was grounded on the *third column*, and that
it related to the nature of the voter's interest in the qualifying property. The objection sought to be proved was that the qualifying
property was situated within a parliamentary borough, occupied so
as to give a borough franchise. *Held* to be a sufficient notice of
objection within the terms of 28 Vic. c. 36, s. 6. (*Simey v. Dixon.*)

In a notice of objection sent to a county voter the objector described himself as " on the register of voters for the township of S,"
which was separated into two polling districts under 31 & 32 Vic.
c. 58, s. 22. It was held that the notice was sufficient, and that it need
not specify on which of the two lists his name appeared. (*Chorlton
v. Tonge.*)

Notices of objection may be sent through the post.

"It shall be sufficient in every case of notice to any person objected to
in any list of county, city, or borough voters, and in the livery list of
the City of London, and also in the case of county voters to the occupying
tenant, whose name and place of abode appears in such respective list, if
the notice so required to be given shall be sent by the post, free of postage,
or the sum chargeable as postage for the same being first paid, directed to
the person to whom the same shall be sent at his place of abode as described
in the list of voters. Whenever any person shall be desirous of sending
any such notice of objection by the post, he shall deliver the same, duly
directed, open and in duplicate, to the postmaster of any post-office
where money orders are received or paid, within such hours as shall
have been previously given notice of at such post-office, and under
such regulations with respect to the registration of such letters and the
fee to be paid for such registration (which fee shall in no case exceed
twopence over and above the ordinary rate of postage) as shall from
time to time be made by the Postmaster-General in that behalf, and in
all cases in which such fee shall have been duly paid the postmaster

shall compare the notice and the duplicate, and on being satisfied that they are alike in their address and in their contents, shall forward one of them to its address by the post, and shall return the other to the party bringing the same, duly stamped with the stamp of the post-office. The production by the party who posted such notice of such stamped duplicate shall be evidence of the notice having been given to the person at the place mentioned in such duplicate on the day on which such notice would in the ordinary course of post have been delivered to such place. If, however, no place of abode of the person objected to shall be described in the list, or if such place of abode shall be situate out of the United Kingdom, then it shall be sufficient if notice shall be given to the overseers, and to such occupying tenant (if any), in the case of a county voter, or in the case of a city or borough voter to the overseers, or to the town clerk, or in the case of a liveryman of the City of London to the secondaries and clerk of the particular company to which the person objected to shall belong, as is in each of the cases required. 6 Vic. c. 18, s. 100.

Where the place of abode of a county voter, as described in the list, was A, the objection reached B, the nearest post town to A, on the 19th August, but there was no delivery of letters at A, and the voter could only obtain his letters by calling, or sending for them. *Held* that no sufficient notice of objection had been given "in the ordinary course of post," on or before the 20th August. (*Lewis v. Evans.*)

Where the objector, in proof of the service of a notice of objection, produced an alleged duplicate notice, stamped by a postmaster in accordance with the provisions of 6 Vic. c. 18, s. 100, the person objected to produced the notice, which he admitted that he had received in due time, but which differed from the alleged duplicate; it was held that the objector might rely on the notice so produced, and his admission, as proof of due service. The notice produced was signed ·"F.N.," place of abode as described on the register. "22, Southampton Street, Bloomsbury, London. W. C.," present place of abode, "110, Guildford Street, Russell Street, W.C." There is only one Guildford Street in the western central postal district of London, and the objector lived there, but there is no Russell Street near it, it was held that "London" might be supplied in the second address, and "Russell Street" rejected as surplusage, and that the notice was sufficient. (*Norris v. Pilcher.*) Any person in the list of Borough Voters may object to any other person on the list.

NOTICES OF OBJECTION IN BOROUGHS.

Objections to Borough Voters, Parliamentary and Municipal, are to be made in the Form I. (Nos. 1, 2, 3, 4), 41 & 42 Vic. c. 26, being substantially the same as required for county voters by 28 Vic. c. 36, ss. 6, 7, 8, and subject to the like incidents. The notice must state specifically the ground or grounds of objection, and each specific ground of objection is to be treated as a "separate" objection. The grounds of objection in the case of a Parliamentary voter are—

1. Cesser of occupation of the qualifying premises.
2. Misdescription of place of residence.
3. Misdescription of situation of the qualifying premises.
4. Being an alien.
5. Being or having been in receipt of parochial relief.
6. Being a duplicate voter.
7. Misdescription of Christian name and surname.
8. Non-occupation for 12 months previous to 15th July last (as tenant).
9. Being in the police.

In the case of a burgess—
1. Non-occupation as owner or tenant for 12 months previous to the 15th July last of the premises, described in the list.
2. The place of abode being incorrectly described.
3. Being dead.
4. Being an alien.
5. Being in the police.

41 & 42 Vic. c. 26, provides that a list of voters shall be prepared in three divisions, the *first* division comprising the names of the persons entitled to vote at Parliamentary and Municipal elections, the *second* division the names of persons entitled to be registered as Parliamentary voters but not to be enrolled as burgesses, and the *third* division the names of the persons entitled to be enrolled as burgesses, but not to be registered as Parliamentary voters, this division in Boroughs, Parliamentary and Municipal, consisting practically of female voters, independently, however, of other lists required to be made out as the list of Claimants, the list of Lodgers, the list of Freeholders in cities and towns being counties, or the list of Freemen.

The note appended to forms 1 and 2 is as follows :—

Note.—If there is more than one list of Parliamentary voters, the notice of objection in each of the above two cases, Nos. 1 and 2, should specify the list to which the objection refers, and if the list referred to is made out in divisions, the notice of objection should specify the division to which the objection refers, and if the list contains two or more persons of the same name, the notice should distinguish the person intended to be objected to.

And the note appended to forms 3 and 4 is as follows :

Note.—If there is more than one burgess list the notice of objection in each of the above two cases, Nos. 3 and 4, should specify the List to which the objection refers; and if the list is made out in divisions, the notice of objection should specify the division to which the objection refers; and if the List contains two or more persons of the same name, the notice should distinguish the person intended to be objected to.

Note.—This form to be used only where the whole part of the area of the municipal borough is co-extensive with, or included in, the area of a Parliamentary Borough.

Great care is therefore required in framing the notice of objection where there is *more than one list*, or *more* than *one division of a list.* (See "*Forms.*")

The following instances which have arisen during the revision of 1879 may be cited in exemplification, although in some instances, doubtless, cases will be stated for the Court of Appeal.

"The Borough of Coventry is composed of three several and distinct parishes, namely, the Parish of St. Michael, the Parish of the Holy Trinity, and the Parish of Stoke. These parishes have separate and distinct Overseers and Churchwardens, and separate rates imposed, and the overseers of each parish, in pursuance of 41 & 42 Vic. c. 26, s. 15, made out a distinct list of persons entitled under any right conferred by 6 Vic. c. 18, and 30 & 31 Vic. c. 102, to be registered as Voters for the Parliamentary borough in respect of the occupation of property situate wholly or partly within that parish, or entitled to be enrolled as burgesses of the municipal borough in respect of the occupation of any property so situate. Before the passing of the 41 & 42 Vic. c. 26, it was provided by 6 Vic. c. 18 that the notice of objection to the overseers only should, if there were more than one list of voters, specify the list to which the objection referred. Several cases were quoted which referred to the notices to the overseers, and it was contended, on the one hand, that as by the 41 & 42 Vic. c. 26, the notices, both to the overseers and to the person objected to, must specify the list to which the objection referred, such cases would now apply to the notice to the person objected to as well as to the overseers; on the other hand, that the notices were sufficient, inasmuch as they specified the *number on the list*, and the polling place, and the name of the list, whether Parliamentary or otherwise.

"The Revising Barrister, after taking time to consider, decided that the notices were invalid, as they did not state the parish (for which the list was made out) in which the name of the person objected to appeared. Notice of appeal was given, and the Revising Barrister said the point was of so much importance that he was anxious to state a case." (See "*Lists*.")

The last instance appears to turn upon a point of *omission, i.e.,* of the name of the parish, and as to whether the Barrister had power to insert the same under 28 s., sub s. 2.

During the revision of the Borough of Birmingham,

One Price was objected to on the list of Parliamentary voters and of burgesses, in St. Stephen's Ward. The notice of objection served on him was in the following form:—

"Notice of Objection:—*Parliamentary Division One*.

"To Mr. Richard Price, Court 10, Hospital-street.

"I hereby give you notice that I object to your name being on the list of persons entitled to vote at the election of a member or members to serve in Parliament for the Parliamentary borough of Birmingham, on the following grounds (1) that on and before the 15th July last you had ceased to occupy the qualifying premises. (2) misdescription of place of residence." Then follow the date, signature, and place of abode of the objector. The notice of objection to the overseers was in a similar form.

The Revising Barrister, after taking time to consider the point, gave his decision as follows:—

"It seemed to me, on inspecting this notice of objection, that inasmuch as there is in St. Stephen's Ward a list of persons claiming for lodgings, in respect of which they are already on the Register, as well as a list of Parliamentary voters and burgesses, the notice was bad, for not specifying the particular list in which the voter's name was to be found, but after carefully considering the provisions of the parliamentary and Municipal Registration Act, 1878, I have come to the conclusion that not only are the notices in question sufficient, but they could not have been framed in more complete harmony with the requirements of the statute."

And after giving his reasons said :

" And I am of opinion that the description ' Division one,' the word 'Parliamentary' preceding it, is quite a sufficient description, the proper division in fact of the list on which the voter's name was to be found. There is, independently of the list of old lodgers, only one list of voters. That list consists in some boroughs of divisions one, two, and three. In this particular borough it consists of division one and division three only. Division three is confined to the burgesses, and division one is the Parliamentary. I consider the heading on this notice to the overseers is sufficient, and that the notices of objection—that served on the voter as well as that served on the overseers—are valid. What I have said with regard to the notices of objection to the Parliamentary list applies also to the municipal."

In the case of objections made to *Lodgers*, if the Overseers have any reasonable cause to believe that any person whose name is entered "on such List, H. 2, is not entitled to be registered, or is dead," they must add on the margin appropriated to "Overseers' Objections" the words *objected to*, or *dead*, and no other words.

During the revision for Westminster, September, 1879, in a case of some importance, where the notices did not contain the name of the parish, or division, in which voters resided,

The Revising Barrister said there was no lodger form of objection, and that illustrated the extreme difficulty of the law.

They had to fall back on the Act of 1843 (6 Vic. c. 18), and that being so, he held that the notices of objection ought to have contained the divisions of the borough in which the voters resided. They must give notice of objection to a lodger just the same as to a householder, the only variation being in the description of the person objected to, and in all other cases the Act of 1843 applied. That, it being the duty of the overseers to make out the old lodger list in ten distinct divisions, it seemed to him that on that principle the notice of objection ought to specify the division. It was, however, a most difficult point to decide, and he should grant a case if it was asked for.

By s. 23 it is enacted that " *in the case of a person claiming to vote as a lodger, the declaration annexed to his claim shall for the purposes of revision be prima facie evidence of his qualification.*" Except, therefore, in the case of overseers' objections, the burden of proof will be thrown on the objector, and he will be subject to the same liability as to costs as in the case of objections to any other class of voters. s. 27 (3).

The notice of objection must state the list on which the objecting party's name appears.

Where, in a notice of objection to a borough voter, the objector was
described as " on the list of voters for the parish of C," his name was not
on the list of the occupiers for that parish, but it was on the list of freemen, and in that list he was described as residing in the parish of C, it
was held that the notice was bad.   *(Tudball v. Town Clerk of Bristol.)*

But where the Borough of Warrington consists of 3 townships, one
being W, each having a separate overseer and a separate list of voters,
the register being composed of three lists, the notice was signed " S. D.
on the list of Voters for G. Street in the borough of W."   The Barrister
found that there was only one G. Street in the borough, and that it
was wholly in the township of W, and that the description of the
abode given would be commonly understood in the borough as
designating the list for the township of W.   It was held that the notice
was sufficient.   *(Allen v. Geddes.)*

It is a question of fact for the Barrister whether the description
of the place of abode of any objector in a notice of objection is
sufficient.   Where the description is such, that a letter so addressed
would reach the objector *by post*, and the person objected to could
easily find him, it is sufficient.   *(Thackway v. Pilcher.)*

A notice of objection, signed by a person who has been in receipt
of medical relief from the parish, and who is, consequently, himself
disqualified, is bad, his name being liable to be struck off, which
would be fatal to his notices of objection.   41 & 42 Vic. c. 26, s.
27, sub-sec. 2, in connection with sub sec. 7.

Notices of objection to "Freemen being Liverymen" of the City
of London are provided for by 6 Vic. c. 18.

Every person whose name shall have been inserted in any list of voters
for the time being of the said city may object to any other person as not
having been entitled on the last day of July then next preceding to have
his name inserted in any such livery list ; and every person so objecting
shall, on or before the 25th day of August, give to such other person,
or leave at his place of abode, as described in such list, a notice according to the form numbered 4 in the said schedule C, or to the like effect,
and shall also give to the secondaries, and to the Clerk of that Company
in the list whereof the name of the person objected to has been inserted,
notice according to the form numbered 5 in the said Schedule C, or to
the like effect. s 20.   (See " *Forms.*")

Notices of objection may be withdrawn by a seven days' notice to
the Clerk and the person objected to. Forms 1, 2. The right of the
original objector (to have given the notice) may be contested
on the hearing of the objection, and any defect in his qualification
will not be satisfied by the more perfect qualification of the party
revising it.

If the objector appears (unless he is an overseer), in addition to
proving his notice, he must give *prima facie* proof of the ground
on which he relies; and if he fails to do so, the person objected to is
not compelled to go into his title, but his name must be retained. If,
however, the objection is by an overseer, the burden of proof is
thrown on the voter.   s. 28 (10-11).

Prima facie proof is defined to be " *if it is shown, to the satisfaction of the Barrister, by evidence, repute, or otherwise, that there is reasonable ground for believing that the objection is well founded, and that by reason of the person objected to not being present for examination, or for some other reason, the objector is prevented from discovering, or proving the truth respecting the entry objected to.*" s. 28 (10).

Sec. 18 of 5 & 6 Will. 4, c. 76, enacts, in regard to Revision—
That the Mayor and two Assessors to be chosen in every year by the Burgesses shall hold an open court within such Borough for the purpose of revising the said burgess lists, at some time between the first day of October and the fifteenth day of October, inclusive, in every year, first, giving three clear days' notice of the holding of such court, to be fixed on or near the outer door of the Town Hall, or in some public and conspicuous situation, and the Town Clerk shall at the opening of the Court produce the said lists, and a copy of the lists of persons then claiming, and of the persons objected to, and the overseers, vestry clerks, and collectors of poor's rates of every parish wholly or in part within every such borough shall attend to the court and shall answer upon oath all questions touching the burgess lists; and the Mayor shall insert in such lists the name of every person who shall be proved to be entitled, and shall retain the names of all persons to whom no objection shall have been duly made, and shall also retain the name of every person who shall have been objected to, unless the party objecting shall appear, by himself, or by some one on his behalf, in support of such objection; and where the name of any person shall have been duly objected to, and the person objecting shall appear by himself, or by some one on his behalf, the court shall require proof of the qualification of the person so objected to; and in case the qualification of such person shall not be proved, the Mayor shall expunge the name of such person from the lists, also the name of every person who shall be proved to be dead, and shall correct any mistake or supply any omission which shall be proved to have been made in any of the lists in respect of the name or place of abode of any person in such lists, or in respect of the local description of his property, provided always that no person's name shall be inserted by the Mayor in any such list, or shall be expunged therefrom, except in the case of death, unless such notice shall have been given as is required.

The Barrister has power to correct any mistake which is proved to him to have been made in any notice of objection. Costs are to be awarded under each head or ground of objection, unless the same be withdrawn, or the Barrister otherwise determines. 41 & 42 Vic. c. 26, s. 27 (3.) (See "*Reviver*"—"*Withdrawal.*")

NOTICE OF TRIAL.—Notice of the time and place of Trial of a Parliamentary Election Petition is to be sent by the Master to the parties, also to the Sheriff, or Mayor, fifteen days before the day on which it is to be commenced—P. Rules, 31, 32—and to the Treasury and Clerk of the Crown in Chancery. (Rule 62.)

Notice of Trial of Municipal Election Petitions. (M. Rules, 31, 32.)

The form of Notice of Trial is given in Rule 33.

No mistake in such form shall affect the result. 35 & 36 Vic. c. 33, s. 13. Nor shall miscarriage by post vitiate the same. Rule 32. (See *"Abatement"—"Presentation."*)

OATH.—The Revising Barrister may administer oaths and affirmations to all persons examined before him, and to all parties whether claiming, or objecting, or objected to. 6 Vic. c. 18, ss. 35, 41, 101.

For Oath for a deaf and dumb person, see *"Interpreter."*

The Presiding Officer, and any Clerk appointed by the Returning Officer to attend at a Polling Station, has power to *ask the questions* and *administer the oath*, authorized by law to be asked and administered.

The only questions that can be asked relate to the Voter's *identity* i.e., whether the voter is the person whose name appears in the Register as So-and-so, the other as to whether the vote has been already given, or not. And the questions must be put in the words of the Act. (*Canterbury Case.*)

1. Are you the same person whose name appears as A. B. on the register of voters now in force for the, &c.
2. Have you already voted, either here or elsewhere, at this election for the county of? &c. or for the, &c.

And if any person shall wilfully make a false answer to either of the questions aforesaid he shall be deemed guilty of a misdemeanor, and shall and may be indicted and punished accordingly, and the returning officer or his deputy, shall, if required, on behalf of any candidate at the time aforesaid, administer an oath to any voter in the following form:—

You do swear (*or* affirm, *as the case may be*) that you are the same whose name appears as A. B. on the register of voters now in force for the county of, &c, *or* for the city *or* borough, &c., and that you have not before voted, either here or elsewhere, at the present election for, &c., "So help you God."

An Oath is to be administered to the Shorthand Writer at the commencement of an Election Petition trial. 31 & 32 Vic. c. 125, s. 24.

OBJECTION.—(See *"Notice of Objection."*)

OBJECTION to Recognizance.—(See *"Recognizance."*)

OCCUPATION is one of the four essentials to some franchises—"tenement," "value," "occupation," and "estate."

There is a marked difference between occupation and either ownership or tenancy, the former being the exercise of the right which is conferred by either of the latter. Where an occupying owner or tenant lets or sublets, his qualification in respect of occupation is gone.

Occupation is necessary for the £50 and £12 rateable franchises for the Freehold and copyhold franchise in Cities and towns being Counties, for the £10 rateable and the Household franchise, whether Parliamentary or Municipal. (See *"Actual Occupation"—"Franchise."*)

The period of qualification in respect of occupation is, in Counties the 31st July, in Boroughs the 15th July.

The occupation as tenants need not be under the same landlord. It is sufficient if the £12 rateable occupier hold, as tenant, several plots of land of the aggregate value of £12. (*Huckle v. Piper.*)

Joint Occupation in Counties.—Where premises are in the joint occupation of *several* persons, as owners or tenants, and the aggregate rateable value of such premises is such as would, if divided amongst them, confer on each of them a vote, then each of such joint occupiers shall, if otherwise qualified, be entitled to be registered, but not more than two persons, being such joint occupiers, shall be entitled to be registered in respect of such premises, unless they shall have derived by descent, succession, marriage, marriage settlement, or devise, or unless they shall be bonâ fide engaged as partners carrying on trade or business thereon. 30 & 31 Vic. c. 102, s. 27.

Successive Occupation in Counties.—Different premises occupied in immediate succession by any person, as owner or tenant, during the twelve calendar months next previous to the last day of July, shall, unless and except as is otherwise provided for, have the same effect as a continued occupation of the same premises. *Ib. s.* 26. (*Smith v. Foreman.*)

The 41 and 42 Vic. c. 26, s. 5, enacts, in regard to occupation in Boroughs, that

" For the purposes of any of the Acts referred to, where an occupier is entitled to the sole and exclusive use of any part of a house, that part shall not be deemed to be occupied otherwise than separately by reason only that the occupier is entitled to the joint use of some other part."

So that any part of a house, however small it be, or however low its value, if occupied *separately* as a dwelling, and the rates are paid, by either landlord, or tenant, confers the franchise.

An important decision was given at the revision for the Borough of Liverpool, September, 1879, affecting such occupiers. The decision was that of Mr. Collins and Mr. M'Connell, and was read by Mr. Collins.

" The question for decision is whether a person who has, for the required period, separately occupied, and paid rent for, a part of a house not structurally severed from the other part, and which has not been separately assessed, is entitled to the franchise, where another person has been rated and paid rates for the whole house. That question now arose for the first time under the provisions of 41 & 42 Vic. c. 6, which came into operation on January 1st, 1879. The essential conditions of the franchise, in boroughs, under former Acts, were the occupation of a house and the personal payment of rates, whereas now, if the contention of the applicants is to prevail, the occupant of a single room, who has not paid rates at all, except in the sense of paying rent for part of a house to a person who pays rates for the whole, may be equally entitled to vote. The principles of the Act 30 & 31 Vic. c. 102, had no doubt already been seriously impinged upon by the 42 & 43 Vic. c. 10, and the interpretation put upon 19, in the case of *Smith v. Seghill,* but the 41 & 42 Vic. c. 26, by giving legislative sanction to that decision, and at the same time altering the definition of 'dwelling-house,' has opened the present question. By s. 19 of 32 & 33 Vic. c. 41, as interpreted by s. 14 of 41 & 42 Vic. c. 26, overseers are bound to enter in the rate book the name of the occupier of every rateable hereditament, whether the rate is collected from the owner or occupier, or the owner is liable to the payment of the rate instead of the occupier, and every such occupier shall be deemed to be duly rated for any qualification or franchise depending upon the payment of the poor rate. This section is to be of *general application.* It follows that if part of a house is a rateable hereditament, the occupation of which for the requisite period is capable of conferring the franchise, the fact that the occupant has not been rated in respect of it will work no disqualification. The definition of 'dwelling-house' in the 30 & 31 Vic. c. 102, included any part of a house occupied as a separate dwelling, and separately rated to the relief of the poor. There had been a difference of opinion amongst the Judges as to what precise degree of severance was necessary to constitute ' a part of a house occupied as a separate dwelling.' This definition and the definition of the 41 & 42 Vic. c. 26 was substituted by the Legislature for that of the Act of 1867 above stated. Section 5 enacts that in and for the purposes of the 30 & 31 Vic. c. 102, the term ' dwelling-house ' should include any part of a house, where that part is separately occupied as a dwelling, and goes on to provide that for the purposes of any of the Acts referred to in the section, where the occupier is entitled to the sole and exclusive use of any part of a house, that part shall not be deemed to be occupied otherwise than separately by reason only that the occupier is entitled to the joint use of some other part. The section concluded by enacting that the substitution of this definition for that of the 30 & 31 Vic. c. 102, shall not affect any of the other provisions of the said Act with respect to rating. This makes it a matter of great nicety to say what is now the distinction, if any, between a lodger and a householder. We are of opinion, however, that, whatever the consequence, the Legislature must have meant to constitute every part of a house separately occupied within the definition 'hereditament capable of conferring a qualification.' We are therefore of opinion that the applications are entitled to be put on the register."

But as notice of appeal was given, the decision has not as yet the authority of a case decided by the Superior Court.

There cannot be *a joint inhabitant occupier* in Boroughs (who can qualify for the franchise) under 30 & 31 Vic. 102, s. 4, but there may be joint £10 occupiers in Boroughs under 2 Will. 4, c. 45, s. 27.

Where six persons were jointly lessees of a house at a rent of £200, but the premises were occupied by a voluntary association called "The Anti-Corn Law League," more than 20 other parties, members of this association, subscribing various sums of money to a common fund for the purposes of the association. The six lessees were subscribers to this fund, out of which the rent and the wages of the servants, who had charge of the premises, were paid. Various members of the association transacted its business on the premises. The lessees, when in London, were daily on the premises, partly transacting the business of the association and partly on their own affairs. It was held that the six lessees occupied as tenants, and that

H

their occupation was sufficient. (*Luckett v. Bright.*) And where premises were occupied by a sole lessee and his 3 partners for their joint business, the three partners were held to occupy as tenants, under 2 Will. 4 c. 5, s. 27. (*Rogers v Harvey.*)

Neither can there be a *joint* occupation qualifying for the *municipal franchise.*

Young persons occupying houses jointly with their parents, but not rated to the poor, are not entitled to the franchise. At the Birmingham Revision, Sept., 1879, Mr. Saint said—

> "A question was put to me last week as to whether men and women of full age, occupying houses jointly with their parents, were entitled to the municipal franchise. I was under the impression at the time that the desired information was simply in relation to the once vexed question of joint occupation, and having in my mind the case of *Reg. v. the Mayor of Exeter,* a case in which it was held that joint occupation qualified a person to be placed on the burgess list, I gave an anwer which is calculated to mislead. Therefore, to prevent any further misapprehension on the matter, I take this opportunity of stating that having referred to 32 & 33 Vic. c. 55, s. 1, I find that persons of the class in question, not being rated occupiers of the premises, are excluded from the municipal franchise."

Occupation may be by merchandise, as where occupation by a bale of goods' was held sufficient. (*Reg. v. St. Mary Kalendar.*) And in a case at the Cambridge Revision Court, 1879, the Rev. E. G. Wood, Curate of St. Clement's, had hired a stable near to his church, but kept no horse or stock of any kind, and rarely went into the stable, in which he had simply a hamper. He admitted that he hired it for the express purpose of getting a vote, and his claim was allowed.

Temporary suspension of occupation will not disqualify.

Occupation may continue although the premises are burned down. A person rated as occupier of houses and yard does not lose his right to be on the register by reason of the houses being destroyed by fire, he still continuing to hold the site on which they stood. (*Cozen's case.*)

And the same in the case of a house being pulled down and rebuilt, there being an intention to occupy the new house when built, and rates are paid without interruption. (*New Windsor Case.*) But where occupation is clearly discontinued, as in the case of a Voter being sent to prison, the Agent of the Landlord obtaining the key, taking possession, doing sundry repairs, and accepting another tenant, the vote was disallowed. (*Jump's Case.*)

The occupation of a freehold house, and land therewith, which confers a Borough franchise, will not entitle the owner to a County vote. 2 Will. 4, c. 45, s. 24.

The occupation of premises by the recipients of a charity, by permission of the trustees of the charity, does not confer the franchise. (*Davies v. Waddington—Heurtley v. Bankes*). (See "*Alms*"— "*Hospital.*")

The occupation, by the outgoing tenant, of a portion of the premises according to the custom of the country, if of sufficient value, is a sufficient occupation, as tenant, although the incoming tenant may have paid the rent for the whole.

Where occupation of premises is part remuneration for services, and where the salary would have been increased had there been no such occupation, or in case the occupier had paid the rates himself, and would have been repaid, he was held to occupy as tenant, and to be entitled, as distinguished from cases where a portion only of the premises is occupied, as in *Hughes v. Chatham*, where the employés of a Dock Company lived in houses, in the dock, rent free, the use of the houses being part of their wages; and so of persons occupying premises for the purpose of discharging *official* duties, *otherwise than as servants*, if rated as occupiers.

> At the revision for the City of London, a Mr. M. was objected to, the ground being that he occupied his offices as Secretary to a Building Society. The voter stated that he was Secretary to a Society, but alleged that the registered office of the Society was at Tottenham, and that he paid half of the yearly rent of £35 for the office in the City, and was responsible for the remainder, though the Building Society was to contribute the other half. It was ruled by the Revising Barrister that this not being the registered office of the company, the name should be retained on the list.

And so of a foreman residing in a house belonging to the works. He was a servant, being foreman of the factory, but there was another servant in charge of the premises. and he might, if he pleased, live elsewhere. He was not absolutely compelled to live there, and he had occupied the house for several years. The claim was allowed.

But the Manager of an Insurance Company, occupying premises for his own business, as well as the Company's, and having a separate entrance to his own offices, but the whole being taken in the name of the Company, was held disqualified for the Parliamentary, though entitled to the Municipal, franchise.

But it is different where the occupation is clearly that of a *servant*, and there is an obligation to live upon the premises.

Where A was the keeper of a Guildhall at B, the house was the residence assigned by the Corporation to the Hallkeeper, in which he was required to reside, and it was necessary for the due performance of the duties as Hallkeeper that he should reside there, it was held that this was an occupation as servant, and not as tenant.

At Birmingham Revision Court, 1879, an objection was made to the list of the name of J. T. on the ground that he was a Chapel keeper and had not a qualification entitling him to be on the list.

> The Barrister said the evidence showed the man was obliged to live in the house in question in order to discharge his duty as Chapel keeper, and that being the case there was no doubt he was not qualified.

H 2

And the same applied to the case of a person who occupied premises adjoining Board Schools. and was objected to because he had official duties to perform in connection with the schools. In answer to the Barrister it was stated that the claimant was employed as the caretaker of the schools. The Barrister said that it was admitted that the claimant was required to live on the premises, which would disqualify him from voting.

The following cases occurred at other revisions:—

Mr. B., master at G. Railway Station, claimed to be on the list for apartments at the Station. He admitted he paid no rent, and the Company compelled him to live there. The claim was disallowed.

J. S., shoemaker at the Royal Hospital Schools, claimed in respect of his quarters in that institution, for which he said he paid £14 a year, his duties being to instruct the lads in the art of shoemaking. The Overseer said Government contributed to the rates in respect of the Royal Naval College and Hospital Schools. The Barrister told the claimant he was bound, by virtue of his situation, to live in the Institution, and therefore his claim could not be allowed. (See "*Actual Occupation.*")

OCCUPIER, An, must be of full age on the last day of the qualifying year. to enable him to qualify under 30 & 31 Vic. c. 102, and 41 & 42 Vic. c. 26. He must be *owner* or *tenant*, and must be rated to the poor *respectively* or *collectively*.

At the Hackney Revision Court, Sept., 1879, a person claimed to be on the register for a house occupied by him, specifying in the claim the portion used, but not mentioning that he was a lodger. In dealing with this the Revising Barrister, Mr. Bathurst, said: If this person had claimed as a lodger I should allow the claim, or if he claimed as a householder I should not refuse him. I confess I am unable to draw any scientific distinction between a lodger and a householder under the new reading of the Act, where a lodger is using unfurnished apartments. Of course if a man calls himself a lodger I allow him to stand in that category, though now he might be placed amongst the householders. There was some difference before the new Act was passed. It is not the mere fact of the occupation of a room that makes a man a householder; he must actively or constructively pay rates for the house he lives in. A man occupying but one room may be a tenant in my view of the case. The rates are paid for that house, either by the man or his landlord, and he is on the rate book, either in his own name or that of his landlord. If the man's name is not on, it is the fault of the overseers. I do not attach any blame to them now in saying this, and if the name is not on, there is a clause in the Act which expressly provides for him having his claim allowed. The practical result of this is, that if there were no such thing as the Lodger Franchise, those people of whom we are now speaking would be entitled to be on the list as inhabitant householders, and I do not see why the existence of the lodger clause should now interfere with them. The claim must be allowed.

Occupiers in Boroughs who are in arrear with rates are to receive Notice. 30 & 31 Vic. c. 102. s 28. (See "*House*"—"*Joint Occupier*"—"*Lodger.*")

OFFENCES at Parliamentary Elections. — (See "*Corrupt Practices.*") Offences at Municipal Elections are governed by 35 & 36 Vic. c. 60. ss. 3.

OFFICE.—A benefice, or office, to be holden for life and having certain fixed emoluments attached to it, *arising out of land*, is a tenement. As it is an incorporeal tenement, the appointment to such an office should properly be by deed. If, however, such an office be held, not for life, or during good behaviour, but merely at the *will of others*, it loses its freehold character.

Where an office is held "*quamdiu se bene gesserit*, the law will not presume that anyone would forfeit the same by misconduct.

Where W. L. was appointed a schoolmaster, "till a person properly qualified should offer," it was held that W. L. had not a freehold office.

The office must be for life, and also have duties attached to it. (*Middlesex Case.*)

In *West v. Robson* it was held that the Fellows of a College, who are entitled as such, to a yearly payment, under a Will do not acquire an estate "by devise," neither is their appointment a promotion to an Office under 2 Will. 4, c. 45, s. 18.

And in the case of *Faulkner v. the Overseers of Boddington*, where lands were conveyed upon trust to divide the rents and profits among the "bedesmen" of D, who held for life, and received over 40s. per annum, but who, neither under the deed nor quâ "bedesmen," had or performed any duties, it was held that they did not acquire an estate "by promotion to any office" within s. 18.

Possession for twelve months is not required in the case of a freehold office of 40s. and upwards, which comes by promotion.

Possession by promotion to an office, which would confer a Borough Vote, does not also necessitate 6 months' residence. (See "*Franchise.*") Stipendiary Curates and Dissenting Ministers have not such an office as will qualify them for the franchise. (See "*Dissenting Minister.*")

On the other hand, a Parish Clerk has been held to hold such an office as will entitle him.

The holder of an office must qualify and vote where the land is situate. The organist of a church in Middlesex, paid out of lands in Surrey, was held to be entitled for Middlesex only. (*Middlesex Case.*)

The holder of a freehold office held or granted by Letters Patent is entitled. (*Dyer v. Gough.*)

OFFICES.—For the purposes of 2 Will. 4, c. 45, and the Municipal Corporation Acts, the terms "House, Warehouse, Counting-house, shop, or other building" shall include any part of a house where that part is separately occupied for the purpose of any trade, business, or profession, and any such part may, for the purpose of describing the qualification, be described as "*Office*," &c. (See "*House*"—"*Dwelling-house.*")

OMISSION from the register for 2 successive years, of any voter under the ancient reserved rights, loses the qualification unless such omission arise from

(1) The receipt of parochial relief within twelve months.

(2) Absence on the Naval or Military service of the Crown.

The omission of the name of the Occupier of a rateable hereditament from the Rate Book is immaterial, by 32 & 33 Vic. c. 41 s. 19, the language of which, viz., " every qualification and franchise depending "*upon rating*" would lead to the inference that there is no longer any franchise dependent on "*the payment of rates*" (see s. 7), but there can be no doubt that the franchise is intended to be conferred on "*rated occupiers*" only, whether the rates be paid individually, or collectively through the landlord.

The omission of the amount of rent paid by a lodger, from his claim, is an informality which is incurable.

The omission of the objecting party's name and address as required by 41 & 42 Vic. c. 26, sch., would appear to render such objection invalid.

A case, however, was granted on the point at the Revision for the Borough of Reading.

ORDER, An, for Costs to be made by the Barrister before proceeding to hear any other objection ; 28 Vic. c. 36, s. 13, not repealing the last proviso in 6 Vic. c. 18, s. 46.

> Provided also, that whenever any Revising Barrister shall have made any such order for the payment of any sum of money for costs by any person who shall have made any objection as aforesaid, it shall not be lawful for the said Barrister to hear or admit proof of any other objection or notice of objection made or signed by the same person until the sum of money so ordered to be paid by him for costs be paid by the person entitled to receive the same, or deposited in the hands of the said Barrister in Court, for the use of the person so entitled.

An order for costs cannot be appealed against.

ORDNANCE MAP.—(See "*Distances.*")

OTHER BUILDINGS.—(See "*Building.*")

OVERSEERS.—(See "*Times to be Observed.*")

OUTLAW.—Outlawry for Treason or Felony disqualifies.

OXFORD.—(See "*Cambridge.*")

OWNER.—The occupation for the £12 rateable franchise in Counties may be *as owner*. (30 & 31 Vic. c. 102, s. 6.)

The owner of a freehold for life, if otherwise qualified, is entitled, though the nature of the appointment be eleemosynary in its character. (*Freyer v Bodenham*). (See "*Hospital.*")

A £10 Rateable Occupier in Boroughs may occupy as owner. 2. Will. 4. c. 45, s. 27. (See "*Franchise.*")

The Inhabitant Householder in Boroughs may also occupy as owner. (30 & 31 Vic. c. 102 (s. 3).

The rateability of owners was abolished by 30 & 31 Vic. c. 102 (s. 7) but was introduced again by 32 & 33 Vic. c. 41. (See *"Abatement"* —*"Occupation."*)

PAID AGENTS.—No Elector who has within six months before the Election been employed, by or on behalf of any candidate for the purposes of election for reward, shall be entitled to vote, or if he votes he shall be guilty of a misdeameanor. (30 & 31 Vic. c. 102, s. 11.)

PARDON.—A convicted felon is disqualified, unless he has received a free or conditional pardon (in which case he must show performance of the condition) or endured the punishment to which he has been adjudged.

PARLIAMENT.—(See *"House of Commons."*)

PAROCHIAL RELIEF is relief given out of funds, which form part of parochial funds for the relief of the poor; also relief given on extraordinary occasions, such as an outbreak of cholera, and funds distributed by a Board of Health, in aid and out of the parochial funds. Medical relief and attendance by the Parish Surgeon is also relief which disfranchise. (*Bewdley's Case—Turner's Case.*)

But medical relief ordered by the police and paid for by the County will not disqualify. (*Oldham Case.*)

Payment of Funeral expenses comes under this head. (*Oldham Case—Northallerton Case.*)

Where a third person supplies a pauper with necessaries and looks for repayment to the parish, the pauper is disqualified. (*Bedford Case.*)

Relief given to the family of a militiaman during actual service will not deprive such militiaman of his vote.

Under 43 Eliz. c. 2, s. 7, a son is liable for the maintenance of his parents, but parochial relief to a parent is not relief to the son so as to disqualify the latter under this section. (*Trotter v. Trevor.—Austis v. Cull.*)

The period of time within which such receipt disqualifies is 12 months; in London 2 years. By 41 & 42 Vic. c. 26, s. 7, it is to be computed by reference to the 15th July, but in s. 28 (7) the pre-existing period, 31st July, remains : there may therefore be cases of persons who might possibly become disqualified between those periods.

PART OF A HOUSE.—(See *"House"*—*"Occupation."*)

PARTNERS.—The 30 & 31 Vic. c. 102, s. 27, provides that *not more than two* joint occupiers shall be entitled to be registered as owners or tenants, unless they shall have derived by descent, &c.,

or shall be bonâ fide engaged as *partners* carrying on a trade or business. "Where A, being a lessee of a mill, for a term of 99 years at £350 rent, terminable on lives, took B, C, and D into partnership in the business which he carried on at the mill, they lived in the house with him, and each paid one-fourth of the expenses, including rent, and received one-fourth of the profits, and all four were rated for the premises, it was held that B, C, and D had each a right to a borough vote, and had properly claimed to have their names inserted on the list of £10 occupiers as for one undivided fourthpart of the house and mill." (*Rogers v. Harvey.*) Where a Company duly registered under 19 & 20 Vic. c. 49, and 20 & 21 Vic. c. 14, hold Freehold land, the shareholders have no interest in such land, entitling them to a County vote. (*Bulmer v. Norris.*)

In the case of unincorporated companies, unless the members of the company are in such occupation as would constitute them tenants at will, they are not entitled.

And though land be held by such Companies it will not assist the members to the franchise.

Where certain lands and buildings, namely, the Corn Exchange at Manchester, were vested in trustees, subject to the trusts of the Companies' deed of settlement, by which it was declared, amongst other things, that the shares in the Exchange were to be legal personal estate, and the Company was provisionally registered under the 7 & 8 Vic. c. 110, s. 58, it was held that the provisional registration did not amount to incorporation; that the Company stood on the footing of an ordinary unincorporated Company; but notwithstanding that, the shareholders, being only entitled to *a share of the profits*, had no sufficient equitable estate in the lands to qualify them to be registered. (*Bennett v. Blain.*)

This case was followed in *Freeman v. Gainsford.* (*Sheffield Case.*)

PAYMENT of Rates is an ingredient of the Borough franchise. The rates payable are those due previous to the preceding 5th January.

Payment may be made individually or collectively by the hands of third persons, as by the landlord, the tenant paying him a higher rate in consideration. (See "*Abatement*"—"*Occupation.*")

A corrupt payment is punishable as bribery. 30 & 31 Vic. c 102, s. 49.

The payment of *Election Bills* by a Candidate himself, and not by his expense Agent, has been held sufficient ground for reporting him to be personally guilty of the bribery proved. (*Cashel Case.*)

Payment is to made into the Bank of England of all monies under the Election Petition Acts.

PENALTIES.—Actions to recover penalties imposed upon Bribery, Treating, and Undue Influence, must be brought within a year of the commission of offence (unless the offenders have absconded) and be prosecuted without delay. 26 Vic. c. 29, ss. 6, 14.

There is no such provision for the recovery of the other penalties imposed by the Act, but the suit must be brought within a year. s. 14.

PERIOD of QUALIFICATION, The, mentioned in 41 & 42 Vic. c. 26, s. 7, has reference to "any period of occupation, residence, possession, receipt of rents and profits, and non-receipt of parochial relief or other alms," but does not apply to the payment of rates, in regard to which the 20th July appears to be the qualifying period, nor does it apply to aliens and minors, who may apparently qualify between the 15th and 20th July, the clause being restricted to the matters mentioned in the second part thereof.

This section will vary and govern the occupation for 12 calendar months next previous to last day of July, joint and successive occupation, receipt of rents and profits by freeholders and burgage tenants for 12 months previous to last day of July, and residence for six months previous to same date, residence of freemen within seven miles for six months previous to last day of July : the same as to reserved rights, receipt of parochial relief, occupation, and rating of dwelling-houses, and the occupation of lodgings. 30 & 31 Vict. c 102, ss. 3. 4.

PERJURY.—Three offences are committed in making a false answer, or declaring or swearing falsely at the poll, viz. Misdemeanor for falsely answering or declaring, Perjury for falsely swearing or affirming, and Personation. (See " Oath.")

PERSONATION.—This offence is a corrupt practice within the meaning of 31 & 32 Vic. c 125.

The definition and punishment as a Felony are given in 35 & 36 Vic. c. 33, s. 24, which incorporates ss. 85 to 89 of 6 Vic. c. 18.

It shall be lawful for any Candidate, at any election of a member or members to serve in Parliament for any county, city, or borough, previous to the time fixed for taking the poll at such election, to denominate and appoint an agent or agents on his behalf to attend at each or any of the booths appointed for taking the poll at such election for the purpose of detecting personation; and such candidate shall give notice in writing to the Returning Officer or his respective deputy of the name and address of the person or persons so appointed by him to act as agents for such purpose, and thereupon it shall be lawful for every such agent to attend during the time of polling at the booth or booths for which he shall have been so appointed. s. 85.

If at any time any person tenders his vote at such election, or after he has voted, and before he leaves the polling booth, any such agent so appointed as aforesaid shall declare to the Returning Officer or his respective deputy, presiding therein, that he verily believes and undertakes to prove, that the said person so voting is not in fact the person in whose name he assumes to vote, or to the like effect ; then and in every such case it shall be lawful for the said Returning Officer, or his said deputy, and he is hereby required immediately after such person shall have voted by word of mouth to order any constable or other peace officer to take the said person so voting into his custody, which said order shall be a sufficient warrant and authority to the said constable or peace officer for so doing. Provided always, that nothing herein contained shall be construed or taken to authorize any Returning Officer, or his deputy, to reject the vote of any person who shall answer the affirmative the questions authorized by this Act to be put to him at the time of polling, and shall take the oaths or make the affirmations authorized and required of him ; but the said returning Officer, or his deputy, shall cause the words " protested against for personation," to be placed against the vote of the person so charged with personation when entered in the poll book. s. 86.

Every such constable or peace officer shall take the person so in custody at the earliest convenient time before some two Justices of the Peace acting in and for the county, city, or borough within which the said person shall have so voted as aforesaid. Provided always that in case the attendance of two such justices as aforesaid cannot be procured within the space of three hours after the close of the poll on the same day on which such person shall have been so taken into custody, it shall be lawful for the said constable or peace officer, and he is hereby required, at the request of such persons so in custody, to take him before any one Justice of the Peace acting as aforesaid, and such justice is hereby authorized and required to liberate such person on his entering into a recognizance. with one sufficient surety, conditioned to appear before any two such justices as aforesaid, at a time and place to be specified in such recognizance, to answer the said charge; and if no Justice shall be found within four hours after the closing of the said poll, then such person shall forthwith be discharged from custody. Provided also, that if in consequence of the absence of such Justices as aforesaid, or for any other cause, the said charge cannot be enquired into within the time aforesaid, it shall be lawful nevertheless for any two such Justices as aforesaid to inquire into the same on the next or on some other subsequent day, and if necessary, to issue their warrant for the apprehension of the person so charged. s. 87.

If on the hearing of the said charge the said two Justices shall be satisfied upon the evidence upon oath of not less than two credible witnesses, that the said person so brought before them has knowingly personated and falsely assumed to vote in the name of some other person within the meaning of this Act, and is not in fact the person in whose name he voted, then it shall be lawful for the said two Justices to commit the said offender to the gaol of the county, city, or borough within which the offence was committed, to take his trial according to law, and to bind over the witnesses in their respective recognizances to appear and give evidence on such trial as in the case of other misdemeanors.

If the said Justices shall on the hearing of the said charge be satisfied that the said person so charged with personation is really and in truth the person in whose name he voted, and that the charge of personation has been made against him without reasonable or just cause, or if the agent so declaring as aforesaid, or some one on his behalf, shall not appear to support such charge before the said Justices, then it shall be lawful for the said Justices, and they are hereby required to make an order in writing under their hands, on the said agent so declaring as aforesaid, to pay to the said person so falsely charged, if he shall consent to accept the same, any sum not exceeding the sum of ten pounds nor less than five pounds, by way of damages and costs ; and if the said sum shall not be paid within twenty-four hours after such order shall have been made, then the same shall be levied, by warrant, under the hand

and seal of any Justice of the Peace acting as aforesaid, by distress and sale of the goods and chattels of the said agent ; and in case no sufficient goods or chattels of the said agent can be found on which such levy can be made, then the same shall be levied in like manner on the goods and chattels of the candidate by whom such agent was so appointed to act ; and in case the said sum shall not be paid or levied in the manner aforesaid, then it shall be lawful for the said person to whom the said sum of money was so ordered to be paid to recover the same from the said agent or candidate, with full costs of suit, in an action of debt to be brought in any one of Her Majesty's Superior Courts of Record at Westminster. Provided always, that if the person so falsely charged shall have declared to the said Justices his consent to accept such sum as aforesaid by way of damages and costs, and if the whole amount of the sum so ordered to be paid shall have been paid or tendered to such person, in every such case, but not otherwise, the said agent, candidate, and every other person shall be released from all actions or other proceedings civil or criminal, for or in respect of the said charge and apprehension. s. 89.

See rules 51 to 55 in the Sched. to 35 & 36 Vic. c. 33 as to appointment of personation Agents in pursuance of the sections of the Act quoted.

35 & 36 Vic. c. 60 s. 11 enacts that these provisions, for the detection of personation, and the apprehension of persons charged therewith, shall apply to *municipal* elections.

Under the 6 Vic. c. 18 personation was not completed, until the vote was actually given; but by 35 & 36 Vic. c. 33, s. & 15, the mere application for a Ballot paper constitutes the offence. (See *Rule* 17.)

And the offence may be committed by a voter applying for a ballot paper in his own name after having once voted.

The Returning Officer may institute proceedings in cases of aiding, abetting, counselling, advising, or procuring the commission of personation as well for the offence itself.

Payment to induce personation is bribery. (*Lisburn Case.*)

Even where a person has been taken into custody on a charge of personation, he is not to be prevented from voting; but the words *"protested against for personation"* are to be written against his name in the Register. 6 Vic. c. 18, s. 86. (See "*Oath*.")

PETITION.—The Court of Common Pleas has jurisdiction over all Election Petitions. Petitions may be

1. Complaining that the respondent was not duly elected, by reason of bribery, treating, or undue influence, or that he had not a majority of votes, and may claim the seat or not.
2. Complaining of the return only.
3. Complaining of no return.
4. Complaining of the conduct of a Returning Officer.
5. Petitions, in defence of the seat. 31 & 32 Vic. c. 125.

Petitions may be written, or printed, or lithographed, but must be signed in writing by the Petitioner himself, and if more than one by all. They are folded, on ordinary Judicature (affidavit) paper, endorsed Common Pleas, with the name of the Borough, and of the Petitioner and Respondent, and are filed in the Rule Office, Room No 83, Royal Courts of Justice.

All interlineation and alteration should be avoided, as requiring explanation, and proof that such were made *before* signature.

The petition should be presented within 21 days after the return has been made, to the Clerk of the Crown in Chancery, of the member to whose election it relates, or *within* 28 *days after the discovery of any illegal payment since the return.*

The petition must state *the right to petition* under 31 & 32 Vic. c. 125 s. 5; also the holding of the election, and the result, and the grounds which are relied upon to sustain the prayer, which should state distinctly the relief or remedy which is claimed. And if it is intended to claim the seat, there should be a distinct claim.

If a scrutiny is claimed, it should state that the petitioner had the majority of legal votes.

The petition need not state any evidence.

A copy is to be left with the Master on presentation, to be sent to the Returning Officer, and by him published.

A petition, where there is more than one Respondent, will be taken as a separate proceeding against each.

If no objection is made to the proposed security, or if the objection is allowed and subsequently removed, or disallowed altogether, the petition is at issue; and the trial will be proceeded with notwithstanding acceptance of office, or prorogation of Parliament.

Petitions relating to the same Election are to be bracketed, at the Master's Office, and tried together.

A petition may not be withdrawn without leave.

Service of a petition must be personal, and be made within 5 days from the presentation, exclusive of the day of presentation, by delivery to the Respondent of a copy, together with a notice of its presentation, and of the nature of the proposed security, except where the Respondent has appointed an Agent or given an address, in which case service may be effected by delivery or by post. And where reasonable efforts have been made to effect personal service, but without success, the Judge may, on application, not later than 5 days after presentation, and on an affidavit showing all that has been done, in order that what has been done shall be considered sufficient, subject to any conditions he may think reasonable. Rules 13, 14.

Municipal Election Petitions are regulated by 35 & 36 Vic. c. 60, and the General Rules made pursuant thereto. (See *Appendix.*)

The provisions of this Act correspond nearly with those of 31 & 32 Vic. c. 125, and the Rules are, *mutatis mutandis*, substantially the same as the General Rules relating to Parliamentary Election Petitions, the principal exception being the rates relating to Agents. Rules 56, 57, 58.

It is, however, enacted by 35 & 36 Vic. c. 60, s. 21 (2) that, so far as that Act, and the Rules made in pursuance do not extend the principles, practice and rules, which are for the time being observed in the case of Election Petitions under 31 & 32 Vic. c. 125, shall be observed in the case of Municipal Election Petitions.

The principles and practice therefore applicable to Parliamentary Petitions before that statute was passed, and which by that statute are still to be followed where not altered by statute or rule, are applicable to Municipal Election Petitions.

PETITIONER.—31 & 32 Vic. c. 125, s. 5, declares who may present a petition.

The persons empowered to present petitions under this Act are identical with the persons who might be petitioners under the Act of 1848. Under 10 Geo. 3, c. 16, (the Grenville Act), any parties whatever were allowed to present petitions complaining of elections. That practice, however, was found to be so vexatious that the House of Commons returned to the rule enacted by 28 Geo. 3, c. 53, and have continued it ever since.

31 & 32 Vic., c. 125, s. 35, enacts—

1. That no petition shall be withdrawn without the leave of the Court.
2. That due notice of an intended withdrawal shall be given in the county or borough to which the petition relates.
3. That the Court may substitute any person who might otherwise have been a petitioner in the place of the withdrawing petitioner, and may further, if it is of opinion that the withdrawal has been induced by a corrupt bargain, make the original petitioner pay to the extent of his security, that is to say, to the extent of £1,000, the costs of the substituted Petitioner. s. 35.

A Petitioner refusing to pay costs, as ordered, will have his recognizance estreated.

The security to be given by a petitioner is to be £500 instead of £1,000.

POLICE—Incapacitated for voting. (See *"Incapacitated."*)

POLL.—The time for opening and closing the poll is not fixed by 35 & 36 Vic. c. 33, but by 16 & 17 Vic. c. 15, s. 2, the Poll in counties is limited to one day, and is to commence at 8 a.m. and terminate at 5 p.m.

In boroughs the poll commences at 8 a.m. and is to be kept open not later than 4 p.m.

The poll in the Universities of Oxford and Cambridge is limited to five days (excluding Sunday, Christmas Day, Good Friday, and Ascension Day), and is to be kept open for 7 hours each day between 8 a.m. and 8 p.m.; in the University of London between 8 a.m. and 4 p.m. and may not be continued more than five days (exclusive as above).

As to a poll being opened before or after the time fixed, or not opened at all in some polling stations, voiding an election, see *Hackney Case and Drogheda Case.*

A poll may be adjourned, in case of rioting, until the following day, 2 Will. 4 c. 45, s. 10, 16 & 17 Vic. c. 15, s. 3, and the presiding officer should give notice of such adjournment to the returning officer, but the poll must not be closed, as once closed it cannot be re-opened and may void the election.

In Municipal Boroughs, the Mayor is to provide everything which in the case of a Parliamentary election is required to be provided by the Returning officer, but the compulsory power of taking *rate aided* schools for the purpose, subject to payment for injury, &c., does not apply. 35 & 36 Vic. c. 33, s. 20.

Where a Parliamentary and Municipal Borough are to any extent coincident in area, the ballot boxes and fittings, &c., provided for Parliamentary Elections may be used free of charge for Municipal Elections. s. 14.

With regard to compartments, form of ballot paper, expenses, &c., see 38 & 39 Vic. c. 40.

35 & 36 Vic. c. 33, s. 20, enacts that nothing in that Act shall be deemed to authorize the appointment of agents, but if a candidate appoints an agent, and gives notice to the returning officer, the Act shall apply to such agent.

POLL CLERKS may not act as Agents, ~~and are incapacitated for voting. 30 & 31 Vic. c. 102, s. 11   35 & 36 Vic. c. 60, s. 26.~~ ✕

The poll clerks are to have read to them sec. 4 of the latter Act, and are to subscribe before the Returning Officer, or a Magistrate, the declaration of secrecy required by Sch. 1, Rule 54.

POOR RATE.—The rating to, and payment of, poor rates as essential to the franchise, has been greatly modified by recent legislation. The voter's name need not appear on the rate book. It is sufficient if the rates are paid in the aggregate by the landlord.

By 32 & 33 Vic. c. 41, s. 19, as explained and extended by 41 & 42 Vic. c. 26, s. 14, Overseers are bound to enter in the rate book the name of the occupier of every rateable hereditament, whether the rate is collected from the owner or occupier, or the owner is liable to the payment of the rate instead of the occupier, and every such occupier shall be deemed to be duly rated for any qualification or franchise depending upon the payment of the poor rate, provided that any occupier whose name has been omitted shall, notwithstanding such omission, and that no claim to be rated has been made by him, be entitled to every qualification and franchise depending upon rating in the same manner as if his name had not been so omitted. This section is of general application;—it follows that if part of a house is a rateable hereditament, the occupation of which for the requisite period is capable of conferring the franchise, the fact that

✕ *Refers only to Agents Messengers and Clerks employed by Candidates.*

the occupant has not been rated in respect of it will work no disqualification

The effect of all this appears to be that no one will in future be excluded from the Borough Franchise except persons who occupy *furnished* rooms *under* 4s. a week, and incapacitated persons. Inquiries will have to be made into the nature and extent of the occupancy of different inmates of the same house under pain of penalties if they omit them, thus increasing the difficulties of Overseers. (See "*Occupation.*")

Borough rates are included in Rates to be paid by Burgesses.

POSSESSION.—(See "*Actual Possession.*")

POST.—Notices of objection sent by post must be posted in time for delivery. (See "*Delivery*"—"*Notice.*")

POSTMASTERS wilfully contravening the Registration Acts are liable to an action. 6 Vic. c. 18.

" Every sheriff, under sheriff, clerk of the peace, town clerk, secondary, returning officer, clerk of the Crown, postmaster, overseer, or other person, or public officer, required by this Act to do any matter or thing, shall for every wilful misfeasance, or wilful act of commission or omission contrary to this Act, forfeit to any party aggrieved the penal sum of £100, or such less sum as the jury before whom may be tried any action to be brought for the recovery of the before-mentioned sum shall consider just to be paid to such party, to be recovered by such party, with full costs of suit, by action for debt in any of Her Majesty's Superior Courts at Westminster. Provided always that nothing herein contained shall be construed to supersede any remedy or action against any returning officer according to any law now in force. s. 97.

POTWALLER.—An inhabitant potwaller is a person who furnishes his own diet. Where for six months previous to the day of election persons who had been inhabitant householders, and had not received parochial relief or other alms for the space of twelve months then last past were entitled to vote, the claimant, who in all other respects was qualified, had ceased to reside for fourteen weeks, and then returned and became again an inhabitant householder; it was contended that the break in the residence under the 33rd section disqualified the claimant. The Revising Barrister having allowed the vote, the Court, on appeal, reversed his decision. *Maule*, C. J., in delivering judgment, said, "The terms of the proviso (s. 33) are very clear, that such persons shall retain the right of voting so long as they shall be qualified, &c. The words ' so long as' being words of time, and importing continuity, certainly do not include a case where the continuity of the qualification has been interrupted." (*Jeffrey v. Kitchener.*)

PRECEPT.—The form of precept to be issued by Clerks of the Peace to Overseers is given in the Schedule to 28 Vic. c. 36. The form is erroneous, but it is the only form given by the Legislature. The form of precept to be given by Town Clerks will be found in the Schedule to 41 & 42 Vic. c. 26.

PRESENTATION.—(See *"Petition."*)

PRISONER.—Where a claimant had been in prison, out of the borough, for five months out of six, previous to the last day of July (the then period of qualification), without the option of paying a fine, he was held to be not qualified, although he carried on his business, and kept a servant at his house during his absence. (*Powell v. Guest.*)

PROMOTION.—(See *"Office."*)

PUBLICATION.—(See 41 & 42 Vic. c. 26, s. 9.)

QUALIFICATION.—(See *"Franchise."*)

QUESTIONS at the Poll.—(See *" Oath."*)

REVIVER OF OBJECTIONS.—An objection by a qualified objector may, after his death, be revived by any other qualified person by a notice in writing to the person objected to, and to the Town Clerk, at or before the time of the revision of the entry to which the objection relates.

A person reviving an objection shall be deemed to have made the objection originally, and he shall be responsible in respect thereof.

The right of the original objector (to have given the notice) may be contested on the hearing of the revised objection, and any defect in his qualification will not be satisfied by the more perfect qualification of the party revising it. s. 27, 1, 2.

REVISING BARRISTER.—By 41 & 42 Vic. c. 26, s. 28, which is to take effect instead of 6 Vic. c 18, s. 40, the Barrister's powers are considerably extended and enlarged.

He may correct any mistake in any claim or objection.

He may exercise the power given by the former Acts of expunging a name in all cases of insufficient qualification, insufficient description, deaths of voters, or omission of name, place of abode, or situation of qualifying property, or incapacity by any law or statute, *whether the person is objected to or not,* but if not objected to, only after such notice as he considers necessary or proper.

In the case of persons objected to, except in objections by Overseers, he must require the objector, in addition to proving his notice of objection, to give evidence of the ground of objection before calling *primâ facie* on the voter to defend his vote.

He may amend the qualification in any list or claim, if any other sufficient qualification is proved before him, and transfer the name of the voter to the list for which the qualification is proved.

He may expunge all double entries, subject to a power in the voter to select by notice in writing given at the opening of the revision, the entry to be retained for voting. The voter may select a different entry for his claim as a Parliamentary voter to that of a burgess, except in the case of freemen, who must be inserted in the Freemen's List. The right to vote as a Parliamentary voter, or a burgess, may be supported by any qualification appearing on the register of Parliamentary voters, or the burgess roll, as the case may be, except as to burgesses, when the lists are made out in wards. In the case of lists made out in divisions, the name must be retained only in the division to which the qualification is proved to belong.

Subject to these provisions, he shall retain the name of every person not objected to, and where the objector does not appear.

And, subject as aforesaid, he shall not, whether the person be objected to or not, receive any evidence of any other qualification than that on the list, or make any correction of the same, except for more accurately and clearly defining it.

The power of fining Overseers not less than twenty shillings, or more than £5 (6 Vic. c. 18, s. 51), is to apply to all cases of wilful refusal, breach or neglect of duty by Overseers, in the execution of any of the duties imposed upon them.

In the case of Overseers' objections, if the party objected to does not appear personally, or by some other person, he shall expunge the name without further evidence. But by 6 Vic. c. 18, *no change is to be made in the qualification stated in the lists.*

"Whether any person shall be objected to or not, no evidence shall be given of any other qualification than that which is described in the "list of voters or claims as the case may be, nor shall the Barrister be at liberty to change the description of the qualification as it appears in the list, except for the purpose of more clearly and accurately defining the same." s. 40.

Where two or more Barristers are appointed for the same County or Borough, they may hold separate Courts. 6 Vic. c. 18, s. 30 (See "*Appeal*"—"*Costs.*")

RIBBONS.—Cockades, ribbons, and other marks of distinction forbidden at elections. 17 & 18 Vic. c. 102, s 7.

RIGHT TO VOTE not affected during an appeal.—(See "*Franchise.*")

RIOT.—Where the rioting is of such a serious and formidable character as to intimidate voters of ordinary courage from going to the poll, from a well grounded apprehension of violence, it will amount to general riot. (*Clare—Morpeth—Westminster—Coventry Cases.*)

Keogh, J., in the *Drogheda Case,* said that if voters were deterred from voting by a prevailing terror, even without violence or a threat thereof being brought to bear upon them personally, the election must be considered void. And when stones are thrown and shots fired among the persons going to record their votes, they are not bound again to imperil their lives, but may claim that the election be declared void.

ROLL, A, is to be kept by the Master of all persons entitled to practise as attorneys, or agents, in cases of Election petitions. (G. R. 56.)

I

By R. 57 the Roll may be subscribed by any person upon the roll of attorneys for the time being, and *might* be signed, during the *then current year*, by Parliamentary agents.

RULES.—The Supreme Court, with the concurrence of a majority of the Judges, of which majority the Lord Chancellor is to be one, may from time to time make, and when made, alter, or annul, the rules for regulating the proceedings in the Revising Barrister's courts, and all such Rules are to be laid before Parliament. 41 & 42 Vic. c. 26, s. 39.

The provisions of 35 & 36 Vic, c. 60, and of the rules of 1872, in regard to Municipal Election Petitions, are nearly similar to those of 31 & 32 Vic. c. 125, and the Rules of 1868, in regard to Parliamentary Election Petitions, and, so far as the former do not extend, the principles, practice, and rules under the latter are to extend.

The rules and principles with regard to *agency* and *evidence*, which apply to Parliamentary, are to apply to Municipal Election Petitions.

SALE.—(See *"Agreement."*)

SCHOOL BOARD fees are not parochial relief, the Education Acts expressly providing that such payment shall not be so considered.

SCHOOLMASTERS may have such a freehold interest in their appointments as to qualify them for the county franchise.

In the case of two Schoolmasters, whose appointment belonged to the Lord of the Manor at Stratton, who thought he had not power to remove the Masters when he had once appointed them, the votes were held good. (2 *Luders* 430.)

Philip Turner voted for a rent charge upon the estate of the Rev. Mr. Hawkins, Rector of Ampthill, who, under a deed settling an estate on the Rector for the time being on condition that he should "apply out of the rents £5 a year to one or more School-masters" for educating 16 children, had appointed the voter to the post, and said he did not know that he was empowered to turn out after he had appointed, and knew no instance of any being dis-placed, the vote was held good. (2 *Luders* 431.)

In the Bedfordshire case, James Taylor, the Schoolmaster of Sharpenhoe, received £10 a year, under a will made in 1686, in which were these words, "the schoolmaster and children, from time to time, to be put in and placed there by the approbation and good liking of J. N. and his heirs." Two instances were proved, in which the Master had been removed without any cause assigned, the vote was held bad. (2 *Luders* 428.)

SECURITY.—(See *"Recognizance."*)

SEPARATE GROUND OF OBJECTION.—(See *"Objection."*)

SEPARATE DWELLING.—41 & 42 Vic. 26, c. enacts that

"In and for the purposes of that Act, the term dwelling-house shall in-clude any part of a house where that part is separately occupied as a dwelling. This interpretation of the 'dwelling-house' is in substitution for the interpretation thereof contained in sec. 61 of the 30 & 31 Vic. c. 2, s. 61, but not so as to affect any of the other provisions of the said Act relating to rating." s. 5.

Thus disposing of the nice distinctions which were drawn in the cases of *Cuthbertson and Butterworth, Thompson and Ward, and Boon and Howard.* And if any part of a house is now occupied separately, either for trade, business, or profession, or as a dwelling-house, it is sufficient.

A very fine line now divides the occupier of a separate dwelling-house and a Lodger.

At the Hackney Revision Court, Sept. 1879, before Mr. Algernon Bathurst, the question of what constituted a Lodger was raised, it being remarked that it would seem there were no lodgers now.

> The Barrister : No ; there are no lodgers. At least, my view of it is this : If a man occupies a room in a house he is householder ; it is only when a person is living in furnished rooms that he can be regarded as a lodger.
> And at the Lambeth Revision, before Mr. Arbuthnot, M. claimed for a *dwelling-house*, at No. 66, Paradise Walk, Lambeth. Upon being questioned, it appeared that the claimant occupied rooms at the above address, and that other persons occupied other rooms in the house, the landlord, who resided next door, paying the rates. The Barrister said he thought he could not allow the claim, as it was impossible, unless a claim was rightly made, to institute proper inquiries into the case. It was submitted to him that under the 12th sub-section of the 28th Vic. he had power to alter the description, so as to allow the claim. Being pressed to decide the case, the Barrister referred to the Act, and ultimately decided to allow all such claims, and amend them so as to make them all "dwelling-houses."

SERVANT.—Ocupation by a servant is insufficient; so the manager of a Co-operative Store, claiming to be on the list of inhabitant householders for a house over the Stores, but where the shareholders paid the rent, he only residing there to carry on the business, his claim was disallowed.

SERVICE of notice of objection may be either personal or through the post. (See *"Notice."*)

SHAREHOLDERS.—(See *"Companies."*)

SHERIFF, The, has the custody of the list of county voters, transmitted to him by the Clerks of the Peace.

The decisions in appeal cases are to be notified to the Sheriff, who is to alter the Register as directed by the Court. 6 Vic. c. 18, s. 47.

The Sheriff is to receive the Judges, on the trial of an election petition, in counties, and in Parliamentary boroughs not under the Municipal Corporation Acts. (See *"Elections."*)

SHORTHAND WRITER, The, of the House of Commons, or his deputy is to attend the trial of Election Petitions. 31 & 32 Vic. c. 125, s. 24.

SIGNATURE, The, of an objector may be written or affixed by a stamp, on which a fac-simile of the name of the objector is engraved. (*Bennett v Brumfitt.*)

The signature to an Election Petition must be in writing.

SPECIAL CASE.—By 41 & 42 Vic. c. 26, s. 37, where the Barrister neglects or refuses to state a case, the party aggrieved may within one month apply to the High Court of Justice, Common Pleas Division, upon an affidavit of facts, to grant a rule to compel the Barrister to show cause why he should not do so, and to make it absolute, or discharge it with or without costs. If the rule is made absolute, the Barrister must state the case, which will be as effectual as if originally stated under the provisions of the 6 Vic. c. 18, ss. 42, 43, as follows :—

It shall be lawful for any person who, under the provisions hereinbefore contained, shall have made any claim to have his name inserted in any list, or made any objection to any other person as not entitled to have his name inserted in any list, or whose name shall have been expunged from any list, and who in any such case shall be aggrieved by or dissatisfied with any decision of any Revising Barrister, on any point of law material to the result of such case, either himself or by some person on his behalf, to give to the Revising Barrister in Court, before the rising of the said court, on the same day on which such decision shall have been pronounced, a notice in writing that he is desirous to appeal, and in such notice shall shortly state the decision against which he desires to appeal; and the said Barrister thereupon, if he thinks it reasonable and proper that such appeal should be entertained, *shall state in writing the facts* which according to his judgment shall have been established by the evidence in the case, and which shall be material to the matter in question, and shall also state in writing his decision upon the whole case, and also his decision upon the point of law in question appealed against ; and such statement shall be made as nearly as conveniently may be in like manner as is now usual in stating any special case for the opinion of the Court of Queen's Bench upon any decision of any Court of Quarter Sessions; and the said Barrister shall read the said statement to the appellant in open court, and shall then and there sign the same ; and the said appellant, or some one on his behalf, shall at the end of the said statement make a declaration in writing under his hand to the following effect ; that is to say, " I appeal from this decision," and the said barrister shall then endorse upon every such statement the name of the county and polling district, of city and borough, and of the parish or township to which the same shall relate, and also the Christian name and surname, and place of abode of the appellant and of the respondent in the matter of the said appeal, and shall sign and date such endorsement ; and the said Barrister shall deliver such statement, with such an indorsement thereon, to the said appellant, to be by him transmitted to Her Majesty's Court of Common Pleas at Westminster in the manner hereinafter mentioned; and the said Barrister shall also deliver a copy of such statement, with the said indorsement thereon, to the respondent in such appeal who shall require the same. In the matter of every such appeal, the party in whose favour the decision appealed against shall have been given shall be the respondent, but if there be no such party, or if such party, or some one on his behalf, shall in open court decline, and state in writing that he declines, to support the decision appealed against as respondent, then, and in every such case, it shall be lawful for the said Revising Barrister to name any person who may be interested in the matter of the said appeal, and who may consent, or the Overseers of any parish or township, or the Town Clerk of any city or borough to be, and such person so consenting, or such overseers or Town Clerk respectively so named, shall be deemed to be, the respondent or respondent in such appeal.

The costs of an appellant, if successful, whether under 6 Vic. c. 18, s. 41 or 41 & 42 Vic. c. 26, s. 37, may be ordered by the Court to be paid by the Clerk of the Peace of the county, or Town Clerk, as the case may be, if named as Respondent, whether he appears or not to defend the decision; and the Barrister may also be required by the appellant to name such officer to be a respondent, if he does so before he makes his declaration, to appeal under 6 Vic. c. 18, s. 42. He may, and if required, he shall, name the Clerk of the Peace, or the Town Clerk, respondent, or add his name to those named in 6 Vic. c. 18, s. 43. The expenses incurred by the Clerk of the Peace, or Town Clerk, are to include costs paid to appellant, in addition to expenses, under 6 Vic. c. 18, sec. 31. The costs of an appeal case are to be in the discretion of the Court.

Where the Revising Barrister died before signing the case, it was held that there was no proof that he had finally settled it, and the appeal was refused. (*Nettleton v. Burrell.*)

The Revising Barrister must sign in open court the endorsement in the statement of facts required, and in the absence of such signature the Master has no authority to enter the appeal nor the court jurisdiction to hear it. (*Wanklyn v. Woollett.*)

But *by consent* of the parties, the case may be remitted to the Revising Barrister for his signature. (*Burton v. Brooks.*)

Alterations cannot be made in the case, by consent of the parties. (*Whithorn v. Thomas.*)

If the case states evidence instead of facts, it will be remitted (*Pitts v. Smedley.*) No objection can be argued upon the hearing of an appeal which is not raised by the case stated by the Revising Barrister. (*Simpson v. Wilkinson.*)

The provisions of s. 42, which relate to single appeals, are made applicable by s. 45 to Consolidated Appeals.

STALLS in a MARKET.—A very important decision was given at the Birmingham Revision, 1879, by Mr. Saint, the Revising Barrister.

"The notice of objection stated 3 grounds of objection—(1) The nature of the alleged qualification; (2) the description thereof; (3) the value. It appeared in evidence that the voter occupied, and had done so for the requisite period, a stall in the Market Hall. This stall he rented from the 'Markets and Fairs Committee.' The voter's stall was separated from the stalls on either side of it by a wooden partition, which stands on a brick structure cemented to the floor. The wooden partition was affixed to the brick structure, but in no very substantial way, being so affixed chiefly by holdfasts. There was no roof or covering to the stall; it had a doorway, but no door. The voter paid £1 9s. 6d. per week for the use of it. He had a right to exclude persons from it so long as he conformed to the conditions under which he occupied it. Byelaw No. 34 enacts that 'all the markets within the Borough be closed on every Sunday, Good Friday, and Christmas Day, and every day appointed for a public feast or thanksgiving.' Other byelaws were of a restrictive character, one of them relating to the keeping of dogs by the occupiers of stalls, and another to smoking; and it appeared that the voter had no right of access to the stall in his occupation after the hours for closing. Mr. Saint said: I am of opinion, on the above facts:—(1) That the stall occupied by the voter does not belong to the class of qualifying tenements specified in s. 27 of the Reform Act, 1852; (2) that, assuming it to be a qualifying tenement within that section, the voter does not occupy it *as tenant*. It is obvious that the stall in question, being used for the purposes of trade, must, if it can qualify at all, qualify as a shop; but it seems to me that the stall in question is not a shop within the meaning of the Act. I do not decide this on the ground that there is no structural severance of that part of the stall on which the stall stands from the residue of the building. In my opinion the question of structural severance does not, strictly speaking, arise on the facts of this case, for, as it seems to me, the stall forms no part of the Market Hall, being a mere erection upon it, having none of the elements of permanence and durability necessary to constitute it a building, and being capable of removal at any time without injury to the freehold. If, however, the stall in question be considered part of the hall, the doctrine as to the necessity of structural severance laid down in *Cook v. Humber* would apply, and the absence of such severance must be held fatal to the vote. But assuming the subject of occupation to be so constructed as to be capable of conferring the franchise on one who occupied it as tenant, I am of opinion that the voter in this case does not occupy it in that capacity. To constitute an occupation as tenant within the meaning of the Act, the occupier of the qualifying premises must either personally, or constructively, occupy such premises during the whole of the prescribed period. The voter in the present case is subject to restrictions which do not allow of his doing so. He cannot use the stall whenever he chooses. He has no right to use it except within certain stated hours, and there are whole days during which he is entirely excluded from it. This limited enjoyment of the stall is incompatible with a tenancy of a nature to qualify for the franchise."

SUB-LESSEES.—By 2 & 3 Will. 4, c. 45, Sub-Lessees, or Assignees of a sub-lease, must be in actual occupation of the premises, to qualify them for the County franchise. In 30 & 31 Vic. c. 102, s. 5, this proviso is omitted. (See *"Assignee"*—*"Lease."*)

SUBSTITUTED PETITIONER.—(See *"Petition."*)

SUCCESSION.—IN COUNTIES.

" Different premises occupied in immediate succession by any person as owner or tenant during the 12 calendar months next previous to the last day of July in any year shall, unless and except as herein is otherwise provided, have the same effect in qualifying such person to vote for a county, *as a continued occupation of the same premises* in the manner herein provided." (30 & 13 Vic. c. 102, s. 26.)

Which is a similar enactment to that respecting £10 Occupiers in Boroughs under 2 Will. 4, c. 45, s. 29, and £50 Occupiers in Counties under 6 Vic. c. 18, s. 73.

In Boroughs.

"The premises in respect of the occupation of which any person shall be entitled to be registered in any year, and to vote in the election for any city or borough, shall not be required to be the same premises, but may be different premises occupied in immediate succession by such person during the twelve calendar months next previous to the 15th day of July in such year, such person having paid on or before the 20th of July in such year all the rates and taxes which shall previously to the 5th of January then next preceding have become payable from him in respect of all such premises so occupied by him in succession. 2 Will. 4. c. 45, s. 28; 41 & 42 Vic. c. 26, s. 7.

The franchise in boroughs, conferred by 2 Will. 4, c. 45, s. 27, in respect of the *continuous* occupation of the premsies, requires that the voter shall *have been rated*, and paid all poor rates, in respect of the premises, but the franchise which depends upon *successive* occupation only requires that the occupier shall have paid all the rates and taxes which shall *have become payable* from him in respect of the premises occupied in succession.

2 Will. 4, c. 45, s. 28, being confirmed by 30 & 31 Vic. c. 102, s. 59, a person occupying premises in immediate succession to premises previously occupied, would be entitled to the franchise under s. 3 of 30 & 31 Vict. c. 102, though he may not have been rated in respect of such premises; for in such case no rates would become payable from him in respect of such premises, and it has been held that the name of a person claiming to be registered for a borough in respect of different premises occupied in immediate succession for 12 months, need not have been entered in the rate book; and that, provided he has paid the rates, he is entitled to be registered. (*Rogers v. Lewis.*)

All the premises occupied "in succession" should be fully set out and described in this claim.

At the City of London Registration Court, 1879, an important question was raised relating to what is understood *as successive occupation*. It appeared a good many of the objections on both sides were taken on the ground that the parties who claimed had not occupied sufficiently long. It frequently, however, happened that they had come from another part of the city, and had really a good qualification if the two addresses were given. The Court was asked whether, under the new powers given to it, it would feel justified in inserting the second address in the fourth column, because, if not, it would be useless to ask these gentlemen to come up. The Barrister said he could not introduce a new qualification; all he could do was to see that the qualification was sufficiently identified. If he were to put in an additional address, he should be importing a new element in the qualification which he had no power to do. The whole thing depended upon the question of law and fact; he could alter in the one case, and not in the other. In other words, he could not supply a new qualification, which he should be doing if he adopted the suggestion.

Possession for the full qualifying period is not required in cases of property coming by *descent, succession,* &c.

" Provided, nevertheless, that, notwithstanding anything hereinbefore contained, no person shall be entitled to vote in the election of a member or members to serve in any future Parliament for any city or borough (other than a city or town being a county of itself in the election for which freeholders or burgage tenants have a right to vote as hereinbefore mentioned), in respect of any estate or interest in any burgage tenement or freehold which shall have been acquired by such person since the 1st day of March 1831, unless the same shall have come to or been acquired by such person since that day, and previously to the passing of this Act, by descent, succession, marriage, marriage settlement, devise or promotion to any benefice in a church, or by promotion to any office." 2. Will. 4, c. 45, ss. 26, 35.

SURETIES.—(See *"Recognizance."*)

TENANT.—The words of 2 Will. 4, c. 45, s. 27, which confer the £10 rateable franchise in Boroughs, are,

Every male person *of full age* and not subject to any *legal incapacity,* who *shall occupy,* within such city or borough, or within any place sharing in the election for such city or borough, *as owner or tenant, any house, warehouse, counting-house, shop, or other building.*

Occupation by a servant will not qualify, when such occupancy is necessary for the performance of the duties, and there is such an obligation to reside that there is no option of residing elsewhere. (*Dodson v. Jones.*)

TENDER.—The name of the voter *tendering* the vote must be entered by the presiding officer in the " tendered voters' list." These are voters who claim to vote in respect of a qualification, for which another has already voted, and those whose are rejected by the returning officer, for any other causes. (35 & 36 Vic. c. 33, Sch 1.)

TIMES to be observed in regard to Registration.

IN COUNTIES.

On or before

June 10. Clerks of the Peace to sign and transmit to Overseers precepts. 28 Vic. c. 36, Sch. A, Form 1. Also forms 6 Vic. c. 18, Sch. A. No 5, 2, 3, 6, Sch. D. No 1. Also copies of the Register. 28 Vic. c. 36. s. 3.

June 20. Overseers to sign and publish notice to voters not on Register to claim. 6 Vic. c. 18, Sch. A. No. 2.
To publish the copy of the Register, which must not be altered. 28 Vic. c. 36 s. 3.

July 20. Occupiers, not on rate book, to claim to be rated.
Persons not on "Property Register" to send in claims; and Voters who have changed their qualification (although the description of the new qualification be the

On or   same as the old), or who have changed their places of
before   abode, to send in *fresh claims* to overseers. 6 Vic. c. 18,
        s. 4. Sch. A. Form 2.

July 31.   Overseers to make out and sign an alphabetical list of
all persons who shall have sent in claims, *in respect of
property*, on or before the 20th of July preceding 6
Vic. c. 18. Sch. A. Form 3. and Sec. 5.

      Also to sign one of the copies of the register
sent them by Clerks of the Peace. 28 Vic. 36—Precept.

      Also to make out a separate list of all persons on
whom a right to vote in respect of £12 occupation is
conferred. (List No. 4.) 6 Vic. c. 18, Sched. B. Form
3; 30 & 31 Vic. c. 102, s. 30; 31 & 32 Vic. c. 58, s. 29.

      Overseers to keep copies of list of objections for
perusal and sale. 6 Vic. c. 18, s. 8.

      Overseers to deliver to Clerks of the Peace "the copy
of the Register," lists of Claimants (property), list
of persons objected to duly signed, list of £12 occupiers and list of claimants thereon. 6 Vic. c. 18, s
9; 28 Vic. c 36, s. 5.

Aug. 1.   Overseers to print and publish "the copy of the
Register" sent them by Clerks of the Peace, "List of
claimants in respect of property" (List No. 3). "List
of £12 occupiers who have paid all poor rates up to
preceding 5th January" (List No 4).

      Overseeers to keep copies of lists of claimants and
of "the copy of the Register" sent to them, and
allow the same to be perused, and to furnish copies,
if required, at price fixed by 6 Vic. c. 18, s. 5, Sched. D.
Table 1, at any time between 10 a.m. and 4 p.m.
on any day except Sunday during first 14 days after
publication.

Aug. 20.   Notices of objection to be given to overseers and
persons objected to. 6 Vic. c. 18, sec, 7, and Sch.
A. Form 4, Sch. A. Form 5. 28 Vic. c. 36, sec. 4,
and Sch. A. Form 2.

Aug. 25th.   Persons omitted from list of £12 occupiers (List
No. 4) to send in claims to overseers in Form No. 6,
Sched. B. 6 Vic. c. 18, s. 15, and 31 & 32 Vic. c. 58,
s. 17.

Sept. 1   Overseers to publish list of persons omitted from £12
list, and who have sent in claims, List No. 5. 31 & 32
Vic. c. 58, s. 17.

On or before   Overseers to make, sign, and publish list of persons against whom they have received notices of objection, (List No 6.) 6 Vic. c. 18, Sch. A. Form 16.

Sept. 14.   Voters, who have changed their residences, to make declarations of true place of abode (before a Justice of the Peace or Commissioner for Oaths) and transmit same to Clerks of the Peace, for delivery by them to the Revising Barristers. 28 Vic. c. 36, s. 10, Sch. B.

Oct. 31.   Last day for holding Revision Courts. 6 Vic. c. 18, s. 32.

Voters whose abodes are not in the same polling district as their qualifying property, *but are in same County*, to claim to vote in districts where their abode is. Voters whose abodes are *out of the County*, to claim to vote at any polling place in the County. Claims to be in writing, signed by voter, delivered to and verified by the Revising Barrister in Court. 6 Vic. c. 18, s. 36.

Nov. 30.   Clerks of the Peace to sign the register, and deliver the same to Sheriff. 6 Vic. c. 18, ss. 47, 49; 30 & 31 Vic. c. 102, s. 38.

IN PARLIAMENTARY AND MUNICIPAL BOROUGHS.

On or before   Registrars of Births and Deaths to send to overseers
Jany. 7.   Lists of Deaths of male persons of full age (and, if required by the overseers, of female persons of full age), who have died within that part of their parish which is included in any Parliamentary or Municipal Borough, and in the Registrar's sub-district, between the preceding 15th Sept. and 31st Dec. 40 & 41 Vic. c. 26, s 11.

Feb. 21.   Clerks of the Peace to send copy register to one of the Secretaries of State. 31 & 32 Vic. c. 58, s. 17.

April 7.   Registrars of Births and Deaths to send in to the Overseers their returns, as above, for the 3 months ending March 31. 40 & 41 Vic. c. 26, sec. 11.

June 10.   Town Clerks to sign, and send to overseers, Precept, Form A., and Forms B. C. D. E. F. G. K. and L. 40 & 41 Vic. c. 26, Schedule, & 6 Vic. c 18, c. 43, s. 10, and Sch. D. No. 1.

June 20.   Overseers to sign and publish notices as to payment of Poor Rates and Assessed Taxes (which shall have become due up to the preceding 5th Jany.) before 20th July. 40 & 41 Vic. c. 26, sec. 9, and Sch. Form B.

Overseers to give notice to every occupier of premises, which confer a Parliamentary or Municipal franchise, whose poor rates (and borough rates if any) due on the preceding 5th Jany. are now unpaid, to pay same on or before 20th July. 6 Vic. c. 18, s. 11; 30 & 31 Vic. c. 102, s. 28; 40 & 41 Vic. c. 26, s. 10, par. 1, 2, 3.

On or before   Registrars of Births and Deaths to send to Over-
July 22.   seers lists of deaths of male persons of full age (and, if
required by overseers of female persons of full age),
who have died between the preceding April 1st and
July 15th. 40 & 41 Vic. c. 26, sec. 11.

Overseers to make out lists of persons whose poor
rates (and Borough rates if any), due on preceding 5th
Jan., have not been paid on 20th June, and shall keep
such lists for perusal (free of charge) for the next 14 days
(Sundays excepted), between 10 a.m. and 4 p.m. 30 &
31 Vic. c. 102, s. 29; 40 & 41 Vic. c. 26, s. 10, par. 5.

July 25.   Claims to be sent in by lodgers who are on the
Register for the time being, and desire to be entered
on the next Register in respect of the same lodgings.
40 & 41 Vic. c. 26, s. 22, Schedule Form H.

July 31.   Overseers to ascertain from the relieving officers the
names of all persons disqualified for the Parliamentary
or Burgess Lists, by reason of having received parochial
relief during the 12 months preceding 15th July. 40
& 41 Vic. 26, s. 42.

July 31.   Overseers to make out a list of persons entitled to be
registered under—

    (a) The Reform Act, 1832. 2 Will. 4, c. 45.
    (b) The Representation of the People Act, 1867.
        30 & 31 Vic. c. 102.
    (c) As Burgesses under Municipal Corporations
        Acts.
    (d) As Lodgers claiming before July 25.
    (e) And of persons entitled to be elected Councillors
        or Aldermen of the Municipal Borough, though
        not entitled to be on the Burgess List. 40 &
        41 Vic. c. 26, s. 15, Sch. Forms D. 1, 2, 3, E.
        F. & G.

Town Clerks to make out Lists of Freemen who were
qualified on previous 15th July. 2 Will. 4, c. 45. s. 32 ;
30 & 31 Vic. c. 102, s. 3; 40 & 41 Vic. c. 26 s. 16.

Aug. 1.   Publication of such lists to be made by Overseers and
Town Clerks respectively.

Aug. 25.   Claims to be sent in to Overseers—

    (a) Parliamentary claims. 40 & 41 Vic. c. 26,
        Sched. Form H. 1.
    (b) Lodgers claims. 40 & 41 Vic. c. 26, Sched. Form
        H. 2.
    (c) Municipal Claims. 40 & 41 Vic. c. 26, Sched.
        Form H. 3.

On or before   Claims as Freemen to be sent in to Town Clerks. Vic. c. 18, Sched. B. Form 5.

Objections to be sent in to Overseers—
Parliamentary Form I, No. 1.
Municipal Form I, No. 3.
And to persons objected to—
Parliamentary Form I, No. 2.
Municipal Form I, No. 4. 40 & 41 Vic. c. 23.
And to Town Clerks as to Freemen. 6 Vic. c. 18, Sch. B. Form 10.

Aug. 29.   Overseers to send to Town Clerks copies of lists made by them, signed.

Sept. 1.   Overseers and Town Clerks to publish their respective lists on or before this date, and to keep the same open for inspection, and furnish copies, if required, on any day (Sundays excepted) until September 14, between 10 a. m. and 4 p. m. (Forms K & L 1, 2, 3.)

Sept. 12.   Last day for sending in Declarations as to misdescriptions, whether as to name, place of abode, nature of qualification, name or situation of qualifying property, or any error or omission in the lists, to Town Clerks. 40 & 41 Vic. c. 26, Sched. Form M.

Sept. 15.   Registrars of Births and Deaths to send to Over-
(variable) seers Lists of Deaths of Male persons of full age (and if required of Female persons of full age) who have died before the preceding 16th July and this date, or between 16th July and such time as the Revising Barrister shall appoint. 40 & 41 Vic. c. 26, sec 19.

Notices of withdrawals of objections to be sent at least 7 days before the day appointed for holding the first Court for the Revision of the list to which such objection applies—

To persons objected to in Form No. 1.

To Town Clerks in Form No. 2. 40 & 41 Vic. c. 26. s. 27. 1.

Notices of revival of objections may be given, to which such objection relates.

To persons objected to. Form O 1.

To Town Clerks. Form O. 2. 40 & 41 Vic. c. 26, s. 27 2. At or before the time of the Revision of the entry to which objection relates.

Oct. 12.   Revision of List of *Burgesses* to be closed.

Nov. 30.   Town Clerks to deliver Register to Returning Officer. 6 Vic. c. 18, s. 48.

IN MUNICIPAL BOROUGHS.

On or before

Sept. 1.   The Overseers to make out an alphabetical list, to be called the burgess list, of all persons who shall be entitled to be enrolled in the burgess roll of that year 5 & 6 Will. 4, c. 76, s. 15, and subsequent Acts.

Sept. 1.   The Overseers to sign such lists and deliver them to the Town Clerk, and to keep true copies thereof, to be perused without payment, up to the 15th September.

Sept. 8th.   The Town Clerk to cause copies of all such lists to be printed, and deliver a copy to any person *on payment*, and also to cause a copy of all such lists to be fixed on or near the outer door of the Town Hall, or in some public and conspicuous situation within the borough on every day up to the 15th day of September.

Sept. 15.   The Overseers to close their lists. 5 & 6 Will. 4, c. 76, s. 17.

The Town Clerk to remove the copies of the Lists from the door of the Town Hall, &c. *Ib.*

Sept. 15.   Persons whose names have been omitted in any such burgess lists, to give notice in writing of their claims to the Town Clerk. *Ib.*

Persons named in the burgess list objecting to any other person's name being therein, to give notice of their objections to the Town Clerk, and also to the person objected to. *Ib.*

Sept. 15 to 22nd.   The Town Clerk to make out a list of all persons so claiming, and a list of all persons so objected to. *Ib.*

Sept. 22   The Town Clerk to cause copies of such lists of persons claiming and objected to respectively to be affixed to the door of the Town Hall, &c., up to and including Sept. 30th, and shall keep copies of such lists, to be perused without payment, up to and including the same day, and for sale. *Ib.*

When the 22nd falls on a Sunday, then on the 21st.

Oct. 1 to 15.   The Mayor and Assessors to hold an open Court for the purpose of revising the said burgess lists, having first given three clear days' notice, to be fixed on the door of the Town Hall, &c. *Ib.* s. 18.

The Town Clerk, Overseers, Vestry Clerks, and Collectors of Poor Rates to attend the Court. The Town Clerk to produce the said lists, and a copy of the lists of persons claiming, and the persons objected to, so made out as aforesaid. Overseers, &c., to answer all questions put to them on oath and produce rate-books for present or any past year. *Ib.* s. 19.

On or before   The Mayor to revise the said lists, and sign each sheet thereof in open court.

Oct. 22.   The Mayor to deliver the lists signed by him to the Town Clerk, who shall keep them, causing them to be copied in one general alphabetical list in a book or books, to be the Burgess Roll for the year commencing Nov. 1.

TITLE.—As to Equitable Title, see *"Agreement."*

TREATING.—Disqualifications by Bribery and Treating existed at common law; that of "Undue Influence" was created, and is dealt with, by 17 & 18 Vic. c. 102, which consolidated and extended the law, and of which the key-note is the word "corruptly." The statutes defining corrupt practices were intended only to give fuller effect to the common law of Parliament; members are still unseated for acts which at common law are corrupt, although not within the definitions of the statutes.

Treating, for the purpose of influencing, *i.e.*, *corruptly*, either single electors or a constituency, is corrupt, but should be distinguished from the refreshment which is prohibited by s. 23, under a penalty of 40s.

To make the doing of an act *corrupt*, it must be done with the knowledge that it is wrong, and with evil feelings and intention. (Martin, J., *Bradford Case.*)

An *intention to influence* is the sting of the corrupt practice.

In the *Bodmin* case, Willes, J. said, "Assuming the feast was given with the view of influencing the election—'corruptly given'—which I should have thought was the same thing as 'with a view of influencing the election,' by attracting poor people, and making them vote otherwise than they would have done, under the impression or expectation that they were to have a dinner at Grose's, assuming that to be made out, there was corrupt treating, and if Grose was an Agent, the election is void, without reference to the question of bribery."

TRIAL.—Notice of the trial of a Parliamentary Election Petition is to be given. 31 & 32 Vic., c. 125, s. 11.

The trial of Municipal Election Petitions, provided for. 35 & 36 Vic. c. 60, s. 15.)

The time and place of trial is to be fixed by the Judges on the Rota.

Unless special circumstances exist which render it desirable that it should be tried elsewhere, every petition is to be tried in the County or Borough to which it relates, and petitions relating to a Metropolitan Borough may take place anywhere in the Metropolitan District.

In the case of illness of the Judge, the trial is to be recommenced and concluded by another Judge.

TRAVELLING ABROAD.—(See *"Abode."*)

TRUSTEES are not entitled to vote,

The *cestui que trust* in actual possession, or in the receipt of the rents and profits thereof, though he may receive the same through the hands of the trustee, shall and may vote for the same, notwithstanding such trust. 6 Vic. c. 18, s. 74.

"Actual possession," in the statute, means in actual possession of the " cestui que trust," as distinguished from the trustee, and not as distinguished from the other "cestuis que trust." (*Gainsford v. Freeman.*)

Where a deed reserved an absolute power of sale to the trustees, it was held that such power of sale did not cut down the freehold interest which was created in the beneficiaries by the earliest part of the deed, inasmuch as it could only be exercised by the Trustees for the benefit of the beneficiaries, and consequently the latter had such a freehold interest as would entitle them to be registered as voters for the county. (*Ashworth v. Hopper.*)

UNDUE INFLUENCE was made a statutable offence by 17 & 18 Vic. c. 102, s. 4. It has been made the subject of resolutions of the House, and of enactments directed against the influence of persons whose position gave them exceptional powers, and rendering them liable to pains and penalties, but without any provisions in reference to the validity of Election.

Of this sort was the interference of Peers, Ministers, military persons holding office under the Crown, and those employed in the Post Office, Excise, and Police; but the 17 & 18 Vic. c. 102, was directed against much more notorious and every-day instances than the above.

There are three kinds of undue influences the subject of sec. 4 of that Act—

(1.) Any force, violence, restraint, or threat thereof.

(2.) Any injury, damage, harm, or loss inflicted, or threat thereof, or other intimidation.

(3.) Any abduction, duress, or any fraudulent device or contrivance which might impede the proper enjoyment of the franchise.

Legal arrest and imprisonment do not amount to abduction, unless it be proved to have been effected for the express purpose of preventing a voter from voting a certain way.

Ejectment by a landlord, if for the purpose of influencing a voter to give his vote or on account of having voted in a certain way, is undue influence.

Personal violence is clearly an infraction of the law, and if done by or with the consent or authority of a candidate, or his agent, with a view of influencing the vote for or against, would render the election void. (See "*Riot*.")

Persons found guilty of undue influence are to be struck out of the Register and inserted in a separate List. s. 6.

VALUE.—The question of value is one of fact on which the decision of the Revising Barrister is conclusive. (*Cogan v. Luckett.*)

The Bedfordshire Committee resolved, "That the value of the freehold, in right of which the owner votes, is the rent which a Tenant would give for it, and not what the owner occupying it himself may possibly acquire from it.

Where a man had been offered £15 a year for a plot of building ground, though the land in its actual condition was not worth 40s. a year, it was held that £15 was the value within the meaning of the Registration Act. (*Astbury v. Henderson.*)

For the purposes of this Act the word "value," shall, in the case of an objection to any person claiming to be retained or inserted in the list as an occupying tenant, mean "amount of rental." 28 Vic. c. 36.

VENDOR.—(See "*Agreement.*")

VEXATIOUS CLAIM or "Objection."

"If in any case it shall appear to the Barrister holding any Court that any person shall have made or attempted to sustain any groundless or frivolous and vexatious claim or objection or title to have any name inserted or retained in any list of voters, he in his discretion may make such order as he shall think fit for the payment by such person of the costs of or any part of the costs of any person or persons in resisting such claim, or objection, or title. In every such case the Barrister shall make an order in writing, specifying the sum which he shall order to be paid for costs, and, by and to whom, and when and where the same sum shall be paid, and date and sign the order, and deliver it to the person or persons to whom the sum shall therein be ordered to be paid. 6 Vic. c. 18, s. 4.

And by 28 Vic. c. 36, s. 13, the sum ordered to be paid by way of costs shall not exceed £5.

VOTING is absolutely free of all costs to the voter, and no payment is necessary by persons making claims, or by persons on the register.

VOTING PAPERS.—(31 & 32 Vic. c. 65. Appendix.)

WAREHOUSE.—The 2 Will. 4, c. 45, s. 27, gives the franchise (subject to registration) to every person who shall *occupy*, either as *owner* or *tenant*, inter alia any warehouse or counting-house of the required value. (See "*Franchise*"—"*House.*")

WAY, Right of, is an easement only, and confers no qualification.

WIFE.—(See "*Curtesy*"—"*Dower.*")

WITHDRAWAL.—An objection may now be withdrawn by a notice to that effect signed by an objector, given to the person objected to, and to the Town Clerk, not less than seven days before the day be appointed for the first court of revision. 41 & 42 Vic. c. 26 s. 27. Form O. 1 2. (See "*Revival.*")

Under the former Act, where notices of objection having been duly served on certain voters, and a notice was published by the objector in the local papers, on the 30th of August, that he withdrew his objections, and he afterwards sent a notice to each voter that the objection was not withdrawn but would be proceeded with, at the revision court the notices of objection were proved, but the voters objected that they ought not to be called upon to support their votes, as the objections had been withdrawn. The Barrister decided that the objections had been withdrawn, and retained the names of the voters objected to without proof of their qualification ; it was held that he was wrong; for that on proof of each notice of objection, he was bound by 6 Vic. c 18, s. 40, to call upon each voter to prove his qualification, and to strike off the name on failure of proof. (*Proudfoot v. Barnes.*)

At the Staffordshire Revision, 1879, the Barrister intimated that he intended to be more strict with regard to ordering costs. In cases where it was clear that the person objected to had a good claim to vote, and the objector knew that to be so, or could have known it by taking the trouble to enquire, he should order the payment of full costs. Later on, a gentleman, who had been objected to, attended and claimed costs. He admitted having received a notice that the objection was withdrawn, but said that the notice was posted at Burton-on-Trent on Saturday, and only received by him on Sunday. The Barrister ordered his costs to be paid.

WITNESS to a Declaration by a Lodger. It is not desirable that these declarations should be witnessed by clerks to party agents. In several instances Revising Barristers have signified their approval of a certificate from the landlord, as to the period, rent, &c., accompanying the declaration.

WOMEN. —The 32 & 33 Vic. c. 55, s. 9, let in female voters to this franchise by words imputing the masculine gender to include the female, but the removal of this disability has no reference to disability by reason of *coverture;* therefore a married woman, though qualified by occupation and payment of rates and inserted in the burgess list, cannot vote at the election of Town Councillors. (*Reg v. Harrald.*)

And a woman rightly on the burgess list, but married before the election, is also disqualified. The Married Women's Property Act does not confer any status.

WRIT.—The old form of the Writ of Summons shows clearly who should be choosers, and who were to be the chosen, and how they were to be chosen ;

" We commend you and strictly enjoin you that (Proclamation being made of the day and place aforesaid in your *next County Court* to be holden after the receipt of this our Writ) two Knights of the most fit and discreet of the said County, girt with swords, and of the University of Oxford two Burgesses, and of every City of the said County two Citizens, and of every Borough in the said County two Burgesses, of the most fit and discreet freely and indifferently, by those who at such proclamations shall be present, according to the form of the Statute, in that case made and provided you cause to be elected.

Writs for the Election of Members are now issued by the Clerk of the Crown in Chancery, in England.

K

CASES ARISING

ON

REGISTRATION APPEALS.

———◇———

Abel v. Lee, L. R., 6 C. P. 365; 40 L. J., C. P. 154.—Excusal of Rates under 54 Geo. 3, c. 170, s. 11, will not obviate objection as to nonpayment.

Ackroyd's case, Wigan, B. & Aust. 189.—A shopkeeper, having a branch business at W., and sometimes sleeping there, held to have a sufficient residence, his principal establishment being at B.

Acland v. Lewis, 30 L. J., C. P. 29; K. & G. 334.—Shareholders in a Company incorporated by a special act vesting lands in the Company have no estate therein, so as to give them the county franchise.

Ahearn v. Wynne, 15 Ir., C. L. R. 359.—Where no name and address was endorsed on the notice of objection posted to the party, it was held to be defective, although the name was written on the duplicate.

Ainsworth v. Creeke, L. R., C. P. 476; 38 L. J., C. P. 58.—Claims to be rated, made through a landlord, should be ratified by the tenant, during the qualifying year, the same being paid by the former in a lump sum.

Aldworth v. Dore, 5 C. B. 89; 2 Lut. 67.—Hearing of Appeals will not be postponed, where ample time has elapsed between the decision and the time appointed, and the Respondent does not appear.

Aldridge v. Medwin, L. R. 4, C.P. 464; 38 L. J., C. P. 45.—An omission to specify the *list* on which an objector's name appears, cured by due publication, but not to form a precedent.

Alexander v. Newman, 2 C. B. 122; 15 L. J., C.P. 134; 1 Lut. 404.—A conveyance for valuable consideration valid, though made to multiply votes, bonâ fide and only those are void which are fraudulent. 10 Anne, c. 23.

Allan v. Liverpool, L. R., 9 B. 191; 43 LJ., M.C. 69.—A lodger in a house, though he has exclusive use of rooms, is not in exclusive occupation, cannot bring an action for trespass, and is not rateable.

Allan v. Waterhouse, 1 Lutw. 92; 13 L. J., C.P. 129.—In special cases Appellant is to deliver paper books to Chief Justice and senior *puisne* Judge. The Respondent to the two junior *puisne* Judges. Delivery of objections to Postmaster's managing Clerk sufficient, open and in duplicate.

Allen, ex parte, 28 L. J., C.P. 256; K. & G. 258.—Where a name is inadvertently struck off the register, the Court cannot by rule order its insertion. This can only be done upon Appeal. But see 41 & 42. Vic. c. 26, s. 37.

Allen v. Geddes, L. R., 5 C.P. 253; 1 Hop. & C. 413.—Where there was more than one List, if the description of the Objector would be commonly understood to refer to the List where his name ought to have appeared, it was held sufficient, but this is a conflicting decision.

Allen v. Greensill, 4 C.B. 100; 16 LJ., C. P. 142; 1 Lut. 592.—Service of a notice of objection, at an Office where the person objected to carried on a business, but did not reside, not a service at the place of abode, and insufficient.

Allen v. House, 1 Lutw. 255; 14 L.J., C. P. 79.—An unnecessary addition in a notice of objection, by way of further describing the list on which the name of the person objected to appears, does not vitiate the notice.

Anelay v. Lewis, 25 L. J., C.P. 121; K. & G. 36.—Where purchase money has been paid for land but no conveyance has been executed, and the purchaser has not been let into possession, neither the vendor nor purchaser are entitled to be registered.

Ashmore v. Lees, 1 Lut. 337; 15 L.J., C. P. 65.—A 40s. freehold qualifies for the county: where lands are situate in two counties, the proportion received from each must amount to 40s.

Ashworth v. Hopper, 45 L. J., C.P. 99; 2 Hop. &c. 283.—An absolute power of sale limited to trustees does not destroy the freehold interest of beneficiaries.

Asthury v. Henderson, 24 L.J., C. P. 20; K. & G. 6.—Land may be estimated by its value for building, although no building erected and no lease granted, in order to confer the county franchise.

Austin v. Cull, L. R., 7 C.P. 28; 41 L. J., C.P. 153.—The rates to be paid before 20 July are those made after 5th Jan. of the year preceding, and payable up to 5th Jan. in the qualifying year.

Autey v. Topham, 1 Lutw. 1—Notice of appeal to the Master of the Court indispensable, within the first 4 days of Mich. Term.

Baye v. Perkins, 1 Lut. 255.—Where Appellant does not appear and Respondent does, the Revising Barrister's decision is affirmed with costs, without hearing the case.

Baker v. Locke, 34 L.J., C.P. 49; 1 Hop. 137.—A person objected to for non-payment of Rates cannot set up that the rate was not signed by a majority of the parish officers, when the rate is good on the face of it.

Bakewell v. Peters, L.R., 4 C.P. 539; 38 L.J., C.P. 266; 1 Hop. 251.—A set of rooms in a College at Oxford or Cambridge held to be a separate dwelling-house, and the occupier not entitled as a lodger, no qualification being conferred.

Ballard v. Gerrard.—The office of Archdeacon held to give a freehold interest in land.

Ballard v. Robins, 47 L.J., C. P. 50; 2 C.P. 92.—The Revising Barrister has power to transfer the names of £12 occupiers, inserted by mistake in list of £50 occupiers, to £12 list.

Barclay v. Parrott, K. & G. 59; 26 L.J., C.P. 77.—An objection to a borough voter need only have a sufficient address on the back. 6 Vic. c. 18, s. 100.

Barnes v. Peters.—See *Bakewell v. Peters*.

Barrow v. Buckmaster, 22 L.J., C.P. 65; 2 Lut. 235.—Apportionment of an overriding chief rent is to be deducted in calculating annual value.

Bartlett v. Gibbs, 5 M. & G. 81; 1 Lut. 73.—No change may be made in the description of qualification, except for more clearly and accurately defining the same; an omission is a misdescription, and cannot be amended under 6 Vic. c. 18, s. 40.

Barton v. Birmingham, 48, L.J., C.P., 87; 2 Hop. & C. 393:—Agreements by owners with occupiers as to payment of rates refer to agreements which need not be in writing, and may be implied, and an abatement will not defeat a qualification. 32 & 33 Vic. c. 41, s. 19; 41 & 42 Vic. c. 26, s. 14.

Baxter v. Newman, 1 Lutw. 287; 14 L.J., C.P. 193.—Shareholders in an incorporated Company (before the Joint Stock Companies Acts) held to have an equitable seisin in sufficient estate to entitle them to the franchise.

Bayley v. Overseers of Nantwich, 2 C.B. 118; 1 Lutw. 363.—Notice of claim may be sent by post, and production of stamped duplicate is conclusive of due delivery, in the ordinary course of post.

Beal v. Ford, 47 L.J., C.P. 56.—It i6 immaterial that the residence is merely *permissive*, and the claimant might be turned out.

Beamish v. Overseers of Stoke, 2 Lut. 189; 21 L.J.,C.P. 9.—Where the monthly payments to a Building Society under a mortgage reduce the annual value to less than 40s. the vote is disallowed. See *Robinson v. Dunkley.*

Beauchamp (Earl) v. Madresfield, L.R., 8 C.P. 245; 42 L. J., C.P. 32.—Revising Barristers to expunge the names of Peers, and incapacitated persons, whether objected to or not.

Beenlen v. Hockin, 1 Lut. 526; 16 L. J., C.P. 49.—Notices of Objection may be served on any Overseer or Assistant Overseer. In dating a Notice of objection, the year may be omitted.

Beeson v. Burton, 22 L.J., C.P. 33; 2 Lut. 225.—An allotment of freemen's land at Leicester, under an Enclosure Act, held by a freeman at a rent over 40s., and held so long as he pays the rent and conforms to regulations, held to be a freehold interest.

Bendle v. Watson, L.R., 7 C.P. 163; 41 L.J., C.P. 15.—The Barrister may alter the number of a house in the list, where the number on the street door had been changed subsequently to list being made out.

Bennett v. Blain, 33 L.J., C. P. 63; 1 Hop. 35.—Shareholders in an unincorporated Company have no direct interest in the land of the Company, but only a right to share in the profits, and are not entitled to the franchise.

Bennett v. Brumfitt L.R., 3 C.P. 28; 37 L.J., C.P. 25.—A fac-simile of the signature of an objector stamped by him on the notice of objection is a sufficient signature within 6 Vic. c. 18, s. 17.

Bennett v. Brumfitt, (Alderson's case), L.R., 4 C.P. 407; 38 L.J., C.P. 65.—A notice of objection to a person on the Overseers' £12 list must specify the grounds of objection. 28 Vic. c. 36, s. 6.

Bennett v. Brumfitt (Ashcroft's case), 1 Hop. & C. 48; L. R., 4 C.P. 399.—The Court has no jurisdiction to hear Appeals improperly consolidated, where the facts are not the same, and one judgment would not govern all.

Beswick v. Alker, L.R., 8 C.P. 265.—Held that a Rector might vote for a county in respect of a freehold interest in pews in a church, assuming that he could have such an interest.

Birch v. Edwards, 5 C.B. 45; 2 Lutw. 37.—The duplicate notice of objection must contain the same direction on the back as the original; an omission is fatal, the service being held not proved.

Birks v. Alison, 32 L.J., C.P. 51; K. & G. 507—Revising Barristers may amend description of qualification by inserting the words "farm, as occupying," before word "tenant."

Bishop v. Helps, 2 C.B. 45-53; 1 Lut. 353.—Production of stamped duplicate notice of objection conclusive evidence of original having been sent, but where no delivery by post, service not proved. *Lewis v. Evans.*

Bishop v Snedley, 1 Lut. 384; 15 L.J., C.P. 73.—A man saying to the Overseer, "If there are rates due, I am prepared to pay them," not a tender.

Blain v. Pilkington, 34 L.J., C.P. 55.—Where a voter objected to did not appear to support his claim, his name was expunged, but appearing at an adjournment and making a reasonable excuse for non-attendance, his name was restored, held this could not be done without the presence of the objector.

Bond v. St. George's, 1 Hop. & C. 427; L.R., 6 C.P. 313.—Lodgings occupied by a claimant when in London, two months out of the year for which they were taken, held a sufficient residence.

Brewer v. McGowan, L.R. 5, C.P. 239; 39 L.J., C.P. 30.—A person duly qualified does not become joint occupier, and lose his qualification, by letting the exclusive use of bedroom and joint use of a sitting room.

Bridgewater v. Durant, 31 L.J., C.P. 46; K. & G. 377.—The claim of a lay clerk who had the option of a house in lieu of salary, but was not obliged to reside in it, and had no power to let, disallowed.

Bright v. Devenish, L.R., 2 C.P. 102; 36 L.J., C.P. 71.—Where an objector described himself as *on the List of Voters for the parish of Clifton*, he being on the list of freemen for the city of Bristol, and there described as in the parish of Clifton, the objection was held inadmissible.

Brown v. Tamplin, L.R., 8 C.P. 241; 42 L.J., C.P. 37.—Where the Respondent had no notice of Appeal until 4th Nov. the case having been signed on the 31st of October, and Appeals were fixed for 13th Nov., the Court refused to hear it, under 6 Vic. c. 18, s. 64.

Brumfitt v. Bremner, 30 L.J., C.P. 331; K.'& G. 352.—County Register not complete until actually signed and delivered by the Clerks of the Peace to the Sheriff. 6 Vic. c. 18, s. 47.

Bulmer v. Norris, 30 L.J., C. P. 25.—Shareholders in incorporated Companies not entitled to vote in respect of any freehold estate held by the Company, their rights being a share in the profits.

Burton v. Brooks, 2 Lut. 197; 21 L.J., C.P. 7.—An Appeal allowed to be argued although the endorsement (upon the statement) only was signed, the Court saying it was presumably signed, and the Respondent consenting that the signature should be obtained afterwards.

Burton v. Grey, 2 Lut. 4; 17 L.J., C.P. 66.—A fresh claim must be made in respect of a fresh qualification though the same description applies, and in default, name struck off on objection.

Burton v. Langham, 17 L.J., C.P. 253.—Committee of a lunatic cannot vote in respect of any land, &c., held by virtue of his office.

Burton v. Ov. of Aston, 2 Lut. 143; 8 C.B. 7.—Land occupied as owner, and a house as tenant, cannot be joined to make up a borough vote, not being under the same landlord.

Bushell v. Eastes, 31 L.J., C.P. 44; K.& G.484.—A parish clerk not entitled to vote by virtue of his office, nor does the receipt of fees on the opening of graves give a freehold interest.

Busher v. Thompson, 1 Lut. 551; 16 L.J., C.P. 57.—"Customary feehold" or "burgage tenure" where the freehold was not shown to be in anyone else, and no record of any Court was shown, allowed as a "freehold."

Capell v. Ov. of Aston, 2 Lut. 148; 19 L.J., C.P. 28.—Freeholds which confer the Borough Franchise will not entitle the owner, who is also the occupier, to the County Franchise.

Caunter v. Adams, 33 L.J., C.P. 68; 1 Hop. 50.—A claim to be rated may be made to an Assistant Overseer, as to an overseer.

Chorlton v. Johnson, L.R., 4 C.P. 426; 1 Hop. &c. 49.—(*Bunting's case*)—Leaseholds in a borough which would confer the borough franchise deprived both owner and occupier of the County Franchise.

Chorlton v. Kessler, L. R., 4 C.P. 397; 1 Hop. &c. 42—Females not entitled to the County Franchise. 2 Will. 4 c. 45.

Chorlton v. Linys, L. R., 4 C. P. 374; 1 Hop. &c. 1.—Females not entitled to the Borough Franchise. 30 & 31 Vic. c. 102, ss. 3-4.

Chorlton v. Ov. of Tonye, L.R., 7 C.P. 178.—Where a township is divided into polling districts, an objector need not specify on which list his name appears; "on the list of voters for the township of   " is sufficient.

Chorlton v. Stretford, L.R., 7 C.P. 198.—Sub-lessee, or assignee of a sub-lessee, must be in "actual occupation."

Clarke v. Ov. Bury St. Edmunds, 26 L. J., C. P. 12.—A servant does not occupy as either owner or tenant, and is not entitled as an inhabitant occupier. 2 Will. 4, c. 45, s. 27.

Collier v. King, K. & G. 385; 31 L.J., C.P. 80.—The qualification of Dissenting ministers depends upon the usage in respect of the *duration* of their office, as a Freehold.

Collins v. Thomas, 2 Lut. 219; 22 L.J., C.P. 38.—Land occupied " therewith," may be so occupied, if lying apart from the house; *time* and not *locality* is the ingredient of the qualification. 2 Will. 4, c. 45, s. 27.

Colvill v. Wood, 1 Lut. 483; 15 L.J., C.P. 160.—Fair annual rent the criterion of " clear yearly value," under that sec.

Colville v. Rochester, 1 Lut. 380; 2 C.B. 60.—Notice of objection posted on Saturday and delivered on Sunday, is sufficient service.

Coogan v. Luckett, B. & Arn. 716; 1 Lut. 447.—Rates paid by landlord should be deducted in calculating " clear yearly value." 2 Will. 4, c. 45, s. 27.

Cook v. Humber, K. & G. 413; 31 L.J., C.P. 77.—An occupier must at least be *tenant.* 2 Will. 4, c. 45, s. 27. There must be "tenement, value, occupation, and estate." One of the " actual severance " cases.

Cook v. Luckett, 2 C.B. 174; 15 L.J., C.P. 78.—Where the landlord pays the rates by agreement it is a legal payment by the tenant.

Cooke v. Butler, L.R., 8 C.P. 256; 42 L.J., C.P. 25.—Rateable value means *true* rateable value, not the value given in the rate book; it is a question for the Barrister. 30 & 31 Vic. c. 102, s. 6 (2).

Cooper v. Ashfield, 28 L.J., C.P. 35; K. & G. 200.—It is sufficient to describe in the 4th column the property out of which a rent charge is payable.

Cooper v. Town Clerk of Cambridge, 7 M. & G 97; 1 Lut. 207.—If a Respondent does not appear, the Court will not reverse the decision without having the appellant's case argued.

Copland v. Bartlett, 2 Lut. 102; 18 L.J., C.P. 50.—Monthly payments under a Mortgage to a Building Society to be deducted, in calculating " clear yearly value," but see *Robinson v. Dunkley.*

Cotton v. Pratt, L.R., 2 C.P. 86; 36 L. J., C.P. 67.—The correct addition of town and county to the voter's address on a notice of objection will not vitiate it.

Courtis v. Blight, K. & G. 475; 31 L.J., C.P. 48.—If an objector has two places of abode he may state either in the notice.

Cross v. Alsop, L.R., 6. C.P. 315; 40 L.J., C.P. 53.—Constructive rating—see 41 & 42 Vic. c. 26, s 14.

Croucher v. Browne, 1 Lut. 388; 15 L.J., C.P. 74.—Freemen being Liverymen of London, may be registered, although admitted by purchase since March 1st, 1831.

Crowther. Oldfield, 1 Salk. 364.—Tenants in " ancient demesne " described.

Crowther v. Bradney, 33 L.J., C.P. 70; H. &. P. 63.—Misdescription of list, on which Objector's name appears, fatal to the objection.

Cull v. Austin. See Austin v. Cull.

Cuming v. Toms, 1 Lut. 151; 14 L.J., C.P. 54.—Production in Court of the stamped duplicate notice of objection by the objector sufficient though posted by an agent.

Daniel v. Camplin, 1 Lut. 264; 14 L.J., C.P. 121.—" House and shop " a good description, without stating the fact of joint occupation.

Daniel v. Coulsting, 1 Lut. 230; 14 L.J., C.P. 70.—A house, let off as warehouses and salesroom, held to be correctly described as " House."

Davies v. Hopkins, 27 L.J., C.P. 6.—Publication by Overseers of notice of claim for a County conclusive evidence of receipt in time.

Davis v. Waddington, 1 Lut. 159; 14 L.J., C.P. 45.—The inmates of a Hospital, removable for " any lawful or reasonable cause," entitled to the freehold franchise, none having ever been removed.

Dawson v. Robins, 46 L.J., C.P. 62.—Rent charge of 50s. granted by the freeholder of lands, let upon a long lease, is sufficient, there being a power of distress and entry, and ample income.

Dewhurst v. Fielden, 1 Lut. 274; 7 M. & G. 182.—Two separate buildings cannot be joined to make up a qualification under 2 Will. 4, c. 45, s. 27.

Dobson v. Jones, 5 M. & G. 112; 13 LJ., C.P. 126.—Occupation of rooms in a Hospital by the surgeon, not occupation as "owner or tenant."

Dodds v. Thompson, L.R., 1 C.P. 133; 35 LJ., C.P. 97.—Power of distress need not be given by deed creating a rent charge, such power being given by 4 Geo. 2, c. 28, s. 5.

Downing v. Luckett, 2 Lut. 33; 17 LJ., C.P. 31.—A counting-house, open only during the daytime, the keys being kept on the premises, is sufficient occupation by a *tenant*, when otherwise qualified.

Durant v. Carter, L.R., 9 C.P. 269; 43 LJ., C.P. 17.—Leaving a house, with an "animus revertendi," for an indefinite period, does not break the residence; but where a man leaves his house for a definite period, with another in possession, he neither "resides," "occupies," nor "inhabits."

Ealen v. Cooper, 11 C.B. 18; 2 Lut. 183.—Barristers may amend an error in a claim, if such as they could amend in a list.

Eckersley v. Barker, 1 Lut. 190.—If the qualifying premises are in a "street, lane, or other like place," it is sufficient to so describe them, and if numbered, the numbers be given. Otherwise the name of the property, if any, or of the occupying tenant.

Elsworth v. Farrer, 1 Lut. 517.—Where a Borough Register is composed of four separate lists, three made out by the overseers of 3 townships, and the fourth a list of freemen, the notice of objection should state on which list the objector appears.

Faulkner v. Ov. of Boddington, 27 LJ., C.P. 20; K. & G. 132.—Beadsmen of Daventry not entitled to be registered.

Fernie v. Scott, L.R, 7 C.P. 202; 41 LJ., C.P. 20.—No freehold interest, if determinable at the will of another, or under a bye-law.

Flint v. Sharp, 25 LJ., C.P. 36; 1 K. & G. 13.—The place of abode as "described in the list," is sufficient direction on a notice of objection.

Flounders v. Donner, 15 LJ., C.P. 81; 1 Lut. 365.—The number of every house occupied in succession should be given in the 4th Column.

Force v. Floud, 33 LJ., C. P. 71.—Writing the surname before the Christian name in a notice of objection, and objection made out to the third person, instead of the second, may be amended.

Ford v. Harington, L.R., 5 C.P. 282.—A member of a corporation aggregate, occupying without intervention, occupies as a corporation sole, and is entitled to a Borough note. Case of a Canon of Exeter.

Ford v. Hart, L.R., 9 C.P. 273.—A freeman, officer in H.M.S., residing with his mother during his leave (3 months in the year), within 7 miles of the Borough, not a sufficient residence.

Ford v. Pye, L. R., 9 C.P. 269; 43 LJ., C.P. 21.—An Incumbent who had exchanged duties and residence with another, loses his qualification, by the break in his residence.

Fox v. Dalby.—Staff Sergeant in the Militia, occupying a house for which 2s. 4d. a week was deducted from his pay, which he would not receive if resident elsewhere, not entitled. L.R, 10 C. P. 285.

Fox v. Overseers of Shaston, 18 LJ., C.P. 48; 2 Lut. 97.—Poor Rates, not allowed by Justices, a nullity.

Freeman v. Gainsford, K. & G. 448.—Inmates of Shrewsbury Hospital, Sheffield, entitled to the County Franchise.

Fryer v. Bodenham, L.R., 4 C. P. 529; 38 LJ., C. P.—Occupation through eleemosynary, does not debar the occupier from the franchise as owner when he has the freehold, and not the Trustees.

Gadsby v. Barrow, 1 Lut. 142.—To qualify as a £50 occupier in a county there must be a *single* rent of land under one landlord.

Gadsby v. Warburton, 14 LJ., C.P. 41; 1 Lut. 136.—An objector is right in describing the place of abode as it appears on the register. It is not necessary to state any place of abode to which he may subsequently have removed. But see *Melbourne v. Greenfield, contra.*

Gainsford v. Freeman, L. R. 1, C. P. 129; 35 L. J., C. P. 92.—The unexpired residue of a term of years, determinable meanwhile by death, does not qualify.

Gale v. Chubb, 1. Lut. 544.—As to "capital burgesses " of Malmesbury.

Garbutt v. Trevor, 33 L. J., C. P. 73.—Customary freeholders at Seaton, in Yorkshire, entitled as being seised of lands " of any other tenure whatever, for life."

Gaydon v. Pencraft, 34 L. J., C. P. 53.—Freemen may claim through a grandfather, or other ancestor, admitted previous to 1st March, 1831.

Gleaves v. Parfitt, 7 C. B. (N. S.), 838.—As to votes of Vicars Choral.

Godsell v. Innons, 17 C. B., 290 ; 25 L. J., C. P. 79.—Where it does not appear when a notice of objection was received by the overseers, but it was acted upon by them, it was sufficient.

Hadfield's case, L. R., 8 C. P. 306 ; 42 L. J., C. P. 146.—Confirming *Heelis v. Blain.*

Hall v. Lewis, K. & G. 499; 31 L. J., C. P. 45.—Preachers in a Cathedral, paid out of chapter revenues, not entitled, though such revenues are in part derived from land.

Hamilton v. Bass, 22 L. J., C. P. 29; 2 Lut. 213.—Premises belonging to 30 persons let at a gross annual rent of £73 15s., reduced by rates, charges, and *repairs* to less than £60, and so not worth 40s. a year to each owner.

Hannaford v. Whiteway, 26 L.J., C.P. 75; K. & G. 61.—The receipt of notices of objection, by a Postmaster, though not within the hours of which notice shall have been previously given, is sufficient.

Hargreaves v. Hopper, 45 L. J.,C. P. 105.—A voter must be of full age on the last day of the qualifying year.

Harris v. Amery, L. R., 1 C. P. 148; 35 L. J., C. P. 89.—Members of a partnership, registered under 25 & 26 Vic. c. 83, cannot claim as occupiers, through their Manager.

Harrison v. Carter, 46 L. J., C. P. 57.—The receipt of a portion of rents annually distributed, " to the poorest inhabitants," disqualifies.

Hayden v. Ov. of Tiverton, 16 L. J., C. P. 88; 1 Lut. 510.—A rent charge, originally created in 1838, was granted on the 19th Jan., 1841, to A., B., and C., in trust for themselves, D., and others. The first quarterly payment was made on the 29th April, 1846. Held that D. was not entitled, not having been in possession six months on the 31st July within 2 Will. 4, c. 45, s. 26— following *Murray v Thorniley.*

Heartly v. Banks, 28 L.J., C.P. 144.—Military Knights of Windsor disqualified not occupying as "owners or tenants."

Heath v. Haynes, 27 L.J., C. P. 50.—Occupation of rooms in an Hospital, by permission of the Trustees, does not entitle as "tenant."

Heelis v. Blain, 34 L. J., C.P. 88; 18 C. B. (N. S) 110.—Grant of a rent charge under the Stat. of Uses, gives immediate possession, and that is " actual possession " within 2 Will. 4, c. 45, s. 26.

Hinde v. Chorlton, L. R., 2 C. P. 104 ; 36 L.J., C. P. 79.—The right to sit in a particular pew, in a church, is an easement only, and does not qualify.

Hinton v. Hinton, 14 L. J., C. P.58 ; 1 Lut. 259.—The name of an objector, W. Nicholas, was spelt *W. Nickless.* Sufficiency of notice a question of fact for the Barrister, not for the Court.

Hitchins v. Brown, 15 L.J., C. P. 38 ; 1 Lut. 328.—The qualification being 2 houses in succession, fully described in the 4th Column but described as " house " only in the 3rd Column held sufficient, the 3rd Column being intended for the *general* nature, the 4th Column for the *particular* nature of the qualification.

Hornsby v. Robson, 26 L.J., C.P. 55 ; K. & G. 66.—Production of the stamped duplicate notice of objection is evidence, though not in fact delivered until after the 25th August.

Huckle v. Piper, L. R., 7 C. P. 143 ; 41 L. J., C. P. 42.—A £12 occupier in Counties need not hold under the " same landlord."

Hughes v. Overseers of Chatham, 13 L. J., C. P. 44 ; 1 Lut. 51.—The occupation by officials of Government residences in part pay for services, they being rated, though the rates were paid by Government, a good qualification.

Jeffrey v. Kitchener, 14 L.J., C.P. 75; 1 Lut. 210.—A person having once lost the *identical* reserved franchise, to which he was entitled under the Reform Act, cannot regain it.

Joliffe v. Rice, 18 L. J., C.P. 2 ; Lut. 90.—A coachhouse and a stable together of the value of £10, separately of less, and having no internal communication, except windows looking from one to the other, held to be " *a building* " under 2 Will. 4, c. 45, s. 27.

Jones v. Innons, 25 L.J., C.P. 78 ; K. & G. 21—If a notice of objection reaches its destination in due course of post, it is evidence that the address is " commonly understood," although by the Act, the County or Borough should be given.

Jones v. Jones, L. R., 4 C.P. 422 ; 38 L.J., C.P. 43.—Leasehold for life, but in case of death within 60 years, then for the residue of the such term, though conferring a freehold interest, held to be sufficiently described as " Leasehold."

Jones v. Pritchard, L.R., 4 C.P. 414 ; 38 L.J., C.P. 67.—Whether the objector has properly described his place of abode a question of fact for the Revising Barrister.

Jump's Case, B. & Aust. 46.—Occupation entirely broken by the voter being committed to prison, and the landlord resuming possession.

Kirton v. Dear, L. R., 5 C. P. 217.—Perpetual curates with an income arising from lands out of the parish, not entitled, and customary fees, for marriages, baptisms, &c., do not qualify

Lambert v. Overseers of New Sarum, 22 L.J., C. P. 31 ; 2 Lut. 222.—Notice of objection to a name being retained on a *certain Parish*, in a certain Division of a County, though not corresponding with the form given in 6 Vic. c. 18, s. 7, held sufficient.

Lawe v. Maillard, L. R., 4 C.P. 547; 38 L. J., C. P. 179.—The Revising Barrister must state all the facts, and not leave it to the Court to find them. The houses in question were extra parochial, and not so found by the Barrister.

Lee v. Hutchinson, 8 C. B. 16 ; 2 Lut. 159.—A mortgagor must retain 40s. a year clear, after deducting all interest, whether the interest be secured by the mortgage or by personal liability.

Lewis v. Evans, L. R., 10 C. P. 297 ; 44 L. J., C. P. 41.—If there is no postal delivery at the place, but only within 2 miles, service of notice is *not proved* to have been made on the last day for service.

Lewis v. Roberts, K. & G. 402 ; 31 L. J., C. P. 51.—Proof of the objector's signature on the *duplicate* notice of objection, sufficient.

Little v. Penrith, L. R., 8. C. P. 259 ; 42 L.J., C. P. 28.—Payment of Rates by " N. A. and Sons " sufficient to qualify father and son jointly.

Luckett v. Bright, 15 L.J., C. P. 85, 1 Lut. 456.—Six members of Political Association (Bright, Cobden, Wilson, Paulton, Moore, and Taylor), joint lessees of a house, and alone liable for the rent, transacting daily their own business, and the business of the association, held to be entitled.

Luckett v. Knowles, 15 L. J., C. P. 87 ; 1 Lut. 451.—An erroneous statement of a place of abode may be corrected by the Revising Barrister, being no part of the qualification.

Mashiter v. Town Clerk of Lancaster, 18 L.J., C.P. 13; 2 Lut. 112.—Excusal from payment of rates is not a disqualification, not being a receipt of parochial relief, or alms, under 2 Will. 4, c 45, s. 36.

Mather v. Overseers of *Allendale,* L. R., 6 C. P. 272 ; 40 L. J., C. P. 76.— Mistake in the heading of an Overseer's List immaterial.

Mayor of Northampton's case, 2 Str., 1238. "Piccage and stallage" does not give the same freehold interest as "tolls."

Medwin v. Streeter, L. R., 4 C. P. 488; 38 L. J., C. P. 180.—Claim to be rated should be made during the qualifying year.

Melbourne v. Greenfield, K. & G. 261 ; 29 L. J., C. P. 81.—Where an objector has removed he must insert his then place of abode, and not the place of abode as described in the Register.

Mills v. Cobb, L. R., 2 C. P. 95 ; 36 L. J., C. P. 75.—Trustees, entitled to a sum of £5 a year each, out of the rents, &c., of an estate, and being in occupation of a portion thereof ; if, on an apportionment, there is not 40s. a year left in their occupation, they are not entitled.

Moore v. Ov. of Carisbrooke, 22 L.J., C. P. 64; 2 Lut. 233.—A plot of freehold land, worth £5 a year, mortgaged with other land for £300, though the interest is apportionable, gives a qualification of more than 40s. and entitles.

Moorhouse v. Gilbertson, 23 L. J., C. P. 19; 2 Lut. 260.—Where the Rates, &c., agreed to be paid by the owners, reduce the clear yearly value of the qualifying premises to less than 40s., the owner not entitled.

Morgan v. Parry, 25 L.J., C.P. 141 ; K. & G. 53.—If Overseers' lists have been published, they must be dealt with, although not signed by all the Overseers. Being directors only, not invalid.

Moss v. Overseers of Lichfield, 14 L. J., C. P. 56 ; 1 Lut. 185.—Where a father and son were joint occupiers and the son's name had been omitted from two out of three rates, the son was disqualified ; also held that there was no misnomer, or insufficient description.

Murray v. Thorniley, 15 L. J., C. P. 155 ; 1. Lut. 496.—Under the grant of a rent charge *at Common Law* there must be a manual receipt thereof, or of some part thereof, to give "actual possession" for the qualifying period.

Norton v. Town Clerk of Salisbury, 1 Lut. 538; 4 C. B. 32.—The Court will not postpone the hearing of an appeal where ample time has elapsed for giving the proper notices; when the decision was given on the 16th October, and the hearing was fixed for the 12th Nov.

Noseworthy v. Buckland-in-the-Moor, L.R., 9 C.P. 233; 43 L. J., C.P. 27.—In counties "the said list" (6 Vic. c. 18, s. 100), is the register sent by the Clerk of the Peace to the overseers, and not that published by them.

Newton v. Overseers of Moberley, 1 Lut. 427 ; 2 C. B. 203.—The Court will not determine a question of fraud, whether *fraud in fact,* as in the granting of a rent charge, or fraudulent violation of 2 Will. 3 c. 25 (multiplication of votes at elections), being a question of fact for the Barrister.

Nichols v. Bulcer, L. R., 6 C. P. 281 ; 40 L. J., C. P. 82.—Freehold rent charge issuing out of freehold houses, a misdescription of qualification, the houses being let on a long lease.

Nicks v. Field, 16 L. J., C. P. 61 ; 1 Lut. 566.—The franchise in the Borough of Warwick was, before the Reform Act, in the inhabitants paying scot and lot. The nonpayment of rates for a subsequent year suspends the right for the time, does not destroy it. See *Jeffrey v. Kitchener.*

Norrish v. Harris, 35 L. J., C. P. 102.—Agricultural, not to be contradistinguished from commercial, industries. 2 Will. 4, c. 45, s. 27.

Norrish v. Pilcher, L. R., 4 C. P. 417 ; 38 L. J., C. P. 69.—Whether an objector's "place of abode" is sufficiently described—a question of fact for the Barrister ; but the Court will not refuse to hear a case on the propriety of the decision.

Nunn v. Denton, 7 M. & G., 66; 1 Lut. 178.—A groundflo or used as a cow-house, with a furnished bedroom over, where a servant of the voter slept, held to be a " house " within 2 Will. 4, c. 45, s. 27.

Onions v. Bowdler, 17 L. J., C. P. 70; 2 Lut. 59.—Where a qualification was for houses "in succession," and so stated in the 3rd column, the Barrister had no power to supply the omission of one of such houses in the 4th Column.

Orme's case—(Webster v. Ov. of Ashton) L.R., 8 C.P. 281; 42 L. J., C.P. 38— Distinction between a grant operating under the Common Law, and under the Stat. of Uses (the latter giving " actual possession " immediately.)

Palmer v. Allen, 18 L. J., C. P. 265.—When the Barrister gave his decision on the 30th Oct., and notice of appeal was given on the 2nd Nov., the appellant's signature not being obtainable before (Sunday intervening), and the 11th Nov. being appointed for the hearing, appellant entitled to a postponement. 2 Lut. 1.

Parient v. Lackett, 15. L. J., C P. 83 ; 1 Lut. 441.—The interlineation of a tenant's name in the Rate Book, immediately after that of his landlord, but not bracketed, and nothing inserted opposite the tenant's name, a sufficient rating.

Passingham v. Pitty, 25 L. J., C. P. 4; 1 K. & G. 26.—Customary Tenants of the Manor of Digswell—freeholders.

Perown v. Peters, L. R., 4 C. P. 539; 38 L. J., C. P. 266.—Rooms in a College at Oxford or Cambridge occupied by a Scholar do not qualify.

Phillips v. Salmon, 47 L.J., C. P. 53.—Lease for lives of waste land a freehold tenement, notwithstanding certain rights of common.

Pinder v. Barr, 4. E. & B., 105.—Appointment of a Parish Clerk, by the locum tenens, during suspension of the Vicar, good.

Powell v. Boraston, 34 L. J., C. P. 73.—A structure adapted for use by man, either for residence or industry, is a building within 2 Will. 4, c. 45, s. 27.

Powell v. Bradley, 34 L. J., C. P. 67.—It is sufficient if a claimant is of age on the last day of the qualifying year, and has occupied during that year.

Powell v. Caswell, 2 Lut. 141.—Unnecessary for Appellant to give Respondent notice of setting down of appeal for hearing; the 10 days' notice of intention to prosecute sufficient.

Powell v. Farmer, 34 L. J., C. P. 71.—A lock-up wooden shed, used by a market gardener for storage, a building within 2 Will. 4, c. 45, s. 27.

Powell v. Guest, 34 L. J., C. P. 69.—Confinement in prison a break in residence.

Powell v. Price, 16 L. J., C. P. 139; 1 Lut. 586.—Shop and bakehouse, separated by a yard communicating by an open passage with the street, cannot be joined to make a qualification under 2 Will. 4, c. 45, s. 27.

Pownall v. Dawson, 21 L. J., C. P. 14; 2 Lut. 177.—Two-stalled stable, with an adjoining building, both of brick, and a wooden annex, all under same roof, and one landlord, held to constitute a building under that sec.

Pring v. Estcourt, 1 Lut. 543.—Decision of the Barrister given on the 16th Oct. Appellant's attorney died on the 7th Nov., having been taken ill the last week in October. No postponement allowed, the statute not contemplating the delay in giving the notice so late as the end of October.

Prior v. Waring, 17 L. J., C. P. 73; 2 Lut. 45.—The Court will not hear a consolidated appeal when the facts are not the same in each case, and a decision in one would not govern the rest, nor can the appeal be remitted to the Barrister.

Proudfoot v. Barnes, L. R., 2 C. P. 88; 36 L.J., C. P. 68.—The Barrister will not enquire whether an objector has, or has not, withdrawn his notices if he appears to support them.

Rawlins v. Ov. of West Derby, 1 Lut. 373.—Where the 20th July falls on Sunday, service upon the Overseers on that day, of notices of claims, is within the statute. Where a Respondent appears, he cannot object to the form of the notice of intention to prosecute.

Reg. v. Harrald, 41 L.J., Q. B. 173.—A married woman, occupying a house, and duly rated, &c., separated from her husband, not entitled to the Municipal Franchise.

Reg. v. Ireland, L.R., 3 Q.B,130.—Relief given to a father cannot be construed as relief to a son.

Reg v. Bolton—Monmouth, 36 L.J., Q. B. 77 ; L. R., 5 Q.B. 251.—Mandamus will be granted to compel Mayors, &c., to hold Courts and hear objections, they having erroneously returned names objected to without an enquiry into the qualification.

Reg. v. Mersey & Irwell Navigation, 9 B. & C. 95.—An incorporeal hereditament cannot be occupied, or rated to the poor, and gives no title to the franchise.

Reg. v. St. Mary Kalendar, 9 A. & E. 626.—Occupation may be without personal residence, as" by a bale of goods." "Suppose a man had gone away without any *animus revertendi,* but had left a person on the premises, would not that have been an occupation: and if so, may not he occupy in the same way by his goods?" *Coleridge, J.*

Reg. v. St. Pancras, 46 L. J., M.C. 250.—Occupation must have in it the character of *permanency*—a way-farer not an occupier.

Rendlesham (Lord) v. Hayward, L.R., 9 C.P.252; 43L.J., C.P.33.—Irish Peer disqualified for the borough franchise.

Rendlesham v. Percival, 34 L. J., C. P.84.—A Barrister may state a case, similar in every respect to a case already decided, but affecting another register or voter.

Robinson v. Ainge, L. R., 4 C. P. 429.—A member of a Benefit Society, entitled to an annuity of sufficient value, not entitled to a freehold interest.

Robinson v. Dunkley, 33 L. J., C. P. 57.—Where a voter makes two payments to a Building Society concurrently, one in reduction of the principal, the other in payment of interest, the latter only is to be deducted in ascertaining the " clear yearly value."

Robinson's case, B., & Aust. 335.—A voter having occupied a house before marriage, his father and mother residing with him, and after marriage ceased to live, but kept it with the furniture for the use of his father and mother, paying all charges, held to be entitled, in respect of continuous occupation.

Rogers v. Harvey, 28 L.J., C.P. 17.—A Leaseholder took three sons into partnership, who all lived on the premises, and were rated jointly. Held that the sons were at least *tenants at will* to the father, and entitled.

Rolleston v. Cope, L. R., 6 C. P. 292; 40 L. J. C. P. 160.—Following *Robinson v. Dunkley.* Two-thirds of the payments to the Building Society being in reducton of principal, and one-third in payment of interest, the former not being deducted in ascertaining the clear yearly value.

Rowledge's case, Wolf & Dews, 199.—Appointment as parish clerk, promotion to an *office.*

Scott v. Durant, 34 L. J., C. P. 81; Hop. & P. 269. Where the parties agreed to waive objections, and no case was stated in Court, and no declaration of appeal made in writing, and the proposed Respondent subsequently declined to sign, the case was struck out, the appeal not being complete.

Shedden v. Butt, 2 Lut. 188.—Where one party to an appeal fails to deliver paper books, the other party should do so, or the case will be struck out See *Allen v. Waterhouse.—Newton v. Moberly.*

Sheldon v. Flatcher, 17 L. J., C. P. 34; 2 Lut. 11.—Whether a notice of objection discloses the objector's true place of abode is a question of law: but whether the description is *sufficient* is one of fact, for the Barrister. The Court will not review his decision.

Sherlock v. Steward, 29 L. J., C. P. 87; K. & G. 286.—Commission paid to an estate agent must be deducted in ascertaining the clear yearly value.

Sherwin v. Whyman, L. R., 9 C. P. 243; 43 L. J., C. P. 36.—" Rent charge on freehold house " a sufficient description of a Freehold rent charge.

Simey v. Dixon, L. R., 7 C. P. 190; 41 L. J., C. P. 18.—Objection to a County vote grounded on the 3rd Column to the nature of the interest, viz., that the qualifying property would confer a Borough vote, held good.

Simey v. Marshall, L. R. 8 C. P. 269; 42 L. J., C. P. 49—Hospital of St James's, Gateshead, " Younger brethren " not entitled as County Voters. Following *Steele v. Bosworth*.

Simpson v. Wilkinson, 1 Lut. 168 ; Burghley Hospital case. Bedesmen entitled to a separate equitable estate of Freehold in their respective rooms.

Smerdon v. Tucker, 29 L J., C. P. 93 ; K. & G. 305.—A tenant of premises whose landlord sells a part of them during the qualifying year, held to be still entitled, as under " the same landlord." 2 Will. 4, c. 45, s. 27.

Smith v. Foreman, 34 L. J., C. P. 93.—Two rents cannot be joined to give a qualification as £50 tenant, under 2 Will. 4, c. 45, s. 20.

Smith v. Hall, 33 L. J., C. P. 59.—Brethren of an Hospital not recipients of *alms*, which would disqualify. (St. John's, Sandwich.)

Smith v. Holloway, 35 L. J., C. P. 100.—Separate notices of objection need not be given to the Overseers in each case. All may be included in one list.

Smith v. Huggett; K. & G. 434; 31 L. J., C. P. 38.—Notices of objection sent by post to the overseers, and acted upon by them ; proof of sending and publication, primâ facie proof of delivery in time without production of stamped duplicate.

Smith v. Over. of Seghill, L. R., 10 Q. B. 432; 44 L. J., M C. 114.—Colliers who occupied cottages of their employers, without paying any rent, but such occupation not being compulsory or necessary, entitled as tenants, notwithstanding that they were omitted from the rate book. 32 & 33 Vic. c. 41, s. 19.

Stamper v. Overseers of Sunderland, L. R., 3 C. P. 388 ; 37 L. J., M. C. 144.—Nature of the Lodger franchise, interpretation substituted by 41 & 42 Vic. c. 26, s. 5.

Stanton v. Jeffrey. See *Jeffrey v. Kitchener.*

Steele v. Bosworth, H. & P. 106; 34 L. J., C. P. 57.—Earl of Rutland's Hospital, Bottesford, the inmates of which were held to have no equitable interest in lands.

Taylor v. St. Mary Abbot, L. R., 6 C. P. 309; 40 L. J., C. P. 45.—A manservant sleeping once a week at the lodgings where his wife and family reside, duly qualified.

Tepper v. Nicholls, 34 L. J., C. P. 61.—Putney Bridge case. No interest in tolls.

Thackray v. Pilcher, L. R., 2 C. P. 100; 36 L. J., C. P. 73.—Whether place of abode of objector sufficiently described a question of fact for the Barrister. H. & P. 378.

Thompson v. Harding, 1 C. B. 940 ; 14 L. J., C. P. 268.—Test whether lands are of freehold or copyhold tenure—interference of the lord on alienation, &c.

Toms v. Cuming, 14 L. J., C. P. 67 ; 1 Lut. 200.—Notice of objection must be signed *by hand;* but see *Bennett v. Brumfitt.*

Townsend v. St. Marylebone, L. R., 7 C. P. 143; 41 L. J., C. P. 25.—" Dwelling-house," a good description of the joint occupation of a dwelling-house under 2 Will. 4, c 45, ss. 27-29, although it is also the description of another qualification under 30 & 31 Vic. c. 102, s. 3.

Trenfield v. Lowe, 38 L. J., C. P. 191.—An allotment a freehold estate for life, notwithstanding right of pasture in other inhabitants.

Trotter v. Walker, 32 L. J., C. P. 66.—Signature of objector, found by the Barrister not to be wholly illegible, sufficient.

Trotter v. Watson, L. R., 4 C. P. 434; 38 L. J., C. P. 100.—Equitable interest in an ascertained legal lease insufficient. Inchoate agreement.

Tudball v. Town Clerk of Bristol, 13 L. J., C. P. 49 ; 1 Lut. 7.—When the objector described himself as on the list of voters for the Parish of Clifton, he being on the list of freemen for the city of Bristol, insufficient, though described in the latter list as " of the Parish of Clifton."

Vance's Case, Alcock 169.—A person having only an equitable interest in a lease is entitled to the franchise notwithstanding that the words " at law or in equity" are not to be found in 2 Will. 4, c. 45, s. 20.

Walker v. Payne, 1 Lut. 324.—Where the voter had for several years been travelling abroad, and had no fixed place of abode, " travelling abroad" a sufficient description for the 2nd Column.

Wanklyn v. Woollett, 1 Lut. 597.—The statement of facts, in an appeal, must be endorsed, and signed by the Barrister in open court. 6 Vic. c. 18, s. 42. If not signed the Master cannot enter it, nor has the Court jurisdiction to hear it. Doubtful whether anyone can be appellant in a consolidated appeal except the person acually interested.

Warburton v. Overseers of Denton, 1 Hop. & Colt. 432; 40 L.J., C. P. 49.—As to the reading of 2 Will. 4, c. 45, s. 20, and 30 & 31 Vic. c. 102, s. 5, together : and the occupation by sub-lessees of an under-lease, and their assignees.

Watson v. Cotton, 2 Lut. 53.—A shed, standing against a wooden paling of a wharf, but not fastened to it, but used for purposes connected with the occupation, as keeping barrows, shovels, &c., a building within 2 Will. 4, c. 45, s. 27.

Watson v. Pitt, 2 Lut. 73.—Whether a notice of objection is properly served, a question for the Barrister, and the Court will not interfere with his decision. Putting a notice under a door, between 9 and 10 at night, on the last day of service, no one answering knocks at the door, an insufficient service.

Webb v. Overseers of Birmingham, 1 Lutw. 18.—Leasehold houses in a Borough, not singly of sufficient value to confer the borough franchise, but collectively of sufficient value to confer the County franchise, a good qualification, not coming within 2 Will. 4, c. 45. s. 25.

Webster v. Ashton-under-Lyne,.—See *Orme's* case.

West v. Robson, 27 L. J., C. P. 262.—Where voters have an interest in lands situate in several counties, the proportion arising from each county must be of sufficient value to confer the franchise.

White v. Pring, 2 Lut. 141.—Where the Respondent appears, and the Appellant does not appear, the Court will affirm the decision of the Barrister, with costs.

Whithorn v. Thomas, 1 Lut. 125.—A wine merchant residing at Gloucester, who was a Freeman of Tewkesbury, more than 7 miles distant, where he hired a room at 9d. a week from a friend, and occasionally slept there, held not to have had a residence there within 2 Will. 4. c. 45, s. 32.

Wills v. Adey, 1 Lut. 481.—An objector whose place of abode appeared in the list as " Fisherton-st." described himself in the notice as " of the parish of Fisherton Anger," there being several other parishes in the Borough, notice held sufficient.

Wilson v. Town Clerk of Salford, L. R., 4 C. P. 398 ; 1 Hop. & Colt. 44.— Women, being legally incapacitated, cannot appeal, under 6 Vic. c. 18, s. 13.

Windsor Case. Glanv. 17.—A house being pulled down and rebuilt continues to confer the franchise.

Wood v. Overseers of Willesden, 1 Lutw. 314.—It is a question of fact for the Barrister whether there is a sufficient description on the face of the register, to identify the qualifying property.

Wood v. Hopper, 45. L. J., C. P. 108.—Rent charges arising from lands in the same county may be joined to give a qualification for the county franchise.

Woollet v. Davis, 1 Lut. 607.—A notice of objection signed J. B. "of the Oaks, on the Register of Voters for the Parish of St. Woollos," he being on the list of voters for that parish, and improperly described as of "the Oaks" in the 4th Column, held insufficient, as not giving a proper description of the "place of abode."

Wright v. Town Clerk of Stockport, 1. Lut. 32.—Rooms in a cotton mill, each tenant having the exclusive use, and also the key of his room, there being a general outer door, which was never locked, held to be "buildings" within 2 Will. 4, c. 45, s. 27.

CASES ARISING

ON

ELECTION PETITIONS.

———o———

Aitkin ex parte, 4 B. & Ald.—Communications made to Solicitors who are retained as Election Agents are not protected from disclosure on the ground of privilege, except such as are made professionally.

Aldridge v. Hurst, L.R, 1 C.P. 410.—An Election Petition cannot be amended, after the expiration of the time limited by the Act for presenting the same, by striking out such portion of his prayer as claims the seat for the Petitioner, or allegations which would apply to a scrutiny and be dependent thereon, as that would affect the constituency.

Appleby, 27 Journ. 443.—Double Return. If on a scrutiny the votes are found equal, election is void.

Ashburton, Wolf & Dew.—Continued agency. That a person is agent for a candidate at an Election cannot be shown from the fact that he was agent for the same candidate at a former Election.

Attorney-General v. Moore, L. R., 3 Ex. 276.—Penalties on summary convictions under 3 & 4 Vic. c. 97, s. 16, are payable to the Borough Treasurer under the Municipal Corporation Acts, the two Acts being read together.

Banbury, Heyw. Co. El. 318.—No Peer, except an Irish Peer who has been actually returned for some County or Borough in Great Britain, may vote at the Election of any member.

Barnstaple, 1 O'Mal. & Hard. 69.—The Legal maxim " Delegatus non potest delegare," does not apply to election agents. Candidates are liable not only for the acts of their agents, but of all persons employed by them.

Beal v. Smith, C. & B.—General allegation of bribery sufficient in a Petition. Order made by the Judge that the Petitioners, three days before the day appointed for the trial, give particulars in writing of all persons alleged to have been bribed, &c., upheld by the Court.

Bedfordshire, 2 Lud. 411.—*Hearsay* evidence allowed as against, but not in favour of, parties whose votes are questioned on a scrutiny.

Beverley, 1 O'Mal. & H. 145.—Assistance given to a man twelve months before an Election to enable him to take up his freedom, not Bribery.

Bewdley, 1 O'Mal. & H. 20.—The omission, by an agent for Election expenses, of important items, from the detailed statement of expenses, is proof of a knowledge, on his part, of corrupt expenditure.

Birmingham, 44 L.J., C.P. 293.—As to what are, and what are not, valid marks upon a ballot paper.

Birkbeck ex parte, L. R., 9 Q. B. 256.—An application to the Court of Queen's Bench for a *quo warranto* calling upon an alderman who had become disqualified to show by what right he claimed, must be made within 12 months after such alderman became disqualified, otherwise the application is too late. 7 Will. 4, & 1 Vic. 78, s. 23.

Blackburn, 1 O'Mal. & H. 198.—The dismissal of voters by their employers, on the ground of political opinion, previous to an election, evidence of undue influence. Intimidation may be direct, or indirect, as by dismissal or by threats of dismissal.

Bodmin, 1 O'Mal. & H.—"Corruptly giving" means giving "with a view of influencing the election;" attracting people to vote otherwise than they would have done, and avoids an Election.

Bolton, 2 O'Mal. & H. 150.—Payment for the conveyance of voters at a Borough Election, contrary to 30 & 31 Vic. c. 102, does not void such Election.

Boston, 2 O'Mal. & H. 161.—A distribution of coals among a number of poor people, several of whom were voters, shortly before an Election, by the expenses agent of an intending candidate, in view of such election, colourable bribery.

Bradford, 1 O'Mal. & H. 32.—Payment of money to a number of Irishmen, with a view of influencing others of their countrymen, held to be bribery.

Bragg's case, K. & O. 191.—Bets made on the result of an Election vitiate the vote of the person making such bets.

Brecon, 2 O'Mal. & H. 45.—Treating *after* an Election, if done corruptly, as if by way of reward, or in pursuance of a preconcerted arrangement, avoids an Election, as if given *previous to*, or *during* an Election.

Bremridge v. Campbell, 5 C. & P. 186.—Where the sum paid for travelling expenses is in excess of the sum actually expended, there is evidence of a corrupt motive.

Bridgewater, 1 O'Mal. & H.—Where votes were canvassed for two candidates on the same cards, where bills were sent into them jointly, and payment made on their joint behalf, there is evidence of coalition.

Bristol, 2 O'Mal. and H. 27.—Treating at a test ballot held to be treating in view of, and with reference to, the subsequent Election.

Britt v. Robinson, L. R., 5 C.P. 503.—Bribery and treating at a *test* ballot are bribery and treating within 17 & 18 Vic. c. 102, ss. 2 (3)—4, and, if proved, will void the subsequent Election.

Budge v. Andrews, L. R., 3. C.P. 510.—Every person whose name appears on the burgess list, pursuant to 5 & 6 Will. 4, c. 76, s. 22, is entitled to be nominated at an Election for Town Councillor on the 1st Nov., whether his name appears on such list at the time of nomination or not.   38 & 38 Vic. c. 40, s. 5.

Bullock v. Dodds, 2 B. & A. 258.—Felons may be elected after pardon, the effect of the pardon being to restore all civil rights.

Cambridge, Wolf & Dew.—Where the sums of money paid to voters were in excess of the sums actually expended, but such sums could not be accurately ascertained, there is evidence to rebut a presumption of corrupt payment.

Canterbury, Knapp & Ombler.—The two questions which may be asked of a voter at the poll must be put in the words of the Act. But whether not answered at all, or improperly answered, the presiding officer cannot refuse to give the voter a ballot paper.

Carnarvon.—Where a recognizance is acknowledged before a Justice, such Justice must have jurisdiction in the place where the acknowledgment is taken.

Carter v. Mills, L. R., 9 C. P. 117.—The dissolution of Parliament, pending the hearing of an Election petition, puts an end to such petition, and the Court will order a return of money deposited by way of security.

Cheltenham, 1 O'Mal. & H.—Particulars allowed to be amended at a trial, on the discovery of fresh evidence.

Cheltenham, 1 O'Mal. & H; 19 L. J., 816.—The employment of an elector, at an election, works a disqualification, independent of any corrupt intention, 30 & 31 Vic. c. 102, s. 11; whether paid at the time, or promised payment after the election.

L

Clementson v. Mason, L. R., 10 C. P. 209.—A candidate may be present at any polling station where his agents may be present, without stating that he is there to assist his agent, or as a substitute.   35 & 36 Vic. c. 33, 1st Sch. R. 51.

Coventry, 1 O'Mal. & H., 97.—To constitute bribery, the allegation of mere offers, of which nothing comes, must be supported by the strongest evidence.

Davies v. Lord Kensington, L. R., 9 C. P. 720.—Parliamentary election expenses are to be paid by the Returning Officer, and to be apportioned by him between the candidates, from whom he is to recover the same.   Prepayment, or security, cannot be demanded as a condition precedent.   Where one of two candidates was refused nomination on such a ground, the return of the other candidate declared void.

Devonport, 1866.—The payment of 10s. each to a number of workmen, subsequently to the election, as for loss of time, they having been allowed half a day for voting, without loss of their wages, voided the election.

Drinkwater v. Deakin (Launceston), L.R., 9 C. P. 626.—A successful candidate having on the day of nomination given leave to his tenants, and others, to kill rabbits on his estate (which was held to be a valuable consideration), and the unsuccessful candidate having given notice that in consequence all votes given for hisopponent would be thrown away, it was held that, although the election of the successful candidate was rendered void through such bribery, the votes given for him were not thrown away in such a sense as to entitle the petitioner to the seat.

Drogheda, 19 L. J., 528.—J. Keogh refused to order particulars of charges of intimidation and undue influence to be delivered before the trial; but this was an exceptional case.

Drogheda, 2 O'Mal. & H. 201.—Where the poll was not opened until 8.45, 8 a.m. being the time appointed, and no voter was prevented from voting in consequence, held that such irregularity was no ground for voiding the election.

Dublin, 1 O'Mal. & H. 272.—A letter written by the candidate's agent, to the secretaries of various District Committees, giving them instructions, &c., as to the appointment of canvassers, makes each member of such committee, and each canvasser so appointed, an agent of the candidate.

Dudley, 2 O'Mal. & H. 119.—No evidence may be given in respect to charges not mentioned in an Election petition.   Where allegations as to riot, &c., are general, questions as to particular persons having acted as canvassers not allowed.

Durham, 1 O'Mal. & H.—The employment of voters and relatives of voters to accompany canvassers, though not as canvassers, but as runners, not within 30 & 31 Vic. c. 102., s. 11, but was strongly condemned by Bramwell, B. as a means of bribery.

East Retford, 1 Peck. 479.—Where a candidate retired, after canvassing the Borough, and his brother came forward, employing the same canvassers, &c., it was held that the brother who retired was not an agent.

Fitzgerald's case, L. R., 5 Q. B.—Commissioners appointed under 15 & 16 Vic. c. 57, to enquire into corrupt practices, may hold their meetings without any formal adjournment, but not for more than a week without the consent of the Home Secretary.

Galway, 1 O'Mal. & H. 303.—A general refusal, or threat of refusal, by the clergy, of the sacraments, &c., of the Church, to persons on account of voting, or not voting, in a particular way at an election, will, without any question of agency, void the election.

Galway, 2 O'M. & H. 53.—A letter written by a candidate arranging for a meeting of clergy, with a view to influence tenants, has the effect of making them all his agents.

Galway, 2. O'M. & H.53, p. 49.—As to the admissibility of the acts or statements of agents after an election ; and a Judge has power to summon and to admit the statements of third parties, as to anything which may have occurred during an election, with a view to the discovery of corrupt practices.

Gloucester, 2 O'Mal. & H. 60.—It seems to be doubtful whether a Judge can order the inspection of ballot papers used at a municipal election for the purposes of an Election petition arising out of a subsequent Parliamentary election.

Grant v. Guinness, 17 C. B. 190.—All claims upon a candidate must be paid through the expense agent, but this does not prevent a candidate from appointing other agents, through whom he may incur liabilities.

Grant v. Overseers of Pagham, L. R., 3 C.P. 80.—A candidate is not to be disqualified from being registered a voter for personal bribery, under 31 & 32. Vic. c. 125, s. 43, from facts stated in a Judge's report ; he must have been found guilty by such report.

Gt. Yarmouth.—Recriminatory evidence admissible, though no claim is made for the seat, to test the credibility of the witness.

Guildford, 1 O'Mal. & H. 15.—General bribery voids an election, without its being traced to any candidate or agent. "Where the case as disclosed by the petition is proper for examination, and is founded on strong primâ facie grounds, and attended with reasonable and proper cause for pursuing the enquiry to the termination," the Court will not give the Respondent his costs, as in case of a "frivolous and vexatious" petition.

Hackney, 2 O'Mal. & H. 77.—Election void, where in consequence of irregularity a great number of electors were prevented from voting, two polling stations being closed during the whole of the polling day, and three others being open for part of the day only, whereby 5,000 electors were prevented from voting.

Hardwick v Brown, L.R , 8 C.P. 406.—A composition with creditors is an absolute disqualification as Town Councillor under 5 & 6. Will. 4, c. 76, s. 52, and the person so becoming disqualified cannot tender his resignation, so as to offer himself again ; " not having paid his debts in full," he is disqualified for re-election.

Hartlepool, 19 L. J., N. S. 821.—When a Petitioner desires to withdraw when the court is sitting, the Court will adjourn, in order that the statutory notices may be given before application made.

Hastings, 1 O'Mal. & H.—Where a voter, on his way to the poll, was told that he might treat himself, and afterwards he would be paid, it was held to be corrupt treating.

Haverfordwest, L. R., 9 C.P. 720.—Where a Returning Officer refused to receive a nomination because the candidate declined either to make a deposit or to give security for payment of his share of the expenses, Election held to be void, but the request being a reasonable one, the Returning Officer was not mulcted in costs.

Hereford, 1 O'Mal. & H. 194.—Where a breakfast was given on the polling day to a number of workpeople and their friends, many of whom were voters, and who were conveyed to the poll from the breakfast, there was held to be a corrupt intention, although the giver, who had previously canvassed at the election, declared that he had no corrupt motive, many of the persons being unknown to him, and some voting on the other side.

Hill v. Peel, L.R., 5. C. P. 172.—The Court is reluctant to interfere with the Master's taxation. Where the Master disallows certain costs the Court will not order him to review the same, unless strong grounds are shown for interference.

Hindmarch, ex parte, L.R., 2. Q.B. 12.—No person is eligible to be a Town Councillor who is not entitled to be on the burgess list, 5 & 6 Will. 4, c. 76,

s. 28 : but the Court refused a rule upon a *quo warranto* information, in
November, 1867, against a person who had been elected in 1866 being on,
though not qualified to be on, the burgess roll, at the time of his election.

Howes v. Turner, L.R, 1 C.P. 670.—Where a Town Clerk, by mistake,
allowed 7 days only, instead of 9, in the notice as to the delivery of nomination papers, under 38 & 39 Vic. c. 40. s. 1, the proceedings were void, and
a new election ordered. A nomination paper, taken away from the Town
Clerk's office, for the purpose of making an immaterial alteration, not a
withdrawal.

Hughes v. Meyrick, L.R., 5 C.P. 407.—Where the Master on taxation disallowed the costs of certain subpœnas, fees to counsel, and of various prelimi-
nary enquiries, following the rule which disallows the costs of preparing for
trial before notice given (the Petition having been withdrawn 7 days after
an order was obtained for the delivery of particulars), the Court ordered the
Master to review the taxation.

Hurdle v. Waring, L.R., 9 C.P. 435 (*Poole Election*).—The return of a
Member to Parliament not complete until the writ, endorsed by the Returning Officer, has been delivered into the hands of the Clerk of the Crown.
The 21 days' time allowed by 31 & 32 Vic. c. 125, s. 6 (2), for the filing of
a Petition dates from such completion.

Kidderminster, 2 O'Mal. & H. 173.—Where the candidate, in a speech made
previously to the election, promised his supporters an entertainment, and afterwards reiterated and confirmed his promise, using the words " when free and
untrammelled by the election law, " and carried out his promise, ordered a
dinner for 2,000 at 5s. a head, and for 200 at £1 a head, and sent 2 cheques for
£500 each, towards defraying the cost, but did not eventually give them, it
was held that the sending of the cheques was a fulfilment of the corrupt
promise made before the election, and that his abandonment of the dinners
did not take away from the corrupt character of the promise.

Lewis v. Carr, L. R., 1 Ex. 484.—Where an Alderman or Councillor becomes
disqualified by reason of any contract with the corporation of which he is a
member, under 5 & 6 Will. 4, c. 76, s. 28, such disqualification only lasts during
the continuance of the contract, and no penalties can be incurred for acting
after its termination.

Limerick, 1 O'Mal. & H. 260.—Held that where a candidate availed himself of
the co-operation of the clergy, who became canvassers for him, and
identified his cause with them, he made himself responsible for their acts
as his agents.

Lovering v. Dawson, L.R., 10 C.P. 711.—An unsuccessful candidate, who was
found guilty of bribery at an election, was not properly made a respondent
to the Petition, under 35 & 36 Vic. c. 60, s. 13, he having objected to be made
such Respondent. But the Petitioner having made him a Respondent, cannot
say that he was not properly a Respondent, and therefore entitled to
his costs.

Malcolm v. Parry, L.R., 10 C. P. 168—A candidate who coalesces with
another in ignorance of any previous corrupt practices by the latter, not
liable by reason of such joint candidature.

Manchester, L.J., 30th Dec. 1876.—At the trial of a Municipal Election
Petition, the Barrister held that a single horizontal stroke of the pen by the
voter before the candidate's name was a sufficient mark.

Maude v. Lowley, L.R., 9 C.P. 165.—A Petition, filed under 35 & 36 Vic. c.
60 (*Municipal Elections Act, 1872*), cannot be amended, after the expiration of
the 21 days limited by s. 13 (2), by the introduction of new charges, such as
allegations of bribery "in other wards."

Maude v. Sir Henry James, L.R., 9 C.P. 702.—Where the decision of the
Judge on the trial of an Election Petition was given, and the certificate and

report were forwarded to the Speaker in the morning, and Parliament was dissolved in the afternoon, the Respondent's right to have his costs taxed continued, although the report and certificate had not reached the Speaker's hands

Mather v. Brown, L.R., 1 C.P. 596.—Where, at an Election for Town Councillor, the candidate's name was inserted in the nomination paper as "Robert V. Mather," instead of Robert Vicars Mather in full, held to be an inaccuracy which could not be amended by 6 & 7 Will. 4, c. 76, s. 142.

Maude v. Lowley, L. R., 9 C.P. 165.—A Petition under 35 & 36 Vic. c. 60, cannot, after the expiration of the 21 days prescribed by s. 13 (2) for its presentation, be amended by the introduction of fresh matters.

A Judge's order, under G. R. 6 (Municipal), for the delivery of particulars, by whom, when, and where persons alleged to have been bribed, &c., had been bribed, &c., allowed by the Court, with the addition of the words "so far as known."

Mayo, 2 O'Mal. & H. 194.—Where the Returning Officer refused a poll, on the ground that the third candidate had not appointed an expenses agent, and returned the other two candidates, the election was declared void, and the candidates who were returned were ordered to pay the petitioner's costs, because their agents had insisted upon the Returning Officer taking such course.

Milnes v. Bale, L.R., 10 C.P. 591.—Where several acts of bribery have been committed at a municipal election, a penalty is recoverable in respect of each.

Molesworth, ex parte, L.R., 7 Q.B. 209—An Assessor, elected under 5 & 6 Will. 4, c. 76, s. 37, is disqualified from holding the office of Town Councillor, but not so of assessors under 7 Will. 4, & 1 Vic. c. 78, s. 4.

Monks v. Jackson, L. R., 1 C.P. 683.—At an election for Town Councillor the nomination paper must be delivered to the Town Clerk by the candidate himself, or by his proposer or seconder, and not by an agent, but the Mayor's decision in allowing an objection may be questioned on Petition.

Muntz v. Sturge, 8 M. & W. 302.—Held that, in the absence of any agreement, a candidate who does not go to the poll is not liable for a share of the expenses.

Neild v. Batty, L. R., 9 C.P. 104.—Where the list of votes objected to under 35 & 36 Vic. c. 60 (Municipal), G. R. 7, is not delivered within the time limited, the Court has no power to allow evidence to be given in respect of such votes, or the subsequent delivery of the list.

Norfolk, 1 O'Mal. & H. 238.—The engagement of any person as agent, or canvasser, who has within 7 years before an election been found guilty of any corrupt practice, voids the election. 31 & 32 Vic. c. 125, s. 44.

Northallerton, 1 O'Mal. & H. 168.—A member of a Nonconformist congregation, who told the Minister that, unless he voted as he desired him to do, he would give up his seat in the chapel, guilty of undue influence.

Norwich, 1 O'Mal. & H.—To void an election, it is not necessary to prove that bribery was committed by an agent with the knowledge of the candidate; and where bribery has been committed by an agent, against the express instructions of a candidate, it is sufficient to work disqualification, and void the election.

Norwich, 2 O'Mal. & H. 42.—The costs of an Election Petition, as a rule, follow the event, but in this case the Respondent was not ordered to pay the Petitioner's costs, on account of the former's purity of conduct, &c., and his efforts to secure purity of election.

Pare v. Hartshorne, 31 L.J. (N.S.) 486.—At the trial of a Municipal Election Petition, the Judge's decision as to costs, endorsed upon the Petition by the Registrar of the Court, held to be a Rule of Court upon which execution may be issued.

Pease v. Norwood (Hull Election).—Security for £1,000 is sufficient under 31 & 32 Vic. c. 125, s. 6, though there be two or more Respondents. The fact of

Petitioners being sureties will not invalidate the security, but is an objection as to sufficiency, which may be cured by a deposit of money.

Pembroke, L.R., 5 C. P. 407.—Where certain particulars were not delivered, the petition being withdrawn, it is in the Master's discretion to decide whether it is reasonable that the Respondent should incur expenses in preparing his defence before suing the charges against him.

Penryn, 1 O'Mal. & H.—A candidate may expend money upon the registration and revision of the lists of voters.

Peterborough, 2 P. R. & D. 259.—A dinner given on the day of the declaration of the poll, the wine being charged to the candidate who was returned, though there was no evidence of a corrupt intention, voided the election.

Pickering v. James, L.R., 8 C.P. 489.—An action may be brought against a presiding officer, at a polling station (at a Municipal Election), for breach of duty, in not being present at such polling station during the election to deliver the voting papers to the voters, and to see that such voting papers bear the official mark, as required by the 35 & 36 Vic. c. 33 (Ballot Act).

Poole, 2 O'Mal. & H.—Drink given, in quantities, to the electors, after an Election, sufficient proof that there was an understanding to do the same at a later election so as to make such treating done "corruptly."

R. v. Blissel, Heyw. Co. Elect.—Votes given for a candidate, with a knowledge that he is disqualified, are thrown away.

R. v. Harrald, L.R., 8. Q.B. 418.—A married woman cannot vote at an election of Town Councillors, and a woman who is on the burgess list loses her qualification on marriage. A voter who is on the list for two wards may vote for either, and if he votes for both, the second vote does not vitiate the first.

R. v. Hulme, L.R, 5. Q.B. 377.—To obtain *a certificate* under 26 & 27 Vic. c. 29, s. 7, a witness must make true answer to all questions put to him by the commissioners; an unsatisfactory certificate not a stay to further proceedings.

R. v. Ireland, L.R., 3 Q.B. 130.—The receipt of parochial relief by a voter's father is not the receipt by the voter himself, so as to work any disqualification as a burgess under s. 9, or Town Councillor under s. 23 of 5 & 6 Will. 4, c. 76.

R. v. Oldham, L.R., 4 Q. B. 290.—The " Regular Minister of a Dissenting congregation" is disqualified as a Town Councillor by 5 & 6 Will 4, c. 76, s. 28 ; but a person engaged in business, and the deacon of a Baptist Chapel in the borough, who agreed to preach in a village ten miles distant from time to time, was held not to come within the disqualification.

R. v. Parkinson, L.R., 3 Q. B. 11.—A voter who nominates a candidate for Town Councillor in a borough divided into wards, must be entitled to vote for that ward for which he nominates. 22 Vic. c. 35, s. 6.

R. v. Plenty, L.R., 4 Q.B. 346.—Where the initial W. was inserted instead of the Christian name of the candidate *William P.*, and there was no other person of that name on the list, it was held to be a misnomer, which might be amended by 22 Vic. c. 35, s. 142, and that the voting papers were valid.

R. v Strachan.—Poll. Voting papers at Universities.

R. v. Mayor of Tewkesbury, L R., 3 Q.B. 629.—Where the Mayor, being the Returning Officer, was also a candidate at an election of Town Councillors in a Borough not divided into wards, there being 4 vacancies and 5 candidates, votes which were given for the Mayor, who was disqualified, were not thrown away, so as to return the fifth candidate.

R. v. Tugwell, L.R., 3 Q. B. 704.—Where a burgess name appears on the list for two wards, and he has not been objected to at the Revision, he may vote for either.

R. v. White, L.R., 2 Q.B. 557.—Where, in a Borough not divided into wards, the Mayor, being Returning Officer, offered himself for re-election as Councillor, and one of the Aldermen was elected to act as returning officer at the election, in his place, held that the Mayor could not act as Returning Officer, though he might be a candidate, and that the appointment of Alderman, &c., was a good one. 5 & 6 Will. 4, c 76, s. 36.

Royse v. Birley (Manchester), L.R., 4 C.P. 296.—Where a contract was made in June, 1868, with the India Office, for the supply of goods for the Indian public service, duly executed on the 23rd Oct. 1868, but no "payment" received until the 18th Jan. 1869, the election of one of the contractors on the 18th Nov., 1868, was not voided thereby.

A contract for the service of a lunatic asylum entered into by a firm, of which one partner was a member of the House, in ignorance that such an asylum was a Government institution, no disqualification.

Salford, 1 O'Mal. & H. 136.—Agency terminates with the Election, so that a canvasser, committing an act of bribery after the close of an election, will not void the same unless done with the cognizance of the candidate.

Where the agent of a candidate had given insignificant sums, 1s. to one voter, 1s. to another, and 6d. to a third, Martin, B., held that to void an election for such acts would bring the law into contempt, though it would be different if there were many such cases.

Shrewsbury, 2 O'Mal. & H.—Held by Channell, B. that a Judge is not at liberty to weigh the importance of an act of bribery, &c., but is bound to apply the express provisions of the Act, differing from the Salford case.

Simpson v. Feend, L.R., 4 Q.B. 626.—A promise to a voter, " that he should be remunerated for any loss of time," is an offer under 17 & 18 Vic. c. 102, s. 2, and 22 Vic. c. 35, s. 12, and is Bribery.

Sligo, 1 O'Mal. & H. 301.—A corrupt practice committed 7 years before an election, as much within the Act as if committed the day before. Keogh, J.

Sterens v. Tillet (Norwich Election), L.R., 6 C.P. 147—The Judge's report at the trial of an Election Petition not final and conclusive, as his certificate in regard to matters contained therein ; and recriminatory charges may be gone into as to corrupt practices discovered subsequently to an election which the Judge had reported to be pure.

Soper v. Mayor of Basingstoke, L.R., 2. C.P. 440.—Where the Mayor had, at an election for Town Councillor, declared a nomination paper to be void, on the ground that the seconder had not correctly described the situation of his property, the name of the street having been recently changed, but being generally well known, held that the Mayor's decision was wrong.

Stafford, 1 O'Mal. & H. 228.—Bribery by an agent voids the election, even if done contrary to the explicit instructions of the candidate, unless it can be shown that such agent acted treacherously, or in collusion with the other side, and even in such case if he did so by the authority of another agent.

St. Ives, 3 O'Mal. & H. 13—The costs of an Election Petition follow the event. Where there had been general bribery, but the Petitioner and Respondent had been equally innocent, the Respondent was ordered to pay the petitioner's costs.

Stroud, 3 O'Mal. & H.—Where the Petitioner or his agents have been to blame, though they may not be deprived of their costs, such costs will be disallowed as relate to matters improperly conducted, &c.

Tamworth, 1 O'Mal. & H. 78.—Where a sub-agent unnecessarily hired 130 men, 39 of them being voters, for the alleged purpose of keeping the peace on the Polling Day, each of them being subsequently paid 10s., but none of them being of any real service, and not influencing any votes, the sub-agent having hired them on his own responsibility and to increase his own influence, inasmuch as the object was not to influence voters, this did not come within the Act. 17 & 18 Vic. c. 102. s. 2.

Taunton, 1 O'Mal. & H. 181.—Where a political association, or body of members, acts in support of a candidate, rendering him substantial assistance, he, accepting their co-operation, and taking the benefit of their proceedings, renders himself liable for their acts as agents; and if some portion of the money expended by them involves them in bribery, the candidateis liable, not having repudiated their acts.

Tillett v. Stracey, L.R., 5. C.P. 185.—The taxation of the costs of a Parliamentary Election Petition is in the Master's discretion, and the Court will not interfere unless a strong case is shown. Where the Master disallowed (*inter alia*) one half the costs paid to the under-sheriff on the trial, the Court refused to interfere.

Waygood v. James (Taunton).—The Judge's decision final. Where on the trial of an Election Petition, claiming the seat for one of the defeated candidates, the Judge decides that such candidate was duly elected, a Petition cannot be afterwards presented against his return.

Westminster, 1 O'Mal. & H. 89.—The providing of refreshments on the polling day for persons bonâ fide engaged at the election, not illegal. Where a son of the Respondent's agent had "been active" in the Election, the Respondent was not rendered liable for his proceedings.

Wigan, 1 O'Mal. & H. 190.—Payment of rates with a corrupt intention does not make a candidate liable unless, he expressly authorized such payment.

Baron Martin said that where he had reason to believe that a candidate himself had done nothing contrary to the law, and honestly wished and intended that his agents should refrain from acting illegally or corruptly, he should require stronger evidence of agency than when a candidate was guilty of corrupt conduct.

Woodward v. Sarsons, L.R., 10.C.P. 733.—Municipal Elections void by the common law applicable to elections, if not conducted under the subsisting election laws, as where such irregularities have prevailed as to afford no opportunity for the majority to elect their candidate. As to non-observance of and non-compliance with the rules of the Ballot Act.

Yates v. Leach, L.R., 9 C.P. 605.--Where A obtained a majority over B., but, being disqualified, B claimed the election, and served on several occasions as Town Councillor, on a petition being presented, A and B being both made respondents, and both giving notice under 35 & 36 Vic. c. 60, s. 18, of intention not to oppose, B's application was refused, on the ground that he was properly made a Respondent.

APPENDIX.

---o---

REGISTRATION

AND

ELECTION ACTS.

17 & 18 Vic. c. 102.

An Act to consolidate and amend the Laws relating to Bribery, Treating, and undue Influence at Elections of Members of Parliament.   [10th *August*, 1854.]

1. *Repeal of Acts mentioned in Schedule A.*

2. The following Persons shall be deemed guilty of Bribery, and shall be punishable accordingly:

1. Every Person who shall, directly or indirectly, by himself, or by any other Person on his behalf, give, lend, or agree to give or lend, or shall offer, promise, or promise to procure or to endeavour to procure, any Money, or valuable Consideration, to or for any Voter, or to or for any Person on behalf of any Voter, or to or for any other person in order to induce any Voter to vote, or refrain from voting, or shall corruptly do any such Act as aforesaid, on account of such Voter having voted or refrained from voting at any election :

2. Every Person who shall, directly or indirectly, by himself or by any other Person on his behalf, give or procure, or agree to give or procure, or offer, promise, or promise to procure or to endeavour to procure any Office, Place, or Employment to or for any Voter, or to or for any Person on behalf of any Voter, or to or for any other Person, in order to induce such Voter to vote, or refrain from voting, or shall corruptly do any such Act as aforesaid, on account of any Voter having voted or refrained from voting at any Election :

3. Every Person who shall, direct or indirectly, by himself or by any other Person on his behalf, make any such Gift, Loan, Offer, Promise,

1   B

Procurement, or Agreement as aforesaid, to or for any Person, in order to induce such Person to procure, or endeavour to procure the return of any Person to serve in Parliament, or the Vote of any Voter at any Election :

4. Every Person who shall, upon, or in consequence of any such Gift, Loan, Offer, Promise, Procurement, or Agreement, procure or engage, promise or endeavour to procure the Return of any Person to serve in Parliament, or the Vote of any Voter at any Election :

5. Every Person who shall advance or pay, or cause to be paid, any Money to or to the Use of any other Person with the Intent that such Money or any part thereof shall be expended in Bribery at any Election, or who shall knowingly pay or cause to be paid any Money to any Person in Discharge or Repayment of any Money wholly or in part expended in Bribery at any Election :

And any Person so offending shall be guilty of Misdemeanor, and in *Scotland* of an offence punishable by Fine and Imprisonment, and shall also be liable to forfeit the Sum of One Hundred Pounds to any Person who shall sue for the same, together with full Costs of the Suit : Provided always, that the aforesaid Enactment shall not extend or be construed to extend to any Money paid or agreed to be paid for or on account of any legal Expenses *bonâ fide* incurred at or concerning any Election.

3. The following Persons shall also be deemed guilty of Bribery, and shall be punishable accordingly :

1. Every Voter who shall, before or during any Election, directly or indirectly, by himself or by any other Person on his Behalf, receive, agree, or contract for any Money, Gift, Loan, or valuable Consideration, Office, Place, or Employment for himself or for any other Person, for voting or agreeing to vote, or for refraining or agreeing to refrain from voting, at any Election :

2. Every Person who shall, after any Election, directly or indirectly, by himself or by any other Person on his Behalf, receive any Money or valuable Consideration on account of any Person having voted or refrained from voting, or having induced any other Person to vote or to refrain from voting at any Election :

Bribery further defined.

2

And any Person so offending shall be guilty of a Misdemeanor, and in *Scotland* of an Offence punishable by Fine and Imprisonment, and shall also be liable to forfeit the Sum of Ten Pounds to any Person who shall sue for the same, together with full Costs of Suit. *Penalty.*

4. Every Candidate at an Election, who shall corruptly by himself, or by or with any Person, or by any other Ways or Means on his Behalf, at any Time, either before, during, or after any Election, directly or indirectly, give or provide, or cause to be given or provided, or shall be accessory to the giving or providing, or shall pay, wholly or in part, any Expenses incurred for any Meat, Drink, Entertainment, or Provision to or for any Person, in order to be elected, or for being elected, or for the Purpose of corruptly influencing such Person or any other Person to give or refrain from giving his vote at such Election, or on account of such Person having voted or refrained from voting, or being about to vote or refrain from voting, at such Election, shall be deemed guilty of the Offence of Treating, and shall forfeit the Sum of Fifty Pounds to any Person who shall sue for the same, with full Costs of Suit; and every Voter who shall corruptly accept or take any such Meat, Drink, Entertainment, or Provision, shall be incapable of voting at such Election, and his Vote, if given, shall be utterly void and of none effect. *Treating defined.* *Penalty.*

5. Every Person who |shall, directly or indirectly, by himself, or by any other Person on his Behalf, make use of, or threaten to make use of, any Force, Violence, or Restraint, or inflict or threaten the Infliction by himself or by or through any other Person, of any Injury, Damage, Harm, or Loss, or in any other Manner practise Intimidation upon or against any Person in order to induce or compel such Person to vote or refrain from voting, or on account of such Person having voted or refrained from voting, at any Election, or who shall, by Abduction, Duress, or any fraudulent Device or Contrivance, impede, prevent, or otherwise interfere with the free exercise of the franchise of any Voter, or shall thereby compel, induce, or prevail upon any Voter, either to give or to refrain from giving his vote at any Election, shall be deemed to have committed the offence of undue influence, and shall be guilty of a misdemeanour, and in Scotland of an offence punishable by fine or imprisonment, and shall also be liable to forfeit the *UndueInfluence defined.*

sum of Fifty Pounds to any person who shall sue for the same, together with full Costs of Suit.

Names of Offenders to be struck out of Register and inserted in separate List.

6. Whenever it shall be proved before the Revising Barrister that any Person who is or claims to be placed on the List or Register of Voters for any County, City, or Borough has been convicted of Bribery or undue Influence at an Election, or that Judgment has been obtained against any such Person for any Penal Sum hereby made recoverable in respect of the Offences of Bribery, Treating, or undue Influence, or either of them, then and in that Case such Revising Barrister shall, in case the Name of such Person is in the List of Voters, expunge the same therefrom, or shall, in case such Person is claiming to have his Name inserted therein, disallow such Claim; and the Names of all Persons whose Names shall be so expunged from the List of Voters, and whose Claims shall be so disallowed, shall be thereupon inserted in a separate List to be entitled "The List of Persons disqualified for Bribery, Treating, or undue Influence," which last-mentioned List shall be appended to the List or Register of Voters, and shall be printed and published therewith, wherever the same shall be or is required to be printed or published.

No Cockades,&c, to be given at Elections.

7. No Candidate before, during, or after any Election shall in regard to such Election, by himself or Agent, directly or indirectly, give or provide to or for any Person having a Vote at such Election, or to or for any Inhabitant of the County, City, Borough, or Place for which such Election is had, any Cockade, Ribbon, or other Mark of Distinction; and every Person so giving or providing shall for every

Penalty.

such Offence forfeit the Sum of Two Pounds to such Person as shall sue for the same, together with full Costs of Suit; and all Payments made for or on account of any Chairing, or any such Cockade, Ribbon, or Mark of Distinction as aforesaid, or of any Bands of Music or Flags or Banners, shall be deemed illegal Payments within this Act.

Voters not to serve as Special Constables during Elections.

8. No Person having a Right to vote at the Election for any County, City, Borough, or other Place shall be liable or compelled to serve as a special Constable at or during any Election for a Member or Members to serve in Parliament for such County, City, Borough, or other Place, unless he shall consent so to act; and he shall not be liable to any Fine,

4

Penalty, or Punishment whatever for refusing so to act, any Statute, Law, or Usage to the contrary notwithstanding.

9. The pecuniary Penalties hereby imposed for the Offences of Bribery, Treating, or undue Influence respectively shall be recoverable by Action or Suit by any Person who shall sue for the same in any of Her Majesty's Superior Courts at *Westminster*, if the Offence be committed in *England* or *Wales*, and in any of Her Majesty's Superior Courts in *Dublin*, if the Offence be committed in *Ireland*, and in or before the Court of Session if the Offence be committed in *Scotland*, and not otherwise.

Penalties how to be recovered.

10. It shall be lawful for any Criminal Court, before which any Prosecution shall be instituted for any Offence against the Provisions of this Act, to order Payment to the Prosecutor of such Costs and Expenses as to the said Court shall appear to have been reasonably incurred in and about the Conduct of such Prosecution: Provided always, that no Indictment for Bribery or undue Influence shall be triable before any Court of Quarter Sessions.

Costs and Expenses of Prosecutions.

11. *Repealed by* 35 & 36 Vic. c. 33.

12. In case of any Indictment or Information by a private Prosecutor for any Offence against the Provisions of this Act, if Judgment shall be given for the Defendant, he shall be entitled to recover from the Prosecutor the Costs sustained by the Defendant by reason of such Indictment or Information, such Costs to be taxed by the proper Officer of the Court in which such Judgment shall be given.

In Cases of private Prosecutions, if Judgment be given for the Defendant, he shall recover costs from the Prosecutor.

13. It shall not be lawful for any Court to order Payment of the Costs of a Prosecution for any Offence against the Provisions of this Act, unless the Prosecutor shall, before or upon the finding of the Indictment or the granting of the Information, enter into a Recognizance, with two sufficient Sureties, in the Sum of Two Hundred Pounds (to be acknowledged in like Manner as is now required in the Cases of Writs of Certiorari awarded at the Instance of a Defendant in an Indictment), with the Conditions following; that is to say, that the Prosecutor shall conduct the Prosecution with Effect, and shall pay to the Defendant or Defendants, in case he or they shall be acquitted, his or their Costs.

Prosecutor not to be entitled to Costs unless he shall have entered into a Recognizance to conduct Prosecution and pay Costs.

14. No Person shall be liable to any Penalty or Forfeiture hereby enacted or imposed, unless some

Limitation of Actions.

Prosecution, Action, or Suit for the Offence committed shall be commenced against such Person within the Space of One Year next after such Offence against this Act shall be committed, and unless such Person shall be summoned or otherwise served with Writ or Process within the same Space of Time, so as such Summons or Service of Writ or Process shall not be prevented by such Person absconding or withdrawing out of the Jurisdiction of the Court out of which such Writ or other Process shall have issued; and in case of any such Prosecution, Suit, or Process as aforesaid, the same shall be proceeded with and carried on without any wilful Delay.

Sections 15 to 22 *repealed by* 26 & 27 Vic. c. 29.

Refreshments to Voters on the days of Nomination or Polling declared illegal.

23. And whereas Doubts have also arisen as to whether the giving of Refreshment to Voters on the Day of Nomination or Day of polling be or be not according to Law, and it is Expedient that such Doubts should be removed : Be it declared and enacted, that the giving or causing to be given to any Voter on the Day of Nomination or Day of polling, on account of such Voter having polled or being about to poll, any Meat, Drink, or Entertainment, by way of Refreshment, or any Money or Ticket to enable such Voter to obtain Refreshment, shall be deemed an illegal Act, and the Person so offending shall forfeit the Sum of Forty Shillings for each Offence to any Person who shall sue for the same, together with full Costs of Suit.

Sections 24 to 32 *repealed by* 26 & 27 Vic. c. 29.

Payments before passing of Act.

33. If any candidate at any Election, or any Member hereafter returned to serve in Parliament, shall before the passing of this Act have paid any Money for or in respect of any Election hereafter to be held, or any Expenses thereof, such Person shall, to the best of his Ability, deliver a full, true, and particular Account of such Payment or Payments to the Election Auditor.

Section 34 *repealed by* 26 & 27 Vic. c. 29.

In Actions for Penalties, Parties, &c., to be competent Witnesses.

35. On the Trial of any Action for Recovery of any pecuniary Penalty under this Act, the Parties to such Action, and the Husbands and Wives of such Parties respectively, shall be competent and compellable to give Evidence in the same Manner as Parties, and their Husbands and Wives, are competent and compellable to give Evidence in Actions

6

and Suits under the Act of the Fourteenth and Fifteenth *Victoria*, Chapter Ninety-nine, and "The Evidence Amendment Act, 1853," but subject to and with the Exceptions contained in such several Acts : Provided always, that any such Evidence shall not thereafter be used in any Indictment or Criminal Proceeding under this Act against the Party giving it.

36. If any Candidate at an Election for any County, City, or Borough shall be declared by any Election Committee guilty by himself or his Agents, of Bribery, Treating, or undue Influence at such Election, such Candidate shall be incapable of being elected or sitting in Parliament for such County, City, or Borough during the Parliament then in existence.

Candidate declared guilty of Bribery incapable of being elected during Parliament then in existence.

37. Short Title—"The Corrupt Practices Prevention Act, 1854."

38. Throughout this Act, in the Construction thereof, except there be something in the Subject or Context repugnant to such construction, the Word "County" shall extend to and mean any County, Riding, Parts, or Division of a County, Stewartry, or combined Counties respectively returning a Member or Members to serve in Parliament; and the Words "City or Borough" shall mean any University, City, Borough, Town Corporate, County of a City, County of a Town, Cinque Port, District of Burghs, or other Place or Combination of Places (not being a County as hereinbefore defined) returning a Member or Members to serve in Parliament; and the Word "Election" shall mean the Election of any Member or Members to serve in Parliament; and the Words "Returning Officer" shall apply to any Person or Persons to whom, by virtue of his or their Office under any Law, Custom, or Statute, the Execution of any Writ or Precept doth or shall belong for the Election of a Member or Members to serve in Parliament by whatever Name or Title such Person or Persons may be called; and the Words "Revising Barrister" shall extend to and include an Assistant Barrister and Chairman, presiding in any Court held for the Revision of the Lists of Voters or his Deputy in *Ireland*, and a Sheriff or Sheriff's Court of Appeal in *Scotland*, and every other Person whose Duty it may be to hold a Court for the Revision and Correction of the List or Registers of Voters in any Part of the United Kingdom, and the Word "Voter" shall mean any Person who has or claims

Interpretation of terms.

to have a Right to vote in the Election of a
Member or Members to serve in Parliament; and
the Words "Candidate at an Election" shall include
all Persons elected as Members to serve in Parliament at such Election, and all Persons nominated as
Candidates, or who shall have declared themselves
Candidates at or before such Election; and the
Words "Personal Expenses," as used herein with
respect to the Expenditure of any Candidate in
relation to any Election, shall include the reasonable
Travelling Expenses of such Candidate, and the
reasonable Expenses of his Living at Hotels or elsewhere for the Purposes of and in relation to such
Election.

22 Vic. c. 35.

An Act to amend the Law relating to Municipal
Elections.   [19th *April*, 1859.]

WHEREAS it is expedient, &c.: Be it enacted, &c.

Sections 1 to 4 *Repealed.*

Notice of Election.

Town Clerk to publish Notice. 5. Seven Days at least before the Day fixed for the
Election of any Councillor or Councillors, the Town
Clerk shall prepare, sign, and publish a Noticein the
Form contained in Schedule (B.) to this Act annexed,
or to the like Effect, by causing the same to be placed
on the Door of the Town Hall and in some other
conspicuous Parts of the Borough or Ward for which
any such Election is to be held. *Repealed.*

Election of Councillors.

Nomination of Candidates. 6. At any Election of Councillors to be held
for any Borough or Ward any Person entitled to
vote may nominate for the Office of Councillor himself
(if duly qualified), or any other Person or Persons
so qualified (not exceeding the Number of Persons
to be elected for the Borough or Ward, as the Case
may be), and every such Nomination shall be in
writing, and shall state the Christian Names and
Surnames of the Persons nominated, with their
respective Places of Abode and Descriptions, and shall
be signed by the Party nominating, and sent to the
Town Clerk at least Two whole days (*Sunday* excluded)
before the Day of Election ; and the Town Clerk
shall at least One whole Day (*Sunday* excluded)
before the said Day of Election cause the Christian

Names and Surnames of the Persons so nominated, with such Statement of their respective Places of abode and Descriptions, and with the Names of the Party nominating them, respectively to be printed and placed on the Door of the Town Hall, and in some other conspicuous Parts of the Borough or Ward for which such Election is to be held. *Repealed.*

7. *Repealed.*

8. At any Election of Councillors to be held for any Borough or Ward :

Election of Councillors.

   1. If the Number of Persons so nominated shall exceed the Number to be elected,
The Councillors to be elected shall be elected from the Persons so nominated, and from them only :

   2. If the Number of Persons so nominated shall be the same as the Number to be elected,
Such Persons shall be deemed to be elected; and the Mayor or Alderman and Two Assessors, as the Case may be, shall publish a List of the Names of the Persons so elected, not later than Eleven of the Clock in the Morning of the said Day of Election :

   3. If the Number of Persons so nominated shall be less than the Number to be elected,
Such Persons shall be deemed to be elected : Such of the retiring Councillors highest on the Poll at their Election, or, if the Poll were equal, or there were no Poll, such as shall be nominated by the Mayor, shall be deemed to be re-elected to make up the Number required to be elected : And the Mayor or Alderman and Two Assessors, as the Case may be, shall publish a List of the Names of all the Persons so elected respectively, not later than Eleven of the Clock in the Morning of the said Day of Election :

   4. If no Persons be so nominated,
The retiring Councillors shall be deemed to be re-elected, and the Mayor or Alderman and Two Assessors, as the Case may be, shall publish a List of the Names of all the Persons so elected, not later than Eleven of the Clock in the Morning of the said Day of Election.

Remaining Sections *Repealed.*

SCHEDULES.

Schedule A.—*Repealed.*
Schedule B.

Borough of } to wit.
in the County of }

Election of Councillors for the [Ward of
in the] Borough of   in the County of

Take notice :

1. That an Election of [*Three*] Councillors will be held for the said Ward [*or* Borough] on
the   Day of   A. D.
in the said Ward [*or* Borough].

2. That any Person entitled to vote may nominate for the said Office himself (if duly qualified), or any other Person or Persons so qualified, not exceeding [*Three*] in Number.

3. That every such Nomination must be in Writing, and must state the Christian Names and Surnames of the Persons nominated, with their respective Places of Abode and Descriptions.

4. That any Nomination Paper must be signed by the Party nominating, and may be in the following Form or to the like Effect [*set out Form as given in Schedule*].

5. That all Nomination Papers must be delivered to the Town Clerk on or before the   Day of   next.

Dated this   Day of   , A. D.
(Signed)   A. B., Town Clerk.
Repealed.

---

26 & 27 Vic. c. 29.

An Act to amend and continue the Law relating to Corrupt Practices at Elections of Members of Parliament.   [*8th June*, 1863.]

17 & 18 Vict. c. 102.

WHEREAS the "Corrupt Practices Prevention Act, 1854," as amended by an Act of the Session holden in the Twenty-first and Twenty-second Years of Her Majesty, Chapter Eighty-seven, is limited to continue in force until the First Day of *September* One thousand eight hundred and sixty-three, and from thence until the End of the next Session of Parliament; and it is expedient further to amend the said

Acts and to continue the same in manner hereinafter mentioned: Be it therefore enacted by the Queen's most Excellent Majesty, by and with the Advice and Consent of the Lords Spiritual and Temporal, and Commons, in this present Parliament assembled, and by the Authority of the same as follows:

1. The Expression "the Corrupt Practices Prevention Acts" shall include this Act and the said Act of the Twenty-first and Twenty-second Years of the Reign of Her present Majesty, and the Corrupt Practices Prevention Act, 1854, as amended by the said other Acts.

Short Title.

Expenses of Elections.

2. No Payment (except in respect of the personal Expenses of a Candidate), and no Advance, Loan, or Deposit shall be made by or on behalf of any Candidate at an Election, before, or during, or after such Election, on account of or in respect of such Election, otherwise than through an Agent or Agents whose Name and Address or Names and Addresses have been declared in Writing to the Returning Officer on or before the Day of Nomination, or through an Agent or Agents to be appointed in his or their Place as herein provided; and any Person making any such Payment, Advance, Loan, or Deposit, otherwise than through such Agent or Agents, shall be guilty of a Misdemeanour, or in *Scotland* of an Offence punishable by Fine and Imprisonment. It shall be the Duty of the Returning Officer to publish, on or before the Day of Nomination, the Name and Address or the Names and Addresses of the Agent or Agents appointed in pursuance of this Section.

No Payment,&c. shall be made by or on behalf of Candidates otherwise than through authorised Agents.

In the event of the Death or legal Incapacity of any Agent appointed in pursuance of this Section, the Candidate shall forthwith appoint another Agent in his Place on giving Notice to the Returning Officer of the Name and Address of the Person so appointed, which shall be forthwith published by the Returning Officer.

3. All Persons who have any Bills, Charges, or Claims upon any Candidate for or in respect of any Election shall send in such Bills, Charges, or Claims within One Month from the Day of the Declaration of the Election to such Agent or Agents as aforesaid, otherwise such Persons shall be barred of their Right to recover such Claims and every or any Part thereof: Provided always, that in case of the Death within the said Month of

Bills, &c., to be sent in within One Month to Agent, or Right to recover barred.

any Person claiming the Amount of such Bill, Charge, or Claim, the legal Representative of such Person shall send in such Bill, Charge, or Claim within One Month after obtaining Probate or Letters of Administration, or Confirmation as Executor, as the Case may be, or the Right to recover such Claim shall be barred as aforesaid : Provided also, that such Bills, Charges, and Claims shall and may be sent in and delivered to the Candidate, if, and so long as, during the said Month, there shall, owing to Death or legal Incapacity, be no such Agent.

As to Publication of Statement of Election Expenses. 4. A detailed Statement of all Election Expenses incurred by or on behalf of any Candidate, including such excepted Payments as aforesaid, shall, within Two Months after the Election (or in Cases where by reason of the Death of the Creditor no Bill has been sent in within such Period of Two Months, then within. One Month after such Bill has been sent in,) be made out and signed by the Agent, or, if there be more than one, by every Agent who has paid the same (including the Candidate in case of Payments made by him), and delivered, with the Bills and Vouchers relative thereto, to the Returning Officer, and the Returning Officer for the Time being shall, at the Expense of the Candidate, within Fourteen Days, insert or cause to be inserted an Abstract of such Statement, with the Signature of the Agent thereto, in some Newspaper published or circulating in the County or Place where the Election was held; and any Agent or Candidate who makes default in delivering to the Returning Officer the Statement required by this Section shall incur a Penalty not exceeding Five Pounds for every Day during which he so makes default; and any Agent or Candidate who wilfully furnishes to the said Returning Officer an untrue Statement shall be guilty of a Misdemeanour, or in *Scotland* of an Offence punishable by Fine and Imprisonment; and the said Returning Officer shall preserve all such Bills and Vouchers, and during Six Months after they have been delivered to him permit any Voter to inspect the same, on Payment of a Fee of One Shilling.

Legal Proceedings.

Section 14 of 17 & 18 Vict. c. 102 extended to Misdemeanours, &c. 5. The Provisions of the Fourteenth Section of the Corrupt Practices Prevention Act, 1854, shall extend to a Misdemeanuor or to any other Offence under the Corrupt Practices Prevention Acts not punishable by a Penalty or Forfeiture, as well as to Proceedings for any Offence punishable by a Penalty or Forfeiture.

6. In any Indictment or Information for Bribery or undue Influence, and in any Action or Proceeding for any Penalty for Bribery, Treating, or undue Influence, it shall be sufficient to allege that the Defendant was at the Election at or in connexion with which the Offence is intended to be alleged to have been committed guilty of Bribery, Treating, or undue Influence (as the Case may require); and in any Criminal or Civil Proceedings in relation to any such Offence the Certificate of the Returning Officer in this Behalf shall be sufficient Evidence of the due holding of the Election, and of any Person therein named having been a Candidate thereat.

General Allegations sufficient in Indictments

7. No Person who is called as a Witness before any Election Committee, or any Commissioners appointed in pursuance of the Act of the Session holden in the Fifteenth and Sixteenth Years of the Reign of Her present Majesty, Chapter Fifty-seven, shall be excused from answering any Question relating to any corrupt Practice at, or connected with, any Election forming the Subject of Inquiry by such Committee or Commissioners, on the Ground that the Answer thereto may criminate or tend to criminate himself: Provided always, that where any witness shall answer every Question relating to the Matters aforesaid which he shall be required by such Committee or Commissioners (as the Case may be) to answer, and the Answer to which may criminate, or tend to criminate him, he shall be entitled to receive from the Committee, under the Hand of their Clerk, or from the Commissioners, under their Hands (as the Case may be), a Certificate stating that such Witness was, upon his Examination, required by the said Committee or Commissioners to answer Questions or a Question relating to the Matters aforesaid, the Answers or Answer to which criminated or tended to criminate him, and had answered all such Questions or such Question; and if any Information, Indictment, or Action be at any Time thereafter pending in any Court against such Witness for any Offence under the Corrupt Practices Prevention Acts, or for which he might have been prosecuted or proceeded against under such Acts committed by him previously to the Time of his giving his Evidence, and at or in relation to the Election concerning or in relation to which the Witness may have been so examined, the Court shall, on Production and Proof of such Certificate, stay the Proceedings in such last-mentioned Information, Indictment, or Action, and may, at its Discretion, award to such Witness such

Evidence of Witness on Election Committee and before Commissioners.

Costs as he may have been put to in such Information, Indictment, or Action : Provided that no Statement made by any Person in answer to any Question put by or oefore such Election Committee or Commissioners shall, except in Cases of Indictments for Perjury, be admissible in Evidence in any Proceeding, Civil or Criminal.

Prosecutions for Bribery. 9. Where an Election Committee has reported to the House of Commons that Certain Persons named by them have been guilty of Bribery or Treating, and where it appears by the Report of any Commission of Inquiry into Corrupt Practices at any Election made to Her Majesty and laid before Parliament that certain Persons named by them have been guilty of the Offences of Bribery or Treating, and have not been furnished by them with Certificates of Indemnity, such Report, with the Evidence taken by the Commission, shall be laid before the Attorney-General, with a view to his instituting a Prosecution against such Persons if the Evidence should, in his Opinion, be sufficient to support a Prosecution.

10. *Repeal* of Acts mentioned.

---

28 Vic. c. 36.

An Act to amend the Law relating to the Registration of County Voters, and to the Powers and Duties of Revising Barristers in certain Cases. [*2nd June*, 1865.]

6 & 7 Vict. c. 18. WHEREAS it is expedient to amend, &c. (6 & Vic. c. 18), so far as relates to the Registration of County Voters, and to the Powers and duties of Revising Barristers : Be it enacted, &c.

Short Title. 1. This Act may be cited as "The County Voters Registration Act, 1865," and shall be construed with and as Part of the said recited Act, hereinafter termed "the Principal Act."

Clerk of Peace to deliver Precept to Overseers of Poor on or before 10th June n every Year. 2. The Clerk of the Peace shall, on or before the Tenth day of *June* in every Year, make and cause to be delivered to the Overseers of the Poor of every Parish and Township within his County his Precept according to the Form No. 1. in Schedule (A.) to this Act, instead of the Precept numbered 1. in Schedule (A.) to the Principal Act, together with the Forms of Notices, List, and Copies of Register in the Principal Act mentioned.

14

3. The Clerk of the Peace of every County shall, together with the Precept, transmit to the Overseers of every Parish or Township within such County a sufficient Number of Copies of the Part or Parts of the Register relating to such Parish or Township; and the Overseers of the Poor of every Parish and Township shall, on or before the Twentieth Day of *June* in every Year, and at the same Time with the Publication of the Notice mentioned in the Fourth Section of the Principal Act, publish a Copy of the Register then in force relating to their Parish or Township, and shall remove the same after a Period including Two *Sundays* at least, and not later than the Twentieth Day of *July*.

Overseers to publish Register.

4. The Twentieth Day of *August* shall be the last Day for giving Notices of Objection to the Overseers and to the Person objected to; and the Seventh Section of the Principal Act shall be read as if the Word "Twentieth" had been substituted therein for the Word "Twenty-fifth."

20th August last Day for giving Notices of Objection.

5. The First Day of *September* shall be the last Day for the Delivery, by the Overseers, to the Clerk of the Peace, of the Papers mentioned in the Ninth Section of the Principal Act; and such Section shall be read as if the Words "First Day of *September*" had been substituted therein for the Words "Twenty-ninth Day of *August*."

1st September last Day for Delivery of Papers to Clerk of Peace.

6. Any Notice of Objection to any person on the List of Claimants for any Parish or Township may be given according to the Provisions of the Seventh Section of the Principal Act, but with that Exception no Notice of Objection given under the Provisions of the said Seventh Section, other than a Notice to the Overseers, shall be valid, unless the Ground or Grounds of Objection be specifically stated therein; and this Provision shall be deemed to be sufficiently satisfied by naming the Column or Columns of the List on which the Objector grounds his Objection: Provided always, that if the Objection be grounded on the third Column, then it shall be necessary to state in the Notice whether the Objection relates to the Nature of the Voter's Interest in the qualifying Property, or to the Value of the qualifying Property, or to both; and each of such last-mentioned Grounds of Objection shall be deemed a separate Ground of Objection, as well as any Objection grounded on any one of the other Columns; and such last-mentioned Notice may be according to the Form numbered 2, in Schedule

Grounds of Objection to be specified in Notice.

(A.) to this Act, or to the like Effect, in substitution for the Form numbered 5 in Schedule (A.) to the Principal Act.

Person objected to only required to give Evidence in support of his Right to vote, &c.

7. No Person objected to under the Provisions of this Act shall be required to give Evidence before the Revising Barrister in support of his Right to be registered, otherwise than as such Right shall be called in question in such Ground or Grounds of Objection.

Each Ground of Objection to be treated by Revising Barrister as a separate Objection.

8. Every separate Ground of Objection shall be treated by the Revising Barrister as a separate Objection; and for every Ground of Objection which, in the Opinion of the Revising Barrister, shall have been groundlessly or frivolously and vexatiously stated in a Notice of objection, he shall, on the Application of the Person objected to, or any one on his Behalf, and upon Production of the Notice of Objection, award Costs against the Objector to the Amount at least of Two Shillings and Sixpence, and this though the Name of the Person objected to be expunged upon some other Ground of Objection stated in the same Notice of Objection.

Sect. 100 of Principal Act to apply to Objections.

9. The Provisions of the Hundredth Section of the Principal Act shall apply to Notices of Objection given under the Provisions of this Act.

Persons changing their Place of Abode, and Persons objected to, may make Declarations.

10. Any Person whose Name appears "on the List of Voters then in force" and whose then Place of Abode is not correctly stated in the said List, or who shall have received a Notice of Objection grounded on the Second Column of the List, and who shall have possessed on the last Day of July the same Qualification in respect of which his Name has been inserted on the List, may, if he think fit, make and subscribe a Declaration before any Justice of the Peace, or any Commissioner or other Person authorized to administer Oaths in any of Her Majesty's Superior Courts at *Westminster*, in the Form contained in Schedule (B.) to this Act, or to the like Effect; and all such Declarations shall be duly dated, and shall, on or before the Fourteenth Day of *September*, be transmitted to the Clerk of the Peace; and it shall be the Duty of the Clerk of the Peace to endorse on every such Declaration the Name of the Polling District, and of the Parish or Township in which the Qualification to which the Declaration relates is situate, and the Name of the Person making the Declaration, and also the Date on which he has received the same, and to affix his Initials to such

16

last-mentioned Endorsement, and to deliver all such Declarations to the Revising Barrister at his First Court, arranged under the Heads of the several Polling Districts according to the alphabetical Order of the Parishes and Townships; and every Revising Barrister shall, for the Purpose of correcting the Statement in the List of the Place of Abode of such Person, receive any such Declaration as Evidence, to be used in Court at the proper Time, if transmitted to the Clerk of the Peace on or before such last-mentioned Day, of which the Endorsement in that Behalf by the Clerk of the Peace shall be *primâ facie* Proof, and if purporting to be subscribed before a Justice of the Peace, or Commissioner, or other Person authorized as aforesaid, without Proof of the Signature of the Person subscribing the same, or of the Justice, Commissioner, or Person before whom the same purports to have been subscribed, unless he shall have good Reason to doubt the Genuineness of any Signature thereto; and all such Declarations may be perused by any Person at the Office of the Clerk of the Peace, without Payment of any Fee, at any Time between the Hours of Ten of the Clock in the Forenoon and Four of the Clock in the Afternoon of any Day, except, *Sunday*, before the Twentieth Day of *September*; and the Clerk of the Peace shall deliver Copies of any such Declaration to all Persons applying for the same, on Payment of the Price of Fourpence *per* Folio of Seventy-two Words.

11. Any Person falsely or fraudulently signing any such Declaration in the Name of any other Person, whether such Person shall be living or dead, and every Person transmitting as genuine any false or falsified Declaration, knowing the same to be false or falsified, and any person knowingly and wilfully making any false Statement of fact in such Declaration, shall be guilty of a Misdemeanor, and punishable by Fine or Imprisonment for a Term not exceeding one Year, and the Revising Barrister shall have Power to impound any such Declaration. *(Penalty for falsely signing such Declaration.)*

12. No Court shall be holden by a Revising Barrister for the Revision of the Lists of any County before the Twentieth Day of September in any Year. *(As to Time for Revision of County Lists.)*

13. Every Order for Costs by a Revising Barrister, whether revising the Lists of a County, City, or Borough, in the Case of any Objection shall be made, before his proceeding to hear any Objection stated *(Orders for Costs.)*

in any other notice of Objection, and such Order may be delivered either to the Person to whom the Costs shall therein be ordered to be paid, or to some other Person on his Behalf: Provided always, that this Section shall not be taken to repeal the last Proviso contained in the Forty-sixth of the Principal Act

Such Costs in no Case to exceed £5. 14. The Sum Ordered to be paid by way of Costs shall not upon any one Vote exceed the Sum of Five Pounds, and the Forty-sixth Section of the Principal Act shall be read as if the Words "Five Pounds" had been substituted therein for the Words "Twenty Shillings."

Revising Barrister to read out Names expunged and inserted. 15. It shall be the Duty of every Revising Barrister; whether revising the Lists of a County, City, or Borough, before signing any Page of any List, as required by the Forty-first Section of the Principal Act, to read out audibly in open Court the Names expunged and inserted by him therein, and all Corrections and Insertions made by him.

Power to remove Persons from Court who interrupt the Proceedings. 16. It shall be lawful for any Revising Barrister, whether revising the Lists of a County, City, or Borough, to order any Person to be removed from his Court who shall interrupt the Business of the Court, or refuse to obey his lawful Orders in respect of the same; and it shall be the Duty of the Chief Constable, Commissioner, or Chief Officer of Police, of the County, City, Borough, or Place in which the Court is held, to take care that an officer of Police do attend that Court during its Sitting, for the Purpose of keeping Order therein, and to carry into effect any Order of the Revising Barrister as aforesaid.

Interpretation of Terms. 17. For the Purposes of this Act the Word "Valuer" shall in the Case of an Objection to any Person claiming to be retained or inserted in the List as an occupying Tenant mean "Amount of Rental."

SCHEDULES TO WHICH THIS ACT REFERS.

SCHEDULE (A.)

No. 1.

PRECEPT of the CLERK of the PEACE to the OVERSEERS.

County of   } To the Overseers of the Poor of the Parish
  to wit.   } of [or of the Township of]

In pursuance of the provisions of the Acts of Parliament in that Behalf, I require your Attention to the following

INSTRUCTIONS.

On or before the Twentieth Day of June you are to publish One of the Copies of the Register for your Parish *or* Township herewith sent, together with a Notice, signed, by you, according to the Form marked No. 2, among the printed Forms herewith sent.

The manner in which you are required to publish that Register and Notice is as follows; (that is to say,) you are to fix One of the printed Copies (each Copy being first signed by you) on or near the Outside of the outer Door or of the outer Wall near the Door of every Church and public Chapel in your Parish or Township, including Chapels which do not belong to the Established Church, or if there should be no such Church or Chapel, then in some public or conspicuous Situation in your Parish [*or* Township,] and it must remain there during a Period including Two Sundays at least, and not later than the Twentieth Day of July.

On or before the last Day of July you are to make out an alphabetical List of all Persons who, on or before the Twentieth Day of July, shall have delivered or sent to you their Claims as Voters for the County [Riding, *etc.*] in which your Parish [*or* Township] lies, in respect of any Property situate wholly or in part within your parish [*or* Township]; and in making out such List you are to write or cause to be written, in the proper Column of the printed Form of List (herewith sent) numbered 3, the Christian name and surname of every such Person, with the Place of his Abode, the Nature of his Qualification, and the local or other Description of the Property, and the name of the Occupier, accordingly as the same shall be stated in the Claim. If you have reasonable Cause to believe that any Person so claiming, or any Person whose name shall appear in the Copy of the Register for your Parish [*or* Township] herewith sent, is not entitled to have his name on the new Register about to be made, you are to add the Word "Objected" before his Name in the Margin of the Copy of the Register or List in which his Name appears; and you are also to add the word "Dead" before the Name of any Person whom you shall have reasonable Cause to believe to be dead. Having done this, you are to sign the List of Claimants, and also one of the Copies of the Register herewith sent, and to cause a sufficient Number of Copies of such Lists to be written or printed, and then, on or before the First Day of August, you are to publish the said Register and Lists, with your marginal Additions, on every Church and Chapel in your Parish [*or* Township] in the same Manner as before mentioned with regard to the Notice.

You are to keep a Copy of the List of Claimants and of the said Register sent to you, with your marginal Additions thereon, signed by you, and to allow them to be perused by every Person desirous of perusing them, at any Time between the Hours of Ten of the Clock in the Forenoon and Four of the Clock in the Afternoon of any Day, except Sunday, during the first Fourteen Days after you have published them, without Payment or demand of any Fee; and you are also to deliver Copies of the List of Claimants and of the said Register, signed by you, to every Person applying for the same, on Payment of a Price for such Copy after the Rate contained in the Table marked Schedule (D.) No. 1., herewith sent.

You are to make out a List, according to the Form numbered 6. (herewith sent), containing the Name of every Person against whom a Notice of Objection shall have been given to you or any one of you, on or before the Twentieth Day of August; and you are to publish Copies of such Lists on or before the First Day of September—on every Church and Chapel in your Parish or Township, in the same manner as before mentioned with regard to the Notice; and you are to keep a Copy of such List of Persons objected to, to be perused by any Person, without Payment or Fee, at any Time between the Hours of Ten of the Clock in the Forenoon and Four of the Clock in the Afternoon of any Day, except Sunday, during the first Fourteen Days of September, both inclusive; and you are to deliver a Copy of such List to any Person requiring the same, on Payment of a Price for such Copy after the Rate contained in the Table marked Schedule (D.) No. 1., herewith sent.

And if you shall find any such Notice, List, Register, or other Document published by you as aforesaid to be destroyed, mutilated, defaced, or removed, you are forthwith to place another to the same effect in its Place.

On or before the First day of September you are to deliver to the Clerk of the Peace of the County [Riding, &c.] wherein your Parish [*or* Township] is situate, the List of Claimants, the Copy of the Part of the Register (Herewith sent), and also a Copy of the List of Persons objected to, signed by you.

You are to attend the Court to be holden by the Barrister appointed to revise the Lists relating to your Parish [*or* Township], of the Time and Place of holding which Notice will be sent to you; and you are there to deliver to the Barrister holding such Court the original Notices of Claim and original Notices of Objection given to you as aforesaid.

Herein if you fail you will be liable to the Penalties in that Case provided. Given under my Hand, this
Day of
Clerk of the Peace for the County of

No. 2.

NOTICE OF OBJECTION to be given to Parties "already on Register" objected to by any Person other than Overseers and to the occupying Tenant of the qualifying Property, where Notice is required to be given to the occupying Tenant.

To Mr.   of   [*here insert the Name and Place of abode of the Person objected to as described in the List, and in the Case of Notice to the Tenant of the qualifying Property insert his Name and Place of Abode as described in the List.*]

Take Notice that I object to your Name [*in the Notice to the Tenant instead of the Words* "your Name," *insert the Name of the Person objected to*] being retained in the [*here insert the Name of the Parish*] List of Voters for the County of
[*or* for the   Riding, *etc.*]

And I ground my Objection,
on the 1st Column of the Register,

or on the 2nd Column,

or on the 3rd Column,
and the Objection relates

to the nature of your interest [*in the Notice to the Tenant, instead of the words* "your Interest," *insert* "the interest of," *here insert the Name of the Person objected to*] in the qualifying property;

or to the Value of the qualifying Property;

or on the 4th Column.

Dated this   day of   one thousand
eight hundred and

Signed A. B. of [*Place of Abode*]
on the Register of Voters for the
parish of

21

SCHEDULE (B.)

FORM of DECLARATION by Voter as to his Place of Abode.

I, A.B., of [*Place of Abode*], on the List of Voters for the Parish or Township of   in the County or Riding or Division of the County of   do solemnly and sincerely declare, That I possessed on the last Day of July now last past the same Qualification in respect of which my Name has been inserted in such List, and that my true Place of Abode is now

(Signed)   A.B.

Place of Abode.

Made and subscribed before me
the   day
of   in the
year

> *C.D.*
> [*Signature of Jus-*
> *tice, etc.*]
> [*Statement of his*
> *Quality, as Justice,*
> *etc.*]

---

30 & 31 Vic. c. 102.

An Act further to amend the Laws relating to the Representation of the People in *England* and *Wales.*   (*15th August, 1867.*)

WHEREAS it is expedient to amend the Laws relating to the Representation of the People in *England* and *Wales:* Be it enacted, &c.

Short Title.   1. This Act shall be cited for all Purposes as "The Representation of the People Act, 1867."

Application of Act.   2. This Act shall not apply to *Scotland* or *Ireland*, nor in anywise affect the Election of Members to serve in Parliament for the Universities of *Oxford* or *Cambridge.*

PART I.

FRANCHISES.

Occupation Franchise for Voters in Boroughs.   3. Every Man shall, in and after the Year One thousand eight hundred and sixty-eight, be entitled to be registered as a Voter, and, when registered, to vote for a Member or Members to serve in Parliament for a Borough, who is qualified as follows : (that is to say),

     1. Is of full Age, and not subject to any legal Incapacity; and

     2. Is on the last Day of *July* in any Year, and has during the whole of the preceding twelve

22

Calendar Months been, an Inhabitant Occupier
as Owner or Tenant of any Dwelling House
within the Borough; and

3. Has during the Time of such Occupation been
rated as an ordinary Occupier in respect of the
Premises so occupied by him within the Borough,
to all Rates (if any) made for the Relief of the
Poor in respect of such Premises; and

4. Has on or before the Twentieth Day of *July*
in the same Year *bonâ fide* paid an equal
Amount in the Pound to that payable by other
ordinary Occupiers in respect of all Poor Rates
that have become payable by him in respect of
the said Premises up to the preceding Fifth
Day of *January*:

Provided that no Man shall under this Section be
entitled to be registered as a Voter by reason of
his being a joint Occupier of any Dwelling House.

4. Every Man shall, in and after the Year One
thousand eight hundred and sixty-eight, be entitled
to be registered as a Voter, and, when registered, to vote
for a Member or Members to serve in Parliament for a
Borough, who is qualified as follows; (that is to say,) **Lodger Franchise for Voters in Boroughs.**

1. Is of full Age and not subject to any legal
Incapacity; and

2. As a Lodger has occupied in the same Borough
separately and as sole Tenant for* the Twelve
Months preceding the last Day of *July* in any Year
the same Lodgings, such Lodgings being Part
of one and the same Dwelling House, and of a
clear yearly Value, if let unfurnished, of Ten
Pounds or upwards; and

3. Has resided in such Lodgings during the Twelve
Months immediately preceding the last Day of
July,* and has claimed to be registered as a
Voter at the next ensuing Registration of Voters.

5. Every Man shall, in and after the Year One
thousand eight hundred and sixty-eight, be entitled
to be registered as a Voter, and, when registered, to
vote for a Member or Members to serve in Parliament for a County, who is qualified as follows;
(that is to say,) **Property Franchise for Voters in Counties.**

1. *Is of full Age* and not subject to any legal
Incapacity, and is seised at Law *or in Equity* of
any Lands or Tenements of Freehold, Copyhold, or any other Tenure whatever, for his
own Life, or for the Life of another, or for

* Now the 15th July.

23

any Lives whatsoever, or for any larger Estate of the clear yearly Value of not less than Five pounds over and above all Rents and Charges payable out of or in respect of the same, or who is entitled either as Lessee or Assignee, to any Lands or Tenements of Freehold or of any other Tenure whatever, for the unexpired Residue, whatever it may be, of any Term originally created for a Period of not less than Sixty Years (whether determinable on a Life or Lives or not), of the clear yearly Value of not less than Five Pounds over and above all Rents and Charges payable out of or in respect of the same.

Provided that no Person shall be registered as a Voter under this Section unless he has complied with the Provisions of the Twenty-sixth Section of the Act of the Second Year of the Reign of His Majesty *William* the Fourth, Chapter Forty-five.

Occupation Franchise for Voters in Counties.

6. Every Man shall, in and after the Year One thousand eight hundred and sixty-eight, be entitled to be registered as a Voter, and, when registered, to vote for a Member or Members to serve in Parliament for a County, who is qualified as follows; (that is to say,)

1. Is of full Age, and not subject to any legal Incapacity; and

2. Is on the last Day of *July* in any Year, and has during the Twelve Months immediately preceding been the Occupier as Owner or Tenant, of Lands or Tenements within the County of the rateable Value of Twelve Pounds or upwards; and

3. Has during the Time of such Occupation been rated in respect to the Premises so occupied by him to all Rates (if any) made for the Relief of the Poor in respect of the said Premises; and

4. Has on or before the Twentieth Day of July in the same Year paid all Poor Rates that have become payable by him in respect of the said Premises up to the preceding Fifth Day of *January*.

Occupiers in Boroughs to be rated, a d not Owners.

7. Where the Owner is rated at the Time of the passing of this Act to the Poor Rate in respect of a Dwelling House or other Tenement situate in a Parish wholly or partly in a Borough, instead of the Occupier his Liability to be rated in any future Poor Rate shall cease, and the following Enactments shall take effect with respect to rating in all Boroughs.

24

1. After the passing of this Act no Owner of any Dwelling House or other Tenement, situate in a Parish either wholly or partly within a Borough shall be rated to the Poor Rate instead of the Occupier except as hereinafter mentioned :

2. The full rateable Value of every Dwelling House or other separate Tenement, and the full Rate in the Pound payable by the Occupier, and the Name of the Occupier, shall be entered in the Rate Book : Where the Dwelling House or Tenement shall be wholly let out in Apartments or Lodgings not separately rated, the Owner of such Dwelling House or Tenement shall be rated in respect thereof to the Poor Rate :

Provided as follows :

Provisoes as to Compositions, &c.

(1) and (2). *Repealed.*

3. That where the Occupier under a Tenancy subsisting at the Time of the passing of this Act of any Dwelling House or other Tenement which has been let to him free from Rates is rated and has paid Rates in pursuance of this Act, he may deduct from any Rent due or accruing due from him in respect of the said Dwelling House or other Tenement any Amount paid by him on account of the Rates to which he may be rendered liable by this Act.

8. *Repealed.*

9. At a contested Election for any County or Borough represented by Three Members no Person shall vote for more than Two Candidates.

10. At a contested Election for the City of *London* no Person shall vote for more than Three Candidates.

Restriction as to Number of Votes in certain Counties and Boroughs and in the City of London.

11. No Elector who within Six Months before or during any Election for any County or Borough shall have been retained, hired, or employed for all or any of the Purposes of the Election for Reward by or on behalf of any Candidate at such Election as Agent, Canvasser, Clerk, Messenger, or in other like Employment, shall be entitled to vote at such Election, and if he shall so vote he shall be guilty of a Misdemeanor

No Elector who has been employed for Reward within Six Months of an Election to be entitled to vote.

12. Boroughs of Totnes, Reigate, Yarmouth, and Lancaster to cease to return Members after end of present Parliament.

13, 14, 15, 16. Persons reported guilty of Bribery in Totnes, Great Yarmouth, Lancaster, and Reigate disqualified.

PART II.

DISTRIBUTION OF SEATS.

17. Boroughs to return One Member each.

18. Boroughs to return Three Members each.

19. New Boroughs, as in Schedule (B), to return One Member each, except Chelsea, which shall return Two.

20. Registers of Voters to be formed for new Boroughs.

21. Merthyr Tydvil and Salford to return Two Members each. Tower Hamlets to be divided into Two Divisions, each Division to return Two Members.

22. Registers of Voters to be formed for the Boroughs of Hackney and the Tower Hamlets.

23. Division of certain Counties.

University of London to return one Member. 24. In all future Parliaments the University of London shall return One Member to serve in Parliament.

Electors for Members of the University of London. 25. Every Man whose Name is for the Time being on the Register of Graduates constituting the Convocation of the University of London shall, if of full Age, and not subject to any legal Incapacity, be entitled to vote in the Election of a Member to serve in any future Parliament for the said University.

PART III.

SUPPLEMENTAL PROVISION.

Incidents of Franchise.

As to successive Occupations. 26. Different Premises occupied in immediate Succession by any Person as Owner or Tenant during the Twelve Calendar Months next previous to the last Day of *July* in any Year shall, unless and except as herein is otherwise provided, have the same Effect in qualifying such Person to vote for a County or Borough as a continued Occupation of the same Premises in the Manner herein provided.

As to Joint Occupation in Counties. 27. In a County where Premises are in the joint Occupation of several Persons as Owners or Tenants, and the aggregate rateable Value of such Premises is such as would, if divided amongst the several Occupiers, so far as the Value is concerned, confer on each of them a Vote, then each of such joint Occupiers shall, if otherwise qualified, and subject to the Conditions of this Act, be entitled to be registered as a Voter, and when registered to vote at an Election for the County: Provided always, that not more than Two Persons, being such joint Occupiers, shall be

26

entitled to be registered in respect of such Premises, unless they shall have derived the same by Descent, Succession, Marriage, Marriage Settlement, or Devise, or unless they shall be *bonâ fide* engaged as Partners carrying on Trade or Business thereon.

28. Where any Poor Rate due on the Fifth Day of *January* in any Year from an Occupier in respect of Premises capable of conferring the Franchise for a Borough remains unpaid on the First Day of *June* following, the Overseers whose Duty it may be to collect such Rate shall, on or before the Twentieth of the same Month of *June*, unless such Rate has previously been paid, or has been duly demanded by a Demand Note, to be served in like Manner as the Notice in this Section referred to, give or cause to be given a notice in the Form set forth in Schedule (E.) to this Act to every such Occupier. The Notice shall be deemed to be duly given if delivered to the Occupier or left at his last or usual Place of Abode, or with some Person on the Premises in respect of which the Rate is payable. Any Overseer who shall wilfully withhold such Notice, with intent to keep such Occupier off the List or Register of Voters for the said Borough, shall be deemed guilty of a Breach of Duty in the Execution of the Registration Acts. *(margin: Notice of Rate in arrear to be given by Overto Voters, in Form as in Schedule (E.))* *(margin: Penalty for wilfully withholding Notice.)*

29. The Overseers of every Parish wholly or partly within a Borough shall, on or before the Twenty-second Day of *July* in every Year, make out a List containing the Name and Place of Abode of every Person who shall not have paid, on or before the Twentieth Day of the same Month, all Poor Rates which shall have become payable from him in respect of any Premises within the said Parish before the Fifth Day of *January* then last past, and the Overseers shall keep the said List, to be perused by any Person, without Payment of any Fee, at any Time between the Hours of Ten of the Clock in the Forenoon and Four of the Clock in the Afternoon of any Day except *Sunday* during the First Fourteen Days after the said Twenty-second day of *July ;* any Overseer wilfully neglecting or refusing to make out such List, or to allow the same to be perused as aforesaid, shall be deemed guilty of a Breach of Duty in the Execution of the Registration Acts. *(margin: Overseers to make out a List of Persons in arrear of Rates, which shall be open to Perusal without Fee.)* *(margin: Penalty on Overseer for Neglect.)*

Registration of Voters.

30. The following Regulations shall in and after the Year One thousand eight hundred and sixty- *(margin: Regulation to be observed as to)*

27

eight be observed with respect to the Registration
of Voters :

1. The Overseers of every Parish or Township shall
make out or cause to be made out a list of all
Persons on whom a Right to vote for a County
in respect of the Occupation of Premises is conferred by this Act, in the same Manner, and subject
to the same Regulations, as nearly as Circumstances
admit, in and subject to which the Overseers of
Parishes and Townships in Boroughs are required
by the Registration Acts to make out or cause
to be made out a List of all Persons entitled
to vote for a Member or Members for a Borough
in respect of the Occupation of Premises of a clear
yearly Value of not less than Ten Pounds :

2. The Claim of every Person desirous of being
registered as a Voter for a Member or Members
to serve for any Borough in respect of the
Occupation of Lodgings shall be in the Form
numbered 1, in Schedule (G.), or to the like
Effect, and shall have annexed thereto a declaration in the Form and be certified in the Manner in the said Schedule mentioned, or as near
thereto as Circumstances admit; and every such
Claim shall after the last Day of *July* and on
or before the Twenty-fifth Day of *August* in
any Year be delivered to the Overseers of the
Parish in which such Lodgings shall be situate,
and the Particulars of such Claim shall be duly
published by such Overseers on or before the
First Day of *September* next ensuing in a separate
List, according to the Form numbered 2, in the
said Schedule (G.):

So much of Section 18, of the Act of the Session of the
Sixth Year of the Reign of Her present Majesty,
Chapter Eighteen, as relates to the Manner of
publishing Lists of Claimants and to the Delivery
of Copies thereof to Persons requiring the same
shall apply to every such Claim and List; and
all the Provisions of the 38th and 39th Sections
of the same Act with respect to the Proof of the
Claims of Persons omitted from the Lists of
Voters, and to Objections thereto, and to the
Hearing thereof, shall "so far as the same are
applicable," apply to Claims and Objections, and
to the Hearing thereof, under this Section.

31. The Word "Expenses" contained in the Sections
Fifty-four and Fifty-five of the said Registration

Act of the Session of the Sixth Year of the Reign of Her present Majesty, Chapter Eighteen, shall be deemed to and shall include and apply to all proper and reasonable Fees and Charges of any Clerk of the Peace of any County, or of any Town Clerk of any City or Borough, to be hereafter made or charged by him in any Year for his Trouble, Care, and Attention in the Performance of the Services and Duties imposed upon him by the same Act or by this Act, in addition to any money actually paid or disbursed by him for or in respect of any such Services or Duties as aforesaid.

Definition of "Expenses of Registration."

32. Whereas several of the Hundreds mentioned in the Third Column of the said Schedule (D.), and therein assigned to *Mid-Lincolnshire*, are situate in the Parts of *Lindsey*, and others are situate in the Parts of *Kesteven*, and the Liberty of *Lincoln*, consisting of the City and the County of the City of *Lincoln*, is situate partly in the Parts of *Lindsey* and partly in the Parts of *Kesteven*, and there are separate Clerks of the Peace for the said Parts of *Lindsey* and *Kesteven :* In forming the Register for the said Division of *Mid-Lincolnshire* the Clerk of the Peace of the Parts of *Lindsey* shall do and perform all such Duties as are by law required to be done by Clerks of the Peace in regard to such of the Hundreds assigned to *Mid-Lincolnshire* as aforesaid as are situate within the said Parts of *Lindsey*, and in regard to so much of the Liberty of *Lincoln* aforesaid as is situate within the said Parts of *Lindsey* ; and the Clerk of the Peace of the Parts of *Kesteven* shall do and perform all such Duties as are by Law required to be done by Clerks of the Peace in regard to such of the said Hundreds assigned to *Mid-Lincolnshire* as aforesaid as are situate within the said Parts of *Kesteven*, and in regard to so much of the Liberty of *Lincoln* aforesaid as is situate within the said Parts of *Kesteven*.

Provision as to Duties of Clerks of Peace in Parts of Lincolnshire.

33. Places for Election and Polling Places.

34. In every County the Justices of the Peace having Jurisdiction therein or in the larger Part thereof, assembled at some Court of General or Quarter Sessions, or at some Adjournment thereof, held after the passing of this Act, may, if they think Convenience requires it, divide such County into Polling Districts, and assign to each District a Polling Place, in such Manner as to enable each Voter, so far as practicable, to have a Polling Place within a

Provision for increased Polling Places in Counties, &c.

convenient Distance of his Residence ; and the Justices shall advertise in such Manner as they think fit a Description of the Polling Districts so constituted by them, and the name of the Polling Place assigned to each District, and shall name the Polling Places at which the Revising Barristers are to hold their Courts, and no Revising Barrister shall be obliged to hold his Courts at any Polling Places not so named: Provided that the Justices of the Peace for the *Isle of Ely*, assembled as aforesaid, shall carry into effect the Provisions of this Section so far as regards the said *Isle of Ely* ; but nothing herein contained shall affect the Powers conferred by any other Act of Parliament of altering Polling Places or Polling Districts, or of creating additional Polling Places or Districts:

Proviso as to Isle of Ely.

The Local Authority of every Borough shall, if they think Convenience requires it, as soon as may be after the passing of this Act, divide such Boroughs into Polling Districts, and the Returning Officer shall in the Case of a contested Election provide at least One Booth or Room for taking the Poll in each Polling District ; and in Cases where a Parliamentary Borough is constituted of Two or more Towns the Distance between Two of which shall exceed Two Miles, there shall be povided a Booth or Room for taking the Poll in each of such Towns:

Where any Parish in a Borough is divided into or forms Part of more than One Polling District, the Overseers shall, so far as practicable, make out the Lists of Voters in such Manner as to divide the Names in conformity with each Polling District:

The Town Clerk, as defined by the Act of the Sixth *Victoria*, Chapter Eighteen, shall cause the Lists of Voters for each Borough to be copied, printed, arranged, and signed, and delivered in the Manner directed by the said Act, so as to correspond with the Division of the Borough into Polling Districts:

A Description of the Polling Districts made or altered in pursuance of this Act shall be advertised by the Local Authority in such Manner as they think fit, and Notice of the Situation, Division, andAllotment of the Polling Booth or Place for each District shall be given in manner now required by Law.

The Local Authority shall mean in every Municipal Borough, and in every Borough any Part of which forms a Municipal Borough, the Town Council of such Borough, and in other Boroughs the Justices of the Peace acting for such Borough, or if there be no such Justices then the Justices acting for the Division of the County in which such Borough or the greater Part thereof is situate ; and in cases where a Parliamentary Borough is constituted by the Combination of Two or more Municipal Boroughs, then the Local Authority shall mean the Town Council of that Municipal Borough in which the Nomination takes place :

The Local Authority may from Time to Time alter any Districts made by them under this Act.

35. *Repealed.*

36. It shall not be lawful for any Candidate, or any One on his Behalf, at any Election for any Borough, except the several Boroughs of *East Retford, Shoreham, Cricklade, Much Wenlock,* and *Aylesbury,* to pay any Money on account of the Conveyance of any Voter to the Poll, either to the Voter himself or to any other Persons ; and if any such Candidate, or any Person on his Behalf, shall pay any Money on account of the Conveyance of any Voter to the Poll, such Payment shall be deemed to be an illegal Payment within the Meaning of "The Corrupt Practices Prevention Act, 1854." *[marginal note: Payment of Expenses of conveying Voters in Boroughs to the Poll illegal, except herein named.]*

37. At every contested Election for any County or Borough, unless some Building or Place belonging to the County or Borough is provided for that Purpose, the Returning Officer shall, whenever it is practicable so to do, instead of erecting a Booth, hire a Building or Room for the Purpose of taking the Poll : *[marginal note: Rooms to be hired for taking Polls wherever they can be obtained.]*

Where in any Place there is any Room the Expense of maintaining which is payable out of any Rates levied in such Place, such Room may, with the Consent of the Person or Corporation having the Control over the same, be used for the Purpose of taking the Poll at such Place. (*a*) *In part repealed by* 35 & 36 Vic. c. 33.

38. The Forty-seventh and Forty-eighth Sections of the Act of the Sixth Year of the Reign of Her present Majesty, Chapter Eighteen, relating to the Transmission and Delivery of the Book or Books *[marginal note: Alteration as to Time for Delivery of Lists and Commencement of Register of Voters.]*

31

containing the Lists of Voters to the Sheriff and Returning Officer, shall be construed as if the Word "*December*" were substituted in those Sections for the Word "*November*," and the said Book or Books shall be the Register of Persons entitled to vote for the County or Borough to which such Register relates at any Election which takes place during the Year commencing on the First Day of *January* next after such Register is made. *Remainder repealed.*

39. *Repealed by* 35 & 36 Vic. c. 33.

40. The Thirty-sixth Section of the Act of the Second Year of King *William* the Fourth, Chapter Forty-five, disqualifying Persons in Receipt of Parochial Relief from being registered as Voters for a Borough, shall apply to a County also, and the said Section shall be construed as if the Word "County" were inserted therein before the Word "City;" and the Overseers of every Parish shall omit from the Lists made out by them of Persons entitled to vote for the Borough and County in which such Parish is situate the Names of all Persons who have received Parochial Relief within Twelve Calendar Months next previous to the last Day of *July* in the Year in which the List is made out.

41—45. Relate to the University of London.

Residence of Electors for the City of London extended to Twenty-five Miles.

46. So much of the Twenty-seventh and Thirty-second Sections of the Act of the Second Year of the Reign of King *William* the Fourth, Chapter Forty-five, and of the Seventy-ninth Section of the Act of the Sixth Year of the Reign of Her present Majesty, Chapter Eighteen, as relates to the Residence of Electors within Seven Miles of any City or Borough, shall be repealed in respect to Electors otherwise qualified to be registered and to vote for Members to serve in Parliament for the City of *London:* Provided always, that no Person shall be registered as an Elector for the said City unless he shall have resided for Six Calendar Months next previous to the last Day of *July* in any Year, nor be entitled to vote at any Election for the said City unless he shall have ever since the last Day of *July* in the Year in which his Name was inserted in the Register then in force have resided, and at the Time of voting shall have continued to reside within the said City or within Twenty-five Miles thereof or any Part thereof.

Miscellaneous.

47. In any Borough named in Schedules (B.) and (C.) to this Act annexed, which is or includes a Municipal Borough, the Mayor of such Municipal Borough shall be the Returning Officer, and in the other Cases the Returning Officer shall be appointed in the same Manner as if such Places were included amongst the Boroughs mentioned in Schedules (C.) and (D.) of the Act of the Second Year of His late Majesty *William* the Fourth, Chapter Forty-five, for which no Persons are mentioned in such Schedules as Returning Officers. *[As to Returning Officers in new Boroughs.]*

48. *Repealed.*

49. Any Person, either directly or indirectly, corruptly paying any Rate on behalf of any Ratepayer for the Purpose of enabling him to be registered as a Voter, thereby to influence his Vote at any future Election, and any Candidate or other Person, either directly or indirectly, paying any Rate on behalf of any Voter for the Purpose of inducing him to vote or refrain from voting, shall be guilty of Bribery, and be punishable accordingly; and any Person on whose Behalf and with whose Privity any such Payment as in this Section is mentioned is made shall also be guilty of Bribery, and punishable accordingly. *[Corrupt Payment of Rates to be punishable as Bribery.]*

50. No Returning Officer for any County or Borough, nor his Deputy, nor any Partner or Clerk of either of them, shall act as Agent for any Candidate in the Management or Conduct of his Election as a Member to serve in Parliament for such County or Borough; and if any Returning Officer, his Deputy, the Partner or Clerk of either of them, shall so act, he shall be guilty of a Misdemeanor. *[Returning Officer, &c. acting as Agent guilty of Misdemeanour.]*

51. Whereas great Inconvenience may arise from the Enactments now in force limiting the Duration of the Parliament in being at the Demise of the Crown: Be it therefore enacted, That the Parliament in being at any future Demise of the Crown shall not be determined or dissolved by such Demise, but shall continue so long as it would have continued but for such Demise, unless it should be sooner prorogued or dissolved by the Crown, anything in the Act passed in the Sixth Year of Her late Majesty Queen *Anne*, Chapter Seven, in any way notwithstanding. *[Not necessary to dissolve Parliament on any future Demise of the Crown.]*

52. Whereas it is expedient to amend the Law relating to Offices of Profit, the Acceptance of which from the Crown vacates the Seats of Members *[Members holding Offices of Profit from the Crown, as in]*

Schedule (H.), not required to vacate their Seats on Acceptance of another Office.

accepting the same, but does not render them incapable of being re-elected: Be it enacted, That where a Person has been returned as a Member to serve in Parliament since the Acceptance by him from the Crown of any Office described in Schedule (H.) to this Act annexed, the subsequent Acceptance by him from the Crown of any other Office or Offices described in such Schedule in lieu of and in immediate Succession the one to the other shall not vacate his Seat.

Copy of Reports of Commissioners as to Boroughs herein named, and printed by Queen's Printer, to be Evidence.

53. Any Copy of any of the said Reports by the said Commissioners appointed for the Purpose of making Inquiry into the Existence of corrupt Practices in any of the said Boroughs of *Totnes*, *Great Yarmouth*, *Lancaster*, or *Reigate*, with the Schedules thereof annexed, and purporting to be printed by the Queen's Printer, shall for the Purposes of this Act be deemed to be sufficient Evidence of any such Report of the said Commissioners, and of the Schedules annexed thereto.

54. *Repealed.*

Temporary Provisions consequent on Formation of new Boroughs.

55. Nothing in this Act contained shall affect the Rights of Persons whose Names are for the Time being on the Register of Voters for any County in which the Boroughs constituted by this Act are situate to vote in any Election for such County in respect of any Vacancy that may take place before the summoning of a future Parliament, but after such summoning no Person shall be entitled to be registered as a Voter or to vote in any Election for any such County who would not be entitled to be so registered or to vote in case the Qualifications held by him were situate in a Borough other than One constituted by this Act. (*Remainder repealed.*)

General saving.

56. The Franchises conferred by this Act shall be in addition to and not in substitution for any existing Franchises, but so that no Person shall be entitled to vote for the same Place in respect of more than One Qualification; and, "subject to the Provisions of this Act," all Laws, Customs, and Enactments now in force conferring any Right to vote, or otherwise relating to the Representation of the People in *England* and *Wales*, and the Registration of Persons entitled to vote, shall remain in full Force, and shall apply, as nearly as Circumstances admit, to any Person hereby authorized to vote, and shall also apply to any Constituency hereby authorized to return a Member or Members to Parliament as if it had heretofore returned such Members to Parlia-

ment and to the Franchises hereby conferred, and to the Registers of Voters hereby required to be formed.

57. From and after the passing of this Act, the County Palatine of *Lancaster* shall cease to be a County Palátine, in so far as respects the Issue, Direction, and Transmission of Writs for the Election of Members to serve in Parliament for any Division of the said County or for any Borough situate in the said County : and such Writs may be issued under the same Seal, be directed to the like Officer, and transmitted in the like Manner, under, to, and in which Writs may be issued, directed, and transmitted in the Case of Divisions of Counties and Boroughs not forming Part of or situate in a County Palatine; and any Writ issued, directed, and transmitted in manner directed by this Section shall be valid accordingly.

As to Issue of Writs to County Palatine of Lancaster.

Extended to Co. Pal. of Durham by 31 & 32 Vict. c. 58, s. 21.

58. All Writs to be issued for the Election of Members to serve in Parliament, and all Mandates, Precepts, Instruments, Proceedings, and Notices consequent upon such Writs or relating to the Registration of Voters, shall be framed and expressed in such Manner and Form as may be necessary for the carrying the Provisions of this Act into effect.

Writs, &c, to be made conformable to this Act.

59. This Act, so far as is consistent with the Tenor thereof, shall be construed as One with the Enactments for the Time being in force relating to the Representation of the People and with the Registration Acts; and in construing the Provisions of the Twenty-fourth and Twenty-fifth Sections of the Act of the Second Year of King *William* the Fourth, Chapter Forty-five, the Expressions "the Provisions hereinafter contained," and "as aforesaid," shall be deemed to refer to the Provisions of this Act conferring Rights to vote as well as to the Provisions of the said Act.

This Act, as far as consistent, to be construed with Enactments now in force.

60. *Repealed.*

61. The following Terms shall in this Act have the Meanings hereinafter assigned to them, unless there is something in the Context repugnant to such Construction; (that is to say),

"Month" shall mean Calendar Month :

"Member" shall include a Knight of the Shire :

"Election" shall mean an Election of a Member or Members to serve in Parliament;

"County" shall not include a County of a City or

Interpretation of Terms:

"Month.'

"Member."

"Election :"

"County :"

County of a Town, but shall mean any County, Riding, Parts or Divisions of a County returning a Member or Members to serve in Parliament:

"Borough:"   "Borough" shall mean any Borough, City, Place or Combination of Places not being a county, as hereinbefore defined, returning a Member or Members to serve in Parliament:

"Dwelling ouse:"   "Dwelling House" shall include any part of a House occupied as a separate Dwelling, and separately rated to the Relief of the Poor. (*Repealed.*)

"The Registration Acts:"   "The Registration Acts" shall mean the Act of the Sixth Year of the Reign of Her present Majesty, Chapter Eighteen, and the Act of the Twenty-eighth Year of the Reign of Her present Majesty, Chapter Thirty-six, and any other Acts or Parts of Acts relating to the Registration of Persons entitled to vote at and Proceedings in the Election of Members to serve in Parliament for *England* and *Wales.*

SCHEDULES.

SCHEDULE (A.)

Relates to Boroughs to return one Member only in future Parliaments.

SCHEDULE (B.)

Relates to New Boroughs.

SCHEDULE (C.)

Relates to New Boroughs formed by Division of the Borough of the Tower Hamlets.
Name of Borough.
Places comprised in the Borough.

SCHEDULE (D.)

Relates to Counties to be divided.

SCHEDULE (E.)

To *A. B.*
City [*or* Borough of]

Take notice that you will not be entitled to have your Name inserted in the List of Voters for this City [*or* Borough] now about to be made in respect of the Premises in your Occupation in

[*Street or Place*] unless you pay on or before the Twentieth Day of July next all the Poor Rates which have become due from you in respect of such Premises up to the Fifth Day of January last, amounting to £

and if you omit to make such Payment you will be incapable of being on the next Register of Voters for this City [*or* Borough.]

Dated the   Day of June 18

C. D. ⎱ Overseers, *or* G. H. ⎱ Assistant
E. F. ⎰   ⎰ Overseer,

or I. K.. Collector.

Schedule (G.)

Superseded by 41 & 42 Vic. c. 26 and Schedule.

Schedule (H.)

Offices of Profit referred to in this Act.

Lord High Treasurer.

Commissioner for executing the Offices of Treasurer of the Exchequer of Great Britain and Lord High Treasurer of Ireland.

President of the Privy Council.

Vice-President of the Committee of Council for Education.

Comptroller of Her Majesty's Household.

Treasurer of Her Majesty's Household.

Vice-Chamberlain of Her Majesty's Household.

Equerry or Groom in Waiting on Her Majesty.

Any Principal Secretary of State.

Chancellor and Under Treasurer of Her Majesty's Exchequer.

Paymaster General, Postmaster General. Lord High Admiral.

Commissioner for executing the Office of Lord High Admiral.

Commissioner of Her Majesty's Works and Public Buildings.

President of the Committee of Privy Council for Trade and Plantations.

Chief Secretary for Ireland.

Commissioner for administering the Laws for the Relief of the Poor in England.

Chancellor of the Duchy of Lancaster, Judge Advocate General.

Attorney General for England, Solicitor General for England.

Lord Advocate for Scotland, Solicitor General for Scotland.

Attorney General for Ireland, Solicitor General for Ireland.

An Act to amend the Law of Registration so far as relates to the Year One thousand eight hundred and sixty-eight, and for other Purposes relating thereto. [16th *July*, 1868.]

WHEREAS it is expedient, &c.: Be it enacted, &c.

Preliminary.

Definition of Principal Act (6 & 7 Vict. c. 18.)

1. "Principal Act" in this Act shall mean the Act 6 & 7 Vic. c. 18, as amended by "The County Voters' Registration Act, 1865."

This and Principal Act construed as One.

2. This Act shall be construed as One with the Principal Act, and may be cited for all Purposes as "The Parliamentary Electors' Registration Act, 1868."

Application of Act.

3. This Act shall not apply to *Scotland* or *Ireland*. Ss. 4 to 16 *Repealed by* 35 and 36 Vic. c. 33.

Amendment of Sect. 30. of 30 & 31 Vict. c. 102.

17. Whereas by the First Enactment contained in the Thirtieth Section of the Representation of the People Act, 1867, it is enacted, that "the Overseers "of every Parish or Township shall make out or "cause to be made out a List of all Persons on "whom a Right to vote for a County in respect of "the occupation of Premises is conferred by this "Act, in the same Manner and subject to the same "Regulations, as nearly as Circumstances admit, in "and subject to which the overseers of Parishes and "Townships in Boroughs are required by the Regis-"tration Acts to make out or cause to be made out a "List of all Persons entitled to vote for a Member "or Members for a Borough in respect of the Occupa-"tion of Premises of a clear yearly Value of not less "than Ten Pounds:" And whereas by the Fifty-ninth Section of the same Act it is further provided that the said Representation of the People Act, 1867, so far as is consistent with the Tenor thereof, shall be construed as One with the Registration Acts: And whereas Doubts are entertained, notwithstanding the said Provisions, whether the Fifteenth Section of the Principal Act, relating to the Claims of Persons omitted from Borough Lists of Voters, or desirous of being registered in respect of a different Qualification from that appearing in such Lists, does or does not apply with the necessary Variations to the Rectification of the Lists of County Voters to be made in pursuance of the said Enactment: It is hereby declared, That the said Fifteenth Section of the Principal Act shall apply to the List of Persons

on whom a Right to vote for a County in respect of the occupation of Premises is conferred by the Representation of the People Act, 1867, in the same Manner as if the List of Voters in the said Fifteenth Section referred to were the List of Voters made in pursuance of the Enactment contained in the Thirtieth Section of the Representation of the People Act instead of the List of Voters for a City or Borough as specified in the said Fifteenth Section.

18. Where a Municipal Borough forms Part of a Parliamentary Borough the Town Clerk of such Municipal Borough shall be deemed to be the Town Clerk within the Meaning of the Thirty-fourth Section of the Representation of the People Act, 1867, and the Acts relating to Registration.

Amendment of Sect. 34 of 30 & 31 Vict. c. 102.

The Local Authority within the Meaning of the same Section, in Boroughs where the Town Council is not the Local Authority, shall be the Justices of the Peace of the Petty Sessional Division in which such Borough is situate, or if such Borough be situate in or comprise more than One Petty Sessional Division then the Justices in General or Quarter Sessions having Jurisdiction over such Borough or the greater Part thereof in Area.

The Power of dividing their County into Polling Districts, and assigning to each District a Polling-Place, vested in the Justices of the Peace by the said Thirty-fourth Section of the Representation of the People Act, 1867, may be exercised by such Justices from Time to Time and as often as they think fit; and the said Power of dividing a County into Polling Districts shall be deemed to include the Power of altering any Polling District or Polling Districts.

19. In the " Lists and Register " of Voters for a County the Names of the Persons in any Parish or Township on whom a Right to vote for a County in respect of the Occupation of Premises in such Parish or Township is conferred by the Representation of the People Act, 1867, shall appear in a separate List after the List of Voters in such Parish or Township otherwise qualified, and such separate List shall be deemed to be Part of the Lists of County Voters of such Parish or Township, and shall be annually made anew by the Overseers of such Parish or Township, subject to this proviso, that the Revising Barrister shall erase from the separate List of such Occupiers as aforesaid all Persons who appear

Provision as to 12l. Occupiers.

to him from the accompanying Lists to be entitled to vote in the same Polling District in respect of some other Qualification to which no Objection is made, except in Cases where any Person whose name is about to be erased object to the Erasure, in which Case such Person shall be deemed to have given due Notice of his Claim to have his Name inserted in the List of Occupiers and shall be dealt with accordingly.

Amendment of Law respecting the Registration of Lodgers.

20. Notwithstanding anything contained in the Thirtieth Section of the Representation of the People Act, 1867, and the Thirty-eighth Section of the Principal Act therein referred to, the Names of the Persons in any Parish or Township on whom a Right to vote for a Member or Members to serve for any Borough in respect of the Occupation of Lodgings is conferred by the Representation of the People Act, 1867, shall, in the Lists and Register of Voters for such Boroughs, appear in a separate List.

As to issue of Writs to the County Palatine of Durham.

21. Section Fifty-seven of the Representation of the People Act, 1867, with respect to the County Palatine of *Lancaster*, and the Issue, Direction, and Transmission of Writs for the Election of Members to serve in Parliament for any Division of the said County or for any Borough situate therein, shall be construed to extend to and include the County Palatine of *Durham*.

Miscellaneous Amendments.

Parish situate in more than One Polling District.

22. Where any Parish in a County, City, or Borough forms Part of more than One Polling District, the Part of such Parish situate in each Polling District shall be deemed to be a separate Parish for the Purposes of the Revision of Voters, and the Lists and Register of Voters, and may be designated by some distinguishing Addition in the List of Voters for such Part of a Parish.

Recovery of Expenses by Town Clerks and Returning Officers.

23. Whereas it is expedient to provide a summary Remedy for the Recovery by Town Clerks and Returning Officers of Sums of Money due to them in respect of Expenses incurred in pursuance of the Registration Acts : Be it enacted, That if the Overseers of any Parish or Township refuse or neglect to pay to the Town Clerk or Returning Officer of any Borough, out of the first Moneys to be collected for the Relief of the Poor, any Contribution or Sum required to be paid to him by the Fifty-fifth Section of the Principal Act, or any Act amending the same, or any Part of such Contribution or Sum, it shall

be lawful for any Justice of the Peace for the County or Place within which such Parish or Township is wholly or in part situate, upon Information and Complaint in Writing, and after Seven Days' Notice in Writing to be served upon such Overseers or One of them, by Warrant under his Hand to levy such Contribution or Sum by Distress and Sale of the Goods of the Offender or Offenders, together with all Costs occasioned by the making of such Complaint, Service of such Summons, and the obtaining and executing such Warrant.

24. *Repealed by* 35 and 36 Vic. c. 33.

25. Where a Borough is situated partly in one Circuit and partly in another the Judge of the Circuit in which the greater Part in Extent of such Borough is situate shall appoint the Revising Barrister for such Borough.

Provision when Borough situate partly in one Circuit and partly in another.

26. *Repealed by* 35 and 36 Vic. c. 33.

27. Appointment of Returning Officer for the Borough of Thirsk.

Appointment of Returning Officer for Borough of Thirsk.

28. The Overseers of every Parish or Township shall produce to the Barrister appointed to revise the Lists of Voters of any County, whilst holding his Court for revising the Lists relating to their Parish or Township, all Rates made for the Relief of the Poor of their Parish or Township between the Fifth Day of *January* in the Year then last past and the last Day of *July* in the then present Year; and any Overseer wilfully refusing or neglecting to produce any such Rates shall be deemed wilfully guilty of a Breach of Duty in the Execution of the Principal Act, and be punishable accordingly.

Production of Rate Books by Overseers. 6 Vict. c. 18. ss. 34, 35.

29. The Barrister appointed to revise the Lists of Voters of any County, whilst holding his Court for revising the Lists relating to a Parish or Township, may require any Overseer or Overseers of a past Year, or other Person having the Custody of any Poor Rate of the then current or any past Year, or any Relieving Officer, to attend before him at any such Court, and they shall attend accordingly, and answer all such Questions as may be put to them by the Barrister; and any Overseer or Relieving Officer wilfully refusing or neglecting to comply with the Requirements authorized to be made by the Revising Barrister in pursuance of this Section shall be punishable in the same Manner in which an Overseer wilfully guilty of a Breach of Duty in the

Power of Revising Barrister to summon Overseers, &c. 6 Vict. c. 18. ss. 34, 35.

Execution of the Principal Act is punishable under the Principal Act.

Application of certain Rating Sections to Counties.

30. The Thirtieth Section of the Act of the Session of the Second Year of King *William* the Fourth, Chapter Forty-five, and the Seventy-fifth Section of the Principal Act, shall apply to all Occupiers of Premises capable of conferring the Franchise for a County under the Representation of the People Act, 1867.

Expenses of Overseers and Relieving Officers.

31. All Expenses properly incurred by an Overseer in pursuance of this Act shall be deemed to be Expenses properly incurred by him in carrying into effect the Provisions of the Principal Act, and any Expense incurred by any Relieving Officer in attending a Revising Barrister in pursuance of this Act (the Amount to be certified by the Revising Barrister) shall be deemed to be Expenses properly incurred by him in the Execution of his Duty as Relieving Officer, and shall be defrayed accordingly.

Certificate of Revising Barrister to be conclusive.

32. The Certificate given to the Overseers by the Revising Barrister under Section Fifty-seven of the Principal Act for the Expenses incurred by them in carrying into effect the Provisions of the Registration Acts shall be final and conclusive; provided nevertheless, that such Certificate shall be signed by the Revising Barrister in open Court, and any Ratepayer present shall have a Right to inspect the Account of Expenses delivered in by the Overseers, and to object to any Item or Items included therein, before such Account is allowed by the Revising Barrister, who shall hear any such Objection and make a Decision respecting the same.

Provision as to Returning Officer in case of Parliamentary Borough becoming a Municipal Borough.

33. Whenever a Borough returning a Member or Members to serve in Parliament becomes a Municipal Borough the Authority of the Person who may for the Time being be acting as Returning Officer shall cease, and the Mayor shall take his place, subject nevertheless to the Repayment to such first-mentioned Returning Officer of any Expenses properly incurred by him in the Execution of the Duties of his Office.

S. 34. *Repealed by* 35 and 36 Vic. c. 33.

Provision as to Officers in case of altered Boundaries of Counties and Boroughs.

35. Where the Boundary of any County or Borough is altered in pursuance of any Act passed during the present Session of Parliament, any Clerk of the Peace, Town Clerk, Returning Officer, or other Officer who would have Jurisdiction in relation to the Registration of Voters, or in relation to the Election of Members to serve in Parliament, within such County or Borough,

if it had remained unaltered, shall have Jurisdiction over the Area constituting such County or Borough as altered by the said Act.

36. *Repealed by* 35 and 36 Vic. c. 33.

37. The Clerk of the Peace of every County, and the Town Clerk or other Officer having charge of the Register of every City or Borough respectively, shall in each and every Year within Twenty-one Days after the First Day of *February* transmit to one of Her Majesty's Principal Secretaries of State, a printed copy of the Register of Voters then in force for such County, City, or Borough.

Copies of Registers to be transmitted to Secretary of State.

---

31 & 32 Vic. c. 65.

An Act to amend the Law relating to the Use of Voting Papers in Elections for the Universities.
[*July* 31st 1868.]

WHEREAS by an Act passed in the Session holden in the Twenty-fourth and Twenty-fifth Years of the Reign of Her present Majesty, Chapter Fifty-three, intituled *An Act to provide that Voters at Elections for the Universities may be recorded by means of Voting Papers,* it is provided that at the Elections for Burgesses to serve in Parliament for the Universities of *Oxford, Cambridge,* and *Dublin,* Votes may be given by means of voting Papers; but it is by the said Act provided that no Voting Paper shall be received or recorded unless the person tendering the same shall make the following declaration, which he shall sign at the Foot or Back thereof:—

24 & 25 Vic. c. 53.

"I solemnly declare that I am personally acquainted with *A. B.* [*the Voter*], and I verily believe that this is the Paper by which he intends to vote, pursuant to the Provisions of the Universities Election Act."

And whereas by virtue of the Representation of the People Act, 1867, the said first-mentioned Act applies to every Election of a member for the University of *London:*

30 & 31 Vic. c. 102.

And whereas it is expedient, &c.: Be it enacted, &c.

1. From and after the passing of this Act the said recited Form of Declaration shall not be required, and there shall be substituted in place thereof the Form of Declaration following; that is to say,

Repeal of Form of Declaration.

"I solemnly declare that I verily believe that this

is the Paper by which *A. B.* [*the Voter*] intends to vote pursuant to the Provisions of the Universities Election Acts, 1861 and 1868."

Amendment of Sect. 2. of first-recited Act.

2. The Second Section of the said first-mentioned Act shall, in reference to the University of *London*, be construed as if the Words "in the Manner heretofore used" were omitted therefrom.

Officers in whose Presence Voting Papers may be signed in the Channel Islands.

3. A Voting Paper for the Election of any Burgess or Member to serve in Parliament for any Universities or University in respect of which the provisions of the said first-mentioned Act may for the Time being be in force, may be signed by a Voter being in one of the Channel Islands in the Presence of the following Officers; that is to say,

1. In *Jersey and Guernsey*, of the Bailiffs or any Lieutenant Bailiff, Jurat, or Juge d'Instruction
2. In *Alderney* of the Judge of *Alderney*, or any Jurat.
3. In *Sark*, of the Seneschal or deputy Seneschal.

And for the purpose of certifying and attesting the Signature of such Voting paper, each of the said Officers shall have all the Power of a Justice of the Peace under the first-mentioned Act, and a Statement of the official Quality of such Officer shall be a sufficient Statement of Quality in pursuance of the Provisions of the said Act.

Short Title.

4. This Act may be cited for all Purposes as "The Universities Elections Act, 1868," and the said first-mentioned Act and this Act may be cited together as "The Unversities Election Acts, 1861 and 1868."

---

31 & 32 Vic. c. 125.

An Act for amending the Laws relating to Election Petitions, and providing more effectually for the Prevention of corrupt Practices at Parliamentary Elections
[31st July 1868.]

WHEREAS it is expedient, &c.: Be it enacted, &c.

Preliminary.

Short Title of Act.

1. This Act may be cited for all Purposes as "The Parliamentary Elections Act, 1868."

Definition and Jurisdiction of Court.

2. The Expression "the Court" shall, for the purposes of this Act, in its application to *England*

mean the Court of Common Pleas at *Westminster*, and in its Application to *Ireland* the court of Common pleas at *Dublin*, and such Court shall, subject to the provisions of this Act, have the same powers, jurisdiction, and authority with reference to an Election Petition and the Proceedings thereon as it would have if such Petition were an ordinary Cause within their Jurisdiction.

3. The following Terms shall in this Act have the Meanings hereinafter assigned to them, unless there is something in the Context repugnant to such Construction; (that is to say,) — Interpretation of Terms.

"Metropolitan District" shall mean the City of *London* and the Liberties thereof, and any Parish or Place subject to the Jurisdiction of the Metropolitan Board of Works : — "Metropolitan District :"

"Election" shall mean an Election of a Member or Members to serve in Parliament : — "Election :"

"County" shall not include a County of a City or County of a Town, but shall mean any County, Riding, Parts or division of a County returning a Member or Members to serve in Parliament : — "County :"

"Borough" shall mean any Borough, University, City, Place, or Combination of Places, not being a County as hereinbefore defined, returning a Member or Members to serve in Parliament : — "Borough :"

"Candidate" shall mean any Person elected to serve in Parliament at an Election, and any Person who has been nominated or declared himself a Candidate at an Election : — "Candidate :"

"Corrupt practices" or "Corrupt practice" shall mean Bribery, Treating, and undue Influence, or any of such Offences, as defined by Act of Parliament, or recognized by the Common Law of Parliament : — "Corrupt Practices :"

"Rules of Court" shall mean Rules to be made as hereinafter mentioned : — "Rules of Court :"

"Prescribed" shall mean "prescribed by the Rules of Court." — "Prescribed."

4. For the Purposes of this Act "Speaker" shall be deemed to include Deputy Speaker; and when the Office of Speaker is vacant, the Clerk of the House of Commons, or any other Officer for the Time being performing the Duties of the Clerk of the House of Commons, shall be deemed to be substituted for and to be included in the Expression "the Speaker." — Provision as to Speaker.

Presentation and the Service of Petition.

To whom and by whom Election Petition may be presented.

5. From and after the next Dissolution of Parliament a Petition complaining of an undue Return or undue Election of a Member to serve in Parliament for a County or Borough may be presented to the Court of Common Pleas at *Westminster* if such County or Borough is situate in *England,* or to the Court of Common Pleas at *Dublin,* if such County or borough is situate in *Ireland,* by any one or more of the following persons :

1. Some person who voted or who had a Right to vote at the Election to which the Petition relates; or,

2. Some person claiming to have had a Right to be returned or elected at such Election; or,

3. Some person alleging hmself to have been a Candidate at such Election :

And such Petition is hereinafter referred to as an Election Petition.

Regulations as to Presentation of Election Petition.

6. The following Enactments shall be made with respect to the Presentation of an Election Petition under this Act :

1. The Petition shall be signed by the Petitioner, or all the Petitioners if more than One :

2. The Petition shall be presented within Twenty-one Days after the Return has been made to the Clerk of the Crown in Chancery in *England,* or to the Clerk of the Crown and Hanaper in *Ireland,* as the Case may be, of the Member to whose Election the Petition relates, unless it question the Return or Election upon an Allegation of corrupt Practices, and specifically alleges a Payment of Money or other Reward to have been made by any Member, or on his Account, or with his Privity, since the Time of such Return, in pursuance or in furtherance of such corrupt Practices, in which Case the Petition may be presented at any Time within Twenty-eight Days after the Date of such Payment :

3. Presentation of a Petition shall be made by delivering it to the prescribed Officer or otherwise dealing with the same in manner prescribed :

4. At the Time of the Presentation of the Petition, or within Three Days afterwards, Security for the Payment all Costs, Charges, and Expenses that may become payable by the Petitioner—

    (*a.*) to any Person summoned as a Witness on his Behalf, or, (*b.*) to the Member whose Election or Return is complained of (who is hereinafter referred to as the Respondent.)

shall be given on behalf of the Petitioner:

5. The Security shall be to an Amount of One Thousand Pounds; it shall be given either by Recognizance to be entered into by any Number of Sureties not exceeding Four, or by a Deposit of Money in manner prescribed, or partly in one way and partly in the other.

7. On Presentation of the Petition the prescribed Officer shall send a copy thereof to the Returning Officer of the County or Borough to which the Petition relates; he shall forthwith publish the same in the County or Borough as the Case may be. *Copy of Petition after Presentation to be sent to Returning Officer.*

8. Notice of the Presentation of a Petition under this Act, and of the Nature of the proposed Security, accompanied with a Copy of the Petition, shall, within the prescribed Time, not exceeding Five Days after the Presentation of the Petition, be served by the Petitioner on the Respondent; and it shall be lawful for the Respondent, where the Security is given wholly or partially by Recognizance, within a prescribed Time, not exceeding Five Days from the Date of the Service on him of the Notice, to object in Writing to such Recognizance, on the Ground that the Sureties, or any of them, are insufficient, or that a Surety is dead, or that he cannot be found or ascertained from the want of a sufficient Description in the Recognizance, or that a Person named in the Recognizance has not duly acknowledged the same. *Recognizance may be objected to.*

9. Any Objection made to the Security given shall be heard and decided on in the prescribed Manner. If an Objection to the Security is allowed it shall be lawful for the Petitioner within a further prescribed time, not exceeding Five Days, to remove such Objection, by a Deposit in the prescribed Manner of such Sum of Money as may be deemed by the Court or Officer having Cognizance of the Matter to make the Security sufficient. *Determination of Objection to Recognizance.*

If on Objection made the security is decided to be insufficient, and such Objection is not removed in Manner hereinbefore mentioned, no further Proceedings shall be laid on the Petition; otherwise, on the Expiration of the Time limited for making Objections, or, after Objection, made, on the Sufficiency of the Security being established, the Petition shall be deemed to be at issue.

10. The prescribed officer shall, as soon as may be, make out a List of all Petitions under this Act presented to the Court of which he is such Officer, and which are at issue, placing them in the Order in which they were presented, and shall keep at his Office a Copy of such List, hereinafter referred to as the Election List, open to the Inspection in the prescribed Manner of any Person making Application.

Such Petitions, as far as conveniently may be, shall be tried in the Order in which they stand in such List.

Trial of a Petition.

Mode of Trial of Election Petitions.

11. The following Enactments shall be made with respect to the trial of Election Petitions under this Act:

1. The Trial of every Election Petition shall be conducted before a Puisne Judge of One of Her Majesty's Superior Courts of Common Law at *Westminster* or *Dublin*, or according as the same shall have been presented to the Court at *Westminster* or *Dublin*, to be selected from at Rota to be formed as hereinafter mentioned.

2. The Members of each of the Courts of Queen's Bench, Common Pleas, and Exchequer in *England* and *Ireland* shall respectively, on or before the Third Day of *Michaelmas* Term in every Year, select, by a Majority of Votes, One of the Puisne Judges of such Court, not being a Member of the House of Lords, to be placed on the Rota for the Trial of Election Petitions during the ensuing Year.

3. If in any Case the Members of the said Court are equally divided in their Choice of a Puisne Judge to be placed on the Rota, the Chief Justice of such Court (including under that Expression the Chief Baron of the Exchequer) shall have a Second or Casting Vote.

4. Any Judge placed on the Rota shall be re-eligible in the succeeding or any subsequent Year.

5. In the event of the Death or the Illness of any Judge for the Time being on the Rota, or his Inability to act for any reasonable Cause, the Court to which he belongs shall fill up the Vacancy by placing on the Rota another Puisne Judge of the same Court.

6. The Judges for the Time being on the Rota shall, according to their Seniority, respectively try the Election Petitions standing for Trial

48

under this Act, unless they otherwise agree among themselves, in which Case the Trial of each Election Petition shall be taken in manner provided by such Agreement.

7. Where it appears to the Judges on the Rota, after due Consideration of the List of Petitions under this Act for the Time being at issue, that the Trial of such Election Petitions will be inconveniently delayed unless an additional Judge or Judges be appointed to assist the Judges on the Rota, each of the said Courts (that is to say), the Court of Exchequer, the Court of Common Pleas, and Court of Queen's Bench, in the Order named, shall, on and according to the Requisition of such Judges on the Rota, select, in manner hereinbefore provided, One of the Puisne Judges of the Court to try Election Petitions for the ensuing Year; and any Judges so selected shall, during that Year, be deemed to be on the Rota for the Trial of Election Petitions:

8. Her Majesty may, in manner heretofore in use, appoint an additional Puisne Judge to each of the Courts of Queen's Bench, the Common Pleas, and the Exchequer in *England*:

9. Every Election Petition shall, except where it raises a Question of Law for the Determination of the Court, as hereinafter mentioned, be tried by One of the Judges hereinbefore in that Behalf mentioned, hereinafter referred to as the Judge sitting in open court without a Jury.

10. Notice of the Time and Place at which an Election Petition will be tried shall be given, not less than Fourteen Days before the Day on which the Trial is held, in the prescribed Manner.

11. The Trial of an Election Petition in the Case of a Petition relating to a Borough Election shall take place in the Borough, and in the Case of a Petition relating to a County Election in the County : Provided always, that if it shall appear to the Court that special Circumstances exist which render it desirable that the Petition should be tried elsewhere than in the Borough or County, it shall be lawful for the Court to appoint such other Place for the Trial as shall appear most convenient : Provided also, that in the Case of

a Petition relating to any of the Boroughs within the Metropolitan District, the Petition may be heard at such Place within the District as the Court may appoint.

12. The Judge presiding at the Trial may adjourn the same from Time to Time and from any one Place to any other Place within the County or Borough, as to him may seem expedient.

13. At the Conclusion of the Trial the Judge who tried the Petition shall determine whether the Member whose Return or Election is complained of, or any and what other Person, was duly returned or elected, or whether the Election was void, and shall forthwith certify in Writing such Determination to the Speaker, and upon such Certificate being given such Determination shall be final to all Intents and Purposes.

14. Where any Charge is made in an Election Petition of any corrupt Practice having been committed at the Election to which the Petition refers, the Judge shall, in addition to such Certificate, and at the same Time, report in Writing to the Speaker as follows :

(a.) Whether any corrupt Practice has or has not been proved to have been committed by or with the Knowledge and Consent of any Candidate at such Election, and the Nature of such corrupt Practice :

(b.) The Names of all Persons (if any) who have been proved at the Trial to have been guilty of any corrupt Practice :

(c.) Whether corrupt practices have, or whether there is reason to believe that corrupt practices have, extensively prevailed at the election to which the petition relates.

15. The Judge may at the same time make a Special Report to the Speaker as to any matters arising in the course of the Trial, an account of which in his judgment ought to be submitted to the House of Commons.

16. Where, upon the applicaton of any party to a Petition made in the prescribed manner to the Court, it appears to the Court that the case raised by the Petition can be conveniently stated as a special case, the Court may direct the same to be stated accordingly, and any such special case shall, as far as may be, be heard before the Court, and

the Decision of the Court shall be final; and the Court shall certify to the Speaker its determination in reference to such special case.

12. Provided always, that if it shall appear to the Judge on the trial of the said petition that any question or questions of law as to the admissibility of evidence or otherwise require further consideration by the Court of Common Pleas, then it shall be lawful for the said Judge to postpone the granting of the said certificate until the determination of such quesiton or questions by the Court, and for this purpose to reserve any such question or questions in like manner as questions are usually reserved by a Judge on a trial at *Nisi Prius.*

Application to the Court respecting trials.

13. *House of Commons to carry out report.*

14. *House of Commons may make order on special report.*

15. If the Judge states in his Report on the trial of an election petition under this Act that corrupt practices have, or that there is reason to believe that corrupt practices have, extensively prevailed in any county or borough at the election to which the Petition relates, such statement shall for all the purposes of the Act of the Session of the fifteenth and sixteenth years of the reign of her present Majesty, Chapter Fifty-seven, intituled *An Act to provide for more effectual Inquiry into the Existence of corrupt Practices at Elections of Members to serve in Parliament,* have the same Effect and may be dealt with in the same Manner as if it were a Report of a Committee of the House of Commons appointed to try an Election Petition, and the Expenses of any Commission of Inquiry which may be issued in accordance with the Provisions of the said Act shall be defrayed as if they were Expenses incurred in the Registration of Voters for such County or Borough.

Report of the Judge as to corrupt practices.

16. The Report of the Judge in respect of Persons guilty of corrupt Practices shall, for the Purpose of the Prosecution of such Persons, in pursuance of Section Nine of the Act of the Twenty-sixth Year of the Reign of Her present Majesty, Chapter Twenty-nine, have the same Effect as the Report of the Election Committee therein mentioned that certain Persons have been guilty of Bribery and Treating.

Report of Judge equivalent to Report of Election Committee.

17. On the Trial of an Election Petition under this Act, unless the Judge otherwise directs, any Charge of a corrupt Practice may be gone into and

Evidence of corrupt Practices how received.

Evidence in relation thereto received before any
Proof has been given of Agency on the Part of any
Candidate in respect of such corrupt Practice.

Acceptance of Office not to stop Petition.
18. The Trial of an Election Petition under this
Act shall be proceeded with notwithstanding the
Acceptance by the Respondent of an Office of Profit
under the Crown.

Prorogation of Parliament.
19. The Trial of an Election Petition under this
Act shall be proceeded with notwithstanding the
Prorogation of Parliament.

Proceedings.

Form of Petition.
20. An Election Petition under this Act shall be
in such Form and state such Matters as may be
prescribed.

Service of Petition.
21. An Election Petition under this Act shall be
served as nearly as may be in the Manner in which
a Writ or Summons is served, or in such other
Manner as may be prescribed.

Joint Respondents to Petition.
22. Two or more Candidates may be made
Respondents to the same Petition, and their Case
may for the sake of Convenience be tried at the
same Time; but for all the Purposes of this Act such
Petition shall be deemed to be a separate Petition
against each Respondent.

Provision in Cases where more than One Petition is presented.
23. Where, under this Act, more Petitions than
One are presented relating to the same Election or
Return, all such Petitions shall in the Election List
be bracketed together, and shall be dealt with as One
Petition, but such Petitions shall stand in the Election
List in the Place where the last of such Petitions
would have stood if it had been the only Petition
presented, unless the Court shall otherwise direct.

Shorthand writer to attend Trial of Election Petition.
24. On the Trial of an Election Petition under
this Act the Shorthand Writer of the House of
Commons or his Deputy shall attend and shall be
sworn by the Judge faithfully and truly to take
down the Evidence given at the Trial, and from
Time to Time as Occasion requires to write or cause
the same to be written in words at Length; and it
shall be the Duty of such Shorthand Writer to take
down such Evidence, and from Time to Time to
write or cause the same to be written at Length,
and a Copy of such Evidence shall accompany the
Certificate made by the Judge to the Speaker; and
the Expenses of the Shorthand Writer shall be deemed
to be Part of the Expenses incurred in receiving
the Judge.

Jurisdiction and Rules of Court.

2 5. The Judges for the Time being on the Rota for the Trial of Election Petitions in *England* and *Ireland* may respectively from Time to Time make, and may from Time to Time revoke and alter, General Rules and Orders (in this Act referred to as the Rules of Court), for the effectual Execution of this Act, and of the Intention and Object thereof, and the Regulation of the Practice, Procedure, and Costs of Election Petitions and the Trial thereof, and the certifying and reporting thereon.

Any General Rules and Orders made as aforesaid shall be deemed to be within the Powers conferred by this Act, and shall be of the same Force as if they were enacted in the Body of this Act.

Any General Rules and Orders made in pursuance of this Section shall be laid before Parliament within Three Weeks after they are made, if Parliament be then sitting, and if Parliament be not then sitting, within Three Weeks after the Beginning of the then next Session of Parliament.

26. Until Rules of Court have been made in pursuance of this Act, and so far as such Rules do not extend, the Principles, Practice, and Rules on which Committees of the House of Commons have heretofore acted in dealing with Election Petitions shall be observed so far as may be by the Court and Judge in the Case of Election Petitions under this Act.

27. The Duties to be performed by the prescribed Officer under this Act shall be performed by such One or more of the Masters of the Court of Common Pleas at *Westminster* as may be determined by the Chief Justice of the said Court of Common Pleas, and by the Master of the Court of Common Pleas at *Dublin*, and there shall be awarded to such Masters respectively, in addition to their existing Salaries, such Remuneration for the Performance of the Duties imposed on them in pursuance of this Act as the Chief Justices of the said Courts of Common Pleas at *Westminster* and *Dublin* may respectively, with the Consent of the Commissioners of the Treasury, determine.

Reception, Expenses, and Jurisdiction of Judge.

28. The Judge shall be received at the Place where he is about to try an Election Petition under this Act with the same State, so far as Circumstances admit, as a Judge of Assize is received at

Marginal notes:

Rules to be made by Court.

Practice of House of Commons to be observed.

Performance of Duties by prescribed Officer.

Reception of Judge.

an Assize Town; he shall be received by the Sheriff in the Case of a Petition relating to a County Election, and in any other Case by the Mayor, in the Case of a Borough having a Mayor, and in the Case of a Borough not having a Mayor by the Sheriff of the County in which the Borough is situate, or by some Person named by such Sheriff.

The travelling and other Expenses of the Judge and all Expenses properly incurred by the Sheriff or by such Mayor or Person named as aforesaid in receiving the Judge and providing him with necessary Accommodation and with a proper Court, shall be defrayed by the Commissioners of the Treasury out of Money to be provided by Parliament.

Power of Judge. 29. On the Trial of an Election Petition under this Act the Judge shall, subject to the Provisions of this Act, have the same Powers, Jurisdiction, and Authority as a Judge of One of the Superior Courts and as a Judge of Assize and Nisi Prius, and the Court held by him shall be a Court of Record.

Attendance on Judge. 30. The Judge shall be attended on the Trial of an Election Petition under this Act in the same Manner as if he were a Judge sitting at Nisi Prius, and the Expenses of such Attendance shall be deemed to be Part of the Expenses of providing a Court.

Summons of Witnesses. 31. Witnesses shall be subpœnaed and sworn in the same Manner as nearly as Circumstances admit as in a Trial at Nisi Prius, and shall be subject to the same Penalties for Perjury.

Judge may summon and examine Witnesses. 32. On the Trial of an Election Petition under this Act the Judge may, by Order under his Hand, compel the Attendance of any Person as a Witness who appears to him to have been concerned in the Election to which the petition refers, and any person refusing to obey such Order shall be guilty of Contempt of Court. The Judge may examine any Witness so compelled to attend or any Person in Court, although such Witness is not called and examined by any Party to the Petition. After the Examination of a Witness as aforesaid by a Judge such Witness may be cross-examined by or on behalf of the Petitioner and Respondent, or either of them.

Indemnity to Witnesses. 33. The Provisions of the Seventh Section of the Act of the Session of the Twenty-sixth and Twenty-seventh Years of the Reign of Her present Majesty, Chapter Twenty-nine, relating to the Examination and Indemnity of Witnesses, shall apply to any

Witness appearing before a Judge on the Trial of an Election Petition under this Act in the same Manner as in the Case of a Trial before a Committee of the House of Commons before the passing of this Act, and the Certificate shall be given under the Hand of the Judge.

34. The reasonable Expenses incurred by any Person in appearing to give Evidence at the Trial of an Election Petition under this Act, according to the Scale allowed to Witnesses on the Trial of Civil Actions at the Assizes, may be allowed to such Persons by a Certificate under the Hand of the Judge or of the prescribed Officer, and such Expenses if the Witness was called and examined by the Judge shall be deemed Part of the Expenses of providing a Court, and in other Cases shall be deemed to be Costs of the Petition.

Expenses of Witnesses.

Withdrawal and Abatement of Election Petitions.

35. An Election Petition under this Act shall not be withdrawn without the Leave of the Court or Judge upon special Application, to be made in and at the prescribed Manner, Time, and Place.

Withdrawal of Petition and Substitution of New Petitioners.

No such Application shall be made for the Withdrawal of a Petition until the prescribed Notice has been given in the County or Borough to which the Petition relates of the Intention of the Petitioner to make an Application for the Withdrawal of his Petition.

On the Hearing of the Application for Withdrawal any Person who might have been a Petitioner in respect of the Election to which the Petition relates may apply to the Court or Judge to be substituted as a Petitioner for the Petitioner so desirous of withdrawing the petition.

The Court or Judge may, if it or he think fit, substitute as a Petitioner any such Applicant as aforesaid ; and may further, if the proposed Withdrawal is in the Opinion of the Court or Judge induced by any corrupt Bargain or Consideration, by Order direct that the Security given on behalf of the original Petitioner shall remain as Security for any Costs that may be incurred by the substituted Petitioner, and that to the Extent of the Sum named in such Security the original Petitioner shall be liable to pay the Costs of the substituted Petitioner.

If no such Order is made with respect to the Security given on behalf of the original Petitioner, Security to the same Amount as would be required in the Case of a new Petition, and subject to the like Conditions, shall be given on behalf of the substituted Petitioner before he proceeds with his Petition, and within the prescribed Time after the Order of Substitution.

Subject as aforesaid, a substituted Petitioner shall stand in the same Position as nearly as may be, and be subject to the same Liabilities, as the original Petitioner.

If a Petition is withdrawn, the Petitioner shall be liable to pay the Costs of the Respondent.

Where there are more Petitioners than One, no Application to withdraw a Petition shall be made except with the Consent of all the Petitioners.

Court to report to the Speaker Circumstances of Withdrawal. 36. In every Case of the Withdrawal of an Election Petition under this Act the Court or Judge shall report to the Speaker whether in its or his Opinion the Withdrawal of such Petition was the Result of any corrupt Arrangement, or in consideration of the Withdrawal of any other Petition, and if so the Circumstances attending the Withdrawal.

Abatement of Petition. 37. An Election Petition under this Act shall be abated by the Death of a sole Petitioner or of the Survivor of several Petitioners.

The Abatement of a Petition shall not affect the Liability of the Petitioner to the Payment of Costs previously incurred.

On the Abatement of a Petition the prescribed Notice of such Abatement having taken place shall be given in the County or Borough to which the Petition relates, and within the prescribed Time after the Notice is given, any Person who might have been a Petitioner in respect of the Election to which the Petition relates may apply to the Court or Judge, in and at the prescribed Manner, Time, and Place, to be substituted as a Petitioner.

The Court or Judge may, if it or he think fit, substitute as a Petitioner any such Applicant who is desirous of being substituted, and on whose Behalf Security to the same Amount is given as is required in the Case of a new Petition.

Admission in certain cases of Voters to be Respondents. 38. If before the Trial of any Election Petition under this Act any of the following Events happen in the Case of the Respondent; (that is to say,)

(1.) If he dies:

(2.) If he is summoned to Parliament as a Peer of *Great Britain* by a Writ issued under the Great Seal of *Great Britain*.

(3.) If the House of Commons have resolved that his Seat is vacant:

(4.) If he gives in and at the prescribed Manner and Time Notice to the Court that he does not intend to oppose the Petition:

Notice of such Event having taken place shall be given in the County or Borough to which the petition relates, and within the prescribed Time after the Notice is given any Person who might have been a Petitioner in respect of the Election to which the Petition relates may apply to the Court or Judge to be admitted as a Respondent to oppose the Petition, and such Person shall on such Application be admitted accordingly, either with the Respondent, if there be a Respondent, or in place of the Respondent; and any Number of Persons not exceeding Three may be so admitted.

39. A Respondent who has given the prescribed Notice that he does not intend to oppose the Petition shall not be allowed to appear or act as a Party against such Petition in any Proceedings thereon, and shall not sit or vote in the House of Commons until the House of Commons has been informed of the Report on the Petition, and the Court or Judge shall in all Cases in which such Notice has been given in the prescribed Time and Manner report the same to the Speaker of the House of Commons. *Respondent not opposing not to appear as Party or to sit.*

40. Where an Election Petition under this Act complains of a double Return and the Respondent has given Notice to the prescribed Officer that it is not his Intention to oppose the Petition, and no Party has been admitted in pursuance of this Act to defend such Return, then the Petitioner, if there be no Petition complaining of the other Member returned on such double Return, may withdraw his Petition by Notice addressed to the prescribed Officer, and upon the Receipt of such Notice the prescribed Officer shall report the Fact of the Withdrawal of such Petition to the Speaker, and the House of Commons shall thereupon give the necessary Directions for amending the said double Return by taking off the File the Indenture by which the Respondent so declining to oppose the Petition was returned. *Provisions for Cases of double Return where the Member complained of declines to defend his Return.*

Remainder repealed by 35 and 36 Vic., c. 33

Costs.

41. All Costs, Charges, and Expenses of and incidental to the Presentation of a Petition under this Act, and to the Proceedings consequent thereon, *General Costs of Petition.*

with the Exception of such Costs, Charges, and Expenses as are by this Act otherwise provided for, shall be defrayed by the Parties to the Petition in such Manner and in such Proportions as the Court or Judge may determine, regard being had to the Disallowance of any Costs, Charges, or Expenses which may, in the Opinion of the Court or Judge, have been caused by vexatious Conduct, unfounded Allegations, or unfounded Objections on the Part either of the Petitioner or the Respondent, and regard being had to the Discouragement of any needless Expense by throwing the Burden of defraying the same on the Parties by whom it has been caused, whether such Parties are or are not on the whole successful.

The Costs may be taxed in the prescribed Manner, but according to the same Principles, as Costs between Attorney and Client are taxed in a Suit in the High Court of Chancery, and such Costs may be recovered in the same Manner as the Costs of an Action at Law, or in such other Manner as may be prescribed.

Recognizance, when to be estreated, &c.

42. If any Petitioner in an Election Petition presented under this Act neglect or refuse for the Space of Six Months after Demand to pay to any Person summoned as a Witness on his Behalf, or to the Respondent, any Sum certified to be due to him for his Costs, Charges, and Expenses, and if such Neglect or Refusal be, within One Year after such Demand, proved to the Satisfaction of the Court of Elections, in every such Case every Person who has entered into a Recognizance relating to such Petition under the Provisions of this Act shall be held to have made default in his said Recognizance, and the prescribed Officer shall thereupon certify such Recognizance to be forfeited, and the same shall be dealt with in *England* in manner provided by the Act of the Third Year of the Reign of King *George* the Fourth, Chapter Forty-six, and in *Ireland* in manner provided by "The Fines Act (*Ireland*), 1851."

Punishment of Corrupt Practices.

Punishment of Candidate guilty of Bribery.

43. Where it is found, by the Report of the Judge upon an Election Petition under this Act, that Bribery has been committed by or with the Knowledge and Consent of any Candidate at an Election, such Candidate shall be deemed to have been personally guilty of Bribery at such Election, and his Election, if he has been elected, shall be void, and he shall be incapable of being elected to and of sitting in the House of Commons during the Seven Years next after the Date of his being found guilty; and he shall further be incapable during the said period of Seven Years—

(1.) Of being registered as a Voter and voting at any Election in the United Kingdom; and

(2.) Of holding any Office under the Act of the Session of the Fifth and Sixth Years of the Reign of His Majesty King *William* the Fourth, Chapter Seventy-six, or of the Session of the Third and Fourth Years of the Reign of Her present Majesty, Chapter One hundred and eight, or any Municipal Office; and

(3.) Of holding any Judicial Office, and of being appointed and of acting as a Justice of the Peace.

Penalty for employing corrupt Agent.

44. If on the Trial of any Election Petition under this Act any Candidate is proved to have personally engaged at the Election to which such Petition relates as a Canvasser or Agent for the Management of the Election, any Person knowing that such Person has within Seven Years previous to such Engagement been found guilty of any corrupt Practice by any competent Legal Tribunal, or been reported guilty of any corrupt Practice by a Committee of the House of Commons, or by the Report of the Judge upon an Election Petition under this Act, or by the Report of Commissioners appointed in pursuance of the Act of the Session of the Fifteenth and Sixteenth Years of the Reign of Her present Majesty, Chapter Fifty-seven, the Election of such Candidate shall be void.

Disqualification of Persons found guilty of Bribery.

45. Any Person, other than a Candidate, found guilty of Bribery in any Proceeding in which after Notice of the Charge he has had an Opportunity of being heard, shall, during the Seven Years next after the Time at which he is so found guilty, be incapable of being elected to and sitting in Parliament; and also be incapable—

(1.) Of being registered as a Voter and voting at any Election in the United Kingdom; and

(2.) Of holding any Office under the Act of the Session of the Fifth and Sixth Years of the Reign of His Majesty King *William* the Fourth, Chapter Seventy-six, or of the Session of the Third and Fourth Years of the Reign of Her present Majesty, Chapter One hundred and eight, or any Municipal Office; and

(3.) Of holding any Judicial Office, and of being appointed and of acting as a Justice of the Peace.

Amendment of the Law relating to the Disqualification of Candidates for corrupt Practices.

46. For the Purpose of disqualifying, in pursuance of the Thirty-sixth Section of "The Corrupt Practices Prevention Act, 1854," a Member guilty of corrupt Practices, other than personal Bribery within the Forty-third Section of this Act, the Report of the Judge on the Trial of an Election Petition shall be deemed to be substituted for the Declaration of an Election Committee, and the said Section shall be construed as if the Words "reported by a Judge on the Trial of an Election Petition" were inserted therein in the Place of the Words " declared by an Election Committee."

Removal of Disqualification on Proof that Disqualification was procured by Perjury.

47. If at any Time after any Person has become disqualified by virtue of this Act, the Witnesses, or any of them, on whose Testimony such Person shall have so become disqualified, shall, upon the Prosecution of such Person, be convicted of Perjury in respect of such Testimony, it shall be lawful for such Person to move the Court to order, and the Court shall, upon being satisfied that such Disqualification was procured by reason of Perjury, order that such Disqualification shall thenceforth cease and determine, and the same shall cease and determine accordingly.

Miscellaneous.

Returning Officer may be sued for neglecting to return any Person duly elected.

48. If any Returning Officer wilfully delays, neglects, or refuses duly to return any Person who ought to be returned to serve in Parliament for any County or Borough, such Person may, in case it has been determined on the Hearing of an Election Petition under this Act that such Person was entitled to have been returned, sue the Officer having so wilfully delayed, neglected, or refused duly to make such Return at his Election in any of Her Majesty's Courts of Record at *Westminster*, and shall recover double the damages he has sustained by reason thereof, together with full Costs of Suit; provided such Action be commenced within One Year after the Commission of the Act on which it is grounded, or within Six Months after the Conclusion of the Trial relating to such Election.

Calculation of Time.

49. In reckoning Time for the Purposes of this Act, *Sunday, Christmas Day, Good Friday*, and any Day set apart for a Public Fast or Public Thanksgiving shall be excluded.

Controverted Elections to be tried under Act.

50. From and after the next Dissolution of Parliament no Election or Return to Parliament shall be questioned except in accordance with the Provisions

of this Act, but until such Dissolution, Elections and Returns to Parliament may be questioned in manner heretofore in use.

51. Where an Election Petition under this Act complains of the Conduct of a Returning Officer, such Returning Officer shall for all the Purposes of this Act, except the Admission of Respondents in his Place, be deemed to be a Respondent. *Returning Officer if complained of to be Respondent*

52. A Petition under this Act complaining of no Return may be presented to the Court, and shall be deemed to be an Election Petition within the Meaning of this Act, and the Court may make such Order thereon as they think expedient for compelling a Return to be made, or may allow such Petition to be heard by the Judge in manner hereinbefore provided with respect to ordinary Election Petitions. *Petition complaining of no Return.*

53. On the Trial of a Petition under this Act complaining of an undue Return and claiming the Seat for some Person, the Respondent may give Evidence to prove that the Election of such Person was undue in the same Manner as if he had presented a Petition complaining of such Election. *Recrimination when Petition for undue Return.*

54. From and after the next Dissolution of Parliament the Acts contained in the Schedule hereto are repealed so far as relates to Elections and Petitions to the Extent therein mentioned; provided that such Repeal shall not affect the Validity or Invalidity of anything already done or suffered, or any Offence already committed, or any Remedy or Proceeding in respect thereof, or the Proof of any past Act or Thing. *Repeal of Acts.*

55. The additional Puisne Judges appointed under this Act to each of the Courts of Queen's Bench, the Common Pleas, and the Exchequer in *England* shall, as to Rank, Salary, Pension, Attendant Officers, Jurisdiction, and all other Privileges and Duties of a Judge, stand in the same Position as the other Puisne Judges of the Court to which he is attached. *Provision as to Payment of additional Judges and Remuneration of Judges for Duties to be performed under this Act.*

Any Puisne Judge of the said Courts appointed in pursuance of or after the passing of this Act shall be authorized to sit, and shall, when requested by the Lord Chancellor, sit as Judge of the Court of Probate and Court of Marriage and Divorce or of the Admiralty Court.

56. If upon a Petition to the House of Commons, presented within Twenty-one Days after the Return to the Clerk of the Crown in Chancery in *England*, or to the Clerk of the Crown and Hanaper in *Ireland*, *Commissions of Inquiry into corrupt Practices.*

of a Member to serve in Parliament for any Borough
or County, or within Fourteen Days after the meeting of Parliament, and signed by any Two or more
Electors of such Borough or County, and alleging
that corrupt Practices have extensively prevailed at
the then last Election for such Borough or County,
or that there is Reason to believe that corrupt
Practices have there so prevailed, an Address be
presented by both Houses of Parliament, praying
that such Allegation may be inquired into, the Crown
may appoint Commissioners to inquire into the same,
and if such Commissioners in such Case be appointed,
they shall inquire in the same Manner and with the
same Powers and subject to all the Provisions of the
Statute of the Fifteenth and Sixteenth of *Victoria*,
Chapter fifty-seven.

Rules as to Agents practising in Cases of Election Petitions. 57. Any Person who at the Time of the passing
of this Act was entitled to practise as Agent,
according to the Principles, Practice, and Rules of
the House of Commons, in Cases of Election Petitions,
and Matters relating to Election of Members of the
House of Commons, shall be entitled to practise as
an Attorney or Agent in Cases of Election Petitions,
and all Matters relating to Elections before the Court
and Judges prescribed by this Act : Provided, that
every such Person so practising as aforesaid shall,
in respect of such Practice and everything relating
thereto, be subject to the Jurisdiction and Order of
the Court as if he were an Attorney of the said
Court : And further, Provided, that no such Person
shall practise as aforesaid until his Name shall have
been entered on a Roll to be made and kept, and
which is hereby authorized to be made and kept, by
the prescribed Officer in the prescribed Manner.

Act continued by 37 *and* 38 Vic. c. 76.

---

32 & 33 Vic. c. 41.

An Act for amending the Law with respect to
the rating of Occupiers for short terms, and
the making and collecting of the Poor's
Rate.   [*26th July*, 1869.]

WHEREAS it is expedient, &c. : Be it therefore
enacted, &c.

Occupiers of tenements let for short terms 1. The occupier of any rateable hereditament let
to him for a term not exceeding three months shall

be entitled to deduct the amount paid by him in respect of any poor rate assessed upon such hereditament from the rent due or accruing due to the owner, and every such payment shall be a valid discharge of the rent to the extent of the rate so paid.

may deduct the poor rate paid by them from their rents.

2. No such occupier shall be compelled to pay to the overseers at one time or within four weeks a greater amount of the rate than would be due for one quarter of the year.

Amount of rate payable by occupier.

3. In case the rateable value of any hereditament does not exceed twenty pounds, if the hereditament is situate in the metropolis, or thirteen pounds if situate in any parish wholly or partly within the borough of Liverpool, or ten pounds if situate in any parish wholly or partly within the city of Manchester or the borough of Birmingham, or eight pounds if situate elsewhere, and the owner of such hereditament is willing to enter into an agreement in writing with the overseers to become liable to them for the poor rates assessed in respect of such hereditament, for any term not being less than one year from the date of such agreement, and to pay the poor rates whether the hereditament is occupied or not, the overseers may, subject nevertheless to the control of the vestry, agree with the owner to receive the rates from him, and to allow to him a commission not exceeding twenty-five per cent. on the whole amount thereof.

Owners may agree to pay the rate, and be allowed a commission.

4. The vestry of any parish may from time to time order that the owners of all rateable hereditaments to which section three of this Act extends, situate within such parish, shall be rated to the poor rate in respect of such rateable hereditaments, instead of the occupiers, on all rates made after the date of such order; and thereupon and so long as such order shall be in force the following enactments shall have effect :

Vestries may order the owner to be rated instead of the occupier.

1. The overseers shall rate the owners instead of the occupiers, and shall allow to them an abatement or deduction of fifteen per centum from the amount of the rate :

2. If the owner of one or more such rateable hereditaments shall give notice to the overseers in writing that he is willing to be rated for any term not being less than one year in respect of all such rateable hereditaments of which he is the owner, whether the same be occupied or

not, the overseers shall rate such owner accordingly, and allow to him a further abatement or deduction not exceeding fifteen per centum from the amount of the rate during the time he is so rated :

3. The vestry may by resolution rescind any such order after a day to be fixed by them, such day being not less than six months after the passing of such resolution; but the order shall continue in force with respect to all rates made before the date on which the resolution takes effect :

Provided that this clause shall not be applicable to any rateable hereditament in which a dwelling house shall not be included.

Owners omitting to pay rates before the fifth day of June to forfeit commission.

5. When an owner who has become liable to pay the poor rate omits or neglects to pay, before the fifth day of June in any year, any rate or any instalment thereof which has become due previously to the preceding fifth day of January, and has been duly demanded by a demand-note delivered to him or left at his usual or last known place of abode, he shall not be entitled to deduct or receive any commission, abatement, or allowance to which he would, except for such omission or neglect, be entitled under this Act, but shall be liable to pay, and shall pay, such rate or instalment in full.

Repeal of 13 and 14 Vict. c. 99, &c., so far as the same apply to the poor rate.

6. The statute thirteenth and fourteenth Victoria, chapter ninety-nine, with respect to the rating of small tenements, and so much of any local statute as relates to the rating of owners instead of occupiers, are hereby repealed, so far as the same apply to any poor rate made after this Act comes into operation.

Constructive payment of the rate.

7. Every payment of a rate by the occupier, notwithstanding the amount thereof may be deducted from his rent as herein provided, and every payment of a rate by the owner, whether he is himself rated instead of the occupier, or has agreed with the occupier or with the overseers to pay such rate, and notwithstanding any allowance or deduction which the overseers are empowered to make from the rate, shall be deemed a payment of the full rate by the occupier for the purpose of any qualification or franchise which as regards rating depends upon the payment of the poor rate.

Where owners omit to pay

8. Where an owner who has undertaken, whether by agreement with the occupier or with the overseers,

to pay the poor rates, or has otherwise become liable to pay the same, omits or neglects to pay any such rate, the occupier may pay the same and deduct the amount from the rent due or accruing due to the owner, and the receipt for such rate shall be a valid discharge of the rent to the extent of the rate so paid.

rates, the occupiers paying the same may deduct the amount from the rent.

9. Every owner who agrees with the overseers to pay the poor rate, or who is rated or liable to be rated for any hereditament instead of the occupier, shall deliver to the overseers, from time to time, when required by them, in writing, a list containing the names of the actual occupiers of the hereditaments comprised in such agreement, or for which he is so rated or liable to be rated; and if any such owner wilfully omits to deliver such list when required to do so, or wilfully omits therefrom or misstates therein the name of any occupier, he shall for every such omission or misstatement be liable, on summary conviction, to a penalty not exceeding two pounds.

Owners to give lists of occupiers, and liable to penalty for wilful omission.

10. Section twenty-eight of "The Representation of the People Act, 1867," with respect to notice to be given of rates in arrear, shall apply to occupiers of premises capable of conferring the parliamentary franchise, although the owners of such premises have become liable for the rates assessed thereon under the provisions of this Act.

Notice to occupiers of rates in arrear.

11. Where the owner has become liable to the payment of the poor rates, the rates due from him, together with the costs and charges of levying and recovering the same, may be levied on the goods of the owner, and be recovered from him in the same way as poor rates may be recovered from the occupier.

Liability of owner under agreement.

12. Notwithstanding the owner of any such rateable hereditament as aforesaid has become liable for payment of the poor rates assessed thereon, the goods and chattels of the occupier shall be liable to be distrained and sold for payment of such rates as may accrue during his occupation of the premises at any time whilst such rates remain unpaid by the owner, subject to the following provisions :

Recovery of rates unpaid by the owner.

1. That no such distress shall be levied unless the rate has been demanded in writing by the overseers from the occupier, and the occupier has failed to pay the same within fourteen days after the service of such demand

2. That no greater sum shall be raised by such distress than shall at the time of making the same be actually due from the occupier for rent of the premises on which the distress is made:

3. That any such occupier shall be entitled to deduct the amount of rates for which such distraint is made, and the expense of distraint, from the rent due or accruing due to the owner, and every such payment shall be a valid discharge of the rent to the extent of the rate and expenses paid.

Owner may appeal against valuation list and rate.

13. Every owner of any hereditament for the rates of which he has become liable shall have the same right of appeal (subject to the same conditions and consequences) against the valuation lists and the poor rates, as if he were the occupier thereof.

The overseer to state the period for which poor rate is made.

Proviso.

14. The overseers of every parish when they make a poor rate shall set forth in the title of the rate the period for which the same is estimated, and if the same is payable by instalments the amount of each instalment and the date at which each instalment is payable; provided that if the necessities of the parish shall require it another rate may be made before such period shall have elapsed.

Overseers may make poor rate payable by instalments.

15. The overseers who make the poor rate for a period exceeding three months may declare that the same shall be paid by instalments at such times as they shall specify, and thereupon each instalment only shall be enforceable as and when it falls due, and the payment of any such instalment shall, as respects any qualification or franchise depending upon the payment of the poor rate, be deemed a payment of such rate in respect of the period to which such instalment applies.

Provision for successive occupiers, and for occupiers coming into unoccupied hereditaments.

16. If the occupier assessed in the rate when made shall cease to occupy before the rate shall have been wholly discharged, or if the hereditament being unoccupied at the time of the making of the rate become occupied during the period for which the rate is made, the overseers shall enter in the rate book the name of the person who succeeds or comes into the occupation, as the case may be, and the date when such occupation commences, so far as the same shall be known to them, and such occupier shall thenceforth be deemed to have been actually rated from the date so entered by the overseer, and

shall be liable to pay so much of the rate as shall be proportionate to the time between the commencement of his occupation and the expiration of the period for which the rate was made, in like manner, and with the like remedy of appeal, as if he had been rated when the rate was made; and an outgoing occupier shall remain liable in like manner for so much and no more of the rate as is proportionate to the time of his occupation within the period for which the rate was made; and the twelfth section of the statute 17 Geo. 2. c. 38 shall be repealed.

17. A poor rate shall be deemed to be made on the day when it is allowed by the justices, and if the justices sever in their allowance then on the day of the last allowance.

When the poor rate shall be deemed to be made.

18. The production of the book purporting to contain a poor rate, with the allowance of the rate by the justices, shall, if the rate is made in the form prescribed by law, be prima facie evidence of the due making and publication of such rate.

Evidence of making and publication of rates.

19. The overseers in making out the poor rate shall, in every case, whether the rate is collected from the owner or occupier, or the owner is liable to the payment of the rate instead of the occupier, enter in the occupiers' column of the rate book the name of the occupier of every rateable hereditament, and such occupier shall be deemed to be duly rated for any qualification or franchise as aforesaid; and if any overseer negligently or wilfully and without reasonable cause omits the name of the occupier of any rateable hereditament from the rate, or negligently or wilfully misstates any name therein, such overseer shall for every such omission or misstatement be liable on summary conviction to a penalty not exceeding two pounds; provided that any occupier whose name has been omitted shall, notwithstanding such omission and that no claim to be rated has been made by him, be entitled to every qualification and franchise depending upon rating, in the same manner as if his name had not been so omitted.

Overseers to insert names of all occupiers in the rate.

Penalty for omission.

Saving of franchises.

20. The word "overseer" shall include every authority that makes an assessment for the poor rate; the words "poor rate" shall mean the assessment for the relief of the poor, and for the other purposes chargeable thereon according to law, and in the metropolis shall extend to every rate

Interpretation of terms.

made by the overseers, and chargeable upon the same
property as the poor rate; the word "owner" shall
mean any person receiving or claiming the rent of
the hereditament for his own use, or receiving
the same for the use of any corporation aggregate,
or of any public company, or of any landlord or lessee
who shall be a minor, a married woman, or insane, or
for the use of any person for whom he is acting as
agent; the word "parish" shall signify every place
for which a separate overseer can be appointed; the
word "vestry" shall include not only the vestry of a
parish existing under the authority of some general
or special Act of Parliament, or by special custom or
otherwise, but also the meeting of the inhabitants
of any township, vill, or place having a separate
overseer, and for which a separate poor rate is
made, held after notice given in like manner as is
required by law in regard to the meetings of vestries;
and the word "metropolis" shall include only the
metropolis as defined by the Metropolis Management
Act, 1855.

Application of
Act.
21. This Act shall not extend to Scotland or
to Ireland.

Short title.
22. This Act may be cited as "The Poor Rate
Commencement
of Act.
Assessment and Collection Act, 1869," and shall
come into operation on the twenty-ninth of
September, one thouand eight hundred and sixty-
nine: Provided that the vestry of any parish may
before that day order that the owners shall be rated
instead of the occupiers under this Act, but no such
order shall take effect until after the said twenty-
ninth day of September, one thousand eight hundred
and sixty-nine.

---

32 & 33 Vic. c. 55.

An Act to shorten the Term of Residence required
as a Qualification for the Municipal Franchise,
and to make provision for other purposes.
[*2nd August*, 1869.]

WHEREAS it is expedient, &c.: Be it therefore
enacted, &c.

Sect. 9 of 5 and 6
W. 4, c. 76 re-
pealed.
1. The ninth section of the Act of the session of
the fifth and sixth years' of King William the Fourth,
chapter seventy-six, shall be repealed, and instead

68

thereof be it enacted, that every person of full age who on the last day of July in any year shall have occupied any house, warehouse, counting-house, shop, or other building within any borough during the whole of the preceding twelve calendar months, and also during the time of such occupation shall have resided within the said borough, or within seven miles of the said borough, shall, if duly enrolled in that year according to the provisions contained in the said Act of the session of the fifth and sixth years of King William the Fourth, chapter seventy-six, and the acts amending the same, be a burgess of such borough and member of the body corporate of the mayor, aldermen, and burgesses of such borough : Provided that no such person shall be so enrolled in any year unless he shall have been rated in respect of such premises so occupied by him within the borough to all rates made for the relief of the poor of the parish wherein such premises are situated during the time of his occupation as aforesaid, and unless he shall have paid on or before the twentieth day of July in such year all such rates, including therein all borough rates, if any, directed to be paid under the provisions of the said Acts, as shall have become payable by him in respect of the said premises up to the preceding fifth day of January : Provided also, that the premises in respect of the occupation of which any person shall have been so rated need not be the same premises or in the same parish, but may be different premises in the same parish or in different parishes : Provided also, that no person being an alien shall be so enrolled in any year, and that no person shall be so enrolled in any year, who, within twelve calendar months next before the said last day of July, shall have received parochial relief or other alms : Provided also, that the respective distances mentioned in this Act shall be measured in the manner directed by section seventy-six of the Act of the session of the sixth and seventh years of Queen Victoria, chapter eighteen.

One year's occupation to entitle persons to Municipal Franchise.

6 and 7 Vic., c. 18.

2. Nothing in this act contained shall affect any existing burgess roll, but every such roll shall continue in force until the first day of November, one thousand eight hundred and sixty-nine.

Saving rights under existing burgess roll.

3. Any such occupier as aforesaid, who shall be rated in respect of premises as in this Act mentioned, shall be entitled to be elected a councillor or an

Councillor or alderman may reside within

fifteen miles of borough.

alderman of any borough, if resident within fifteen miles of said borough, although by reason of his residence beyond seven miles of the borough he is not entitled to be on the burgess roll of such borough, provided that he is otherwise qualified to be on the burgess roll, and to be elected a councillor or an alderman for such borough, and the following enactments shall take effect with respect to such occupiers:

1. The overseers shall make out and publish a separate list containing the name of every such occupier at the same time and in the same manner as the burgess list, and all the provisions of the said Act of the fifth and sixth William the Fourth, chapter seventy-six, and the Acts amending the same with respect to objections and claims shall, as nearly as circumstances admit, apply to such separate list.

2. The separate list so made out shall be revised in the like manner as the burgess list, and when so revised shall be delivered to the town clerk and copied as a separate list at the end of the burgess roll.

Qualification for aldermen and councillors.

4. When any borough, consisting of less than four wards, shall at any time hereafter be divided into a greater number of wards, the qualification for an alderman or councillor of such borough shall not be increased or altered in consequence of such division, but shall continue the same as if such borough consisted of less than four wards.

Proprietors of shares in companies not to be deemed contractors, &c., and not to be disqualified from election to municipal offices by reason of such holding.

5. From and after the passing of this Act no person shall be deemed to have had or to have an interest in a contract or employment with, by, or on behalf of the council of any borough by reason only of his having had or having a share or interest in any railway company or in any company incorporated by Act of Parliament or by Royal Charter, or under "The Companies Act, 1862," and no councillor, alderman, or mayor in any municipal corporation shall be deemed to have been or to be disqualified to be elected, or to be such councillor, alderman, or mayor by reason only of his having had or having any share or interest in any railway company or in any company incorporated by Act of Parliament or Royal Charter, or under "the Companies Act, 1862," but all elections of councillors, aldermen, or mayors as aforesaid shall be deemed and taken to have been and to be valid, notwithstanding any such share or interest as aforesaid.

6. At any election of auditors, revising assessors, or ward assessors, any person entitled to vote may nominate for the office of auditor or assessor, in like manner as such person can nominate for the office of councillor under and by virtue of the provisions in that behalf contained in the twenty-second Victoria, chapter thirty-five, and the proceedings in relation to such nomination and election shall be in all respects the same as are prescribed in the said Act in relation to the election of councillors.

Who may nominate for office of auditor and assessor.

7. Every nomination for the office of councillor, assessor, or auditor must be sent to the town clerk, so that the same shall be received in his office before five o'clock in the afternoon of the last day on which any such nomination may by law be made.

Time for receipt of nominations.

8. If an extraordinary vacancy shall happen in the office of assessor, and at the same time a vacancy shall exist or arise in the office of councillor which cannot be legally filled up before the vacant office of assessor has been or can be by law filled up, the election to supply such vacant office of councillor shall be held before the alderman of the ward, or the mayor where the borough is not divided into wards, the continuing assessor, and such burgess (not being a burgess representing or enrolled on the burgess list for that ward, if the borough is divided into wards), as the mayor shall by writing under his hand appoint.

Elections to supply extraordinary vacancies.

9. In this Act and the said recited Act of the fifth and sixth years of King William the Fourth, chapter seventy six, and the Acts amending the same, wherever words occur which import the masculine gender the same shall be held to include females for all purposes connected with and having reference to the right to vote in the election of councillors, auditors, and assessors.

Words importing the masculine gender to include females.

10. This Act shall be construed as one with the said Act of the Session of the fifth and sixth years of King William the Fourth, chapter seventy-six, and the Acts amending the same, except so far as the same are altered or repealed by this Act, and the words used in this Act shall have the same meaning as in the said Acts.

Act to be construed with 5 & 6 W. 4, c. 76, &c.

11. This Act shall not apply to Scotland or Ireland.

Extent of Act.

An Act to amend the Law relating to Procedure
at Parliamentary and Municipal Elections.
[18th July, 1872.]

WHEREAS it is expedient, &c.: Be it enacted, &c.

PART I.

PARLIAMENTARY ELECTIONS.

Procedure at Elections.

Nomination of candidates for Parliamentary elections.

1. A candidate for election to serve in Parliament for a county or borough shall be nominated in writing. The writing shall be subscribed by two registered electors of such county or borough as proposer and seconder, and by eight other registered electors of the same county or borough as assenting to the nomination, and shall be delivered during the time appointed for the election to the returning officer by the candidate himself, or his proposer or seconder.

If at the expiration of one hour after the time appointed for the election no more candidates stand nominated than there are vacancies to be filled up, the returning officer shall forthwith declare the candidates who may stand nominated to be elected, and return their names to the Clerk of the Crown in Chancery; but if at the expiration of such hour more candidates stand nominated than there are vacancies to be filled up, the returning officer shall adjourn the election and shall take a poll in manner in this Act mentioned.

A candidate may, during the time appointed for the election, but not afterwards, withdraw from his candidature by giving a notice to that effect, signed by him, to the returning officer: Provided that the proposer of a candidate nominated in his absence out of the United Kingdom may withdraw such candidate by a written notice signed by him and delivered to the returning officer, together with a written declaration of such absence of the candidate.

If after the adjournment of an election by the returning officer for the purpose of taking a poll one of the candidates nominated shall die before the poll has commenced, the returning officer shall, upon being satisfied of the fact of such death, countermand notice of the poll, and all the proceedings with reference to the election shall be commenced afresh in all respects as if the writ had been received by the returning officer on the day on which proof was given to him of such death; provided that no fresh nomination shall be necessary in the case of a candidate who stood nominated at the time of the countermand of the poll.

2. In the case of a poll at an election the votes shall be given by ballot. The ballot of each voter shall consist of a paper (in this Act called a ballot paper) showing the names and description of the candidates. Each ballot paper shall have a number printed on the back, and shall have attached a counterfoil with the same number printed on the face. At the time of voting, the ballot paper shall be marked on both sides with an official mark, and delivered to the voter within the polling station, and the number of such voter on the register of voters shall be marked on the counterfoil, and the voter having secretly marked his vote on the paper, and folded it up so as to conceal his vote, shall place it in a closed box in the presence of the officer presiding at the polling station (in this Act called "the presiding officer") after having shown to him the official mark at the back.

Any ballot paper which has not on its back the official mark, or on which votes are given to more candidates than the voter is entitled to vote for, or on which anything, except the said number on the back is written or marked by which the voter can be identified, shall be void and not counted.

After the close of the poll the ballot boxes shall be sealed up, so as to prevent the introduction of additional ballot papers, and shall be taken charge of by the returning officer, and that officer shall, in the presence of such agents, if any, of the candidates as may be in attendance, open the ballot boxes and ascertain the result of the poll by counting the votes given to each candidate, and shall forthwith declare to be elected the candidates or candidate to whom the majority of votes have been given, and return their names to the Clerk of the Crown in Chancery. The decision of the returning officer as to any question arising in respect of any ballot paper shall be final, subject to reversal on petition questioning the election or return.

Where an equality of votes is found to exist between any candidate at an election for a county or borough, and the addition of a vote would entitle any of such candidates to be declared elected, the returning officer, if a registered elector of such county or borough, may give such additional vote, but shall not in any other case be entitled to vote at an election for which he is returning officer.

Offences at Elections.

Offences in respect of nomination papers, ballot papers, and ballot boxes.

3. Every person who,—

1. Forges or fraudulently defaces or fraudulently destroys any nomination paper, or delivers to the returning officer any nomination paper, knowing the same to be forged; or
2. Forges or counterfeits or fraudulently defaces or fraudulently destroys any ballot paper, or the official mark on any ballot paper; or
3. Without due authority supplies any ballot papers to any person; or
4. Fraudulently puts into any ballot box any paper other than the ballot paper which he is authorised by law to put in; or
5. Fraudulently takes out of the polling station any ballot paper; or
6. Without due authority destroys, takes, opens, or otherwise interferes with any ballot box or packet of ballot papers then in use for the purposes of the election;

shall be guilty of a misdemeanor, and be liable, if he is a returning officer or an officer or clerk in attendance at a polling station, to imprisonment for any term not exceeding two years, with or without hard labour, and if he is any other person, to imprisonment for any term not exceeding six months, with or without hard labour.

Any attempt to commit any offence specified in this section shall be punishable in the manner in which the offence itself is punishable.

In any indictment or other prosecution for an offence in relation to the nomination papers, ballot boxes, ballot papers, and marking instruments at an election, the property in such papers, boxes, and instruments may be stated to be in the returning officer at such election, as well as the property in the counterfoils.

Infringement of secrecy.

4. Every officer, clerk, and agent in attendance at a polling station shall maintain and aid in maintaining the secrecy of the voting in such station, and shall not communicate except for some purpose authorised by law, before the poll is closed, to any person any information as to the name or number on the register of voters of any elector who has or has not applied for a ballot paper or voted at that station, or as to the official mark, and no such officer, clerk, or agent, and no person

whosoever, shall interfere with or attempt to interfere with a voter when marking his vote, or otherwise attempt to obtain in the polling station information as to the candidate for whom any voter in such station is about to vote or has voted, or communicate at any time to any person any information obtained in a polling station as to the candidate for whom any voter in such station is about to vote or has voted, or as to the number on the back of the ballot paper given to any voter at such station. Every officer, clerk, and agent in attendance at the counting of the votes shall maintain and aid in maintaining the secrecy of the voting, and shall not attempt to ascertain at such counting the number on the back of any ballot paper, or communicate any information obtained at such counting as to the candidate for whom any vote is given in any particular ballot paper. No person shall directly or indirectly induce any voter to display his ballot paper after he shall have marked the same, so as to make known to any person the name of the candidate for or against whom he has so marked his vote.

Every person who acts in contravention of the provisions of this section shall be liable, on summary conviction before two justices of the peace, to imprisonment for any term not exceeding six months, with or without hard labour.

Amendment of Law.

5. The local authority (as hereinafter defined) of every county shall by order, as soon as may be practicable after the passing of this Act, divide such county into polling districts, and assign a polling place to each district, in such manner that, so far as is reasonably practicable, every elector resident in the county shall have a polling place within a distance not exceeding four miles from his residence; so, nevertheless, that a polling district need not in any case be constituted containing less than one hundred registered electors.

Division of counties and boroughs into polling districts.

The local authority (as hereinafter defined) of every borough shall take into consideration the division of such boroughs into polling districts, and, if they think it desirable, by order, divide such borough into polling districts in such manner as they may think most convenient for taking the votes of the electors at a poll.

The local authority of every county and borough shall, on or before the first day of May one thousand eight hundred and seventy-three, send to one of Her

Majesty's Principal Secretaries of State, to be laid by
him before both Houses of Parliament, a copy of any
order made by such authority in pursuance of this
section, and a report, in such form as he may require,
stating how far the provisions of this Act with respect
to polling districts have been complied with in their
county or borough ; and if they make any order
after the first day of May one thousand eight hundred
and seventy-three, with respect to polling districts
or polling places in their county or borough, they
shall send a copy of such order to the said Secretary
of State, to be laid by him before both Houses of
Parliament.

The local authority of a county or borough in this
section means the authority having power
to divide such county or borough into polling
districts under section thirty-four of the Representation
of the People Act, 1867, and any enactments amending
that section ; and such authority shall exercise the
powers thereby given to them for the purposes of
this section ; and the provisions of the said section
as to the local authority of a borough constituted by
the combination of two or more municipal boroughs
shall apply to a borough constituted by the combination of a municipal borough and other places,
whether municipal boroughs or not ; and in the case
of a borough of which a town council is not the
local authority and which is not wholly situate within
one petty sessional division, the justices of the peace
for the county in which such borough or the larger
part thereof in area is situate, assembled at some court
of general or quarter sessions, or at some adjournment
thereof, shall be the local authority thereof, and shall
for this purpose have jurisdiction over the whole of
such borough ; and in the case of such borough and
of a county, a court of general sessions shall be
assembled within twenty-one days after the passing
of this Act, and any such court may be assembled
and adjourned from time to time for the purpose.

No election shall be questioned by reason of any
non-compliance with this section or any informality
relative to polling districts or polling places, and any
order made by a local authority in relation to polling
districts or polling places, shall apply only to lists of
voters made subsequently to its date, and to registers
of voters formed out of such lists, and to elections held
after the time at which a register of voters so formed
has came into force: Provided that where any such

order is made between the first day of July and the first day of November in any year, and does not create any new division between two or more polling districts of any parish for which a separate poor rate is or can be made, such order shall apply to the register of voters which comes into force next after such order is made, and to elections held after that register so comes into force; and the clerk of the peace or town clerk, as the case may be, shall copy, print, and arrange the lists of voters for the purpose of such register in accordance with such order.

6. The returning officer at a parliamentary election may use, free of charge, for the purpose of taking the poll at such election, any room in a school receiving a grant out of moneys provided by Parliament, and any room the expense of maintaining which is payable out of any local rate, but he shall make good any damage done to such room, and defray any expense incurred by the person or body of persons, corporate or unincorporate, having control over the same on account of its being used for the purpose of taking the poll as aforesaid. *Use of school and public room for poll.*

The use of any room in an unoccupied house for the purpose of taking the poll shall not render any person liable to be rated or to pay any rate for such house.

7. At any election for a county or borough, a person shall not be entitled to vote unless his name is on the register of voters for the time being in force for such county or borough, and every person whose name is on such register shall be entitled to demand and receive a ballot paper and to vote: Provided that nothing in this section shall entitle any person to vote who is prohibited from voting by any statute, or by the common law of Parliament, or relieve such person from any penalties to which he may be liable for voting. *Conclusiveness of register of voters.*

Duties of Returning and Election Officers.

8. Subject to the provisions of this Act, every returning officer shall provide such nomination papers, polling stations, ballot boxes, ballot papers, stamping instruments, copies of register of voters, and other things, appoint and pay such officers, and do such other acts and things as may be necessary for effectually conducting an election in manner provided by this Act. *General powers and duties of returning officer.*

All expenses properly incurred by any returning officer in carrying into effect the provisions of this

Act, in the case of any parliamentary election, shall be payable in the same manner as expenses incurred in the erection of polling booths at such election are by law payable.

Where the sheriff is returning officer for more than one county as defined for the purposes of parliamentary elections, he may, without prejudice to any other power, by writing under his hand, appoint a fit person to be his deputy for all or any of the purposes relating to an election in any such county, and may, by himself or such deputy, exercise any powers and do any things which the returning officer is authorised or required to exercise or do in relation to such election. Every such deputy, and also any under sheriff, shall, in so far as he acts as returning officer, be deemed to be included in the term returning officer in the provisions of this Act relating to parliamentary elections, and the enactments with which this part of this Act is to be construed as one.

Keeping of order in station.

9. If any person misconducts himself in the polling station, or fails to obey the lawful orders of the presiding officer, he may immediately, by order of the presiding officer, be removed from the polling station by any constable in or near that station, or any other person authorised in writing by the returning officer to remove him; and the person so removed shall not, unless with the permission of the presiding officer, again be allowed to enter the polling station during the day.

Any person so removed as aforesaid, if charged with the commission in such station of any offence, may be kept in custody until he can be brought before a justice of the peace.

Provided that the powers conferred by this section shall not be exercised so as to prevent any elector who is otherwise entitled to vote at any polling station from having an opportunity of voting at such station.

Powers of presiding officer and administration of oaths, &c.

10. For the purpose of the adjournment of the poll, and of every other enactment relating to the poll, a presiding officer shall have the power by law belonging to a deputy returning officer; and any presiding officer and any clerk appointed by the returning officer to attend at a polling station shall have the power of asking the questions and administering the oath authorised by law to be asked of and administered to voters, and any justice of the

peace and any returning officer may take and receive
any declaration authorised by this Act to be taken
before him.

11. Every returning officer, presiding officer, and
clerk who is guilty of any wilful misfeasance or any
wilful act or omission in contravention of this Act
shall, in addition to any other penalty or liability to
which he may be subject, forfeit to any person
aggrieved by such misfeasance, act, or omission, a
penal sum not exceeding one hundred pounds.

Liability of officers for misconduct.

Section fifty of the Representation of the People
Act, 1867 (which relates to the acting of any returning
officer, or his partner or clerk, as agent for a candidate),
shall apply to any returning officer or officer appointed
by him in pursuance of this Act, and to his partner
or clerk.

30 and 31 Vict. c. 102.

Miscellaneous.

12. No person who has voted at an election shall,
in any legal proceeding to question the election or
return, be required to state for whom he has voted.

Prohibition of disclosure of vote.

13. No election shall be declared invalid by reason
of a non-compliance with the rules contained in the
First Schedule to this Act, or any mistake in the use
of the forms in the Second Schedule to this Act, if
it appears to the tribunal having cognizance of the
question that the election was conducted in accordance
with the principles laid down in the body of this
Act, and that such non-compliance or mistake did
not affect the result of the election.

Non-compliance with rules.

14. Where a parliamentary borough and municipal
borough occupy the whole or any part of the same
area, any ballot boxes or fittings for polling stations
and compartments provided for such parliamentary
borough or such municipal borough may be used in
any municipal or parliamentary election in such
borough free of charge, and any damage other than
reasonable wear and tear caused to the same shall be
paid as part of the expenses of the election at which
they are so used.

Use of municipal ballot boxes, &c., for parliamentary election, and vice versâ.

15. This part of this Act shall, so far as is
consistent with the tenor thereof, be construed as
one with the enactments for the time being in force
relating to the representation of the people, and to
the registration of persons entitled to vote at the
election of members to serve in Parliament, and with
any enactments otherwise relating to the subject
matter of this part of this Act, and terms used in
this part of this Act shall have the same meaning as

Construction of Act.

in the said enactments; and in construing the said enactments relating to an election or to the poll or taking the votes by poll, the mode of election and of taking the poll established by this Act shall for the purposes of the said enactments be deemed to be substituted for the mode of election or poll, or taking the votes by poll, referred to in the said enactments; and any person applying for a ballot paper under this Act shall be deemed "to tender his vote," or "to assume to vote," within the meaning of the said enactments; and any application for a ballot paper under this Act, or expressions relative thereto, shall be equivalent to "voting" in the said enactments, and any expressions relative thereto; and the term "polling booth" as used in the said enactments shall be deemed to include a polling station; and the term "proclamation" as used in the said enactments shall be deemed to include a public notice given in pursuance of this Act.

16. Application of part of Act to Scotland.

17, 18, and 19. Application of part of Act to Ireland.

PART II.

MUNICIPAL ELECTIONS.

Application to municipal election of enactments relating to the poll at parliamentary elections.

20. The poll at every contested municipal election shall, so far as circumstances admit, be conducted in the manner in which the poll is by this Act directed to be conducted at a contested parliamentary election, and, subject to the modifications expressed in the schedules annexed hereto, such provisions of this Act and of the said schedules as relate to or are concerned with a poll at a parliamentary election shall apply to a poll at a contested municipal election: Provided as follows:

1. The term "returning officer" shall mean the mayor or other officer who, under the law relating to municipal elections, presides at such elections:

2. The term "petition questioning the election or return" shall mean any proceeding in which a municipal election can be questioned:

3. The mayor shall provide everything which in the case of a parliamentary election is required to be provided by the returning officer for the purpose of a poll:

4. All expenses shall be defrayed in manner provided by law with respect to the expenses of a municipal election:

5. No return shall be made to the Clerk of the Crown in Chancery:

6. Nothing in this Act shall be deemed to authorise the appointment of any agents of a candidate in a municipal election, but if in the case of a municipal election any agent of a candidate is appointed, and a notice in writing of such appointment is given to the returning officer, the provisions of this Act with respect to agents of candidates shall, so far as respects such agent, apply in the case of that election :

7. The provisions of this Act with respect to—
    (a.) The voting of a returning officer; and
    (b.) The use of a room for taking a poll; and
    (c.) The right to vote of persons whose names are on the register of voters;
shall not apply in the case of a municipal election.

A municipal election shall, except in so far as relates to the taking of the poll in the event of its being contested, be conducted in the manner in which it would have been conducted if this Act had not passed.

21. Assessors shall not be elected in any ward of any municipal borough, and a municipal election need not be held before the assesssors or their deputies, but may be held before the mayor, alderman, or other returning officer only. *Abolition of ward assessors.*

22. Application of part of Act to Scotland.
23. Application of part of Act to Ireland.

PART III.
PERSONATION.

24. The following enactments shall be made with respect to personation at parliamentary and municipal elections: *Definition and punishment of personation.*

A person shall for all purposes of the laws relating to parliamentary and municipal elections be deemed to be guilty of the offence of personation who at an election for a county or borough, or at a municipal election applies for a ballot paper in the name of some other person, whether that name be that of a person living or dead or of a fictitious person, or who having voted once at any such election applies at the same election for a ballot paper in his own name.

The offence of personation, or of aiding, abetting, counselling, or procuring the commission of the offence of personation by any person, shall be a felony, and any person convicted thereof shall be punished by imprisonment for a term not exceeding two years together with hard labour. It shall be the duty of the returning officer to institute a prosecution against any person whom he may believe to have been guilty of personation, or of aiding, abetting, counselling, or procuring the commission of the offence of personation by any person, at the election for which he is returning officer, and the costs and expenses of the prosecutor and the witnesses in such case, together with compensation for their trouble and loss of time, shall be allowed by the court in the same manner in which courts are empowered to allow the same in cases of felony.

The provisions of the Registration Acts, specified in the third Schedule to this Act, shall in England and Ireland respectively apply to personation under this Act in the same manner as they apply to a person who knowingly personates and falsely assumes to vote in the name of another person as mentioned in the said Acts.

The offence of personation shall be deemed to be a corrupt practice within the meaning of the Parliamentary Elections Act, 1868.

If, on the trial of any election petition questioning the election or return for any county or borough, any candidate is found by the report of the judge by himself or his agents to have been guilty of personation, or by himself or his agents to have aided, abetted, counselled, or procured the commission at such election of the offence of personation by any person, such candidate shall be incapable of being elected or sitting in Parliament for such county or borough during the Parliament then in existence.

Vote to be struck off for bribery, treating, or undue Influence.

25. Where a candidate, on the trial of an election petition claiming the seat for any person, is proved to have been guilty, by himself or by any person on his behalf, of bribery, treating, or undue influence in respect of any person who voted at such election, or where any person retained or employed for reward by or on behalf of such candidate for all or any of the purposes of such election, as agent, clerk, messenger, or in any other employment, is proved on such trial to have voted at such election, there shall, on a scrutiny, be struck off from the number of

votes appearing to have been given to such candidate one vote for every person who voted at such election and is proved to have been bribed, treated, or unduly influenced, or so retained or employed for reward as aforesaid.

26. *This part of this Act to apply to Scotland, subject as therein mentioned.*

Alterations in Act as applying to Scotland.

27. This part of this Act, so far as regards parliamentary elections, shall be construed as one with " The Parliamentary Elections Act, 1868," and shall apply to an election for a university or combination of universities.

Construction of part of Act.

PART IV.
MISCELLANEOUS.

28. The schedules to this Act, and the notes thereto, and directions therein, shall be construed and have effect as part of this Act.

Effect of schedules.

29. In this Act—

Definitions.

The expression "municipal borough" means any place for the time being subject to the Municipal Corporation Acts, or any of them:

" Municipal borough"

The expression "Municipal Corporation Acts" means—

" Municipal Corporation Acts:"

(a) As regards England, the Act of the session of the fifth and sixth years of the reign of King William the Fourth, chapter seventy-six, intituled "An Act to provide for the regulation of municipal corporations in England and Wales," and the Acts amending the same:

(b) (As regards Scotland.)

(c) (As regards Ireland.)

The expression "municipal election" means—

(a) As regards England, an election of any person to serve the office of councillor, auditor, or assessor of any municipal borough, or of councillor for a ward of a municipal borough; and

" Municipal election."

(b) (As regards Scotland.)

(c) (As regards Ireland.)

30. This Act shall apply to any parliamentary or municipal election which may be held after the passing thereof.

Application of Act.

31. Nothing in this Act, except Part III. thereof, shall apply to any election for a university or combination of universities.

Saving.

32. Repeal of Acts in schedules.

33. This Act may be cited as the Ballot Act, 1872, and shall continue in force till the thirty-first day of December, one thousand eight hundred and eighty,

Short title.

and no longer, unless Parliament shall otherwise
determine; and on the said day the Acts in the fourth,
fifth, and sixth schedules shall be thereupon revived;
provided that such revival shall not affect any act
done, any rights acquired, any liability or penalty
incurred, or any proceeding pending under this Act,
but such proceeding shall be carried on as if this
Act had continued in force.

SCHEDULES.

FIRST SCHEDULE.

PART 1.
RULES FOR PARLIAMENTARY ELECTIONS.
Election.

1. The returning officer shall, in the case of a county
election, within two days after the day on which he
receives the writ and in the case of a borough
election on the day on which he receives the writ, or
the following day, give public notice, between the
hours of nine in the morning and four in the afternoon, of the day on which and the place at which
he will proceed to an election, and of the time
appointed for the election, and of the day on which the
poll will be taken in case the election is contested, and
of the time and place at which forms of nomination
papers may be obtained, and in the case of a county
election shall send one of such notices by post under
cover to the postmaster of the principal post-office
of each polling place in the county, endorsed with
the words "Notice of election," and the same shall
be forwarded free of charge; and the postmaster
receiving the same shall forthwith publish the same
in the manner in which post-office notices are usually
published.

2. The day of election shall be fixed by the returning officer as follows; that is to say, in the case of
an election for a county or a district borough not
later than the ninth day after the day on which he
receives the writ, with an interval of not less than
three clear days between the day on which he gives
the notice and the day of election; and in the case
of an election for any borough other than a district
borough not later than the fourth day after the day
on which he receives the writ, with an interval of
not less than two clear days between the day on
which he gives the notice and the day of election.

3 .The place of election shall be a convenient room situate in the town in which such election would have been held if this Act had not passed, or where the election would not have been held in a town, then situate in such town in the county as the returning officer may from time to time determine as being in his opinion most convenient for the electors.

4. The time appointed for the election shall be such two hours between the hours of ten in the forenoon and three in the afternoon as may be appointed by the returning officer, and the returning officer shall attend during those two hours and for one hour after.

5. Each candidate shall be nominated by a separate nomination paper, but the same electors or any of them may subscribe as many nomination papers as there are vacancies to be filled, but no more.

6. Each candidate shall be described in the nomination paper in such manner as in the opinion of the returning officer is calculated to sufficiently identify such candidate; the description shall include his name, his abode, and his rank, profession, or calling, and his surname shall come first in the list of his names. No objection to a nomination paper on the ground of the description of the candidate therein being insufficient, or not being in compliance with this rule, shall be allowed or deemed valid, unless such objection is made by the returning officer, or by some other person, at or immediately after the time of the delivery of the nomination paper.

7. The returning officer shall supply form of nomination paper to any registered elector requiring the same during such two hours as the returning officer may fix, between the hours of ten in the morning and two in the afternoon on each day intervening between the day on which notice of the election was given and the day of election, and during the time appointed for the election; but nothing in this Act shall render obligatory the use of a nomination paper supplied by the returning officer, so, however, that the paper be in the form prescribed by this Act.

8. The nomination papers shall be delivered to the returning officer at the place of election during the time appointed for the election; and the candidate nominated by each nomination paper, and his proposer and seconder, and one other person selected by the candidate, and no person other than aforesaid, shall except for the purpose of assisting the return-

ing officer, be entitled to attend the proceedings during the time appointed for the election.

9. If the election is contested the returning officer shall, as soon as practicable after adjourning the election, give public notice of the day on which the poll will be taken, and of the candidates described as in their respective nomination papers, and of the names of the persons who subscribed the nomination paper of each candidate, and of the order in which the names of the candidates will be printed in the ballot paper, and, in the case of an election for a county, deliver to the postmaster of the principal post office of the town in which is situate the place of election a paper, signed by himself, containing the names of the candidates nominated, and stating the day on which the poll is to be taken, and the postmaster shall forward the information contained in such paper by telegraph, free of charge, to the several postal telegraph offices situate in the county for which the election is to be held, and such information shall be published forthwith at each such office in the manner in which post-office notices are usually published.

10. If any candidate nominated during the time appointed for the election is withdrawn in pursuance of this Act, the returning officer shall give public notice of the name of such candidate, and the names of the persons who subscribed the nomination paper of such candidate, as well as of the candidates who stood nominated or were elected.

11. The returning officer shall, on the nomination paper being delivered to him, forthwith publish notice of the name of the person nominated as a candidate, and of the names of his proposer and seconder, by placarding or causing to be placarded the names of the candidate and his proposer and seconder in a conspicuous position outside the building in which the room is situate appointed for the election.

12. A person shall not be entitled to have his name inserted in any ballot paper as a candidate unless he has been nominated in manner provided by this Act, and every person whose nomination paper has been delivered to the returning officer during the time appointed for the election shall be deemed to have been nominated in manner provided by this Act, unless objection be made to his nomination paper by the returning officer or some other person before the expiration of the time appointed for the election or within one hour afterwards.

13. The returning officer shall decide on the validity of every objection made to a nomination paper, and his decision, if disallowing the objection, shall be final; but if allowing the same shall be subject to reversal on petition questioning the election of return.

The Poll.

14. The poll shall take place on such day as the returning officer may appoint, not being in the case of an election for a county or a district borough less than two nor more than six clear days, and not being in the case of an election for a borough other than a district borough more than three clear days after the day fixed for the election.

15. At every polling place the returning officer shall provide a sufficient number of polling stations for the accommodation of the electors entitled to vote at such polling place, and shall distribute the polling stations amongst those electors in such manner as he thinks most convenient, provided that in a district borough there shall be at least one polling station at each contributory place of such borough.

16. Each polling station shall be furnished with such number of compartments in which the voters can mark their votes screened from observation, as the returning officer thinks necessary, so that at least one compartment be provided for every one hundred and fifty electors entitled to vote at such polling station.

17. A separate room or separate booth may contain a separate polling station, or several polling stations may be constructed in the same room or booth.

18. No person shall be admitted to vote at any polling station except the one allotted to him.

19. The returning officer shall give public notice of the situation of polling stations and the description of voters entitled to vote at each station, and of the mode in which electors are to vote.

20. The returning officer shall provide each polling station with materials for voters to mark the ballot papers with instruments for stamping thereon the official mark and with copies of the register of voters or such part thereof as contains the names of the voters allotted to vote at such station. He shall keep the official mark secret, and an interval of not less than seven years shall intervene between the use of the same official mark at elections for the same county or borough.

21. The returning officer shall appoint a presiding officer to preside at each station, and the officer so appointed shall keep order at his station, shall regulate the number of electors to be admitted at a time, and shall exclude all other persons except the clerks, the agents of the candidates, and the constables on duty.

22. Every ballot paper shall contain a list of the candidates described as in their respective nomination papers and arranged alphabetically in the order of their surnames, and (if there are two or more candidates with the same surname) of their other names. It shall be in the form set forth in the Second Schedule to this Act or as near thereto as circumstances admit, and shall be capable of being folded up.

23. Every ballot box shall be so constructed that the ballot papers can be introduced therein but cannot be withdrawn therefrom without the box being unlocked. The presiding officer at any polling station just before the commencement of the poll shall show the ballot box empty to such persons, if any, as may be present in such station, so that they may see that it is empty, and shall then lock it up and place his seal upon it in such manner as to prevent its being opened without breaking such seal, and shall place it in his view for the receipt of ballot papers and keep it so locked and sealed.

24. Immediately before a ballot paper is delivered to an elector it shall be marked on both sides with the official mark, either stamped or perforated, and the number, name, and description of the elector, as stated in the copy of the register, shall be called out, and the number of such elector shall be marked on the counterfoil, and a mark shall be placed in the register against the number of the elector, to denote that he has received a ballot paper, but without showing the particular ballot paper which he has received.

25. The elector, on receiving the ballot paper, shall forthwith proceed into one of the compartments in the polling station, and there mark his paper, and fold it up so as to conceal his vote, and shall then put his ballot paper, so folded up, into the ballot box; he shall vote without undue delay, and shall quit the polling station as soon as he has put his ballot paper into the ballot box.

26. The presiding officer, on the application of any voter who is incapacitated by blindness or other physical cause from voting in manner prescribed in

this Act or (if the poll be taken on Saturday) of any voter who declares that he is of the Jewish persuasion, and objects on religious grounds to vote in manner prescribed by this Act, or of any voter who makes such a declaration as hereinafter mentioned that he is unable to read, shall, in the presence of the agents of the candidates, cause the vote of such voter to be marked on a ballot paper in manner directed by such voter, and the ballot paper to be placed in the ballot box, and the name and number on the register of voters of every voter whose vote is marked in pursuance of this rule, and the reason why it is so marked shall be entered on a list in this Act called "the list of votes marked by the presiding officer."

The said declaration, in this Act referred to as "the declaration of inability to read," shall be made by the voter at the time of polling, before the presiding officer, who shall attest it in the form hereinafter mentioned, and no fee, stamp, or other payment shall be charged in respect of such declaration, and the said declaration shall be given to the presiding officer at the time of voting.

27. If a person, representing himself to be a particular elector named on the register, applies for a ballot paper after another person has voted as such elector, the applicant shall, upon duly answering the questions and taking the oath permitted by law to be asked of and to be administered to voters at the time of polling, be entitled to mark a ballot paper in the same manner as any other voter, but the ballot paper (in this Act called a tendered ballot paper) shall be of a colour differing from the other ballot papers, and instead of being put into the ballot box, shall be given to the presiding officer and endorsed by him with the name of the voter and his number in the register of voters, and set aside in a separate packet, and shall not be counted by the returning officer. And the name of the voter and his number on the register shall be entered on a list in this Act called the tendered votes list.

28. A voter who has inadvertently dealt with this ballot paper in such manner that it cannot be conveniently used as a ballot paper, may, on delivering to the presiding officer the ballot paper so inadvertently dealt with, and proving the fact of the inadvertence to the satisfaction of the presiding officer, obtain another ballot paper in the place of

89

the ballot paper so delivered up (in this Act called a spoilt ballot paper), and the spoilt ballot paper shall be immediately cancelled.

29. The presiding officer of each station, as soon as practicable after the close of the poll, shall, in the presence of the agents of the candidates, make up into separate packets, sealed with his own seal and the seal of such agents of the candidates as desire to affix their seals, —

1. Each ballot box in use at his station, un-opened but with the key attached; and

2. The unused and spoilt ballot papers, placed together; and

3. The tendered ballot papers; and

4. The marked copies of the register of voters, and the counterfoils of the ballot papers; and

5. The tendered votes list, and the list of votes marked by the presiding officer, and a statement of the number of the voters whose votes are so marked by the presiding officer under the heads " physical incapacity," " Jews," and " unable to read," and the declarations of inability to read;

and shall deliver such packets to the returning officer.

30. The packets shall be accompanied by a statement made by such presiding officer, showing the number of ballot papers entrusted to him, and accounting for them under the heads of ballot papers in the ballot box, unused, spoilt, and tendered ballot papers, which statement is in this Act referred to as the ballot paper account.

Counting Votes.

31. The candidates may respectively appoint agents to attend the counting of the votes.

32. The returning officer shall make arrangements for counting the votes in the presence of the agents of the candidates as soon as practicable after the close of the poll, and shall give to the agents of the candidates appointed to attend at the counting of the votes notice in writing of the time and place at which he will begin to count the same.

33. The returning officer, his assistants and clerks and the agents of the candidates, and no other person, except with the sanction of the returning officer, may be present at the counting of the votes.

34. Before the returning officer proceeds to count the votes, he shall, in the presence of the

agents of the candidates, open each ballot box, and, taking out the papers therein, shall count and record the number thereof, and then mix together the whole of the ballot papers contained in the ballot boxes. The returning officer, while counting and recording the number of ballot papers and counting the votes, shall keep the ballot papers with their faces upwards, and take all proper precautions for preventing any person from seeing the numbers printed on the backs of such papers.

35. The returning officer shall, so far as practicable, proceed continuously with counting the votes, allowing only time for refreshment, and excluding (except so far as he and the agents otherwise agree) the hours between seven o'clock at night and nine o'clock on the succeeding morning. During the excluded time the returning officer shall place the ballot papers and other documents relating to the election under his own seal and the seals of such of the agents of the candidates as desire to affix their seals, and shall otherwise take proper precautions for the security of such papers and documents.

36. The returning officer shall endorse "rejected" on any ballot paper which he may reject as invalid, and shall add to the endorsement "rejection objected to," if an objection be in fact made by any agent to his decision. The returning officer shall report to the Clerk of the Crown in Chancery the numbers of ballot papers rejected and not counted by him under the several heads of—

1. Want of official mark;
2. Voting for more candidates than entitled to;
3. Writing or mark by which voter could be identified;
4. Unmarked or void for uncertainty;

and shall on request allow any agents of the candidates, before such report is sent, to copy it.

37. Upon the completion of the counting, the returning officer shall seal up in separate packets the counted and rejected ballot papers. He shall not open the sealed packet of tendered ballot papers or marked copy of the register of voters and counterfoils, but shall proceed, in the presence of the agents of the candidates, to verify the ballot paper account given by each presiding officer by comparing it with the number of ballot papers recorded by him as aforesaid, and the unused and spoilt ballot papers in his possession and the tendered votes list, and shall reseal

each sealed packet after examination. The returning officer shall report to the Clerk of the Crown in Chancery the result of such verification, and shall, on request, allow any agents of the candidates, before such report is sent, to copy it.

38. Lastly, the returning officer shall forward to the Clerk of the Crown in Chancery (in manner in which the poll books are by any existing enactment required to be forwarded to such clerk, or as near thereto as circumstances admit) all the packets of ballot papers in his possession, together with the said reports, the ballot paper accounts, tendered votes lists, lists of votes marked by the presiding officer, statements relating thereto, declarations of inability to read, and packets of counterfoils, and marked copies of registers, sent by each presiding officer, endorsing on each packet a description of its contents and the date of the election to which they relate, and the name of the county or borough for which such election was held; and the term poll book in any such enactment shall be construed to include any document forwarded in pursuance of this rule.

39. The Clerk of the Crown shall retain for a year all documents relating to an election forwarded to him in pursuance of this Act by a returning officer, and then, unless otherwise directed by an order of the House of Commons, or of one of Her Majesty's Superior Courts, shall cause them to be destroyed.

40. No person shall be allowed to inspect any rejected ballot papers in the custody of the clerk of the Crown in Chancery, except under the order of the House of Commons or under the order of one of Her Majesty's Superior Courts, to be granted by such court on being satisfied by evidence on oath that the inspection or production of such ballot papers is required for the purpose of instituting or maintaining a prosecution for an offence in relation to ballot papers, or for the purpose of a petition questioning an election or return; and any such order for the inspection or production of ballot papers may be made subject to such conditions as to persons, time, place, and mode of inspection or production as the House or court making the same may think expedient, and shall be obeyed by the Clerk of the Crown in Chancery. Any power given to a court by this rule may be exercised by any judge of such court at chambers.

41. No person shall, except by order of the House of Commons or any tribunal having cognizance of petitions complaining of undue returns or undue elections, open the sealed packet of counterfoils after the same has been once sealed up, or be allowed to inspect any counted ballot papers in the custody of the Clerk of the Crown in Chancery; such order may be made subject to such conditions as to persons, time, place, and mode of opening or inspection as the House or tribunal making the order may think expedient; provided that on making and carrying into effect any such order care shall be taken that the mode in which any particular elector has voted shall not be discovered until he has been proved to have voted, and his vote has been declared by a competent court to be invalid.

42. All documents forwarded by a returning officer in pursuance of this Act to the Clerk of the Crown in Chancery, other than ballot papers and counterfoils, shall be open to public inspection at such time and under such regulations as may be prescribed by the Clerk of the Crown in Chancery with the consent of the Speaker of the House of Commons, and the Clerk of the Crown shall supply copies of or extracts from the said documents to any person demanding the same, on payment of such fees and subject to such regulations as may be sanctioned by the Treasury.

43. Where an order is made for the production by the Clerk of the Crown in Chancery of any document in his possession relating to any specified election, the production by such clerk, or his agent of the document ordered, in such manner as may be directed by such order, or by a rule of the court having power to make such order, shall be conclusive evidence that such document relates to the specified election; and any endorsement appearing in any packet of ballot papers produced by such Clerk of the Crown or his agent shall be evidence of such papers being what they are stated to be by the endorsement. The production from proper custody of a ballot paper purporting to have been used at any election, and of a counterfoil marked with the same printed number and having a number marked thereon in writing, shall be primâ facie evidence that the person who voted by such ballot paper was the person who at the time of such election had affixed to his name in the register of voters at such election the same number as the number written on such counterfoil. .

General Provisions.

44. The return of a member or members elected to serve in Parliament for any county or borough shall be made by a certificate of the names of such member or members under the hand of the returning officer endorsed on the writ of election for such county or borough, and such certificate shall have effect and be dealt with in like manner as the return under the existing law, and the returning officer may, if he think fit, deliver the writ with such certificate endorsed to the postmaster of the principal post office of the place of election, or his deputy, and in that case he shall take a receipt from the postmaster or his deputy for the same; and such postmaster or his deputy shall then forward the same by the first post, free of charge, under cover, to the Clerk of the Crown, with the words " Election Writ and Return " endorsed thereon.

45. The returning officer shall, as soon as possible, give public notice of the names of the candidates elected, and, in the case of a contested election, of the total number of votes given for each candidate, whether elected or not.

46. Where the returning officer is required or authorised by this Act to give any public notice, he shall carry such requirement into effect by advertisements, placards, handbills,' or such other means as he thinks best calculated to afford information to the electors.

47. The returning officer may, if he think fit, preside at any polling station, and the provisions of this Act relating to a presiding officer shall apply to such returning officer with the necessary modifications as to things to be done by the returning officer to the presiding officer, or the presiding officer to the returning officer.

48. In the case of a contested election for any county or borough, the returning officer may, in addition to any clerks, appoint competent persons to assist him in counting the votes.

49. No person shall be appointed by a returning officer for the purposes of an election who has been employed by any other person in or about the election,

50. The presiding officer may do, by the clerks appointed to assist him, any act which he is required or authorised to do by this Act at a polling station,

except ordering the arrest, exclusion, or ejection from the polling station of any person.

51. A candidate may himself undertake the duties which any agent of his if appointed might have undertaken, or may assist his agent in the performance of such duties, and may be present at any place at which his agent may, in pursuance of this Act, attend.

52. The name and address of every agent of a candidate appointed to attend the counting of the votes shall be transmitted to the returning officer one clear day at the least before the opening of the poll; and the returning officer may refuse to admit to the place where the votes are counted any agent whose name and address has not been so transmitted, notwithstanding that his appointment may be otherwise valid, and any notice required to be given to an agent by the returning officer may be delivered at or sent by post to such address.

53. If any person appointed an agent by a candidate for the purposes of attending at the polling station or at the counting of the votes dies, or becomes incapable of acting during the time of the election, the candidate may appoint another agent in his place, and shall forthwith give to the returning officer notice in writing of the name and address of the agent so appointed.

54. Every returning officer, and every officer, clerk, or agent authorised to attend at a polling station, or at the counting of the votes, shall, before the opening of the poll, make a statutory declaration of secrecy, in the presence, if he is the returning officer, of a justice of the peace, and if he is any other officer or an agent, of a justice of the peace or of the returning officer; but no such returning officer, officer, clerk, or agent as aforesaid shall, save as aforesaid, be required, as such, to make any declaration or take any oath on the occasion of any election.

55. Where in this Act any expressions are used requiring or authorising or inferring that any act or thing is to be done in the presence of the agents of the candidates, such expressions shall be deemed to refer to the presence of such agents of the candidates as may be authorized to attend, and as have in fact attended, at the time and place where such act or thing is being done, and the non-attendance of any agent or agents at such time and place shall

not, if such act or thing be otherwise duly done, in anywise invalidate the act or thing done.

56. In reckoning time for the purposes of this Act, Sunday, Christmas Day, Good Friday, and any day set apart for a public fast or public thanksgiving, shall be excluded; and where anything is required by this Act to be done on any day which falls on the above-mentioned days such thing may be done on the next day, unless it is one of the days excluded as above mentioned.

57. In this Act—

> The expression "district borough" means the borough of Monmouth and any of the boroughs specified in Schedule E. to the Act of the session of the second and third years of the reign of King William the Fourth, chapter forty-five, intituled "An Act to amend the Representation of the People in England and Wales"; and

> The expression "polling place" means, in the case of a borough, such borough or any part thereof in which a separate booth is required or authorized by law to be provided; and

> The expression "agents of the candidates," used in relation to a polling station, means agents appointed in pursuance of section eighty-five of the Act of the session of the sixth and seventh years of the reign of Her present Majesty, chapter eighteen.

58—61. *Modifications in Application of Part One of Schedule to Scotland.*

62—63. *Modifications in Application of Part One of Schedule to Ireland.*

PART II.

RULES FOR MUNICIPAL ELECTIONS.

64. In the application of the provisions of this schedule to municipal elections the following modifications shall be made :—

> (a.) The expression "register of voters" means the burgess roll of the burgesses of the borough, or, in the case of an election for the ward of a borough, the ward list; and the mayor shall provide true copies of such register for each polling station :

> (b.) All ballot papers and other documents which, in the case of a parliamentary election are forwarded to the Clerk of the Crown in Chan-

cery shall be delivered to the town clerk of the municipal borough in which the election is held, and shall be kept by him among the records of the borough; and the provisions of part one of this schedule with respect to the inspection, production, and destruction of such ballot papers and documents, and to the copies of such documents, shall apply respectively to the ballot papers and documents so in the custody of the town clerk, with these modifications; namely,

(a.) An order of the county court having jurisdiction in the borough, or any part thereof, or of any tribunal in which a municipal election is questioned, shall be substituted for an order of the House of Commons or of one of Her Majesty's Superior Courts; but an appeal from such county court may be had in like manner as in other cases in such county court;

(b.) The regulations for the inspection of documents and the fees for the supply of copies of documents of which copies are directed to be supplied, shall be prescribed by the council of the borough with the consent of one of Her Majesty's Principal Secretaries of State; and, subject as aforesaid, the town clerk, in respect of the custody and destruction of the ballot papers and other documents coming into his possession in pursuance of this Act, shall be subject to the directions of the council of the borough:

(c.) Nothing in this schedule with respect to the day of the poll shall apply to a municipal election.

65. *Modifications in Application of Part Two of Schedule to Scotland.*

66. *Modifications in Application of Part Two of Schedule to Ireland.*

SECOND SCHEDULE.

Note. —The forms contained in this schedule, or forms as nearly resembling the same as circumstances will admit, shall be used in all cases to which they refer and are applicable, and when so used shall be sufficient in law.

Writ for a County or Borough at a Parliamentary Election.

* The name of the Sovereign may be altered when necessary.

† Insert "sheriff" or other returning officer.

‡ This preamble to be omitted except in case of a general election.

§ Except in a general election, insert here in the place of A.B., deceased, or otherwise, stating the cause of vacancy.

* Victoria, by the Grace of God, of the United Kingdom of Great Britain and Ireland, Queen, Defender of the Faith, to the † of the county [or borough] of , greeting:

‡ Whereas by the advice of our Council we have ordered a Parliament to be holden at Westminster on the day of next. We command you that, notice of the time and place of election being first duly given, you do cause election to be made according to law of members [or a member] to serve in Parliament for the said county [or the division of the said county, or the borough, or as the case may be] of § and that you do cause the names of such members [or member] when so elected, whether they [or he] be present or absent, to be certified to us, in our Chancery, without delay.

Witness ourself at Westminster, the day of in the year of our reign, and in the year of our Lord 18

Label or direction of Writ.

To the of
A writ of a new election of members [or member] for the said county [or division of a county or borough, or as the case may be.]

Endorsement.

Received the within writ on the day of 18

(Signed) A. B.,

High Sheriff [or Sheriff] or Mayor, or as the case may be.]

Certificate endorsed on the Writ.

I hereby certify, that the members [or member] elected for in pursuance of the within-written writ, are [or is] A. B. of in the county of and C. D. of in the county of

(Signed) A. B.,

High Sheriff [or Sheriff, or Mayor, or as the case may be].

Note.—A separate writ will be issued for each county defined for the purposes of a parliamentary election.

Form of Notice of Parliamentary Election.

The returning officer of the   of
will, on the   day of   now next ensuing,
between the hours of   and   proceed to the
nomination, and, if there is no opposition, to the
election, of a member [*or* members] for the said county
or division of a county or borough at the*

> * *Note.* Insert description of place and room.

Forms of nomination paper may be obtained at
, * between the hours of   and   on   .

Every nomination paper must be signed by two
registered electors as proposer and seconder, and by
eight other registered electors as assenting to the
nomination.

Every nomination paper must be delivered to the
returning officer by the candidate proposed, or by
his proposer and seconder, between the said hours
of   and   on the said
day of   at the said   *.

Each candidate nominated, and his proposer and
seconder, and one other person selected by the
candidate, and no other persons, are entitled to be
admitted to the room.

In the event of the election being contested, the
poll will take place on the   day of   .

(Signed) *A.B.*,

Sheriff [*or* Mayor, *or as the case may be*]
day of   18   .

Take notice, that all persons who are guilty of
bribery, treating, undue influence, personation, or other
corrupt practices at the said election will, on
conviction of such offence, be liable to the penalties
mentioned in that behalf in "The Corrupt Practices
Prevention Act, 1854," and the Ballot Act, 1872, and
the Acts amending the said Acts.

Form of Nomination Paper in Parliamentary Election.

We, the undersigned, *A.B.* of   in the
of   and *C.D.* of   in the   of
being electors for the   of   , do
hereby nominate the following person as a proper
person to serve as member for the said   in
Parliament:

99   H 2

Surname.	Other Names.	Abode.	Rank, Profession, or Occupation.
BROWN	JOHN - - -	52, George St., Bristol.	Merchant.
JONES	*or* WILLIAM DAVID -	High Elms, Wilts	Esquire.
MERTON	*or* Hon. GEORGE TRAVIS, commonly called Viscount.	Swanworth, Berks	Viscount.
SMITH	*or* HENRY SYDNEY, -	72, High St., Bath.	Attorney.

(Signed) *A. B.*

C. D.

We, the undersigned, being registered electors of the   , do hereby assent to the nomination of the above-mentioned *John Brown* as a proper person to serve as member for the said   in Parliament.

(Signed) *E.F.* of	*M.N.* of
G. H. of	*O.P.* of
I. J. of	*Q.R.* of
K L. of	*S. T.* of

Note. —Where a candidate is an Irish peer, or is commonly known by some title, he may be described by his title as if it were his surname.

Form of Nomination Paper in Municipal Election.

Note. —The form of nomination paper in a municipal election shall, as nearly as circumstances admit, be the same as in the case of a parliamentary election.

Form of Ballot Paper.
Form of Front of Ballot Paper.

Counterfoll No.		
1	**BROWN** (John Brown, of 52, George St., Bristol, merchant.)	
2	**JONES** (William David Jones, of High Elms, Wilts, Esq.)	
3	**MERTON** (Hon. George Travis, commonly called Viscount Merton, of Swanworth, Berks.)	
4	**SMITH** (Henry Sydney Smith, of 72, High Street, Bath, attorney.)	

NOTE :
The counterfoil is to have a number to correspond with that on the back of the Ballot Paper

Form of Back of Ballot Paper.

No.
Election for　　　　county [*or* borough *or* ward.]
18　　.
Note.—The number on the ballot paper is to correspond with that in the counterfoil.

Directions as to printing Ballot Paper.

Nothing is to be printed on the ballot paper except in accordance with this schedule.

The surname of each candidate, and if there are two or more candidates of the same surname, also the other names of such candidates, shall be printed in large characters, as shown in the form, and the names, addresses, and descriptions, and the number on the back of the paper, shall be printed in small characters.

Form of Directions for the Guidance of the Voter in voting, which shall be printed in conspicuous Characters, and placarded outside every Polling Station and in every Compartment of every Polling Station.

The voter may vote for　　　　candidate
The voter will go into one of the compartments, and, with the pencil provided in the compartment,

place a cross on the right hand side, opposite the name of each candidate for whom he votes, thus X.

The voter will then fold up the ballot paper so as to show the official mark on the back, and leaving the compartment will, without showing the front of the paper to any person, show the official mark on the back to the presiding officer, and then, in the presence of the presiding officer, put the paper into the ballot box and forthwith quit the polling station.

If the voter inadvertently spoil a ballot paper, he can return it to the officer, who will, if satisfied of such inadvertence, give him another paper.

If the voter votes for more than   candidate, or places any mark on the paper by which he may be afterwards identified, his ballot paper will be void and will not be counted.

If a voter takes a ballot paper out of the polling station, or deposits in the ballot box any other paper than the one given him by the officer, he will be guilty of a misdemeanor, and be subject to imprisonment for any term not exceeding six months, with or without hard labour.

Note.—These directions shall be illustrated by examples of the ballot paper.

Form of Statutory Declaration of Secrecy.

I solemnly promise and declare, that I will not at this election for   do anything forbidden by section four of the Ballot Act, 1872, which has been read to me.

Note.—The section must be read to the declarant by the person taking the declaration.

Form of Declaration of Inability to Read.

I, *A. B.*, of   , being numbered   on the Register of Voters for the county [*or* borough] of   do hereby declare that I am unable to read.

                                   A. B.,   his mark.
            day of   .

I, the undersigned, being the presiding officer for the   polling station for the county [*or* borough] of   , do hereby certify that the above declaration, having been first read to the above-named *A.B.*, was signed by him in my presence with his mark.

Signed *C. D.*

Presiding officer for　　　　　　polling
station for the county [*or* borough]
of　　　　　　day of

THIRD SCHEDULE.

Provisions of Registration Acts referred to in Part III. of the foregoing Act.

Session and Chapter.	Title.	Part applied.
	As to England.	
6 and 7 Vict. c. 18.	An Act to amend the law for the registration of persons entitled to vote, and to define certain rights of voting, and to regulate certain proceedings in the elections of members to serve in Parliament for England and Wales.	ss. 85 to 89, both inclusive.

FOURTH SCHEDULE.
(Acts relating to England repealed.)

FIFTH SCHEDULE.
(Acts relating to Scotland repealed.)

SIXTH SCHEDULE.
(Acts relating to Ireland repealed, Ballot Act, p. 36.)

---

35 & 36 Vic. c. 60.

An Act for the better prevention of Corrupt Practices at Municipal Elections, and for establishing a Tribunal for the trial of the validity of such elections. [*6th August*, 1872.]

WHEREAS it is expedient to make provision for the better prevention of corrupt practices at municipal elections and for establishing a tribunal for the trial of the validity of such elections:

Be it enacted by the Queen's most Excellent Majesty, by and with the advice and consent of the Lords Spiritual and Temporal, and Commons, in this present Parliament assembled, and by the authority of the same as follows:

Short title.   1. This Act may be cited for all purposes as the
"Corrupt Practices (Municipal Elections) Act, 1872."

Definitions.   2. In this Act, except where the context otherwise
requires, the following words and expressions shall
respectively be construed as follows, viz.:

    1. "Borough" means a place for the time being
subject to the provisions of the Act of the
fifth and sixth of William the Fourth, chapter
seventy-six, intituled "An Act to provide
for the regulation of municipal corporations
in England and Wales," as amended by the
Acts amending the said Act:

"Office" means the office of mayor, alderman,
councillor, auditor, or assessor, of a borough
or ward of a borough:

"Election" means an election to an office:

"Candidate" means a person elected, or who
has been nominated or has declared himself
a candidate for election to an office:

"Canvasser" means any person who solicits
or persuades, or attempts to persuade, any
person to vote or to abstain from voting at
an election, or to vote or to abstain from
voting for any candidate at an election:

"Register" includes a burgess roll or ward list:

"Voter" means a person included in a register,
or who voted or claimed to vote at an election:

"Returning officer" means a person under whatever designation presiding at an election:

"Election court" means an election court constituted and acting under the provisions of
this Act for the trial of a petition respecting
an election:

"Superior court" means the Court of Common
Pleas at Westminster:

"Prescribed" means prescribed by general rules
to be made under the provisions of this Act.

    2. This Act shall so far as is consistent with the
tenor thereof be construed as one with the Acts
for the time being in force relating to boroughs
and to elections in boroughs.

Part I.

Corrupt Practices at Municipal Elections.

As to corrupt practices at municipal elections.   3. The offences of bribery, treating, undue influence,
and personation, shall be deemed to be corrupt practices
at an election for the purposes of this Act.

The terms "bribery," "treating," "undue influence," and "personation," shall respectively include anything committed or done before, at, after, or with respect to an election which if done before, at, after, or with respect to an election of members to serve in Parliament would render the person committing or doing the same liable to any penalties, punishments, or disqualifications, for bribery, treating, undue influence, or personation, as the case may be, under any Act for the time being in force with respect to elections of members to serve in Parliament.

Any person who is guilty of a corrupt practice at an election shall be liable to the like actions, prosecutions, penalties, forfeitures, and punishments, as if the corrupt practice had been committed at an election of members to serve in Parliament.

4. Where it is found by the report of an election court acting under the provisions of this Act that any corrupt practice has been committed by or with the knowledge and consent of any candidate at an election, such candidate shall be deemed to have been personally guilty of corrupt practices at the election, and his election, if he has been elected, shall be void, and he shall (whether he was elected or not) during seven years from the date of the report be subject to the following disqualifications, viz., *Disqualifications of candidates personally guilty of corrupt practices.*

1. He shall be incapable of holding or exercising any municipal office or franchise, and of having his name placed on the register, or voting at any municipal election :
2. He shall be incapable of acting as a justice of the peace and of holding any judicial office :
3. He shall be incapable of being elected to and of sitting or voting in Parliament :
4. He shall be incapable of being registered or voting as a parliamentary voter :
5. He shall be incapable of being employed by any candidate in any parliamentary or municipal election :
6. He shall be incapable of acting as overseer or as guardian of the poor.

If any person is upon an indictment or information found guilty of any corrupt practice at an election, or is in any action or proceeding adjudged to pay a penalty or forfeiture for any corrupt practice at an election, he shall, whether he was a candidate at the election or not, be subject during seven years from the date of the conviction or judgment to all the disqualifications mentioned in this section.

If at any time after any person has become disqualified by virtue of this Act, the witnesses, or any of them, on whose testimony such person has so become disqualified, are upon the prosecution of such person convicted of perjury in respect of such testimony, it shall be lawful for such person to move the superior court to order, and the superior court shall, upon being satisfied that such disqualification was procured by reason of perjury, order that such disqualification shall thenceforth cease and determine, and the same shall cease and determine accordingly.

Avoidance of election for corrupt practices by agents, and for offences against this Act.

5. If it is found by an election court acting under the provisions of this Act, that a candidate has by an agent been guilty of any corrupt practice at an election, or that any act herein after in this Act declared to be an offence against this Act has been committed at an election by a candidate or by an agent for a candidate with the candidate's knowledge and consent, the candidate shall during the period for which he was elected to serve, or for which, if elected, he might have served, be disqualified for being elected to and for holding any municipal office in the borough for which the election was held, and if he was elected his election shall be void.

Avoidance of election on the ground of general corruption, &c.

6. An election for a borough or a ward thereof shall be wholly avoided by such general corruption, bribery, treating, or intimidation at the election for such borough or ward as would by the common law of Parliament avoid an election of members to serve in Parliament for a parliamentary borough.

Prohibition of paid canvassers.

7. No person who is included in a register for a borough or ward thereof as a burgess or citizen shall be retained or employed for payment or reward by or on behalf of a candidate at an election for such borough or any ward thereof as a canvasser for the purposes of the election.

If any person is retained or employed by or on behalf of a candidate at an election in contravention of this prohibition, such person and also the candidate or other person by whom he is retained or employed shall be deemed to be guilty of an offence against this Act, and shall be liable on summary conviction before two justices of the peace to a penalty not exceeding ten pounds.

An agent or canvasser who is retained or employed for payment or reward for any of the purposes of an election shall not vote at the election, and if he votes he shall be guilty of an offence against this Act, and shall be liable on summary conviction before two justices of the peace to a penalty not exceeding ten pounds.

8. If a candidate or an agent for a candidate pays or agrees to pay any money on account of the conveyance of a voter to or from the poll, such candidate or agent shall be deemed to be guilty of an offence against this Act, and shall be liable on summary conviction before two justices of the peace to a penalty not exceeding five pounds.

Prohibition of payment for conveyance of voters.

9. The costs and expenses of a prosecutor and his witnesses in the prosecution of any person for either of the corrupt practices of bribery, undue influence, or personation at an election, together with compensation for trouble and loss of time, shall, unless the court before which such person is prosecuted othewise directs, be allowed, paid, and borne in the same manner in which they may be allowed, paid, and borne in cases of felony.

Prosecutions for corrupt practices.

The clerk of the peace of the county in which a borough is situate, or in the case of a borough which is a county of a city or a county of a town or in which there is a clerk of the peace, the clerk of the peace of such county of a city or county of a town or borough shall, if he is directed by an election court acting under the provisions of this Act to prosecute any person for either of the corrupt practices of bribery, undue influence, or personation at the election in respect of which the court acts, or to sue or proceed against any person for penalties for bribery, treating, undue influence, or any offence against this Act at such election, prosecute, sue, or proceed against such person accordingly.

10. The votes of persons in respect of whom any corrupt practice is proved to have been committed shall be struck off on a scrutiny. Subject to the provisions of this section a register shall for all purposes be conclusive as to the right of the persons included therein to vote at an election for the purposes whereof such register is in force; but nothing in this section shall entitle any person to vote who is by any Act or law prohibited from voting at an election on the ground of any disqualification by office or disability, nor shall relieve any such person from any penalty, liability, or punishment to which he may by law be subject by reason of his voting at an election.

Provisions for striking off votes.

As to alleged personation.

11. The provisions of the Acts for the time being in force for the detection of personation and for the apprehension of persons charged with personation at a parliamentary election shall apply in the case of a municipal election.

Part II.

Election Petitions.

Municipal elections may be questioned by petition.

12. The election of any person at an election for a borough or ward may be questioned by petition before an election court constituted as hereinafter in this Act provided, and hereinafter in this Act referred to as the "Court," on the ground that the election was as to the borough or ward wholly avoided by general bribery, treating, undue influence, or personation, or on the ground that the election of such person was avoided by corrupt practices or offences against this Act committed at the election, or on the ground that he was at the time of the election disqualified for election to the office for which the election was held, or on the ground that he was not duly elected by a majority of lawful votes.

An election shall not, except in the manner provided by this Act, be questioned upon an information in the nature of a quo warranto or by or in any process or manner whatsoever for a matter for which it might be questioned under the provisions of this Act.

Presentation of petition.

13. The following provisions shall have effect with reference to the presentation of a petition complaining of an undue election (hereinafter in this Act referred to as a "petition") :

1. A petition may be presented either by four or more persons who voted or who had a right to vote at the election or by a person alleging himself to have been a candidate at the election ;

A petition shall be in the prescribed form and shall be signed by the petitioner or petitioners, and shall be presented to the superior court in the prescribed manner, and the prescribed officer shall send a copy thereof to the town clerk of the borough to which it relates, who shall forthwith publish it in the borough ;

The terms "petitioner" and "respondent" as hereinafter used in this Act, include respectively any one or more persons by whom a petition is presented, and any one or more persons against whose election a petition is presented:

108

2. A petition shall be presented within twenty-one days after the day on which the election was held, unless it complain of the election on the ground of corrupt practices, and specifically allege a payment of money or other reward to have been made or promised since the election by a person elected at the election, or on his account or with his privity, in pursuance or furtherance of such corrupt practices, in which case it may be presented at any time within twenty-eight days after the date of the alleged payment or promise, whether or not any other petition against such person has been previously presented or tried :

3. At the time of presenting a petition or within three days afterwards, the petitioner shall give security for all costs, charges, and expenses which may become payable by him to any witness summoned on his behalf, or to any respondent. The security shall be to the amount of five hundred pounds, and shall be given in the prescribed manner either by a deposit of money or by recognizance entered into by not exceeding four sureties, or partly in one way and partly in the other:

4. Within five days after the presentation of a petition the petitioner shall in the prescribed manner serve on the respondent a notice of the presentation and of the nature of the proposed security, and a copy of the petition ; and the respondent may within five days from the service of the notice object in writing to any security by way of recognizance on the ground that any surety is insufficient or is dead, or cannot be found or ascertained for want of a sufficient description in the recognizance, or that a person named in the recognizance has not duly acknowledged the same. An objection to a recognizance shall be decided in the prescribed manner :

5. If an objection to the security is allowed it shall be lawful for the petitioner, within a further prescribed time not exceeing five days, to remove such objection by a deposit in the prescribed manner of such sum of money as may be deemed by the court or officer having cognizance of the matter to make the security sufficient ;

If on objection made the security is decided to be insufficient, and the objection is not removed in manner hereinbefore mentioned, no further proceedings shall be had on the petition; but otherwise on the expiration of the time limited for making objections, or, after objection made, on the sufficiency of the security being established, the petition shall be deemed to be at issue:

6. Where a petition complains of the conduct of a returning officer, he shall be deemed to be a respondent:

7. The prescribed officer shall so soon as may be make out a list of all petitions under this Act presented to the superior court which are at issue, placing them in the order in which they were presented, and shall keep at his office a copy of such list, hereinafter referred to as the "Municipal Election List," open to the inspection in the prescribed manner of any person making application to inspect the same:

8. The petitions shall, so far as conveniently may be, be tried in the order in which they stand in such list:

9. Two or more candidates may be made respondents to the same petition, and their cases may be tried at the same time, but for all the purposes of this Act such petition shall be deemed to be a separate petition against each respondent:

10. Where more petitions than one are presented relating to the same election, or to elections held at the same time for different wards of the same borough, all such petitions shall in the municipal election list be bracketed together as one petition, but such petitions shall stand in the list in the place where the last of such petitions would have stood if it had been the only petition relating to that election, unless the superior court otherwise directs.

Constitution of election court.

14. An election court for the trial of petitions under this Act shall be constituted as follows:

1. A petition shall be tried by a barrister qualified and appointed as hereinafter provided, without a jury:

2. So soon as may be after a municipal election list is made out a copy thereof shall by the prescribed officer be transmitted to each of the judges for the time being on the rota for the trial of election petitions under the provisions of the Parliamentary Elections Act, 1868, and the said judges or any two of them shall forth-

with determine the number of barristers, not exceeding five at any one time, necessary to be appointed for the trial of the petitions at issue, and shall appoint such number of barristers accordingly, and shall assign the petitions to be tried by them respectively:

3. No barrister shall be appointed or act for the purposes of this Act who is of less than fifteen years standing, or who is a member of Parliament, or who holds any office or place of profit under the Crown, other than that of a recorder, and no barrister shall try a petition relating to any borough for which he is recorder, or in which he resides, or which is included in a circuit of Her Majesty's judges on which he practises as a barrister:

. If a barrister to whom the trial of a petition is assigned, dies, or declines, or becomes incapable to act, the said judges or any two of them may assign the trial to be conducted or continued by any other of the barristers appointed as aforesaid:

5. The court shall for the purposes of the trial of a petition have all the same powers and privileges which a judge may have on the trial of an election petition under the provisions of the Parliamentary Elections Act, 1868, with this modification, that any fine or order of committal by the court may upon motion by the person aggrieved be discharged or varied by the superior court, or in vacation by a judge thereof, upon such terms, if any, as such superior court or judge thinks fit.

15. The following provisions shall have effect with respect to the trial of a petition: Trial of a petition.

1. A petition shall be tried in open court, and notice of the time and place at which the petition will be tried shall be given not less than seven days before the day on which the trial is held, in the prescribed manner:

2. A petition shall be tried within the borough to which it relates; provided that, if it appear to to the superior court that special circumstances exist which render it desirable that the petition should be tried elsewhere than in the borough, it shall be lawful for the superior court to appoint such other place for the trial as appears most convenient:

3   The court may adjourn the trial from time to time, and from any one place to any other place within the borough or place where it is held, as may seem expedient:

4. At the conclusion of the trial the court shall determine whether the person whose election is complained of, or any and what other person, was duly elected, or whether the election was void, and shall forthwith certify in writing the determination to the superior court, and upon the certificate being given the determination shall be final to all intents and purposes as to the matters at issue on the petition:

5. Where any charge is made in a petition of any corrupt practice or offence against this Act having been committed at the election to which the petition refers, the court shall, in addition to the certificate, and at the same time, report in writing to the superior court as follows:

> (*a.*) Whether any corrupt practice or offence against this Act has or has not been proved to have been committed by or with the knowledge and consent of any candidate at the election, and the nature of such corrupt practice or offence against this Act;
>
> (*b.*) The names of all persons (if any) who have been proved at the trial to have been guilty of any corrupt practice or offence against this Act;
>
> (*c.*) Whether any corrupt practices have, or whether there is reason to believe that any corrupt practices have extensively prevailed at the election to which the petition relates, in the borough or in any ward thereof;
>
> The court may at the same time make a special report to the superior court as to any matters arising in the course of the trial, an account of which, in the judgment of the court, ought to be submitted to the superior court:

6. Where, upon the application of any party to a petition made in the prescribed manner to the superior court, it appears to that court that the case raised by the petition can be

conveniently stated as a special case, that court may direct the same to be stated accordingly, and any such special case shall be heard before the superior court, and the decision of the superior court shall be final:

7. If it appear to the court on the trial of a petition that any question of law as to the admissibility of evidence, or otherwise, requires further consideration by the superior court, the court may postpone the granting of a certificate until such question has been determined by the superior court, and for this purpose may reserve any such question in like manner in which questions may be reserved by a judge on a trial at nisi prius :

8. On the trial of a petition, unless the court otherwise directs, any charge of a corrupt practice or offence against this Act may be gone into, and evidence in relation thereto received before any proof has been given of agency on behalf of any candidate in respect of such corrupt practice or offence :

9. On the trial of a petition complaining of an undue election and claiming the office for some person, the respondent may give evidence to prove that such person was not duly elected, in the same manner as if he had presented a petition against the election of such person :

10. The trial of a petition shall be proceeded with notwithstanding that the respondent has ceased to hold the office his election to which is questioned by the petition :

11. A copy of any certificate or report made to the superior court upon the trial of a petition or a statement of any decision made by the superior court shall by the superior court be transmitted to one of Her Majesty's Principal Secretaries of State :

12. A copy of any certificate made by the court to the superior court, or in the case of a decision by the superior court upon a special case, a statement of such decision shall be certified by the superior court, under the hands of two or more judges of the superior court, to the town clerk of the borough to which the petition relates.

16. The following provisions shall have effect with respect to witnesses at the trial of a petition : Provisions as to witnesses.

1. Witnesses shall be summoned and sworn in the same manner, as nearly as circumstances admit, as witnesses at a trial at nisi prius, and shall be liable to the same penalties for perjury:

2. On the trial of a petition the court may, by order in writing, compel the attendance of any person as a witness who appears to the court to have been concerned in the election to which the petition refers, and any person refusing to obey such order shall be guilty of contempt of court. The election court may examine any witness so compelled to attend, or any person in court although such witness is not called and examined by any party to the petition. After the examination of a witness by the election court such witness may be cross-examined by or on behalf of the petitioner and respondent or either of them :

3. The provisions of the seventh section of the Act of the twenty-sixth and twenty-seventh of Her Majesty, chapter twenty-nine, relating to the examination and indemnity of witnesses, shall apply to any witness appearing before the court on the trial of a petition under this Act, and the certificate shall be given by the court ; provided always, that the giving or refusal to give such certificate by the court shall be final and conclusive, and shall not be questioned by any proceeding or in any court whatsoever :

4. The reasonable expenses incurred by any person in appearing to give evidence at the trial of a petition according to the scale allowed to witnesses on the trial of civil actions at the assizes, may be allowed to such person by a certificate of the court or of the prescribed officer, and such expenses, if the witness was called and examined by the court, shall be deemed part of the expenses of providing a court, and in other cases shall be deemed to be costs of the petition.

Withdrawal and abatement of petitions.

17. The following provisions shall have effect with respect to the withdrawal and abatement of petitions:

1. A petition shall not be withdrawn without the leave of the court or superior court upon special application, to be made in and at the prescribed manner, time, and place ;

No such application shall be made for the withdrawal of a petition until the prescribed notice has been given in the borough to which the petition relates, of the intention of the petitioner to make an application for the withdrawal of his petition :

2. On the hearing of the application for withdrawal any person who might have been a petitioner in respect of the election to which the petition relates, may apply to the court or superior court to be substituted as a petitioner for the petitioner so desirous of withdrawing the petition ;

The court or superior court may, if it think fit, substitute as a petitioner any such applicant as aforesaid; and may further, if the proposed withdrawal is in the opinon of the court or superior court induced by any corrupt bargain or consideration, by order direct that the security given on behalf of the original petitioner shall remain as security for any costs that may be incurred by the substituted petitioner, and that to the extent of the sum named in such security the original petitioner and his sureties shall be liable to pay the costs of the substituted petitioner :

3. If no such order is made with respect to the security given on behalf of the original petitioner, security to the same amount as would be required in the case of a new petition, and subject to the like conditions, shall be given on behalf of the substituted petitioner before he proceeds with his petition, and within the prescribed time after the order of substitution :

4. Subject as aforesaid, a substituted petitioner shall stand in the same position as nearly as may be, and be subject to the same liabilities, as the original petitioner ;

If a petition is withdrawn, the petitioner shall be liable to pay the costs of the respondent ;

Where there are more petitioners than one, no application to withdraw a petition shall be made except with the consent of all the petitioners :

5. A petition shall be abated by the death of a sole petitioner or of the survivor of several petitioners :

The abatement of a petition shall not affect the liability of the petitioner or of any other person to the payment of costs previously incurred ;

On the abatement of a petition the prescribed

notice of such abatement having taken place shall be given in the borough to which the petition relates, and within the prescribed time after the notice is given, any person who might have been a petitioner in respect of the election to which the petition relates may apply to the court or superior court in and at the prescribed manner, time, and place to be substituted as a petitioner;

The court or superior court may, if it think fit, substitute as a petitioner any such applicant who is desirous of being substituted and on whose behalf security to the same amount is given as is required in the case of a new petition.

Withdrawal and substitution of respondents.

18. The following provisions shall have effect with respect to the withdrawal and substitution of respondents upon a petition :

1. If before the trial of a petition either of the following events happens in the case of a respondent other than a returning officer; viz.,

    (*a.*) If he dies, resigns, or otherwise ceases to hold the office to which the petition relates ; or

    (*b.*) If he gives the prescribed notice that he does not intend to oppose the petition ;

Notice of such event having taken place shall be given in the borough to which the petition relates, and within the prescribed time after the notice is given any person who might have been a petitioner in respect of the election to which the petition relates may apply to the court or superior court to be admitted as a respondent to oppose the petition, and such person shall be admitted accordingly, and any number of persons not exceeding three may be so admitted:

2. A respondent who has given the prescribed notice that he does not intend to oppose the petition, shall not be allowed to appear or act as a party against such petition in any proceedings thereon.

Costs on petitions.

19. The following provisions shall have effect with respect to costs on the trial of a petition :

1. All costs, charges, and expenses of and incidental to the presentation of a petition, and to the proceedings consequent thereon, with the exception of such costs, charges, and

expenses as are by this Act otherwise provided for, shall be defrayed by the parties to the petition in such manner and in such proportions as the court by which the petition is tried may determine; and in particular any cost, charges, or expenses which in the opinion of the court by which the petition is tried have been caused by vexatious conduct, unfounded allegations, or unfounded objections on the part either of the petitioner or the respondent, and any needless expense incurred or caused on the part of petitioner or respondent, may be ordered to be defrayed by the parties by whom it has been incurred or caused, whether such parties are or are not on the whole successful :

2. The costs may be taxed in the prescribed manner, but according to the same principles, as costs between attorney and client in a suit in the High Court of Chancery, and such costs may be recovered in the same manner as the costs of an action at law, or in such other manner as may be prescribed :

3. If any petitioner neglect or refuse for the space of three months after demand to pay to any person summoned as a witness on his behalf, or to the respondent, any sum certified to be due to him for his costs, charges, and expenses, and if such neglect or refusal be, within one year after such demand, proved to the satisfaction of the superior court, every person who has entered into a recognizance relating to such petition under the provisions of this Act shall be held to have made default in his said recognizance, and the prescribed officer shall thereupon certify such recognizance to be forfeited, and the same shall be dealt with in the same manner as a forfeited recognizance under the provisions of the Parliamentary Elections Act, 1868.

20. The following provisions shall have effect with reference to the reception of the court upon the trial of a petition : *Reception of and attendance on the court.*

1. The town clerk of a borough in respect of which a petition is to be tried shall provide proper accommodation for holding the election court; and any expenses incurred by him for the purposes of this section shall be paid by the

117

treasurer of the borough out of the borough fund or rate:

2. All superintendents of police, chief constables, headboroughs, gaolers, constables, and bailiffs shall give their assistance to the court in the execution of the duties of the said court, and if any gaoler or officer of a prison makes default in receiving or detaining a prisoner committed thereto in pursuance of the provisions of this Act, he shall incur a penalty not exceeding five pounds for every day during which such default continues:

3, The court may employ such officers and clerks as may be allowed by general rules to be made under the provisions of this Act:

4. A shorthand writer shall attend at the trial of a petition, and shall be sworn by the court faithfully and truly to take down the evidence given at the trial, and shall take down the evidence at length, and a copy of the evidence so taken shall accompany the certificate of the said court, and the expenses of the shorthand writer, according to a scale to be prescribed, shall be deemed to be part of the expenses incurred in receiving the court.

Jurisdiction and general rules.

21. The following provisions shall have effect with respect to jurisdiction, and to general rules :

1. The judges for the time being on rota for the trial of election petitions under the provisions of the Parliamentary Elections Act, 1868, may from time to time make, revoke, and alter general rules for the effectual execution of this Act, and of the intention and object thereof, and the regulation of the practice, procedure, and costs of petitions, and the trial thereof, and the certifying and reporting thereon;

Any general rules made as aforesaid shall, in so far as they are not inconsistent with any of the provisions of this Act, be deemed to be within the powers conferred by this Act, and shall be of the same force as if they were enacted in the body of this Act;

Any general rules made in pursuance of this section shall be laid before Parliament within three weeks after they are made, if Parliament be then sitting, and if Parliament be not then sitting, within three weeks after the beginning of the then next session of Parliament :

2. Until general rules have been made in pursuance of this Act, and so far as such rules (when made), and the provisions of this Act, do not extend, the principles, practice, and rules which are for the time being observed in the case of election petitions under the provisions of the Parliamentary Elections Act, 1868, shall be observed so far as may be by the court and superior court in the case of petitions under this Act :

3. The duties to be performed by the prescribed officer under this Act shall be performed by the prescribed officer of the superior court :

4. The rules and principles with regard to agency and evidence, and with regard to a scrutiny, and with regard to the declaring any person to be elected in the room of any other person who is declared to have been not duly elected, which are applicable in the case of parliamentary election petitions, shall be applied so far as they are applicable in the case of a petition under this Act :

5. The superior court shall, subject to the provisions of this Act, have the same powers, jurisdiction, and authority with reference to an election petition and the proceedings thereon as it would have if the petition were an ordinary cause within its jurisdiction.

Miscellaneous Provisions.

22. The remuneration and allowances to be paid to a barrister for his services in respect of the trial of a petition, and to any officers, clerks, or shorthand writers employed under the provisions of this Act, shall be fixed by scale which shall be made and may be varied from time to time by the election judges on the rota for the trial of election petitions under the provisions of the Parliamentary Elections Act, 1868, with the approval of the Commissioners of Her Majesty's Treasury, or any two or more of them, and the amount of any such remuneration and allowances shall be paid by the said Commissioners, and shall be repaid to the said Commissioners on their certificate, by the treasurer of the borough to which the petition relates, out of the borough fund or rate :

Expenses of the court.

Provided that the court at its discretion may order that the whole or any part of such remuneration and allowances, or the whole or any part of the expenses incurred by a town clerk for receiving the court under the provisions of this Act, shall be repaid to the said commissioners or to the town clerk, as the case may be, in the cases, by the persons, in the manner following ; viz.,

(a.) When in the opinion of the court a petition is frivolous and vexatious, then by the petitioner;

(b.) When in the opinion of the court a respondent has been personally guilty of corrupt practices at the election, then by such respondent :

And any order so made for the repayment of any sum by a petitioner or respondent may be enforced in the same way as an order for payment of costs; but any other costs or expenses payable by such petitioner or respondent to any party to the petition shall be satisfied out of any deposit or security made or given under the provisions of this Act before such deposit or security is applied for the repayment of any sum under an order made in pursuance of this section.

Acts done pending a petition not to be invalidated.
23. Where a candidate who has been elected to an office at an election is by a certificate of the court, or by a decision of the superior court, declared not to have been duly elected, acts done by him in execution of such office before the time when the certificate or decision is certified to the town clerk, shall not be invalidated by reason of his being so declared not to have been duly elected.

Provisions as to elections in the room of persons unseated on petition.
24. Where upon a petition the election of any person to an office has been declared void, and no other person has been declared elected in his room, a new election shall forthwith be held to supply the vacancy, in the same manner as in the case of an extraordinary vacancy in the office; and for the purposes of any such new election any duties to be performed by a mayor, alderman, or any officer, shall, if such mayor, alderman, or officer has been declared not elected, be performed by a deputy or other person who might have acted for him if he had been incapacitated by illness.

Computation of time.
25. In reckoning time for the purposes of this Act, Sunday, Christmas Day, Good Friday, and any day set apart for a public fast or public thanksgiving shall be excluded.

Prohibition of disclosure of vote.
26. No person who has voted at an election by ballot shall in any proceeding to question the election be required to state for whom he has voted.

Act not to apply to Scotland.
27. This Act shall not apply to Scotland.

SCHEDULE.

ACTS REPEALED.

5 & 6 Will. 4. c. 76. ss. 54 to 56, both inclusive.

22 Vict. c. 35. ss. 9 to 14, both inclusive.

3 & 4 Vict. c. 108. ss. 90, 91.

---

38 & 39 Vic. c. 40.

An Act to amend the Law regulating Municipal Elections.   [19th July, 1875.]

Be it enacted, &c.

1. The following provisions shall be enacted and apply to nominations at all municipal elections of councillors, auditors, and assessors after the passing of this Act: *Provisions applicable to municipal elections.*

1. Nine days at least before any such election the town clerk shall prepare, sign, and publish a notice in the form No. 1. set forth in the First Schedule to this Act, or to the like effect, by causing the same to be placed on the door of the Town Hall, and in some conspicuous parts of the borough or ward for which any such election is to be held.

2. At any such election every candidate shall be nominated in writing; the writing shall be subscribed by two enrolled burgesses of such borough or ward as proposer and seconder, and by eight other enrolled burgesses of such borough or ward as assenting to the nomination. Each candidate shall be nominated by a separate nomination paper; but the same burgesses, or any of them, may subscribe as many nomination papers as there are vacancies to be filled, but no more. Every person nominated shall be enrolled on the burgess roll of the borough, or a person whose name is inserted in the separate list at the end of the burgess roll, as provided by section three of the Act thirty-two and thirty-three Victoria, chapter fifty-five, and shall be otherwise qualified to be elected. The nomination paper shall state the surname and other names of the person

nominated, with his place of abode and description, and shall be in the form No. 2, set forth in the First Schedule to this Act, or to the like effect. And the town clerk shall provide nomination papers, and shall supply any enrolled burgess with as many nomination papers as may be required, and shall, at the request of any such person, fill up a nomination paper in manner prescribed by this Act.

3. Every nomination paper subscribed as aforesaid shall be delivered by the candidate himself, or his proposer or seconder, to the town clerk, seven days at least before the day of election, and before five o'clock in the afternoon of the last day on which any such nomination paper may by law be delivered; the town clerk shall forthwith send notice of such nomination to each person nominated. The mayor shall attend at the Town Hall on the day next after the last day for the delivery of nominations to the town clerk between the hours of two and four in the afternoon, and shall decide on the validity of every objection made to a nomination paper, such objection to be made in writing. The candidate nominated by each nomination paper, and one other person, appointed by or on behalf of the candidate as hereinafter mentioned, and no person other than aforesaid, shall, except for the purpose of assisting the mayor, be entitled to attend such proceedings, and each candidate and the person appointed by him shall, during the time appointed for the attendance of the mayor for the purposes of this section, have respectively power to object to the nomination paper of every person nominated at the same election. The decision of the mayor, which shall be given in writing, shall, if disallowing any objection to a nomination paper, be final, but if allowing the same shall be subject to reversal on petition questioning the election or return. The appointment by or on behalf of candidates of persons as aforesaid shall be made in writing under the hand of the candidate, or in case he is absent from the United Kingdom, then under the hand of his proposer or seconder, and shall be delivered to the town clerk before five o'clock in the afternoon of the last day on which nomination papers may by law be delivered.

The town clerk shall at least four days before the day of election cause the surnames and other names of all persons duly nominated, with their respective places of abode and descriptions, and the names of the persons subscribing their respective nomination papers as proposers and seconders, to be printed and placed on the door of the Town Hall, and in some conspicuous part of the borough or ward for which such election is to be held.

4. Section eight of the Act of twenty-second Victoria, chapter thirty-five, so far as the same is now in force, shall apply to nominations of councillors, auditors, and assessors, duly made and allowed under this Act.

Section three of the Ballot Act, 1872, shall apply to nomination papers under this Act, and so applied, the word "returning officer" shall be taken to include town clerk in reference to the delivery of such nomination papers.

2. The nomination of a person who is absent from the United Kingdom shall be void, unless his written consent given within one month of the day of his nomination before two witnesses be produced at the time of his nomination. *Candidates out of United Kingdom ineligible*

3. At any municipal election of councillors, auditors, or assessors, the power and duty of the mayor, under section twenty of the Ballot Act of 1872, to provide everything which in the case of a parliamentary election is required to be provided by the returning officer for the purpose of a poll, shall (save as to the appointment of the alderman as returning officer for any ward) extend to the appointment of officers for taking the poll and counting the votes recorded at such election. *Mayor to appoint officers for taking the poll.*

4. The provisions contained in rules 16 and 19 of the first schedule to the Ballot Act, 1872, shall not apply to any such election, but the mayor shall furnish every polling station with such number of compartments in which the voters can mark their votes screened from observation, and furnish each presiding officer with such number of ballot papers, as in the judgment of the mayor shall be necessary for effectually taking the poll at such election in other respects in the manner provided by the Ballot Act, 1872. Where more candidates are nominated than there are vacancies to be supplied, the mayor shall, at least four days before the day of *Amendment of law.*

election, give such public notice as may be required by law of the situation, division, and allotment of polling places for taking the poll at any municipal election, and of the description of persons entitled to vote thereat and at the several polling stations.

Conclusiveness of burgess roll.

5. At any municipal election a person shall not be entitled to sign or subscribe any nomination paper, or to vote, unless his name is on the burgess roll for the time being in force in the borough, or on the ward list for the time being in force for the ward, for which such election shall be held; and every person whose name is on such burgess roll or ward list, as the case may be, shall be entitled to sign or subscribe any nomination paper, and to demand and receive a ballot paper, and to vote; provided that nothing in this section shall entitle any person to do any of the acts aforesaid who is prohibited from doing such acts or any of them by law, or relieve such person from any penalties to which he may he liable for doing any such act.

One poll to be taken for auditors and assessors.

6. At the poll at any election of auditors and assessors one ballot paper only shall be used by any person voting   In such ballot paper the names of the candidates for the respective offices shall be separate and distinguished, so as to show the office for which they are respectively candidates, and the ballot paper shall be in the Form No. 3 set forth in the First Schedule to this Act or to the like effect, and the provisions of the Ballot Act, 1872, shall at any such election be altered and varied accordingly; provided always, that in counting the votes every such ballot paper shall be deemed to be a separate ballot paper in respect of each office, and any objections thereto shall be considered and dealt with accordingly.

Withdrawal of candidates.

7. Where more candidates are nominated at any municipal election than there are vacancies to be filled at such election, any of such candidates may withdraw from his candidature by notice signed by him and delivered to the town clerk not later than two o'clock in the afternoon of the day next after the last day for the delivery of nomination papers to the town clerk; provided that such notices shall take effect in the order in which they are delivered to the town clerk, and that no such notice shall have effect so as to reduce the number of candidates ultimately standing nominated below the number of the vacancies to be filled.

8. Any notice required by law to be given or published by the mayor or other returning officer or town clerk in connection with any municipal election may, as to auditors and assessors, be comprised in one notice, and with respect to the election of councillors in any borough divided into wards, may comprise the matter necessary to such notice for the several wards in the borough, and it shall not be necessary to issue a separate notice for each ward.

Notices by mayor or town clerk may comprise the several wards of borough.

9. Section eleven of the Act sixteenth and seventeenth Victoria, chapter seventy-nine, shall be read as if fourteen days were therein inserted instead of ten days, and the day for holding the election in the case of any extraordinary vacancy in the office of councillor, auditor, or assessor in any borough (whether such borough shall be divided into wards or not) shall be fixed by the mayor.

Time of holding elections on extraordinary vacancies.

10. The town council of any borough may by order divide any such borough or any ward or wards of such borough into polling districts in such manner as they may think most convenient for taking the votes of the burgesses at a poll, and the overseers shall, so far as practicable, make out the lists of burgesses in such manner as to divide the names in conformity with such polling districts.

Power to town council to divide wards into polling places as they may think fit.

11. In reckoning time for the purpose of this Act, Sunday, Christmas Day, Good Friday, and any day set apart for a public holiday, fast, or public thanksgiving, shall be excluded.

Computation of time under the Act.

12. The several Acts of Parliament mentioned in the Second Schedule to this Act shall be repealed to the extent specified in the third column of such schedule, but such repeal shall not affect the validity or invalidity of anything already done or suffered, or any remedy or proceeding in respect thereof, or the proof of any past act or thing.

Repeal of parts of Acts in Second Schedule.

13. This Act shall, as far as consistent with the tenor thereof, be construed as one with the Act fifth and sixth William the Fourth, chapter seventy-six, and the Acts amending the same, and the Acts for the time being in force relating to elections of councillors, auditors, and assessors in boroughs.

Act to be construed with Municipal Corporation Acts.

14. This Act may for all purposes be cited as "The Municipal Elections Act, 1875."

Short title.

15. This Act shall continue in force for so long only as the Ballot Act, 1872, continues in force

Duration of Act.

First Schedule.

Form No. 1.

Notice.

Borough of   .   Election of [Councillors,
or Auditors, *or* Assessors, *as the case may be*] for the
[Ward or several Wards of the]   Borough.

Take Notice,

1. That an election of [*here insert the number of
Councillors, Auditors, or Assessors, as the case may be*] for
the [Ward or several Wards
of the] said Borough will be held on the   day
of   .

2. Candidates must be nominated by writing,
subscribed by two enrolled burgesses as proposer or
seconder, and by eight other enrolled burgesses as
assenting to the nomination.

3. Candidates must be duly qualified for the office
to which they are nominated, and the nomination
paper must state the surname and other names of the
person nominated, with his place of abode and
description, and may be in the following form, or to
the like effect:

(Set out Form No. 2.)

4. Each candidate must be nominated by a
separate nomination paper, but the same burgesses
or any of them may subscribe as many nomination
papers as there are vacancies to be filled for the
borough [*or* ward,] but no more.

5. Every person who forges a nomination paper,
or delivers any nomination paper, knowing the same
to be forged, will be guilty of misdemeanor, and
be liable to imprisonment for any term not exceeding
six months, with or without hard labour.

6. Nomination papers must be delivered by the
candidate himself, or his proposer or seconder, to
the town clerk, at his office, before five o'clock in the
afternoon of   day the   day of
next.

7. The mayor will attend at the Town Hall on
        day the   day of   from two
to four o'clock in the afternoon, to hear and decide
objections to nomination papers.

8. Forms of nomination papers may be obtained at the town clerk's office; and the town clerk will, at the request of any enrolled burgess, fill up a nomination paper.

Dated this   day of   18   .

A. B., Town Clerk.

Form No. 2.

NOMINATION PAPER.

Borough of   .   Election of Councillors, Auditors, or Assessors for   Ward in the said Borough [*or* the said Borough,] to be held on the   day of   18   .

We, the undersigned, being respectively enrolled burgesses, hereby nominate the following person as a candidate at the said election.

Surname.	Other Names.	Abode.	Description.

(Signed)   *A. B.* of°

C. D. of°

We, the undersigned, being respectively enrolled burgesses, do hereby assent to the nomination of the above person as a candidate at the said election.

Dated this   day of   18   .

(Signed)   *E. F.* of°

G. H. of°

I. J. of°

K. L. of°

M. N. of°

O. P. of°

Q. R. of°

S. T. of°

° The number on the Burgess Roll of the Burgess subscribing, with the situation of the property in respect of which he is enrolled on the Burgess Roll.

FORM No. 3.

BALLOT PAPER.

FORM of Front of Ballot Paper.

For Auditors.

Counterfoil.		
No.	1	CADE. (Charles Cade, of 22, Wellclose Place, Accountant.)
Note.—The Counterfoil is to have a Number to correspond with that on the back of the Ballot Paper.	2	JOHNSON. (Charles Johnson, of 7, Albion Street, Gentleman.)
	3	THOMPSON. (William Thompson, of 14, Queen Street. Silversmith.)

For Revising Assessor.

1	BACON. (Charles Bacon, 29, New Street, Solicitor.)
2	BYRON. (James Byron, of 45, George Street, Commission Agent.)
3	WILSON. (George Wilson, of 22, Hanover Square, Gentleman.)

FORM of Back of Ballot Paper.

No.   Election of Auditors [*or* Assessors] for the Borough of   to be held on the day of   18   .

The Number on the back of the Ballot Paper is to correspond with that on the Counterfoil.

SECOND SCHEDULE.

Repeal of Acts.

An Act to regulate the Expenses and to control the Charges of Returning Officers at Parliamentary Elections.

[13*th August*, 1875.]

WHEREAS it is expedient, &c. : Be it enacted, &c.

1. The Ballot Act, 1872, as modified by this Act, and this Act shall be construed as one Act.

Construction of Act.

This Act shall apply only to parliamentary elections.

2. The returning officer at an election shall be entitled to his reasonable charges, not exceeding the sums mentioned in the first schedule to this Act, in respect of services and expenses of the several kinds mentioned in the said schedule, which have been properly rendered or incurred by him for the purposes of the election.

Payments to returning officers.

The amount of such charges shall be paid by the candidates at the election in equal several shares, or where there is only one candidate, by such candidate. If a candidate is nominated without his consent, the persons by whom his nomination is subscribed shall be jointly and severally liable for the share of the charges for which he would be liable if he were nominated with his consent.

A returning officer shall not be entitled to payment for any other services or expenses, or at any greater rates, than as in the said schedule mentioned, any law or usage to the contrary notwithstanding.

3. The returning officer, if he think fit, may, as hereinafter provided, require security to be given for the charges which may become payable under the provisions of this Act in respect of any election.

Returning officer may require deposit or security.

The total amount of the security which may be required in respect of all the candidates at an election shall not in any case exceed the sums prescribed in the third schedule to this Act.

Where security is required by the returning officer it shall be apportioned and given as follows; viz.,

1. At the end of the two hours appointed for the election the returning officer shall forthwith declare the number of the candidates who then stand nominated, and shall, if there be more candidates nominated than there are vacancies to be filled up, apportion equally among them the total amount of the required security:

2. Within one hour after the end of the two hours aforesaid, security shall be given, by or in

respect of each candidate then standing nominated for the amount so apportioned to him :

3. If in the case of any candidate security is not given or tendered as herein mentioned, he shall be deemed to be withdrawn within the provisions of the Ballot Act, 1872 :

4. A tender of security in respect of a candidate may be made by any person :

5. Security may be given by deposit of any legal tender or of notes of any bank being commonly current in the county or borough for which the election is held, or, with the consent of the returning officer, in any other manner :

6. The balance (if any) of a deposit beyond the amount to which the returning officer is entitled in respect of any candidate shall be repaid to the person or persons by whom the deposit was made.

The accounts of a returning officer may be taxed.

4. Within twenty-one days after the day on which the return is made of the persons elected at the election, the returning officer shall transmit to every candidate or other person from whom he claims payment either out of any deposit or otherwise of any charges in respect of the election, or to the agent for election expenses of any such candidate, a detailed account showing the amounts of all the charges claimed by the returning officer in respect of the election, and the share thereof which he claims from the person to whom the account is transmitted. He shall annex to the account a notice of the place where the vouchers relating to the account may be seen, and he shall at all reasonable times and without charge allow the person from whom payment is claimed, or any agent of such person, to inspect and take copies of the vouchers.

The returning officer shall not be entitled to any changes which are not duly included in his account.

If the person from whom payment is claimed objects to any part of the claim, he may, at any time within fourteen days from the time when the account is transmitted to him, apply to the court as defined in this section for a taxation of the account and the court shall have jurisdiction to tax the account in such manner and at such time and place as the court thinks fit, and finally to determine the amount payable to the returning officer and to give and enforce judgment for the same, as if such judgment were a judgment in an action in such court, and with or without costs at the discretion of the court.

The court for the purposes of this Act shall be in the city of London the Lord Mayor's Court, and elsewhere in England the County Court, and in Ireland the Civil Bill Court, having jurisdiction at the place of nomination for the election to which the proceedings relate.

5. Every person having any claim against a returning officer for work, labour, materials, services, or expenses in respect of any contract made with him by or on behalf of the returning officer for the purposes of an election, except for publication of accounts of election expenses, shall, within fourteen days after the day on which the return is made of the person or persons elected at the election, transmit to the returning officer the detailed particulars of such claim in writing, and the returning officer shall not be liable in respect of anything which is not duly stated in such particulars. *Claims against a returning officer.*

The court may depute any of its powers or duties under this Act to the registrar or other principal officer of the court.

Nothing in this section shall apply to the charge of the returning officer for publication of accounts of election expenses.

Where application is made for taxation of the accounts of a returning officer, he may apply to the court as defined in this Act to examine any claim transmitted to him by any person in pursuance of this section, and the court after notice given to such person, and after hearing him, and any evidence tendered by him, may allow or disallow, or reduce the claim objected to, with or without costs, and the determination of the court shall be final for all purposes, and as against all persons.

6. In any case to which the fourteenth section of the Ballot Act, 1872, is applicable, it shall be the duty of the returning officer, so far as is practicable, to make use of ballot boxes, fittings, and compartments provided for municipal or school board elections, and the court, upon taxation of his accounts, shall have regard to the provisions of this section. *Use of ballot boxes, &c., provided for municipal elections.*

7. There shall be added to every notice of election to be published under the provisions of the Ballot Act, 1872, the notification contained in the second schedule to this Act with respect to claims against returning officers. *Notices to be given by returning officers.*

Saving of the universities.

8. Nothing in this Act shall apply to an election for any university or combination of universities.

Commencement and duration of Act.

9. This Act shall come into operation on the first day of October, one thousand eight hundred and seventy-five, and continue in force until the thirty-first day of December, one thousand eight hundred and eighty, and no longer, unless Parliament shall otherwise determine.

Short title.

10. This Act may be cited for all purposes as the "Parliamentary Elections (Returning Officers) Act, 1875."

Not to apply to Scotland.

11. This Act shall not apply to Scotland.

First Schedule.

Charges of Returning Officers.

The following are the maximum charges to be made by the returning officer, but the charges are in no case to exceed the sums actually and necessarily paid or payable.

Part I.—Counties and District or Contributory Boroughs.

This Part of this Schedule applies to an election for a county, or for either of the boroughs of Aylesbury, Cricklade, Monmouth, East Retford, Stroud, and New Shoreham, or for any borough or burgh consisting of a combination of separate boroughs, burghs, or towns.

	£	s.	d.
For preparing and publishing the notice of election	2	2	0
For preparing and supplying the nomination papers	1	1	0
For travelling to and from the place of nomination, or of declaring the poll at a contested election, per mile.	0	1	0
For hire or necessary fitting up of rooms or buildings for polling, or damage or expenses by or for use of such rooms or buildings. ..	The necessary expenses, not exceeding at any one polling station the charge for constructing and fitting a polling station,		

	£	s.	d.
For constructing a polling station, with its fittings and compartments, in England.	7	7	0
For each ballot box required to be purchased	1	1	0
For the use of each ballot box, when hired	0	5	0
For stationery at each polling station	0	10	0
For printing and providing ballot papers, per thousand	1	10	0
For each stamping instrument ..	0	10	0
For copies of the register	The sums payable by statute for the necessary copies.		
For each presiding officer	3	3	0
For one clerk at each polling station where not more than 500 voters are assigned to such station ..	1	1	0
For an additional clerk at a polling station for every number of 500 voters, or fraction thereof beyond the first 500 assigned to such polling station.	1	1	0
For every person employed in counting votes, not exceeding six such persons where the number of registered electors does not exceed 3,000, and one for every additional 2,000 electors. ..	1	1	0
For making the return to the clerk of the Crown	1	1	0
For the preparation and publication of notices (other than the notice of election.)	Not exceeding for the whole of such notices 20l., and 1l. for every additional 1,000 electors above 3,000.		
For conveyance of ballot boxes from the polling stations to the place where the ballot papers are to be counted, per mile	0	1	0

	£ s. d.
For professional and other assistance in and about the conduct of the election.	In a contested election not exceeding 25*l.*, and an additional 3*l.* for every 1,000 registered electors or fraction thereof above 3,000 and up to 10,000, and 2*l.* for every 1,000 or fraction thereof above 10,000. In an uncontested election one-fifth of the above sums.
For travelling expenses of presiding officers and clerks, per mile ..	0 1 0
For services and expenses in relation to receiving and publishing accounts of election expenses, in respect of each candidate	2 2 0
For all other expenses	In a contested election, not exceeding 10*l.*, and an additional 1*l.* for every 1,000 electors or fraction thereof above 1,000. In an uncontested election nil.

NOTE.—*Travelling expenses are not to be allowed in the case of any person unless for distances exceeding two miles from the place at which he resides.*

PART II. BOROUGHS.

This part of the Schedule applies to all boroughs not included in Part I. of this Schedule.

	£ s. d.
For preparing and publishing the notice of election	2 2 0
For preparing and supplying the nomination papers	1 1 0
For hire or necessary fitting up of rooms or buildings for polling, or damage or expenses by or for use of such rooms or buildings ..	The necessary expenses, not exceeding at any one polling station the charge for constructing and fitting a polling station.

134

	£ s. d.
In England for constructing a polling station, with its fittings and compartments, not exceeding two in number	7 7 0
For each compartment required to be constructed, when more than two be used	1 1 0
For the use of each compartment hired, when more than two are used	0 5 0
For each ballot box required to be purchased.	1 1 0
For the use of each ballot box, when hired.	0 5 0
For stationery at each polling station	0 10 0
For printing and providing ballot papers, per thousand	1 10 0
For each stamping instrument ..	0 10 0
For copies of the register	The sums payable by statute for the necessary copies.
For each presiding officer	3 3 0
For one clerk at each polling station where not more than 500 voters are assigned to such station ..	1 1 0
For an additional clerk at a polling station for every number of 500 voters, or fraction thereof beyond the first 500 assigned to such station.	1 1 0
For every person employed in counting votes, not exceeding six such persons where the number of registered electors does not exceed 3,000, and one for every additional 2,000 electors	1 1 0
For making the return to the clerk of the Crown	1 1 0
For the preparation and publication of notices (other than the notice of election.)	Not exceeding for the whole of such notices 10l., and 1l. for every additional 1,000 electors above 10,000.

	£ s. d.
For professional and other assistance in and about the conduct of the election.	In a contested election, not exceeding 20*l.*, an additional 2*l.* for every 1,000 registered electors or fraction thereof above 1,000 and up to 10,000, and 1*l.* additional for every 1,000 or fraction thereof above 13,000. In an uncontested election one-fifth of the above sum.
For services and expenses in relation to receiving and publishing accounts of election expenses, in respect of each candidate	1 1 0
For all other expenses	Not exceeding 10*l.*, and an additional 1*l.* for every 1,000 electors above the first 1,000.

NOTE to PARTS I. and II. of SCHEDULE I.

The above sums are the aggregate charges, the amount of which is to be apportioned among the several candidates or other persons liable for the same.

SECOND SCHEDULE.

1. NOTIFICATION to be added to the NOTICE of ELECTION.

Take notice, that by the Parliamentary Elections (Returning Officers) Act, 1875, it is provided that every person having any claim against a returning officer for work, labour, materials, services, or expenses in respect of any contract made with him by or on behalf of the returning officer, for the purposes of an election (except for publications of account of election expenses), shall, within fourteen days after the day on which the return is made of the person or persons elected at the election, transmit to the returning officer the detailed particulars of such claim in writing, and the returning officer shall not be liable in respect of anything which is not duly stated in such particulars.

THIRD SCHEDULE.

MAXIMUM Amount of SECURITY which may be required by a RETURNING OFFICER.

	County or District of Contributory Borough.	Borough.
	£	£
Where the registered electors do not exceed 1,000	150	100
Where the registered electors exceed 1,000 but do not exceed 2,000.	200	150
Where the registered electors exceed 2,000 but do not exceed 4,000.	275	200
Where the registered electors exceed 4,000 but do not exceed 7,000.	400	250
Where the registered electors exceed 7,000 but do not exceed 10,000.	550	300
Where the registered electors exceed 10,000 but do not exceed 15,000.	700	450
Where the registered electors exceed 15,000 but do not exceed 20,000.	800	500
Where the registered electors exceed 20,000 but do not exceed 30,000.	900	600
Where the registered electors exceed 30,000.	1,000	700

If at the end of the two hours appointed for the election, not more candidates stand nominated than there are vacancies to be filled up, the maximum amount which may be required is one-fifth of the maximum according to the above scale.

---

41 Vic. c. 3.

An Act to relieve certain Occupiers of Dwelling-houses from being disqualified from the right of voting in the Election of Members to serve in Parliament by reason of their underletting such Dwelling-houses for short terms.

[*25th February*, 1878.]

WHEREAS questions have arisen upon the occupation required by the third section of the Representation of the People Act, 1867: Be it therefore enacted, &c. 30 and 31 Vict., c. 102.

Short title, 1. This Act shall be cited for all purposes as the House Occupiers Disqualification Removal Act, 1878.

Letting as furnished house for certain periods not to disqualify. 2. From and after the passing of this Act every man shall be entitled to be registered and to vote under the provisions of the said section, notwithstanding that during a part of the qualifying period not exceeding four months in the whole he shall by letting or otherwise have permitted the qualifying premises to be occupied as a furnished house by some other person.

---

41 & 42 Vic. c. 26.

An Act to amend the Law relating to the Registration of Voters in Parliamentary Boroughs and the Enrolment of Burgesses in Municipal Boroughs, and relating to certain rights of voting and proceedings before and appeals from Revising Barristers.

[*22nd July*, 1878.]

BE it enacted, &c.

Short Titles. 1. This Act may be cited as the Parliamentary and Municipal Registration Act, 1878.

The Acts referred to in this Act by short titles may be cited for all purposes by those titles respectively.

Extent of Act. 2. This Act shall not extend to Scotland or Ireland.

Commencement of Act. 3. This Act shall come into operation on the first day of February, one thousand eight hundred and seventy-nine, which date is in this Act referred to as the commencement of this Act.

Definitions. 4. In this Act—

The term "Reform Act, 1832," means the Act of the session of the second and third years of the reign of King William the Fourth, chapter forty-five, " to amend the representation of the people in England and Wales : "

5 and 6 W. 4, c. 76.
40 and 41 Vict., c. 69. The term "Municipal Corporation Acts" means the Municipal Corporation Act, 1835, and the Acts amending the same : The term "Parliamentary Registration Act, 1843," means the Act of the session of the sixth and seventh years of the reign of Her present Majesty, chapter eighteen,

138

to amend the law "for the registration of
persons entitled to vote, and to define "certain
rights of voting and to regulate certain proceedings in the election of members to serve in
Parliament for England and Wales:"

The term "Parliamentary Registration Acts" means
the Parliamentary Registration Act, 1843, and
any enactment amending the same or otherwise
relating to the registration of parliamentary
electors:

The term "parliamentary borough" means any
borough, city, county of a city, county of a town,
place, or combination of places returning a
member or members to serve in Parliament and
not being a county at large, or riding, part, or
division, of a county at large:

The term "municipal borough" means any place
for the time being subject to the Municipal
Corporation Acts:

The term "parliamentary voter" means a person
entitled to be registered as a voter and when
registered to vote at the election of a member
or members to serve in Parliament for a
parliamentary borough:

The term "burgess" has the same meaning as in
the Municipal Corporation Acts:

The term "parish" means a place for which a
separate poor rate is or can be made or for
which a separate overseer is or can be appointed:

Other terms used in this Act have the same
meaning as in the Paliamentary Registration
Acts.

5. In and for the purposes of the Reform Act, *Explanation of*
1832, and the Municipal Corporation Acts, the term *terms.*
"house, warehouse, counting-house, shop, or other *"House," &c.*
building," shall include any part of a house where *2 and 3 W. 4, c.*
that part is separately occupied for the purpose *45, s. 27.*
of any trade, business, or profession; and any such
part may for the purpose of describing the qualification
be described as "office," "chambers," "studio," or by
any like term applicable to the case.

In and for the purposes of the Representation of *30 and 31 Vict.,*
the People Act, 1867, the term "dwelling-house" *c. 102.*
shall include any part of a house where that part *"Dwelling-*
is separately occupied as a dwelling, and the term *house."*
"lodgings" shall include any apartments or place of *"Lodgings."*
residence, whether furnished or unfurnished, in a
dwelling-house.

Separate occu-
pation of part
notwithstand-
ing joint occu-
pation of other
part.

For the purposes of any of the Acts referred to in this section, where an occupier is entitled to the sole and exclusive use of any part of a house, that part shall not be deemed to be occupied otherwise than separately by reason only that the occupier is entitled to the joint use of some other part.

30 and 31 Vict.,
c. 102, s. 61.

The interpretation contained in this section of "dwelling-house" shall be in substitution for the interpretation thereof contained in section sixty-one of the Representation of the People Act, 1867, but not so as to affect any of the other provisions of the said Act relating to rating.

Additional lodg-
ings.

6.—(1.) Lodgings occupied by a person in any year or two successive years shall not be deemed to be different lodgings by reason only that in that year or in either of those years he has occupied some other rooms or place in addition to his original lodgings.

Successive lodg-
ings in the same
house.

(2.) For the purpose of qualifying a lodger to vote the occupation in immediate succession of different lodgings of the requisite value in the same house shall have the same effect as continued occupation of the same lodgings.

Joint occupa-
tion of lodgings.

(3.) Where lodgings are jointly occupied by more than one lodger, and the clear yearly value of the lodgings if let unfurnished is of an amount which when divided by the number of the lodgers gives a sum of not less than ten pounds for each lodger, then each lodger, if otherwise qualified and subject

30 and 31 Vict.,
c. 102.

to the conditions of the Representation of the People Act, 1867, shall be entitled to be registered, and when registered to vote as a lodger, provided that not more than two persons being such joint lodgers shall be entitled to be registered in respect of such lodgings.

Period of quali-
fication.

7. In every parliamentary borough and in every municipal borough every period of qualification for parliamentary voters and burgesses respectively which is now computed by reference to the last day of July, shall, instead of being so computed, be computed by reference to the fifteenth day of July.

The term "period of qualification" in this section shall include any period of occupation, residence, possession, receipt of rents and profits, and non-receipt of parochial relief or other alms.

Forms relating
to registration
in parliamen-
tary boroughs

8. In every parliamentary borough and in every municipal borough the whole or part of the area whereof is co-extensive with or included in the area

140

of a parliamentary borough, the forms in the schedule to this Act, or forms to the like effect, varied as circumstances require, shall be used for the purposes for which the same are applicable respectively, and shall for the purposes of the Parliamentary Registration Acts and this Act be deemed to be substituted for any corresponding forms in the schedules to the Parliamentary Registration Acts.

and burgess lists in certain municipal boroughs.

The said schedule and the notes thereto shall be construed and have effect as if enacted in the body of this Act.

All precepts, instructions, proceedings, notices, and lists relating to the registration of parliamentary voters or enrolment of burgesses shall be expressed in such manner and form as may be necessary to carry the provisions of this Act into effect.

9. In every parliamentary borough and in every municipal borough the whole or part of the area whereof is co-extensive with or included in the area of a parliamentary borough, any notice or list which is by the Parliamentary Registration Acts or this Act directed to be published by overseers shall be published by them not only in the manner directed by those Acts, but also by being affixed and kept in some public and conspicuous position in or near every post office and telegraph office occupied by or on behalf of Her Majesty's Postmaster General, and in or near every public or municipal or parochial office within the parish to which the list relates.

Publication of notices and lists in post and telegraph offices, &c.

All the provisions of those Acts with respect to the publication of notices or lists shall apply to the publication to be made under this section.

10. Where the whole or part of the area of a municipal borough is co-extensive with or included in the area of a parliamentary borough, section eleven of the Parliamentary Registration Act, 1843, and section twenty-eight of the Representation of the People Act, 1867 (which relate to the notices to be published and given with respect to rates and taxes in arrear), shall, as amended by this Act, extend with the necessary modifications to the rates of which the payment is required as a condition of enrolment on the burgess roll, and all the provisions of those sections as so amended shall apply to the overseers of parishes situate wholly or partly in a municipal borough accordingly.

Notice of rates in arrear.

6 and 7 Vict., c. 18, s. 11. §

30 and 31 Vict. c. 102, s. 28.

Any notice required to be given under this section shall be deemed to be duly given if delivered to the occupier or left at his last or usual place of abode, or with some person on the premises in respect of which the rate is payable.

In case no such person can be found, then the notice required to be given under this section or under section twenty-eight of the Representation of the People Act, 1867, shall be deemed to be duly given if affixed upon some conspicuous part of the premises.

Any overseer who with intent to keep an occupier off the list or register of voters for a parliamentary borough, or off the burgess lists or burgess roll of a municipal borough, shall wilfully withhold any notice required by this section to be given to such occupier, shall be deemed guilty of a breach of duty in the execution of this Act.

Section twenty-nine of the Representation of the People Act, 1867, shall extend and be applicable to every parish situate wholly or partly within a municipal borough whose burgess lists are revised under this Act.

11. Every registrar of births and deaths whose sub-district includes the whole or part of any parliamentary borough or any municipal borough the whole or part of the area whereof is co-extensive with or included in the area of a parliamentary borough, shall transmit by post or otherwise to the overseers of every parish the whole or any part of which is included in the parliamentary borough or municipal borough, and also in his sub-district. a return certified under his hand to be a true return of the names, ages, and residences of all male persons of full age dying within that parish or part, and also when and as required by those overseers of the names, ages, and residences of all women of full age dying within that parish or part.

The returns shall state the names of all such persons in full (where the names are known) and the dates of their deaths, and the names and residences of the persons by whom information of the deaths was given to the registrar.

The returns shall be made four times a year; tha t is to say,

On or before the seventh day of April for the three months ending with the preceding thirty-first day of March;

On or before the twenty-second day of July for the period beginning with the preceding first

Marginal notes:

30 and 31 Vict., c. 102, s. 28.

30 and 31 Vict., c. 102, s. 29.

Registrars to furnish returns of deaths to overseers.

142

day of April and ending with the fifteenth day of July;

On or before the fifteenth day of September, or at such other time before the completion of the revision of the lists of the parliamentary borough or municipal borough to the area of which the return relates as the barrister revising the same shall appoint in ˙that behalf for the period beginning with the preceding sixteenth day of July, and ending with the time when such return is made, or as near thereto as practicable;

And on or before the seventh day of January for the period beginning with the preceding fifteenth day of September or from the time for which the last preceding return was made, and ending with the thirty-first day of December:

The registrar making any such return shall be entitled to fees at the rate specified in the twenty-eighth section of the Births and Deaths Registration Act, 1874, in respect of the returns therein mentioned, and such fees shall be paid by the overseers as part of the expenses of carrying into effect the provisions of this Act with respect to the lists of parliamentary voters and burgess lists.

37 and 38 Vict., c 88, s. 28.

The overseers shall omit from any list made by them the name of any person who appears from such returns to be dead, and shall allow any person who is registered as a parliamentary voter of the parliamentary borough or enrolled as a burgess of the muncipal borough to which the returns relate to inspect any such returns in their custody at all reasonable times free of charge.

12. The overseers of every parish situate wholly or partly either in a parliamentary borough or in a muncipal borough the whole or part of the area whereof is co-extensive with or included in the area of a parliamentary borough, shall ascertain from the relieving officer acting for that parish the names of all persons who are disqualified for being inserted in the lists of parliamentary voters or burgess lists for that parish by reason of having received parochial relief, and the relieving officer, upon application from the overseers, shall produce to them at such place within the parish, and at such time as is required by them, the books in his possession containing the names of those persons.

List of person- disqualified by parochial relief.

Inspection of rate books.

13. In every parish situate wholly or partly either in a parliamentary borough or in a municipal borough the whole or part of the area whereof is co-extensive with or included in the area of a parliamentary borough, the books containing the poor rates made for the parish within the previous two years shall at all reasonable times be open, free of charge, to the inspection of any person who is registered as a parliamentary voter for the parliamentary borough, or enrolled as a burgess of the municipal borough, and any such voter or burgess may make any copy thereof or take any extract therefrom.

Explanation of 32 and 33 Vict., c. 41, sec. 19, as to entering occupier's name in rate book.

14. Whereas by section nineteen of the Poor Rate Assessment and Collection Act, 1869, the overseers in making out the poor rate are required in every case, whether the rate is collected from the owner or occupier, or the owner is liable to the payment of the rate instead of the occupier, to enter in the occupier's column of the rate book the name of the occupier of every rateable hereditament, and it is thereby declared that every such occupier shall be deemed to be duly rated for any qualification or franchise as therein mentioned; and whereas doubts have been entertained as to the application of this enactment and it is expedient to remove them: Be it therefore enacted that the recited enactment shall not be deemed to apply exclusively to cases where an agreement has been made under section three of the same Act, or where an order has been made under section four of the same Act, but shall be of general application.

Preparation of lists of parliamentary voters and burgess lists together in certain cases.

15. Where the whole or part of the area of a municipal borough is co-extensive with or included in the area of a parliamentary borough, the lists of parliamentary voters and the burgess lists shall so far as practicable be made out and revised together.

In every such case the overseers of every parish situate wholly or partly either in the parliamentary borough or in the municipal borough shall, on or before the last day of July in every year, make out a list of all persons entitled under any right conferred by

2 and 3 W. 4, c. 45.

30 and 31 Vict., c. 102, s. 3.

the Reform Act, 1832, or by section three of the Representation of the People Act, 1867, to be registered as voters for the parliamentary borough in respect of the occupation of property situate wholly or partly within that parish, or entitled to be enrolled as burgesses of the municipal borough in respect of the occupation of any property so situate.

With respect to every list so made out the following provisions shall have effect:

1. The lists shall be in substitution for the lists of persons so entitled, which are required to be made out under the Parliamentary Registration Acts and the Municipal Corporation Acts:

2. Where the parish is situate wholly or partly both in the parliamentary borough and in the municipal borough the list for the parish shall be made out in three divisions:

Division One shall comprise the names of the persons entitled both to be registered as parliamentary voters under a right conferred as aforesaid, and to be enrolled as burgesses;

Division Two shall comprise the names of the persons entitled to be registered as parliamentary voters under a right conferred as aforesaid, but not to be enrolled as burgesses;

Division Three shall comprise the names of the persons entitled to be enrolled as burgesses, but not to be registered as parliamentary voters under a right conferred as aforesaid:

3. Each list shall state the surname and other name or names of every person whose name is inserted therein, his place of abode, the nature of his qualification, and the situation and description of the property in respect of which he is entitled:

4. Each list shall be signed and otherwise dealt with in manner directed by the Paliamentary Registration Acts with respect to the alphabetical lists mentioned in section thirteen of the Parliamentary Registration Act, 1843: *6 and 7 Vict., c. 18, s. 13.*

5. Where no part of the parish is situate within the municipal borough, the list for the parish shall be deemed to be a list of voters for the parliamentary borough:

6. Where no part of the parish is situate within the parliamentary borough, the list for the parish shall be deemed to be a burgess list for the municipal borough:

7. Where the list is made out in divisions, Divisions One and Two shall be deemed to be lists of voters for the parliamentary borough, and Divisions One and Three shall be deemed to be burgess lists for the municipal borough:

8. The lists, and if the lists are made out in divisions, each division thereof, shall, if and so far as the local authority from time to time

direct, according to convenience for use, be framed in parts for polling districts or wards; and where the polling districts and wards are not conterminous, in such manner that the parts may be conveniently compiled or put together to serve either as lists for polling districts or as ward lists.

Freemen's and other rights.

2 and 3 W. 4, c. 45.

30 and 31 Vict. c. 102, s. 3.

16. In the case of any parliamentary borough in which any persons are entitled to be registered as freemen, or under any right other then a right conferred by the Reform Act, 1832, or the third section of the Representation of the People Act, 1867, the registration of such persons shall be carried out in the manner directed by the Parliamentary Registration Acts, as modified by this Act.

Provision where several municipal boroughs included in one parliamentary borough.

17. In the case of a parliamentary borough which includes in whole or in part more municipal boroughs than one, each such municipal borough shall, for the purposes of this Act, be dealt with separately and as if each were the only municipal borough included in whole or in part in such parliamentary borough, and if any parish is partly in one and partly in another or others of such municipal boroughs, so much thereof as is in any one of such municipal boroughs shall, for the purposes of this Act, be dealt with as a separate parish.

The town clerks of each such municipal borough shall, so far as regards the area of such municipal borough, issue the precepts and perform the other duties to be performed by the town clerk under and shall be the town clerk for the purposes of the Parliamentary Registration Acts and this Act.

Application of Parliamentary Registration Acts to burgess lists made out under this Act.

18. The Municipal Corporation Acts shall not, as to anything prior to the completion of the revision of the burgess lists, apply to any burgess list made out under this Act, and instead thereof the Parliamentary Registration Acts, as modified by this Act, shall, up to the completion of the revision of the burgess lists, apply to every such burgess list, as if it were a list of parliamentary voters made out under those Acts, and as if the municipal borough to which such burgess lists relate were a parliamentary borough: Provided as follows:

1. Nothing in this Act shall authorise a person entered on a burgess list, not being also entered on a list of parliamentary voters, to make any objection in respect of a list of parliamentary voters, or authorise any person entered on a

146

list of parliamentary voters, not being also entered on a burgess list, to make any objection in respect of a burgess list;

2. The last day for revising a burgess list made out under this Act shall be the twelfth day of October; and

3. The burgess lists when revised shall be copied for the burgess roll in manner directed by the Municipal Corporation Acts.

19. Where the whole or part of the area of a municipal borough is co-extensive with or included in the area of a parliamentary borough, the separate lists of the persons entitled to be elected councillors or aldermen of the municipal borough, though not entitled to be on the burgess roll, shall be made out at the same time and in the same manner as the burgess lists, and all the provisions of this Act with respect to the burgess lists shall apply to those separate lists. *Lists of persons qualified to be aldermen or councillors, but not to be burgesses.*

20. After the commencement of this Act assessors shall not be elected in any municipal borough which as regards the whole or part of its area is co-extensive with or included in the area of a parliamentary borough, and any assessors elected in any such municipal borough before the commencement of this Act shall cease to hold office upon the commencement of this Act. *Abolition of assessors in certain municipal boroughs.*

21. If and so far as the local authority so direct, the lists of parliamentary voters and registers of parliamentary voters in parliamentary boroughs, and the burgess lists and burgess rolls in municipal boroughs, and the lists of claimants and persons objected to in parliamentary boroughs and municipal boroughs respectively, or any of those documents, shall, so far as they relate to persons qualified in respect of the ownership or occupation of property (including persons qualified in respect of lodgings), be arranged in the same order in which the qualifying premises appear in the rate book for the parish in which those premises are situate, or as nearly thereto as will cause those lists, registers, and rolls to record the qualifying premises in successive order in the street or other place in which they are situated, subject in the case of a municipal borough divided into wards to the division of the burgess roll into ward lists. The local authority in this Act means as regards a parliamentary borough the authority having power to divide the parliamentary borough into polling *Lists and registers may be arranged according to streets*

districts, and as regards a municipal borough the council of the municipal borough.

Claim by lodger retaining same lodgings in successive years.

22. Where a person is entered in respect of lodgings on the register of voters for the time being in force, and desires to be entered on the next register in respect of the same lodgings, he may claim to be so entered by sending notice of his claim to the overseers of the parish in which his lodgings are situate on or before the twenty-fifth day of July.

The overseers shall on or before the last day of July make out a list of all persons so claiming, and if they have reasonable cause to believe that any person whose name is entered on the list is not entitled to be registered or is dead, shall add in the margin of the list opposite his name the words "objected to" or "dead" as the case may be.

The lists so made out shall be signed, published, and otherwise dealt with in the same manner as the alphabetical list mentioned in section thirteen

6 and 7 Vict., c. 18.

of the Parliamentary Registration Act, 1843, and shall for the purposes of the Parliamentary Registration Acts be deemed to be lists of voters, and the provisions of the Parliamentary Registration Acts as to objections shall apply to such lists, and the persons against whose names the overseers have so written the words "objected to" or "dead" shall be deemed to be duly objected to.

Declaration of lodger to be primâ facie evidence.

23. In the case of a person claiming to vote as a lodger, the declaration annexed to his notice of claim shall, for the purposes of revision, be primâ facie evidence of his qualification.

Declaration as to misdescription.

24. Any person who is entered on any list of voters for a parliamentary borough or any burgess list, subject to revision under this Act, for a municipal borough, and whose name or place of abode or the nature of whose qualification or the name or situation of whose qualifying property is not correctly stated in such list, or in respect of whom there is any other error or omission in the said list, may, whether he has received a notice of objection or not, if he thinks fit, make and subscribe a declaration in the form in that behalf in the schedule to this Act, or as near thereto as the circumstances will admit, before any justice of the peace or any commissioner or other person authorised to administer oaths in the Supreme Court of Judicature.

The declaration shall be duly dated and shall on or before the twelfth day of September be sent to the town clerk, who forthwith shall indorse on the declaration a memorandum signed or initialed by him, stating the date when he received it, and naming the declarant and the list to which the declaration refers, and shall deliver all such declarations to the revising barrister at his first court.

If the declaration is sent as aforesaid in due time (of which the said indorsement shall be primâ facie proof), the revising barrister shall receive the declaration as evidence of the facts declared to, and that without proof of the signature of the declarant, or of the justice, commissioner, or person before whom the declaration purports to have been subscribed, unless he has good reason to doubt the genuineness of any signature thereto.

The declarations shall be open free of charge to public inspection at the office of the said town clerk, at any time between the hours of ten of the clock in the forenoon and four of the clock in the afternoon of any day except Sunday, before the fifteenth day of September, and he shall deliver copies thereof on application and payment of the price of fourpence per folio of seventy-two words.

25. If any person falsely or fraudulently signs any such declaration as last aforesaid, or any declaration either as claimant or witness in respect of a claim to vote as a lodger in the name of any other person, whether that person is living or dead, or in a fictitious name, or sends as genuine any false or falsified declaration knowing the same to be false or falsified, or knowingly and wilfully makes any false statement of fact in any declaration of the nature aforesaid, he shall be guilty of a misdemeanor and punishable by fine or by imprisonment for a term not exceeding one year, and the revising barrister shall have power to impound the declaration. *Penalty for false declaration.*

26. The notice required by the seventeenth and twentieth sections of the Parliamentary Registration Act, 1843, to be given to persons objected to in boroughs for the purposes of the revision of the lists of voters for a parliamentary borough and the burgess lists for a municipal borough whose burgess lists are revised under this Act, shall state specifically the ground or grounds of objection, and sections seven and eight of the County Voters Registration Act, 1865, shall extend to such objections. *Notice of objection to state specific grounds of objection, &c.* *6 and 7 Vict., c. 18, ss. 17, 20.* *28 and 29 Vict., c. 36, ss. 7, 8.*

Revision of lists of voters.

27. For the purposes of the revision of the lists of voters for a parliamentary borough, and the burgess lists for a municipal borough whose burgess lists are revised under this Act

Objections may be withdrawn.

1. An objection may be withdrawn by a notice to that effect in writing, signed by the objector, and given to the person objected to and to the town clerk not less than seven days before the day which shall be appointed for the holding of the first court of revision of the list to which the objection relates:

Reviver of objections on death of objector.

2. Any objection by a qualified objector may, after his death, be revived by any other person qualified to have made the objection originally by a notice to that effect in writing signed by him, and given to the person objected to and to the town clerk at or before the time of the revision of the entry to which the objection relates:

A person reviving an objection shall be deemed to have made the objection originally, and he shall be responsible in respect thereof, and the proceedings thereon shall be continued accordingly:

Costs of objections.

3. Where objection is made otherwise than by an overseer to any person whose name appears on a list of voters or burgesses and the name is retained on the list, the revising barrister shall, unless he is of opinion that the objection was reasonably made either because of a defect or error in the entry to which the objection relates, or because of a difficulty in verifying or identifying the particulars comprised in such entry, or unless the objection is duly withdrawn, or unless for some other special reason he otherwise determines, order costs not exceeding forty shillings to be paid by the objector to the person objected to.

Duties and powers of revising barrister.

28. A revising barrister shall, with respect to the list of voters for a parliamentary borough and the burgess lists for a municipal borough which he is appointed to revise, perform the duties and have the powers following:

1. He shall correct any mistake which is proved to him to have been made in any list:

2. He may correct any mistake which is proved to him to have been made in any claim or notice of objection:

3. He shall expunge the name of every person, whether objected to or not, whose qualification stated in any list is insufficient in law to entitle such person to be included therein :

4. He shall expunge the name of every person who, whether objected to or not, is proved to the revising barrister to be dead :

5. Where an entry in any list and an entry in a return made to the overseer of deaths appear to relate to the same person, the revising barrister shall inquire whether such entries relate to the same person, and on proof being made to him that the entries relate to the same person shall expunge the entry in the list therefrom :

6. The revising barrister shall expunge the name of every person, whether objected to or not, whose name or place of abode, or the nature of whose qualification, or the name or situation of whose qualifying property if the qualification is in respect of property, or any other particulars respecting whom by law required to be stated in the list, is or are either wholly omitted or in the judgment of the revising barrister insufficiently described for the purpose of being identified, unless the matter or matters so omitted or insufficiently described be supplied to the satisfaction of the revising barrister before he shall have completed the revision of the list in which the omission or insufficient description occurs, and in case such matter or matters shall be so supplied, he shall then and there insert the same in such list :

7. He shall expunge the name of every person, whether objected to or not, where it is proved to the revising barrister that such person was, on the last day of July then next preceding, incapacitated by any law or statute from voting at an election for the parliamentary borough or an election for the municipal borough, as the case may be, to which the list relates :

8. Before expunging from a list the name of any person not objected to, the revising barrister shall cause such notice, if any, as shall appear to him necessary or proper under the circumstances of the proposal to expunge

the name, to be given to or left at the usual
or last known place of abode of such person :

9. Subject as herein and otherwise by law provided, the revising barrister shall retain the
name of every person not objected to, and
also of every person objected to, unless the
objector appears by himself or by some person
on his behalf in support of his objection :

10. If the objector so appears the revising
barrister shall require him, unless he is an
overseer, to prove that he gave the notice or
notices of objection required by law to be
given by him, and to give primâ facie proof
of the ground of objection, and for that
purpose may himself examine and allow the
objector to examine the overseers of any other
person on oath touching the alleged ground
of objection, and unless such proof is given to
his satisfaction shall, subject as herein and
otherwise by law provided, retain the name of
the person objected to :

An objection made under this Act by overseers
shall be deemed to cast upon the person
objected to the burden of proving his right
to be on the list :

The primâ facie proof shall be deemed to be
given by the objector if it is shown to the satisfaction of the revising barrister by evidence, repute,
or otherwise that there is reasonable ground
for believing that the objection is well founded,
and that by reason of the person objected to not
being present for examination, or for some other
reason, the objector is prevented from discovering or proving the truth respecting the entry
objected to :

11. If such proof is given by the objector as
herein prescribed, or if the objection is by
overseers, then unless the person objected to
appears by himself or by some person on his
behalf, and proves that he was entitled on
the last day of July then next preceding
to have his name inserted in the list in
respect of the qualification described in such
list, the revising barrister shall expunge the
name of the person objected to :

12. Where the matter stated in a list or claim,
or proved to the revising barrister in relation
to any alleged right to be on any list, is in

the judgment of the revising barrister insufficient in law to constitute a qualification of the
nature or description stated or claimed, but
sufficient in law to constitute a qualification of
some other nature or description, the revising
barrister, if the name is entered in a list for
which such true qualification in law is appropriate, shall correct such entry by inserting such
qualification accordingly, and in any other case
shall insert the name with such qualification
in the appropriate list, and shall expunge it from
the other list, if any, in which it is entered:

13. Except as herein provided, and whether any
person is objected to or not, no evidence shall
be given of any other qualification than that
which is described in the list or claim, as the
case may be, nor shall the revising barrister
be at liberty to change the description of the
qualification as it appears in the list, except for
the purpose of more clearly and accurately
defining the same:

14. Where the name of any person appears to
be entered more than once as a parliamentary
voter on the list of voters for the same parliamentary borough, or more than once as a
burgess on the burgess lists for the same
municipal borough the revising barrister shall
inquire whether such entries relate to the same
person, and on proof being made to him that
such entries relate to the same person, shall
retain one of the entries for voting, and
place against the other or others a note to the
effect that the person is not entitled to vote
in respect of the qualification therein contained
for the parliamentary borough or for the
municipal borough, as the case may be, he being
on the list for voting in respect of another
qualification :

Any such person may, by notice in writing
delivered to the revising barrister at the opening
of his first revision court, select the entry to be
retained for voting, and in making such selection may select one entry to be retained for
voting for the parliamentary borough, and
another entry to be retained for voting as a
burgess for the municipal borough, but if he
does not make any selection the entry to be
so retained shall be selected by the revising

barrister, except in the case of freemen, in which case the entry to be retained by the revising barrister for voting shall be that on the freeman's list:

If any question on appeal, or otherwise, arise as to the validity of the qualification for which the parliamentary voter or burgess is on the list for voting, recourse may be had for supporting the right of the voter or burgess to be on the parliamentary register or burgess roll for voting to any other qualification of such person appearing on the register or burgess roll:

Provided always, that in the case of a municipal borough divided into wards a vote given in or the right to vote in one ward shall not be supported by a qualification appearing on the burgess roll for some other ward:

15. Where a list is made out in divisions the revising barrister shall place the name of any person in the division in which it should appear according to the result of the revision, regard being had to the title of the person to be on the list both as a parliamentary voter and as a burgess, or only in one of those capacities, and shall expunge the name from the other division (if any) in which it appears.

This section shall, as regards every parliamentary borough and every municipal borough whose burgess lists are revised under this Act, take effect instead of section forty of the Parliamentary Registration Act, 1843.

6 and 7 Vict., c. 18, s. 40.

Power to fine overseers for neglect of duty.

29. The provisions of the fifty-first section of the Parliamentary Registration Act, 1843, relating to the power of the revising barrister to fine overseers for neglect of duty, shall extend to every wilful refusal, neglect, or breach of duty, on the part of overseers in the execution of this Act.

6 and 7 Vict., c. 18, s. 51.

Expenses and receipts.

30. Where the whole or part of the area of a municipal borough is co-extensive with or included in the area of a parliamentary borough, the expenses properly incurred by the town clerk (including in his expenses the matters mentioned in section thirty-one of the Representation of the People Act, 1867), and the expenses properly incurred by the overseers in carrying into effect the provisions of this Act with respect to the lists of parliamentary voters and burgess lists, and all moneys received in respect of any of those lists, or in respect of any fine imposed by the

30 and 31 Vict., c. 102, s. 31.

revising barrister on the revision of the lists, shall
be respectively paid and applied as follows:

1. If the area of the parliamentary borough and
the area of the municipal borough are co-extensive, one half of the expenses shall be defrayed
in the manner provided by the Parliamentary
Registration Acts as expenses incurred thereunder, and the other half shall be defrayed out
of the borough fund, and one half of the moneys
received as aforesaid shall be applied in the
manner directed in those Acts, and the other
half shall be paid to the borough fund:

2. In all other cases the expenses and receipts
in respect of the area common to the parliamentary borough and to a municipal borough shall,
as to one half thereof, be defrayed and applied
as expenses and receipts under the Parliamentary Registration Acts, and shall as to the other
half thereof be defrayed out of and paid to the
borough fund of such municipal borough:

And the expenses and receipts in respect of an
area exclusively parliamentary shall be defrayed
and applied as expenses and receipts under the
Parliamentary Registration Acts:

And the expenses and receipts of an area exclusively
municipal shall be defrayed out of and paid to
the borough fund of the municipal borough comprising such area:

Any expenses and receipts incurred or arising in
respect of more than one such area shall be apportioned between the several areas in respect of
which they are incurred or arise, in the proportion as nearly as may be in which the same are
incurred and arise in respect of the several areas,
regard being had to the number of parliamentary
voters or burgesses in each area, or any other
circumstances occasioning the expenses or giving
rise to the receipts:

The revising barrister shall, as part of the business
of the revision, determine, if necessary, in respect
of what area or areas any expenses or receipts
are incurred or arise, and how much thereof is
attributable to each area.

The remuneration of the revising barrister shall be
paid as heretofore under the Parliamentary Registration Acts: Provided always, that in the case of a
municipal borough whose burgess lists are revised

under this Act, there shall be paid out of the borough fund to the revising barrister, by way of additional remuneration in respect of his additional work on account of the municipal revision for such municipal borough, a remuneration at the rate mentioned in the third section of the Municipal Corporation Act, 1859.

22 Vict., c. 35, s. 3.

Delivery and custody of revised lists.

31. The lists, if made out in divisions under this Act, shall when revised be delivered to the town clerk to whom in respect of the area to which the lists relate revised parliamentary lists ought to be delivered.

The revising barrister shall as part of the business of the revision, at the request of the town clerk of any municipal borough, the whole or part of the area of which is co-extensive with or included in the area of a parliamentary borough, sign and deliver to him a duplicate of the whole or part of any revised list made out in divisions and relating to that municipal borough.

Every such duplicate shall be prepared by the town clerk at whose request it is so signed, and shall be kept by him for use for municipal purposes.

Commencement and duration of parliamentary register.

32. The register made up from revised lists under the Parliamentary Registration Acts and this Act of voters for any parliamentary borough shall come into operation on the first day of January next after the revision, and shall continue in operation for the year commencing with such first day of January.

Commencement and duration of burgess roll.

33. The burgess roll made up from revised lists under this Act of burgesses for any municipal borough shall come into operation on the first day of November next after the revision, and shall continue in operation for the year commencing with such first day of November.

Certain expressions in 38 and 39 Vict., c. 40, to refer to new burgess roll or ward list.

34. For all the purposes of the Municipal Elections Act, 1875, relating to the qualification of candidates, or of persons signing or subscribing nomination papers, expressions referring to the burgess roll of the borough, or to the burgess roll or ward list for the time being in force in the borough or ward, shall, for the purposes of any election to be held on or after the first day of November in any year, be deemed to refer to the new burgess roll or ward list to come into force on the first day of November in that year.

35. Where burgess lists are revised under this Act, the provisions of the Parliamentary Registration Acts as to appeal from the decision of the revising barrister shall apply to a decision on the revision of the burgess lists, and the provisions of the said Acts as to the alteration or correction of the register in pursuance of any judgment or order of the court of appeal shall apply to the alteration or correction of the burgess roll made up from the burgess lists, as if it were a register of parliamentary voters, except that the notice of the judgment or order shall be given to the town clerk having the custody of the burgess roll, and the alteration or correction shall be made and signed by him.

Appeal and correction of burgess roll where burgess lists are revised under this Act.

36. A revising barrister may by summons under his hand require any person to attend at the court and give evidence or produce documents for the purpose of the revision, and any person who, after the tender to him of a reasonable amount for his expenses, fails so to attend, or who fails to answer any question put to him by the revising barrister in pursuance of this section, or to produce any document which he is required in pursuance of this section to produce, shall be liable to pay such fine not exceeding five pounds as may be imposed by the revising barrister, and such fine may be recovered, and when recovered shall be applied in like manner as any other fine imposed by the revising barrister under the Parliamentary Registration Acts.

Power for revising barrister to summon witnesses.

37. If any person feels aggrieved by a revising barrister neglecting or refusing to state any case, he may, within one month after such neglect or refusal, apply to the High Court of Justice upon affidavit of the facts for a rule calling on the revising barrister, and also on the person, if any, in whose favour the decision from which the applicant desires to appeal was given, to show cause why a rule should not be made directing the appeal to be entertained and the case to be stated, and thereupon the High Court, or any judge thereof in chambers, may make such rule to show cause, and make the same absolute, or discharge it with or without payment of costs as seems just, and the revising barrister on being served with any such rule absolute shall state the case accordingly, and the case shall be stated and the appeal entertained and heard, notwithstanding any limitations of time or place contained in the Parliamentary Registration Act, 1843.

Appeal where revising barrister neglects or refuses to state case.

6 and 7 Vict., c. 18.

Costs of Appeal.

38. The cost of an appellant against a decision of a revising barrister may, if the appeal is successful, be ordered by the court hearing the appeal to be paid by the clerk of the peace or town clerk named as respondent in the said appeal, whether he shall or shall not appear before the said court in support of the decision.

For enabling an appellant to obtain such an order he may at or before the time of making his declaration of appeal under section forty-two of the Parliamentary Registration Act, 1843, require the revising barrister to name the clerk of the peace for the county or the town clerk for the parliamentary borough or municipal borough, as the case may be, to which the appeal relates to be respondent in the appeal.

6 and 7 Vict., c. 18, s. 42.

The revising barrister if so required shall, and in any case may, name such clerk of the peace or town clerk, as the case may be, to be respondent in an appeal, either alone or in addition to any other person referred to in section forty-three of the Parliamentary Registration Act, 1843.

6 and 7 Vict., c. 18, s. 43.

The expenses properly incurred by a clerk of the peace or town clerk as respondent, including any costs which he may be ordered to pay to the appellant in any such appeal, shall be allowed to him as part of the expenses incurred by him in respect of the revision of the list to which the appeal relates. The term "expenses" in this section shall include all matters mentioned in section thirty-one of the Representation of the People Act, 1867.

30 and 31 Vict., c. 102, s. 31.

The cost of an appeal against a decision of a revising barrister shall be in the discretion of the court hearing the appeal, subject, except as aforesaid, to the proviso contained in section seventy of the Parliamentary Registration Act, 1843.

6 and 7 Vict., c. 18, s. 70.

Power to make rules for proceedings at revision courts.

39. The authority having power to make rules for regulating the practice and procedure in Her Majesty's High Court of Justice may from time to time make, and when made alter and annul, rules for regulating the practice and procedure in the courts of revising barristers for the purposes of the Parliamentary Registration Acts and of this Act.

Rules to be laid before Parliament.

All rules made under this section shall be laid before each House of Parliament within forty days next after the same are made, if Parliament is then sitting, and if not within forty days after the begin-

ing of the then next sitting of Parliament, and if
an address is presented to Her Majesty by either of
the said Houses within the next subsequent forty
days on which the said House shall have sat praying
that any such rule be annulled, Her Majesty may
by order in council annul the same, and any
rule so annulled shall thenceforth be of no effect,
but without prejudice to the validity of any proceeding in the meantime taken thereunder.

All such rules shall while in force have effect as
if enacted in this Act.

40. The provisions of section one hundred and
one of the Parliamentary Electors Registration Act,
1843, as to the service of notices shall apply to the
service of notices under this Act.

Service of notices.

6 & 7 Vict. c. 18. s. 101.

The term "notice" in the Parliamentary Registration Acts and this Act shall include any document
required to be sent or delivered.

41. Section thirteen of the Ballot Act, 1872, shall,
with respect to any municipal election, apply to non-
compliance with any of the provisions of or mistake
or error in the use of any of the forms prescribed
by the Municipal Elections Act, 1875.

Application of 35 & 36 Vict. c. 33. s. 13.

38 & 39 Vict. c. 40.

42. Nothing in this Act shall affect any register
of parliamentary voters or burgess roll in force at
the commencement of this Act.

Saving for existing registers and burgess rolls.

43. Nothing in this Act shall affect the provisions
contained in section seventy-eight of the Reform Act,
1832.

Saving for 2 & 3 W. 4, c. 45. s. 78.

SCHEDULE.

FORM (A).

FORM of PRECEPT of the TOWN CLERK or other OFFICER
issuing the PRECEPT to the OVERSEERS of any
PARISH situate wholly or partly in a PARLIA-
MENTARY BOROUGH, or partly in a MUNICIPAL
BOROUGH, the whole of the Area of which is
co-extensive with or included in the PARLIA-
MENTARY BOROUGH.

†Parliamentary borough of † To the overseers of the
*Municipal borough of *   poor of the parish of
to wit.   [or township of]

*Omit part be-
tween crosses if
no part of
parish is in a
Parliamentary
borough.
Omit part
between
asterisks if no
part of parish
is in a munici-
pal borough.*

In pursuance of the provisions of the Parliamentary
and Municipal Registration Act, 1878, and the Act
therein referred to, I require your attention to the
following:

159

Instructions.

On or before the Twentieth day of June you are to publish a notice [or notices], signed by you according to the form marked B. among the printed forms herewith sent.

The manner in which you are required to publish that notice is as follows; (that is to say,) you are to fix one of the printed copies (each copy being first signed by you) on or near the outside of the outer door or of the outer wall near the door of every church and public chapel in your parish [or township], including chapels which do not belong to the Established Church, and also in some public and conspicuous position on or near every post office or telegraph office occupied by or on behalf of Her Majesty's Postmaster General, and every public or municipal or parochial office in your parish [or township] or if there is no such church, chapel, or office, then in some public situation in your parish [or township] and it must remain there during a period including two Sundays at the least.

Where any poor rate was on the First day of June due from an occupier in respect of any premises capable of conferring the franchise for the said †Parliamentary *or† municipal* borough, you are on or before the Twentieth day of June to give to that occupier a notice in the form marked C. sent herewith, by delivering it to the occupier, or leaving it at his last or usual place of abode, or with some person on the premises in respect of which the rate is payable, and in case no such person can be found, then by affixing the notice upon some conspicuous part of such premises. You need not give this notice if the rate has been previously duly demanded by a demand note served in the like manner as the last-mentioned notice.

On or before the Twenty-second day of July next you are to make out a list containing the name and place of abode of every person who has not paid on or before the Twentieth day of the same month all poor rates which have become due from him in respect of any premises within your parish [or township] before the Fifth day of January last, and you are to keep that list to be perused by any person gratis at any time between 10 a. m. and 4 p.m. on any day, except Sunday, during the first fourteen days after the said Twenty-second day of July.

On or before the last day of July you are to make out a list of all persons† entitled under any right conferred by the Reform Act, 1832 (2 & 3 Will. 4, c. 45), or by section three of the Representation of the People Act, 1867, to be registered as Parliamentary voters to vote at the election of a member [or members] to serve in Parliament for the Parliamentary borough of   in respect of the occupation of property situate wholly or partly within your parish [or township] *or† entitled to be enrolled as burgesses of the municipal borough of   in respect of the occupation of property situate wholly or partly within your parish [or township]. *

Omit part between crosses if no part of parish is in a Parliamentary borough.

Omit part between asterisks if no part of parish is in a municipal borough.

*This list is to be made out in three divisions :

Division one is to comprise the names of the persons entitled both to be registered as Parliamentary voters under a right conferred as aforesaid, and to be enrolled as burgesses.

Division two is to comprise the names of the persons entitled to be registered as Parliamentary voters under a right conferred as aforesaid, but not to be enrolled as burgesses.

Division three is to comprise the names of the persons entitled to be enrolled as burgesses, but not to be registered as Parliamentary voters under a right conferred as aforesaid. *

Omit part between asterisks if no part of parish is in a municipal borough, or if no part of parish is in a Parliamentary borough.

†On or before the last day of July you are also to make out a list of all persons who are entitled within your parish [or township] to be registered as Parliamentary voters to vote at the election of a member [or members] to serve in Parliament for the said Parliamentary borough in respect of any other right than a right conferred by the Reform Act, 1832, or by section three of the Representation of the People Act, 1867 (except as freemen or as lodgers).

Omit part between crosses if no part of parish is in a Parliamentary borough.

On or before the last day of July you are also to make out a list of all persons who, being on the register of voters now in force for the said Parliamentary borough in respect of residence in lodgings within your parish [or township], have duly claimed, on or before the Twenty-fifth day of July, to have their names inserted in the lists of Parliamentary voters for the said borough in respect of residence in the same lodgings. †

These lists are [or this list is] to be in the form D. (or, as the case may be, E. or F.) sent herewith.

Note.—The appropriate form must be sent.

Omit part between asterisks if no part of parish is in a municipal borough, but unless it is omitted, send Form G.

Note.—A printed copy of the directions in the Schedule for the guidance of overseers in making out the lists must be enclosed.

Omit part between crosses if no part of parish is in a Parliamentary borough.

Note.—A printed copy of the Table No. 1 in Schedule (D.) to the Parliamentary Registration Act, 1843, 6 & 7 Vict. c. 18, must be enclosed.

Note—Forms marked K. and L. must be sent.

*On or before the last day of July you are also to make out a list, in the Form G. sent herewith) of all persons who are entitled, in respect of the occupation of property within your parish [*or* township] to be elected councillors or aldermen of the said municipal borough, but who are not entitled to be on the burgess roll thereof. *

In making out each of these lists you will follow the directions of which a copy is enclosed.

On or before the first day of August you are to sign and publish written or printed copies of these lists, in the same manner as before mentioned with respect to the notice.

You are to keep a copy of these lists signed by you, †and also a copy of the lists of defaulters in payment of asessed taxes sent to you by the collector of taxes,† to be open to public inspection at any time between the hours of ten o'clock in the forenoon and four o'clock in the afternoon of any day, except Sunday, during the first fourteen days after the publication of the said lists, and to deliver copies of any such lists to any person on payment of a price for each copy after the rate contained in the table marked " Parliamentary Registration Act, 1843, Schedule (D.), No. 1," sent herewith.

You are to make out lists according to the forms marked K. sent herewith, containing the names of every person who has given or caused to be given to you, or any one of you, on or before the Twenty-fifth day of August, notice of his claim to have his name inserted in any lists of voters, making separate lists of—

1. Persons claiming to be entered in the lists of Parliamentary voters otherwise than as freemen or lodgers; and,

2. Persons claiming to be entered in the lists of Parliamentary voters as lodgers who are not comprised in the above-mentioned lists of lodger voters; *and,

Omit part between asterisks if no part of parish is in a municipal borough.

3. Persons claiming to be entered in the burgess lists. *

You are also to make out lists according to the forms marked L., sent herewith, containing the names of every person against whom a notice of

162

objection has been given to you, or any of you, on or before the Twenty-fifth day of August, as not being entitled to have his name retained in any list for your parish (or township), giving in separate lists the objections made to—

1. Any persons on the lists of Parliamentary voters other than the above-mentioned lists of lodger voters:
2. Any person on the above-mentioned list of lodger voters:
* 3. Any person on the burgess list. *

On or before the Twenty-ninth day of August you are to deliver to me copies of the lists so respectively made out and signed by you as aforesaid.

On or before the First day of September you are to sign and publish each of the lists of claimants and persons objected to in the same manner as before mentioned with respect to the notice.

You are to keep a copy of each of the lists of claimants and persons objected to, signed by you, and these copies and also the original notices of claims and of objections are to be open to public inspection at any time between the hours of ten of the clock in the forenoon and four of the clock in the afternoon of any day, except Sunday, during the first Fourteen days of September, and you are to deliver copies of each of these lists to any person on payment of a price for each copy after the rate contained in the table marked "Parliamentary Registration Act, 1843, Schedule (D.), No. 1," sent herewith.

If you find any such notice, list, or other document published by you as aforesaid to be destroyed, mutilated, effaced, or removed, you are forthwith to place another in its room to the same effect.

You are to attend at the court to be holden for the revision of the said lists, of the time of holding which notice will be given; and at the opening of the court you are there to deliver to the barrister before whom the same is holden the several lists made out and signed by you, and the original notices of claims and of objections given to you.

Herein if you fail you will be liable to the penalties in that case provided.

> Omit part between asterisks if no part of parish is in a municipal borough.

Dated the   day of   18 .

(Signed)   *A. B.*,

Town Clerk of the Municipal Borough of

> If the officer issuing precept is not the town clerk of a municipal borough, he should append to his signature his proper official description.

FORM (B).

NOTICE to be Published by the OVERSEERS in a PARLIAMENTARY BOROUGH.

Parliamentary borough of

to wit.

} We hereby give notice, that no person will be entitled to have his name

inserted in any list of Parliamentary voters for the Parliamentary borough of   now about to be made in respect of the occupation of any property situate wholly or partly within this parish [*or* township] unless he pays on or before the Twentieth day of July all the poor rates which have become due from him in respect of those premises up to the Fifth day of January last past; or to have his name inserted in any such list under any right conferred by the Reform Act, 1832, in respect of the occupation of any property situate as aforesaid, unless he pays on or before the Twentieth day of July all assessed taxes which have become due from him in respect of those premises up to the Fifth day of January last past; and all persons who omit to make such payments will be incapable of being upon the next register of Parliamentary voters for this borough in respect of those premises.

Dated the   day of June, 18 .

(Signed)   *A.B.* } Overseers of the Parish [*or*
            C.D. }   township] of

NOTICE to be Published by the OVERSEERS in a MUNICIPAL BOROUGH.

Note.—This form is to be used only where the whole or part of the area of the municipal borough is co-extensive with or included in tLe area of a Parliamentary borough.

Municipal borough of

to wit.

} We hereby give notice, that no person will be entitled to have

his name inserted in any list of burgesses of the municipal borough of   now about to be made in respect of the occupation of any property situate wholly or partly within this parish [*or* township], unless he pays on or before the Twentieth day of July all poor rates and borough rates (if any) which have become due from him in respect of those premises up to the Fifth day of January last past; and all persons who omit to make such payment will be incapable of being upon tho next burgess roll for this borough in respect of those premises.

Dated the   day of June 18 .

(Signed)   A.B. } Overseers of the Parish [or
            C.D. } township] of

Note.—Where a parish is situate within both a Parliamentary borough and a municipal borough, both the above notices must be issued.

FORM (C).

To *A. B.*

† Parliamentary borough of †

* Municipal borough of *

Take notice, that you will not be entitled to have your name inserted † in the list of Parliamentary voters for the Parliamentary borough of
* or† in the burgess lists for the municipal borough
          * now about to be made in respect of the premises in your occupation in [*street or place*], unless you pay on or before the Twentieth day of July next all the poor rates* (including borough rates, if any)* due from you in respect of those premises up to the Fifth day of January last, amounting to £   , and if you omit to make such payment you will be incapable of being on the next † register of Parliamentary voters for the said Parliamentary borough * or † burgess roll for the said municipal borough. *

Dated the   day of June, 18 .

(Signed)   C.D. } Overseers,
            E.F. }

or

G. H., Assistant Overseer,

or

I. K., Collector

of the Parish [*or* Township of]

Note.—This form is to be used in every Parliamentary borough, but only in a municipal borough the whole or part of the area of which is co-extensive with or included in the area of a Parliamentary borough. If no part of the parish is in a Parliamentary borough, the parts between crosses are to be omitted. If no part of the parish is in a municipal borough, the parts between asterisks are to be omitted. Where a borough rate is levied as a separate rate and not as part of the poor rate, the form should be altered accordingly, so as to distinguish the borough rate from the poor rate, and to state that omission to pay the borough rate will disqualify for enrolment as a burgess.

FORM (D).

FORM OF LISTS of PARLIAMENTARY VOTERS and
BURGESSES for a PARISH wholly or partly situate
both in a PARLIAMENTARY BOROUGH and in a
MUNICIPAL BOROUGH.

No. 1.—LIST OF

N.B.—This list (No. 1) does not contain the names of any Parliamentary voters except those entitled under some right conferred by the Reform Act, 1832, or by Section 3 of the Representation of the People Act, 1867.

† The persons entitled under any right conferred
by the Reform Act, 1832, or by section three of the
Representation of the People Act, 1867, to be registered as Parliamentary voters to vote at the election
of a member [*or* members] to serve in Parliament
for the Parliamentary borough of   in
respect of the occupation of property situate wholly
or partly within this parish [*or* township], * and †
the persons entitled to be enrolled as burgesses for
the municipal borough of   in respect
of the occupation of property situate wholly or
partly within this parish [*or* township]. *

*Division One.   Persons entitled both to be Registered as
Parliamentary Voters under a right conferred as
aforesaid, and to be Enrolled as Burgesses.*

1	2	3	4
Names of Voters in full, Surname being First.	Place of Abode.	Nature of Qualification.	Name and Situation of Qualifying Property.
Abrahams, Samuel	4, Brick Street	House (joint)	4, Brick Street
Brown, Thomas	4, Brick Street	Shop	4, Brick Street
Masters, Abel	1, Brick Street	House	1, Brick Street
Smith, William	Wood Villa, Gainsborough.	Building	2, Brick Street

*Division Two.   Persons entitled to be Registered as
Parliamentary Voters under a right conferred as
aforesaid, but not to be Enrolled as Burgesses.*

Names of Voters in full, Surname being first.	Place of Abode.	Nature of Qualification.	Name and Situation of Qualifying Property.
Adams, John	24, Duke Street	House	7, Brick Street
Stubbs, Thomas	10, High Street	Shop	4, Brick Street

Division Three. Persons entitled to be Enrolled as Burgesses, but not to be Registered as Parliamentary Voters under a right conferred as aforesaid.

Names of Voters in full, Surname being first.	Place of Abode.	Nature of Qualification.	Name and Situation of Qualifying Property.
Gardener, Mary -	10, Brick Street	House -	-10, Brick Street
Thompson, Henry	14. John Street	Warehouse	-3, Brick Street

(Signed)　　　*A.B.* ⎰ Overseers of the Parish [*or*
　　　　　　　C.D. ⎱　Township] of　　　　　.

No. 2.—LIST OF

The persons entitled to be registered as Parliamentary Voters to vote at the election of a member [*or* members] to serve in Parliament for the Parliamentary borough of　　　in respect of any other right than a right conferred by the Reform Act, 1832, or by section 3 of the Representation of the People Act, 1867 (except as freemen or as lodgers).

Names of Voters in full, Surname being first.	Place of Abode.	Nature of Qualification.	Name and Situation of Qualifying Property (if any).
Smith, John -	-15, Brick Street	Inhabitant householder, paying scot and lot.	

(Signed)　　　*A.B.* ⎰ Overseers of the Parish [*or*
　　　　　　　C.D. ⎱　Township] of

No. 3.—LIST OF

The persons who, being on the register of voters now in force for the Parliamentary borough of in respect of residence in lodgings within the parish [*or* township] of　　　claim, in respect of residence in the same lodgings, to have their names inserted in the list of persons entitled to vote in the election of a member [or members] to serve in Parliament for the said borough.

167

Names of Claimants in full, Surname being first.	Description of Rooms occupied, and whether Furnished or not.	Street, Lane, or other Place, and Number (if any) of House in which Lodgings are situate.	Amount of Rent paid.	Name and Address of Landlord or other person to whom Rent is paid.	Objections by Overseers.

(Signed)   *A.B.* } Overseers of the Parish [*or*
                C.F. }   Township] of   .

FORM (E).

FORM of LIST of Parliamentary Voters for a PARISH wholly or partly situate in a PARLIAMENTARY BOROUGH, but not in a MUNICIPAL BOROUGH.

This form is to be the same as Form D., omitting from list No. 1 the parts between asterisks, and omitting the words "*Division One. Persons entitled, &c.,*" forming the heading of Division One, and omitting Divisions Two and Three. (*n.*)

(*n.*) See additional Form No. 1.

FORM (F).

Note.—This form is to be used only where the whole or part of the area of the municipal borough is co-extensive with or included in the area of a Parliamentary borough.

FORM OF LIST of Burgesses for a PARISH wholly or partly situate in a MUNICIPAL BOROUGH, but not in a PARLIAMENTARY BOROUGH.

This form is to be the same as Form D., No. 1, omitting the parts between crosses, and omitting the words "*Division One. Persons entitled, &c.,*" forming the heading of Division One, and omitting Divisions Two and Three. (*n.*)

(*n.*) See additional Form No. 2.

FORM (G).

Note.—This form is to be used only where the whole or part of the area of the municipal borough is co-extensive with or included in the area of a Parliamentary borough.

Form of List of Occupiers in any Parish entitled to be elected Councillors or Aldermen of a Municipal Borough, though not entitled to be on the Burgess Roll of that Borough.

List of the persons who are entitled to be elected councillors or aldermen of the municipal borough of   in respect of the occupation, within the

parish [*or* township] of
of any property, but who are not entitled to be on
the Burgess Roll of that borough.

1. Name of Persons in full, Surname being first.	2. Place of Abode.	3. Nature of Qualification.	4. Name and Situation of Qualifying Property.

(Signed) *A. B.* } Overseers of the Parish [*or*
C. D. }   township] of   .

Form (H).

Form of Notice of Claim.

No. 1.—Parliamentary (General).

To the overseers of the parish [*or* township] of

I claim to have my name inserted in the list
made by you of persons entitled to vote at the
election of a member [*or* members] to serve in Parliament for the Parliamentary borough of   in
respect of the qualification named below.

Dated the   day of   18 .

Name of Claimant in full, Surname being first.	Place of Abode.	Nature of Qualification.	Name and Situation of Qualifying Property.

(Signed) *A. B.*

No. 2.—Parliamentary (Lodgers).

To the overseers of the parish [*or* township] of

I claim to have my name inserted in the list of
persons entitled to vote at the election of a member
[*or* members] to serve in Parliament for the Parliamentary borough of   in respect of the
qualification named below.

Name of Claimant in full, Surname being first.	Description of Rooms occupied, and whether Furnished or not.	Street, Lane, or other Place and Number (if any) of House in which Lodgings situate.	Amount of Rent paid.	Name and Address of Landlord or other Person to whom Rent is paid.
Stevens, John William.	Two rooms, first floor, furnished.	51, Brick Street.	16s. a week	William Johnson, High Street.

I hereby declare that I have during the twelve calendar months immediately preceding the Fifteenth day of July in this year occupied as sole tenant [*or* as joint tenant with   ], and resided in the above mentioned lodgings, and that those lodgings are of a clear yearly value, if let unfurnished, of ten [*or* twenty] pounds or

Omit the words between crosses if they are not applicable.

upwards, † and I hereby declare that I am on the register of Parliamentary voters for the said Parliamentary borough in respect of the same lodgings as above mentioned, and I desire to have my name inserted in the list of lodger voters published on or before the first day of August. †

Dated the   day of   18 .

(Signed)   *A.B.* (the Claimant).

I, the undersigned, hereby declare that I have witnessed the above signature of the above-named [*here state name of claimant*] at the date stated above, and that I believe the above claim to be correct.

Dated the   day of   18 .

(Signed)   *C. D.*, of
[*state residence and calling of witness*].

Note.—If the claim is in respect of different rooms successively occupied as lodgings in the same house, the notice of claim must specify each room, or set of rooms, so occupied. If the claimant is on the register in respect of the same lodgings, and desires to have his name inserted in the list of lodger voters published on or before the First day of August, he must send in his claim on or before the Twenty-fifth day of July. In any other case he must send it in after the last day of July, and on or before the Twenty-fifth day of August. If there are two joint lodgers, the yearly value of the lodgings must be twenty pounds or upwards.

No. 3.—Municipal.

To the overseers of the parish [*or* township] of

I claim to have my name inserted in the list made by you of burgesses of the municipal borough of in respect of the qualification named below.

Dated the   day of   18 .

Name of Claimant in full, Surname being first.	Place of Abode.	Nature of Qualification.	Name and Situation of Qualifying Property.

Note.—This form is to be used only where the whole or part of the area of the municipal borough is co-extensive with or included in the area of a Parliamentary borough.

(Signed)   *A.B.*

FORM (I).

Form of Notice of Objection.

No. 1 (Parliamentary).

Notice of Objection to be given to Overseers.

To the Overseers of the parish [*or* township] of

I hereby give you notice that I object to the name of   being retained on the lists of persons entitled to vote at the election of a member [*or* members] to serve in Parliament for the Parliamentary borough of

Dated the   day of   18 .

(Signed) *A. B.* [*place of abode*] on the List of Parliamentary voters for the parish of   .

No. 2. (Parliamentary).

Notice of objection to be given to Person objected to.

To Mr.

I hereby give you notice that I object to your name being retained on the lists of persons entitled to vote at the election of members (*or* a member) to serve in Parliament for the Parliamentary borough of   on the following grounds, viz :—

1. *e.g.*, that you have not occupied for twelve months to July 15th.
2. That
3.

Dated the   day of   18 .

(Signed)   *A. B.* of [*place of abode*] on the List of Parliamentary voters for tho parish of

171

Note.—If there is more than one list of Parliamentary voters, the notice of objection in each of the above two cases, Nos. 1 and 2, should specify the list to which the objection refers, and if the list referred to is made out in divisions, the notice of objection should specify the division to which the objection refers; and if the list contains two or more persons of the same name, the notice should distinguish the person intended to be objected to.

No. 3. (Municipal.)

Note.—This form is to be used only where the whole or part of the area of the municipal borough is co-extensive with or included in the area of a Parliamentary borough.

Notice of Objection to be given to Overseers.

To the Overseers of the parish [*or* township] of

I hereby give you notice that I object to the name of
being retained on the list of burgesses of the municipal borough of   .
Dated the   day of   18 .

(Signed)   *A. B.* of [*place of abode*]
on the List of burgesses for the
parish of   .

No. 4 (Municipal).

NOTICE of OBJECTION to be given to PERSONS
objected to.

Note.—This form is to be used only where the whole or part of the area of the municipal borough is co-extensive with or included in the area of a Parliamentary borough.

To Mr.

I hereby give you notice that I object to your name being retained on the lists of burgesses of the municipal borough of   , on the following grounds, viz. :—

1. *e.g.*, that you have not occupied for twelve months to July 15th.
2. That
3.

Dated the   day of   18 .
(Signed)   *A.B.*, of [*place of abode*], on the List
of Burgesses for the parish of

Note. —If there is more than one burgess list the notice of objection in each of the above two cases, Nos. 3 and 4, should specify the list to which the objection refers, and if the list is made out in divisions, the notice of objection should specify the division to which the objection refers; and if the list contains two or more persons of the same name, the notice should distinguish the person intended to be objected to.

FORM (K).

FORM of LIST of CLAIMANTS to be Published by the Overseers.

No. 1.—GENERAL LIST of CLAIMANTS (PARLIAMENTARY).

The following persons claim otherwise than as lodgers to have their names inserted in the lists of persons entitled to vote at the election of a member [or members] to serve in Parliament for the Parliamentary borough of

Name of Claimant in full, Surname being first.	Place of Abode.	Nature of Qualification.	Name and Situation of Qualifying Property.

(Signed)   *A.B.* | Overseers of the Parish [or
             C.D. | Township] of

No. 2.—LIST of LODGER CLAIMANTS (PARLIAMENTARY).

The following persons claim as lodgers to have their names inserted in the lists of persons entitled to vote at the election of a member [or members] to serve in Parliament for the Parliamentary borough of

Name of Claimant in full, Surname being first.	Description of Rooms occupied and whether Furnished or not.	Street, Lane, or other Place, and Number (if any) of House in which Lodgings are situate.	Amount of Rent paid.	Name and Address of Landlord or other Person to whom Rent is paid.

(Signed)   *A.B.* | Overseers of the Parish [or
             C.D. | Township] of

No. 3.—LIST of CLAIMANTS (MUNICIPAL).

The following persons claim to have their names inserted in the Burgess Roll for the municipal borough of   •

Note.—This form is to be used only where the whole or part of the area of the municipal borough is co-extensive with or included in a Parliamentary borough.

Name of Claimant in full, Surname being first.	Place of Abode.	Nature of Qualification.	Name and Situation of Qualifying Property.

(Signed)   *A.B.* } Overseers of the Parish [*or*
           C.D. }   Township], of

FORM (L).

FORM of LIST of PERSONS Objected to to be Published by the Overseers.

No. 1.—LIST of PERSONS objected to (PARLIAMENTARY).

The following persons have been objected to as not being entitled to have their names retained on the lists of persons entitled to vote at the election of a member [*or* members] to serve in Parliament for the Parliamentary borough of   .

Name of Person objected to in full, Surname being first.	Place of Abode.	Nature of the supposed Qualification.	Name and Situation of Qualifying Property.

(Signed)   *A.B.* } Overseers of the Parish [*or*
           C.D. }   Township] of

No. 2.—LIST of LODGERS objected to (PARLIAMENTARY).

The following persons have been objected to as not being entitled to have their names retained on the list of persons entitled to vote in respect of residence in lodgings at the election of member [*or* members] to serve in Parliament for the Parliamentary borough of

Name of Person objected to in full, Surname being first.	Description of Rooms occupied, and whether Furnished or not.	Street, Lane, or other Place, and Number (if any) of House in which Lodgings are situate.	Amount of Rent paid.	Name and Address of Landlord or other Person to whom Rent is paid.

(Signed)   *A.B.* } Overseers of the Parish [*or*
           C.D. }   Township] of

Note.—This form applies only to lodgers on the list of lodger claimants who claimed on or before the Twenty-fifth day of July, and were then on the register in respect of the same lodgings, and who are objected to. The list of such lodgers should form a separate list from that of other persons objected to.

No. 3.—LIST of PERSONS objected to (MUNICIPAL).

The following persons have been objected to as not being entitled to have their names retained on the Burgess Lists for the municipal borough of

Note.—This form is to be used only where the whole or part of the area of the municipal borough is co-extensive with or included in a Parliamentary borough.

Name of Person objected to in full, Surname being first.	Place of Abode.	Nature of the supposed Qualification.	Name and Situation of Qualifying Property.

(Signed)   *A. B.* }   Overseers of the Parish [*or*
           C.D. }   Township] of

FORM (M).

DECLARATION for correcting misdescription in List.

I,   of No.   in the parish of   in the Parliamentary borough of and in the municipal borough of
[*as the case may be*], do solemnly and sincerely declare as follows :—

1. I am the person referred to in Division of the List of Parliamentary Voters and Burgesses made out in Divisions [or in the list of   ] (*specifying the particular list*) made out for the parish of   , by an entry as follows :—

Name as described in List.	Place of Abode as described in List.	Nature of Qualification as described in List.	Name and Situation of Qualifying Property.
Brown, John - -	High Street -	Shop -	-2, Shire Lane.

2. My correct name and place of abode, and the correct particulars respecting my qualification, are, and ought to be stated for the purposes of the Register about to be made up of voters for the Parliamentary borough of   , and the Burgess Roll about to be made up of burgesses for the municipal borough of
(*as the case may be*), as follows :—

Correct Name.	Correct place of Abode.	Correct nature of Qualification.	Correct Name and Situation of Qualifying Property.
Brown, Joseph	15, High Street	House	24, Shire Lane.

Dated this   day of   18 .

(Signed)

Made and subscribed before }
    me this   day }
of   18 . }

The person before whom the declaration is made should affix his official description.

A B.,

Justice of the Peace for

FORM (N).

NOTICE of WITHDRAWAL of OBJECTION.

No. 1.—NOTICE to the PERSON objected to.

To Mr.

The list should be referred to in the manner prescribed for the notice of objection.
Omit the words between crosses if the objection is wholly withdrawn.
The notice should be signed in the manner prescribed for the notice of objection.

I hereby give you notice that I withdraw my objection to your name being retained on the list of † so far as regards the ground of objection numbered   in my notice to you of such objection.†

Dated the   day of   18 .

(Signed)

No. 2.—NOTICE to the TOWN CLERK.

To the Town Clerk of

The list should be referred to in the manner prescribed for the notice of objection.
Omit the words between crosses if the objection is wholly withdrawn.
The notice should be signed in the manner prescribed for the notice of objection.

I hereby give you notice that I withdraw my objection to the name of   being retained on the list of † so far as regards the ground of objection numbered   in my notice to him of such objection.†

Dated the   day of   18

(Signed)

FORM (O).
NOTICE of REVIVING an OBJECTION.
No. 1.—NOTICE to the PERSON objected to.

To Mr.

I hereby give you notice that I revive the objection which was made by   , since deceased, to your name being retained on the list of

†so far as regards the ground of objection numbered   in the notice to you of such objection.†

Dated the   day of   18 .

(Signed)

No. 2.—NOTICE to the TOWN CLERK.

To the Town Clerk of

I hereby give you notice that I revive the objection which was made by   , since deceased, to the name of

being retained on the list of

† so far as regards the ground of objection numbered   in the notice to the person objected to of such objection.†

Dated the   day of   18 .

(Signed)

The list should be referred to in the manner prescribed for the notice of objection. Omit the words between crosses if the objection is wholly revived. The notice should be signed in the manner prescribed for the notice of objection.

The list should be referred to in the manner prescribed for the notice of objection. Omit the words between crosses if the objection is wholly revived. The notice should be signed in the manner prescribed for the notice of objection.

NOTE (P).
DIRECTIONS for the Guidance of OVERSEERS in making out the Lists.

The following directions should be observed by overseers in making out the lists of Parliamentary voters and burgesses, and also the lists of claimants and persons objected to as Parliamentary voters and burgesses.

(1.) The surname and other name or names of each person are to be written at full length, the surname being placed first.

(2.) Each list, and, where the list is made out in divisions, each divison of each list, should be made out in alphabetical order.

(3.) The place of abode should be entered with the name of the street, lane, or other locality, and the number in such street, lane, or other locality of such place of abode, where there is any such name or number, and should be entered in all cases in

Note.—If the local authority has given any special directions as to the mode of making out the list, the town clerk, or other officer issuing the precepts, must modify direction (2) accordingly.

177   N

such a manner as will afford a full and sufficient address for a person entered if a letter is addressed to him by post.

(4.) The nature of the qualification should be entered as nearly as possible in the words of the statute conferring the franchise, for instance:—

> (a) The nature of the qualification of a person under the Reform Act, 1832 (2 & 3 Will. 4, c. 45), or under the Municipal Corporation Acts, should be stated thus: "house," or, in the case of a joint occupation, "house (joint)," or "warehouse," "counting-house," "shop," or "building," or in the manner provided by the Parliamentary and Municipal Registration Act, 1878, as the case may be :

> (b) The nature of the qualification of a person under section 3 of the Representation of the People Act, 1867, should be stated thus, "dwelling-house."

(5.) The name and situation of the qualifying property, if the qualification is in respect of property, should be entered with the name of the street, lane, or other locality, and the number in such street, lane, or other locality of such property, where there is any such name or number, and should be entered in all cases in such a manner as will afford full and sufficient means of identifying such property.

(6.) Where several qualifications are possessed by the same person, the particulars respecting each qualification should be stated in the list; and in the case of a list made out in divisions, where a person is entered in Division 1 in respect of one qualification for Parliamentary purposes, and in respect of another qualification for municipal purposes, each such qualification should be distinguished in the list by a note to the effect that the qualification is for Parliamentary purposes only, or for municipal purposes only, as the case may be.

(7.) In making out the list of lodger claimants who claim on or before the Twenty-fifth day of July, and are then on the register in respect of the same lodgings, if you have reason to believe that any person whose name is entered on that list is dead, or is not entitled to vote, you should make a note to that effect in the last column of the list, being the column headed " Objections by overseers."

(8.) You should omit from any list of Parliamentary voters or burgesses the name of any person who appears from the returns furnished by the registrar of births and deaths to be dead, and the name of any person who is ascertained to be disqualified for being inserted in the list by reason of having received parochial relief or other alms.

Note (Q).

Directions for Guidance in the formation of the Parliamentary Register and Burgess Roll.

In copying and printing Divisions 1 and 2 for the Parliamentary Register, and Divisions 1 and 3 for the Burgess Roll, of any revised list made out in divisions under this Act, the two divisions in each set may, and, if and so far as the local authority under the Act shall so direct, shall be combined or kept separate, and be arranged according to convenience for use in parts for polling districts or wards, and where the polling districts and wards are not conterminous in such manner that the parts may be conveniently compiled or put together to serve either as lists for polling districts or as ward lists; and the names may, and, if and so far as the said local authority shall so direct, shall be distinguished by a number either alone or in combination with a letter or other distinguishing mark according to the parts, and any arrangement may, and, if and so far as the said local authority shall so direct, shall be adopted according to convenience, so that one print or edition of Division 1 may be available for both sets.

Each entry for voting on the Parliamentary register of every Parliamentary borough, and on the burgess roll of every municipal borough whose burgess lists are revised under this Act, is to be distinguished by a number, either alone or in combination with a letter or distinguishing mark.

Any entry of a person not entitled to vote in respect of the qualification therein contained, he being on the list for voting in respect of another qualification, is to be denoted by an asterisk in the manner provided by section forty-seven of the Parliamentary Registration Act, 1843, with respect to similar entries in the registers for counties.

The officer having the custody of any revised lists under this Act shall permit access thereto for the purpose of the same being copied for the Parliamentary register of the Parliamentary borough, and for the Burgess Roll of any municipal borough to which such revised lists relate.

42 & 43 Vic. c. 10.

An Act to amend the Poor Rate Assessment and Collection Act, 1869.   [23rd *May*, 1879.]

Short title and construction. 32 & 33 Vict. c. 41.

1. This Act may be cited as the Assessed Rates Act, 1879, and shall be construed as one with the Poor Rate Assessment and Collection Act, 1869, in this Act called the principal Act.

Effect of allowance or deduction as regards qualification or franchise.

2. Where by way of commission or abatement or deduction under the principal Act, or purporting or assumed to be under the principal Act, an allowance or deduction has, before the passing of this Act, been or shall hereafter be actually made, the same shall, for the purpose of every qualification or franchise depending upon rating or upon payment of rates, be deemed to have been duly made in pursuance of every or any agreement, order, notice, or proceeding necessary for the validity thereof under the principal Act, and to have been and to be an allowance or deduction which the overseers were and are empowered to make from the rate under the principal Act; and no qualification or franchise depending upon rating or upon payment of rates shall be defeated by reason of such allowance or deduction not having been made in pursuance of an agreement in writing, order in writing, or notice in writing, or by reason of the want or insufficiency of any agreement, order, notice, or proceeding necessary for the validity thereof under the principal Act, or by reason of any informality or defect in the making thereof; provided always, that this Act shall not relieve any overseers from any liability which they have incurred or may incur by making an allowance or deduction otherwise than in pursuance of the provisions of the principal Act, or affect any remedy for the recovery of the amount of such allowance or deduction.

---

42 & 43 Vic. c. 54.

An Act to make better provision for the adjustment of Parish Boundaries, and to make further amendments in the Acts relating to the relief of the Poor in England.

[15th *August*, 1879.]

Short title.

1. This Act may be cited as the Poor Law Act, 1879.

2. This Act shall not extend to Scotland or Ireland. *Extent of Act.*

3. This Act shall come into operation on the first *Commencement* day of September one thousand eight hundred and *of Act.* seventy-nine, which day is in this Act referred to as the commencement of this Act.

Parish Boundaries.

4. Where part of a parish is on one side while the *Applying cer-* residue of the parish is on the other side of the *tain provisions of 39 & 40 Vict.* boundary of a municipal borough or county, or of a *c. 61 to incon-* river, estuary, or branch of the sea, or where part of a *venient divi-* parish is so situate as to be nearly detached from the *sions of pa-rishes.* residue of the parishes, or otherwise so situate as to render the administration of the relief of the poor in or the local government of such part in conjunction with the residue of the parish inconvenient, the said parish shall be deemed to be a divided parish within the meaning of section one of the Divided Parishes and Poor Law Amendment Act, 1876, and the provisions *39 & 40 Vict.* of that Act shall apply accordingly in like manner as if *c. 61.* the said part were isolated as mentioned in that section.

5. Whereas by section one of the Divided Parishes *Removing* and Poor Law Amendment Act, 1876, an order may be *doubts as to con-* made "for constituting separate parishes out of the *struction of 39 & 40 Vict. c. 61,* Divided Parish, or for amalgamating some of the *s. 1.* parts thereof with the parish or parishes in which the same may be locally included, or to which they may be annexed;" and doubts have arisen with respect to the construction of the said provision, and it is expedient to remove such doubts: Be it therefore enacted as follows :

An order under the said Act may deal with several divided parishes at the same time, and may constitute separate parishes out of any of such divided parishes or out of parts of several divided parishes, and may unite any parts of a divided parish or several divided parishes with each other, and amalgamate the part so united with any adjoining parish, and may amalgamate any part of a divided parish or parts of several divided parishes with an adjoining parish or adjoining parishes.

6. Where a parish was at the time of the passing of *Extension of 39* the Act of the twentieth year of Her present Majesty, *& 40 Vict. c. 61* chapter nineteen, intituled "An Act to provide for *to certain places formerly extra-* the relief of the Poor in extra-parochial places," an *parochial.* extra-parochial place, and a representation is made to the Local Government Board that, by reason of the

relative size and shape of such parish, and its position in respect to other parishes, the relief of the poor could be better administered if the same, or any part or parts thereof, were amalgamated with the adjoining parish or parishes, an order may be made in pursuance of the Divided Parishes and Poor Law Amendment Act, 1876, in relation to such parish, in like manner as if the said parish were a divided parish.

39 & 40 Vict.
c. 61.

---

42 & 43 Vic. c. 75.

An Act to amend and continue the Acts relating to Election Petitions, and to the prevention of Corrupt Practices at Parliamentary Elections.   [*15th August 1879.*]

Short title.

1. This Act may be cited as the Parliamentary Elections and Corrupt Practices Act, 1879.

Trial of election petition to be conducted before two judges.

2. The trial of every election petition and the hearing of an application for the withdrawal of an election petition shall be conducted before two judges instead of one, and the Parliamentary Elections Act, 1868, shall be construed as if for the purpose of hearing and determining the petition at the trial and of hearing and determining any application for the withdrawal of an election petition two judges were mentioned, and additional judges shall, if necessary, be placed on the rota accordingly.

Every certificate and every report sent to the Speaker in pursuance of the said Act shall be under the hands of both judges, and if the judges differ as to whether the member whose return or election is complained of was duly returned, or elected, they shall certify that difference, and the member shall be deemed to be duly elected or returned ; and if the judges determine that such member was not duly elected or returned, but differ as to the rest of the determination, they shall certify that difference, and the election shall be deemed to be void; and if the judges differ as to the subject of a report to the Speaker, they shall certify that difference and make no report on the subject on which they so differ.

Save as aforesaid, any order, act, application, or thing for the purpose of the said Act may continue to be made or done by, to, or before one judge. The expenses incident to the sitting of two judges shall be defrayed as the expenses of one judge are payable under the provisions of the said Act.

3. This Act and the Acts mentioned in the schedule to this Act, so far as they are unrepealed, shall continue in force until the thirty-first day of December one thousand eight hundred and eighty, and any enactments amending or affecting the enactments continued by this Act shall, in so far as they are temporary in their duration, be continued in like manner.

Continuance of Acts.

Session and Chapter.	Title.
	PART I.
17 & 18 Vict. c. 102 -	The Corrupt Practices Prevention Act, 1854.
21 & 22 Vict. c. 87 -	An Act to continue and amend the corrupt Practices Prevention Act, 1854.
26 & 27 Vict. c. 29 -	An Act to amend and continue the Law relating to Corrupt Practices at Elections of Members of Parliament.
	PART II.
31 & 32 Vict. c. 125 -	The Parliamentary Elections Act, 1868.
32 & 33 Vict. c. 21 -	The Corrupt Practices Commission Expenses Act, 1869.
31 & 35 Vict. c. 61 -	The Election Commissioners Expenses Act. 1871.

PARLIAMENTARY ELECTION PETITION RULES.

General Rules made 21st November, 1868.

1. The presentation of an Election Petition shall be made by leaving it at the office of the Master nominated by the Chief Justice of the Common Pleas; and such Master or his clerk shall (if required) give a receipt, which may be in the following form :—

> Received on the   day of   at the Master's office, a Petition touching the election of A.B., a Member for   , purporting to be signed by [*insert the names of Petitioners*].
>
> C. D., Master's Clerk.

With the Petition shall also be left a copy thereof for the Master to send to the returning officer, pursuant to Section 7 of the Act.

2. An Election Petition shall contain the following statements :—

   1. It shall state the right of the Petitioner to petition within Section 5 of the Act.
   2. It shall state the holding and result of the election, and shall briefly state the facts and grounds relied on to sustain the prayer.

3. The Petition shall be divided into paragraphs, each of which, as nearly as may be, shall be confined to a distinct portion of the subject; and every paragraph shall be numbered consecutively; and no costs shall be allowed of drawing or copying any Petition not substantially in compliance with this rule, unless otherwise ordered by the Court or a Judge.

4. The Petition shall conclude with a prayer, as, for instance, that some specified person should be declared duly returned or elected, or that the election shall be declared void, or that a return may be enforced (as the case may be), and shall be signed by all the Petitioners.

5. The following form, or one to the like effect, shall be sufficient:—

In the Common Pleas.

"The Parliamentary Elections Act, 1868."
Election for [*state the place*], holden on the
day of　　　　　　　　, A.D.
The Petition of A., of　　[*or* of A., of　　, and
B., of　　　　*as the case may be*], whose names are
subscribed.

1. Your Petitioner, A., is a person who voted [*or* had a right to vote, *as the case may be*] at the above election [*or* claims to have had a right to be returned at the above election ; *or* was a candidate at the above election], and your Petitioner, B. [*here state in like manner the right of each Petitioner*].

2. And your Petitioners state that the Election was holden on the　　　　　　　　　day of
　　　　A.D.,　　　when A. B., C. D., and E. F. were candidates, and the returning officer has returned A. B and C. D. as being duly elected.

3. And your Petitioners say that [*here state the facts and grounds on which the Petitioners rely*].

Wherefore your Petitioners pray that it may be determined that the said A. B. was not duly elected or returned, and that the Election was void [*or* that the said E. F. was duly elected and ought to have been returned, *or as the case may be.*]

　　　　　　　　　(Signed)　　　A.
　　　　　　　　　　　　　　　　B.

6. Evidence need not be stated in the Petition, but the Court or a Judge may order such particulars as may be necessary to prevent surprise and unnecessary expense, and to insure a fair and effectual trial, in the same way as in ordinary proceedings in the Court of Common Pleas, and upon such terms, as to costs and otherwise, as may be ordered.

7. When a Petitioner claims the seat for an unsuccessful candidate, alleging that he had a majority of lawful votes, the party complaining of or defending the election or return shall, six days before the day appointed for trial, deliver to the Master, and also at the address (if any) given by the Petitioners and Respondent, as the case may be, a list of the votes intended to be objected to, and of the heads of objection to each such vote; and the Master shall allow inspection and office copies of such lists to all parties concerned; and no evidence shall be given against the validity of any

vote, nor upon any head of objection not specified in the list, except by leave of the Court or Judge, upon such terms as to amendment of the list, postponement of the inquiry, and payment of costs, as may be ordered.

8. When the Respondent in a petition under the Act, complaining of an undue return, and claiming the seat for some person, intends to give evidence to prove that the election of such person was undue, pursuant to the 53rd section of the Act, such Respondent shall, six days before the day appointed for trial, deliver to the Master, and also at the address (if any) given by the Petitioner, a list of the objections to the election upon which he intends to rely; and the Master shall allow inspection and office copies of such lists to all parties concerned; and no evidence shall be given by a Respondent of any objection to the election not specified in the list, except by leave of the Court or Judge, upon such terms as to amendments of the list, postponement of the inquiry. and payment of costs, as may be ordered.

9. With the Petition Petitioners shall leave at the office of the Master a writing, signed by them or on their behalf, giving the name of some person entitled to practise as an attorney or agent in cases of Election Petitions whom they authorise to act as their agent, or stating that they act for themselves, as the case may be, and in either case giving an address within three miles from the General Post Office, at which notices addressed to them may be left; and if no such writing be left or address given, then notice of objection to the recognizances, and all other notices and proceedings may be given by sticking up the same at the Master's office.

10. Any person returned as a Member may at any time after he is returned send or leave at the office of the Master a writing signed by him or on his behalf, appointing a person entitled to practise as an attorney or agent in cases of Election Petitions, to act as his agent in case there should be a Petition against him, or stating that he intends to act for himself, and in either case giving an address within three miles from the General Post Office at which notices may be left; and in default of such writing being left in a week after service of the Petition, notices and proceedings may be given and served respectively by sticking up the same at the Master's office.

11. The Master shall keep a book or books at his office in which he shall enter all addresses and the names of agents given under either of the preceding rules, which book shall be open to inspection by any person during office hours.

12. The Master shall upon the presentation of the Petition forthwith send a copy of the Petition to the returning officer, pursuant to section 7 of the Act, and shall therewith send the name of the Petitioners' agent, if any, and of the address, if any, given as prescribed; and also of the name of the Respondent's agent, and the address, if any, given as prescribed; and the returning officer shall forthwith publish those particulars along with the Petition.

The cost of publication of this and any other matter required to be published by the returning officer shall be paid by the Petitioner or person moving in the matter, and shall form part of the general cost of the Petition.

13. The time for giving notice of the presentation of a Petition and of the nature of the proposed security shall be five days, exclusive of the day of presentation.

14. Where the Respondent has named an agent or given an address, the service of an Election Petition may be by delivery of it to the agent, or by posting it in a registered letter to the address given at such time that, in the ordinary course of post, it would be delivered within the prescribed time.

In other cases the service must be personal on the Respondent, unless a Judge, on an application made to him not later than five days after the Petition is presented on affidavit showing what has been done, shall be satisfied that all reasonable effort has been made to effect personal service and cause the matter to come to the knowledge of the Respondent, including when practicable service upon an agent for election expenses, in which case the Judge may order that what has been done shall be considered sufficient service, subject to such conditions as he may think reasonable.

15. In case of evasion of service the sticking up a notice in the office of the Master of the Petition having been presented stating the Petitioner, the prayer, and the nature of the proposed security, shall be deemed equivalent to personal service if so ordered by a Judge.

16. The deposit of money by way of security for payment of costs, charges, and expenses payable by

the Petitioner, shall be made by payment into the Bank of England to an account to be opened there by the description of, " The Parliamentary Elections Act, 1868, Security Fund," which shall be vested in and drawn upon, from time to time, by the Chief Justice of the Common Pleas for the time being, for the purposes for which security is required by the said Act, and a bank receipt or certificate for the same shall be forthwith left at the Master's office.

17. The Master shall file such receipt or certificate, and keep a book open to inspection of all parties concerned, in which shall be entered, from time to time, the amount and the Petition to which it is applicable.

18. The recognizance as security for costs may be acknowledged before a Judge at Chambers or the Master in town, or a Justice of the Peace in the country.

There may be one recognizance acknowledged by all the sureties or separate recognizances by one or more, as may be convenient.

19. The recognizance shall contain the name and usual place of abode of each surety, with such sufficient description as shall enable him to be found or ascertained, and may be as follows :—

Be it remembered that on the   day of   , in the year of our Lord 18   , before me [*name and description*] came A.B., of [*name and description as above prescribed*] and acknowledged himself [*or severally acknowledged themselves*] to owe to our Sovereign Lady the Queen the sum of one thousand pounds [*or the following sums*] (that is to say) the said C.D., the sum of £   , the said E.F. the sum of £   , the said G.H. the sum of £   and the said J.K. the sum of £   , to be levied on his [*or their respective*] goods and chattels, land and tenements, to the use of our said Sovereign Lady the Queen, Her heirs, and successors.

The condition of his recognizance is that if [*here insert the names of all the Petitioners, and if more than one add* or any of them] shall well and truly pay all costs. charges, and expenses, in respect of the Election Petition signed by him [*or them*] relating to the [*here insert the name of the borough or county*] which shall become payable by the said Petitioner [*or Petitioners, or any of them*] under " The Parliamentary Elections Act,

1868," to any person or persons, then this recognizance to be void, otherwise to stand in full force.

(Signed)
[*Signature of Sureties.*]

Taken and acknowledged by the above-named [*names of sureties*] on the   day of   , at , before me,

C. D.

A justice of the Peace [*or as the case may be*].

20. The recognizance or recognizances shall be left at the Master's office by or on behalf of the Petitioner in like manner as before prescribed for the leaving of a Petition forthwith after being acknowledged.

21. The time for giving notice of any objection to a recognizance under the 8th section of the Act shall be within five days from the date of service of the notice of the Petition and of the nature of the security exclusive of the day of service.

22. An objection to the recognizance must state the ground or grounds thereof, as that the sureties, or any and which of them, are insufficient, or that a surety is dead, or that he cannot be found, or that a person named in the recognizance has not duly acknowledged the same.

23. Any objection made to the security shall be heard and decided by the Master, subject to appeal within five days to a judge upon summons taken out by either party to declare the security sufficient or insufficient.

24. Such hearing and decision may be either upon affidavit or personal examination of witnesses or both, as the Master or Judge may think fit.

25. If by order made upon such summons the security be declared sufficient, its sufficiency shall be deemed to be established within the meaning of the 9th section of the said Act, and the Petition shall be at issue.

26. If by order made upon such summons an objection be allowed and the security be declared insufficient, the Master or Judge shall in such order state what amount he deems requisite to make the security sufficient; and the further prescribed time to remove the objection by deposit shall be within five days from the date of the order, not including the day of the date, and such deposit shall be made in the manner already prescribed.

27. The costs of hearing and deciding the objections made to the security given shall be paid as ordered by the Master or Judge, and in default of such order shall form part of the general costs of the Petition.

28. The costs of hearing and deciding an objection upon the ground of insufficiency of a surety or sureties shall be paid by the Petitioner, and a clause to that effect shall be inserted in the order declaring its sufficiency or insufficiency, unless at the time of leaving the recognizance with the Master there be also left with the Master an affidavit of the sufficiency of the surety or sureties sworn by each surety before a Justice of the Peace, which affidavit any Justice of the Peace is hereby authorised to take, or before some person authorised to take affidavits in the Court of Common Pleas, that he is seised or possessed of real or personal estate, or both, above what will satisfy his debts of the clear value of the sum for which he is bound by his recognizance, which affidavit may be as follows:

In the Common Pleas.
"Parliamentary Elections Act, 1868."

I, A.B., of [*as in recognizance*] make oath and say that I am seised or possessed of real [*or* personal] estate above what will satisfy my debts of the clear value of £   Sworn, &c.

29. The order of the Master for payment of costs shall have the same force as an order made by a Judge, and may be made a Rule of the Court of Common Pleas, and enforced in like manner as a Judge's order.

30. The Master shall make out the election list. In it he shall insert the name of the agents of the Petitioners and Respondent, and the addresses to which notices may be sent, if any. The list may be inspected at the Master's office at any time during office hours, and shall be put up for that purpose upon a notice board appropriated to proceedings under the said Act, and headed "Parliamentary Elections Act, 1868."

31. The time and place of the trial of each Election Petition shall be fixed by the Judges on the rota, and notice thereof shall be given in writing by the Master by sticking notice up in his office, sending one copy by the post to the address given by the Petitioner, another to the address given by the Respondent, if any, and a copy by the post to the sheriff, or in case of a borough having a mayor, to the mayor of that borough, 15 days before the day appointed for the trial.

The sheriff or mayor, as the case may be, shall forthwith publish the same in the county or borough.

32. The sticking up of the notice of trial at the office of the Master shall be deemed and taken to be notice in the prescribed manner within the meaning of the Act, and such notice shall not be vitiated by any miscarriage of, or relating to, the copy or copies thereof to be sent as already directed.

33. The notice of trial may be in the following form :—

"Parliamentary Elections Act, 1868."

Election Petition of   county or borough] of

Take notice that the above petition [*or* petitions] will be tried at   on the day of   and on such other subsequent days as may be needful.

Dated the   day of

Signed, by order,
A.B.,

The Master appointed under the above Act.

34. A Judge may from time to time, by order made upon the application of a party to the Petition, or by notice in such form as the Judge may direct to be sent to the sheriff or mayor, as the case may be, postpone the beginning of the trial to such day as he may name, and such notice when received shall be forthwith made public by the sheriff or mayor.

35. In the event of the Judge not having arrived at the time appointed for the trial, or to which the trial is postponed, the commencement of the trial shall *ipso facto* stand adjourned to the ensuing day, and so from day to day.

36. No formal adjournment of the Court for the trial of an Election Petition shall be necessary, but the trial is to be deemed adjourned, and may be continued from day to day until the inquiry is concluded; and in the event of the Judge who begins the trial being disabled by illness or otherwise, it may be recommenced and concluded by another Judge.

37. The application to state a special case may be made by rule in the Court of Common Pleas when sitting, or by summons before a Judge at Chambers upon hearing the parties

38. The title of the Court of Record held for the trial of an Election Petition may be as follows :—

Court for the trial of an Election Petition for the [county of   or borough of
as may be] between
Petitioner and
Respondent, and it shall be sufficient so to entitle all proceedings in that Court.

39. An officer shall be appointed for each Court for the trial of an Election Petition, who shall attend at the trial in like manner as the clerks of assize and of arraigns attend at the assizes.

Such officer may be called the Registrar of that Court. He by himself, or in case of need his sufficient deputy, shall perform all the functions incident to the officer of a Court of Record, and also such duties as may be prescribed to him.

40. The reasonable costs of any witness shall be ascertained by the Registrar of the Court, and the certificate allowing them shall be under his hand.

41. The order of a Judge to compel the attendance of a person, as a witness, may be in the following form :—

Court for the trial of an Election Petition for [*complete the title of the Court*] the
day of   To A.B. [*describe the person*] You are hereby required to attend before the above Court at [*place*] on the
day of   at the hour of [*or* forthwith, *as the case may be*] to be examined as a witness in the matter of the said Petition, and to attend the said Court until your examination shall have been completed.

As witness my hand,
A.B.
Judge of the said Court.

42. In the event of its being necessary to commit any person for contempt, the warrant may be as follows :—

At a Court holden on   at
for the trial of an Election Petition
for the county [*or borough*] of
before Sir Samuel Martin, Knight, one of the Barons of Her Majesty's Court of Exchequer, and one of the Judges for the time being for the trial of Election Petitions in England, pursuant to " The Parliamentary Elections Act, 1868,"

Whereas A.B. has this day been guilty, and is
by the said Court adjudged to be guilty, of a contempt thereof, the said Court does therefore
sentence the said A.B. for his said contempt to be
imprisoned in the   gaol for
                      calendar months, and to pay
to our Lady the Queen a fine of £
and to be further imprisoned in the said gaol until
the said fine be paid; and the Court further orders
that the sheriff of the said county [*or as the case
may be*], and all constables and officers of the peace
of any county or place where the said A.B. may
be found, shall take the said A.B. into custody and
convey him to the said gaol, and there deliver him
into the custody of the gaoler thereof, to undergo
his said sentence; and the Court further orders the
said gaoler to receive the said A.B. into his custody,
and that he shall be detained in the said gaol in
pursuance of the said sentence.

A.D.

Signed the   day of

S.M.

43. Such warrant may be made out and directed to
the sheriff or other person having the execution of
process of the Superior Courts, as the case may be,
and to all constables and officers of the peace of the
county or place where the person adjudged guilty of
contempt may be found, and such warrant shall be
sufficient without further particularity, and shall and
may be executed by the persons to whom it is directed,
or any or either of them.

44. All interlocutory questions and matters, except
as to the sufficiency of the security, shall be heard and
disposed of before a Judge, who shall have the same
control over the proceedings under " The Parliamentary Elections Act, 1868," as a Judge at Chambers in
the ordinary proceedings of the Superior Courts, and
such questions and matters shall be heard and disposed
of by one of the Judges upon the rota, if practicable,
and if not, then by any Judge at Chambers.

45. Notice of an application for leave to withdraw a
Petition shall be in writing, and signed by the
Petitioners or their agent.

It shall state the ground on which the application is
intended to be supported.

The following Form shall be sufficient :—

"Parliamentary Elections Act, 1868."

County [*or* borough] of   Petition
of [*state Petitioners*]
presented   day of
The Petitioner proposes to apply to withdraw his
Petition upon the following ground [*here state the
ground*] and prays that a day may be appointed for
hearing his application.

Dated this   day of
(Signed)

46. The notice of application for leave to withdraw
shall be left at the Master's office.

47. A copy of such notice of the intention of the
Petitioner to apply for leave to withdraw his Petition
shall be given by the Petitioner to the Respondent,
and to the Returning Officer, who shall make it public
in the county or borough to which it relates, and
shall be forthwith published by the Petitioner in at
least one newspaper circulating in the place.

The following may be the form of such notice :—

" Parliamentary Elections Act, 1868."

In the Election Petition for   in which
is Petitioner and   Respondent.

Notice is hereby given, that the above Petitioner
has on the   day of
lodged at the Master's office, notice of an application
to withdraw the Petition, of which notice the following
is a copy [*set it out*].

And take notice that, by the rule made by the
Judges, any person who might have been a Petitioner
in respect of the said eection may within five days
after publication by the Returning Officer of this
notice give notice in writing of his intention on the
hearing to apply for leave to be substituted as a
Petitioner.

(Signed)

48. Any person who might have been a Petitioner
in respect of the election to which the Petition relates
may, within five days after such notice is published by
the Returning Officer, give notice, in writing, signed by
him or on his behalf, to the Master, of his intention to
apply at the hearing to be substituted for the Petitioner,
but the want of such notice shall not defeat such
application, if in fact made at the hearing.

49. The time and place for hearing the application shall be fixed by a Judge, and whether before the Court of Common Pleas or before a Judge, as he may deem advisable, but shall not be less than a week after the notice of the intention to apply has been given to the Master as hereinbefore provided, and notice of the time and place appointed for the hearing shall be given to such person or persons, if any, as shall have given notice to the Master of an intention to apply to be substituted as Petitioners, and otherwise in such manner and at such time as the Judge directs.

50. Notice of abatement of a Petition, by death of the Petitioner or surviving Petitioner, under section 37 of the said Act, shall be given by the party or person interested in the same manner as notice of an application to withdraw a Petition, and the time within which application may be made to the Court or a Judge, by motion or summons at Chambers, to be substituted as a Petitioner, shall be one calendar month, or such further time as upon consideration of any special circumstances the Court or a Judge may allow.

51. If the Respondent dies or is summoned to Parliament as a Peer of Great Britain by a writ issued under the Great Seal of Great Britain, or if the House of Commons have resolved that his seat is vacant, any person entitled to be a Petitioner under the Act in respect of the election to which the Petitioner relates may give notice of the fact in the county or borough by causing such notice to be published in at least one newspaper circulating therein, if any, and by leaving a copy of such notice signed by him or on his behalf with the Returning Officer, and a like copy with the Master.

52. The manner and time of the Respondent's giving notice to the Court that he does not intend to oppose the Petition shall be by leaving notice thereof in writing at the office of the Master, signed by the Respondent, six days before the day appointed for trial exclusive of the day of leaving such notice.

53. Upon such notice being left at the Master's office, the Master shall forthwith send a copy thereof by the post to the Petitioner or his agent, and to the sheriff or mayor, as the case may be, who shall cause the same to be published in the county or borough.

54. The time for applying to be admitted as a Respondent in either of the events mentioned in the 38th section of the Act shall be within ten days after such notice is given as hereinbefore directed, or such further time as the Court or a Judge may allow.

55. Costs shall be taxed by the Master or, at his request, by any Master of a Superior Court, upon the rule of Court or Judge's order by which the costs are payable, and costs when taxed may be recovered by execution issued upon the Rule of Court ordering them to be paid; or if payable by the order of a Judge, then by making such order a Rule of Court in the ordinary way and issuing execution upon such rule against the person by whom the costs are ordered to be paid, or in case there be money in the Bank available for the purpose, then to the extent of such money by order of the Chief Justice of the Common Pleas for the time being, upon a duplicate of the Rule of Court. The office fees payable for Inspection Office copies, enrolment, and other proceedings under the Act; and these rules shall be the same as those payable, if any, for like proceedings according to the present practice of the Court of Common Pleas.

56. The Master shall prepare and keep a roll properly headed for entering the names of all persons entitled to practise as Attorney or Agent in cases of Election Petitions, and all matters relating to elections before the Court and Judges pursuant to the 57th section of the said Act, which Roll shall be kept and dealt with in all respects as the Roll of Attorneys of the Court of Common Pleas, and shall be under the control of that Court, as to striking off the Roll and otherwise.

57. The entry upon the Roll shall be written and subscribed by the attorney or agent, or some attorney authorised by him in writing to sign on his behalf, who shall therein set forth the name, description, and address in full.

58. The Master may allow any person upon the Roll of Attorneys for the time being, and during the present year any person whose name or the name of whose firm is in the Law List of the present year as a Parliamentary Agent to subscribe the Roll, and permission to subscribe the Roll may be granted to any other person by the Court or a Judge upon affidavit showing the facts which entitle the applicant to practise as agent according to the principles, practice, and rules of the House of Commons in cases of Election Petitions.

59. An agent employed for the Petitioner or Respondent shall forthwith leave written notice at the office of the Master of his appointment to act as such agent,

and service of notices and proceedings upon such
agent shall be sufficient for all purposes.

60. No proceeding under "The Parliamentary
Elections Act, 1868," shall be defeated by any formal
objection.

61. Any rule made or to be made in pursuance of
the Act, if made in term time, shall be published by being read by the Master in the Court of
Common Pleas, and if made out of term, by a copy
thereof being put up at the Master's office.

Additional General Rule made the 19th day of
December 1868.

62. That notice of the time and place of the trial
of each Election Petition shall be transmitted by the
Master to the Treasury, and to the Clerk of the
Crown in Chancery; and that the Clerk of the Crown
in Chancery shall, on or before the day fixed for the
trial, deliver, or cause to be delivered, to the
Registrar of the Judge who is to try the Petition, or
his deputy, the poll books, for which the registrar or
his deputy shall give, if required, a receipt: And that
the registrar shall keep in safe custody the said poll
books until the trial is over, and then return the same
to the Crown Office.

Additional General Rules made the 25th day of March,
1869.

63. All claims at law or in equity to money deposited
or to be deposited in the Bank of England for payment
of costs, charges, and expenses payable by the
Petitioners, pursuant to the 16th General Rule, made
the 21st of November 1868, by the Judges for the
trial of Election Petitions in England, shall be disposed
of by the Court of Common Pleas or a Judge.

64. Money so deposited shall, if and when the same
is no longer needed for securing payment of such
costs, charges, and expenses, be returned or otherwise
disposed of as justice may require, by rule of the Court
of Common Pleas or order of a Judge.

65. Such rule or order may be made after such
notice of intention to apply, and proof that all just
claims have been satisfied or otherwise sufficiently
provided for as the court or judge may require.

66. The rule or order may direct payment either to
the party in whose name the same is deposited or to
any person entitled to receive the same.

67. Upon such rule or order being made, the amount may be drawn for by the Chief Justice of the Common Pleas for the time being.

68. The draft of the Chief ·Justice of the Common Pleas for the time being shall, in all cases, be a sufficient warrant to the Bank of England for all payments made thereunder.

Additional General Rules made 27th January 1875.

69. A copy of every order (other than an order giving further time for delivering particulars, or for costs only), or, if the Master shall so direct, the order itself or a duplicate thereof, also a copy of every particular delivered, shall be forthwith filed with the Master, and the same shall be produced at the trial by the Registrar, stamped with the official seal. Such order and particular respectively shall be filed by the party obtaining the same.

70. The petitioner or his agent shall, immediately after notice of the presentation of a petition and of the nature of the proposed security shall have been served, file with the Master an affidavit of the time and manner of service thereof.

71. The days mentioned in rules 7 and 8, and in any rule of court or Judge's order, whereby particulars are ordered to be delivered, or any act is directed to be done, so many days before the day appointed for trial, shall be reckoned exclusively of the day of delivery, or of doing the act ordered and the day appointed for trial, and exclusively also of Sunday, Christmas Day, Good Friday, and any day set apart for a public fast or public thanksgiving.

72. When the last day for presenting petitions, or filing lists of votes or objections, under rules 7 and 8, or recognizances or any other matter required to be filed within a given time, shall happen to fall on a holiday, the petition or other matter shall be deemed duly filed if put into the letter box at the Master's office at any time during such day; but an affidavit, stating with reasonable precision the time when such delivery was made, shall be filed on the first day after the expiration of the holidays.

73. Rule 40 is hereby revoked, and in lieu thereof it is ordered that the amount to be paid to any witness whose expenses shall be allowed by the Judge shall be ascertained and certified by the Registrar; or in the event of his becoming incapacitated from giving such certificate, by the Judge.

74. After receiving notice of the petitioner's intention to apply for leave to withdraw, or of the respondent's intention not to oppose, or of the abatement of the petition by death, or of the happening of any of the events mentioned in the 38th section of the Act, if such notice be received after notice of trial shall have been given, and before the trial has commenced, the Master shall forthwith countermand the notice of trial. The countermand shall be given in the same manner, as near as may be, as the notice of trial.

MUNICIPAL
ELECTION PETITION RULES.

General Rules for the Effectual Execution of "The Corrupt Practices (Municipal Elections) Act, 1872," made 20th November, 1872, pursuant to the Parliamentary Elections Act, 1868.

1. The presentation of a Municipal Election Petition shall be made by leaving it at the office of the Master for the time being nominated by the Chief Justice of the Common Pleas, under the Parliamentary Elections Act, 1868, and such Master or his clerk shall (if required) give a receipt which may be in the following form :—

> Received on the   day of   at the Master's office a petition touching the election of A.B., alderman, councillor [&c. *as the case may be*] for the borough of
> purporting to be signed by [*insert the names of petitioners*].
>
> C. D., Master's Clerk.

With the petition shall also be left a copy thereof for the Master to send to the town clerk, pursuant to section 13, sub-section (1), of the Municipal Elections Act.

2. A municipal election petition shall contain the following statements :—

1. It shall state the right of the petitioner or petitioners to petition within section 13, sub-section (1), of the Act:

2. It shall state the holding and result of the election, and shall briefly state the facts and grounds relied on to sustain the prayer.

3. The petition shall be divided into paragraphs, each of which, as nearly as may be, shall be confined to a distinct portion of the subject, and every paragraph shall be numbered consecutively, and no costs shall be allowed of drawing or copying any petition not substantially in compliance with this rule, unless otherwise ordered by the Court of Common Pleas or a judge at chambers.

4. The petition shall conclude with a prayer, as, for instance, that some specified person should be declared duly returned or elected, or that the election should be declared void, or that a return may be enforced (as the case may be), and shall be signed by all the petitioners.

5. The following form, or one to the like effect, shall be sufficient :—

In the Common Pleas.

"The Municipal Elections Act, 1872."

Election for [*state the place and office for which election held*]
holden on the   day of   A. D.

The petition of *A.* of   [*or of A.* of
                , and *B.* of
as the case may be] whose names are subscribed.

1. Your petitioner *A.* is a person who voted [*or* had a right to vote, *as the case may be*] at the abov᠎ election [*or* was a candidate at the above election] ; and your petitioner *B.* [*here state in like manner the right of each petitioner*].

2. And your petitioners state that the election was holden on the   day of   A.D.
                , when *A. B.*, *C. D.*, and *E. F.*, were candidates, and that *A. B.* and *C. D.* have been in the usual manner declared to be duly elected.

3. And your petitioners say that [*here state the facts and grounds on which the petitioners rely*].

Wherefore your petitioners pray that it may be determined that the said *A. B.* was not duly elected, and that the election was void [*or that the said E. F.* was duly elected and ought to have been returned, *or as the case may be*].

(Signed)   *A.*
                B.

201

6. Evidence need not be stated in the petition, but the Court of Common Pleas or a judge at chambers may order such particulars as may be necessary to prevent surprise and unnecessary expense, and to insure a fair and effectual trial in the same way as in ordinary proceedings in the Court of Common Pleas, and upon such terms as to costs and otherwise as may be ordered.

7. When a petitioner claims the office for an unsuccessful candidate, alleging that he had a majority of lawful votes, the party complaining of or defending the election shall, six days before the day appointed for trial, deliver to the Master and also at the address, if any, given by the petitioners and respondent, as the case may be, a list of votes intended to be objected to, and of the heads of objection to each such vote, and the Master shall allow inspection and office copies of such lists to all parties concerned; and no evidence shall be given against the validity of any vote, nor upon any head of objection not specified in the list, except by leave of the Court of Common Pleas or a judge at chambers, upon such terms as to amendment of the list, postponement of the inquiry, and payment of costs as may be ordered.

8. When the respondent in a petition under the Act complaining of an undue election, and claiming the office for some person, intends to give evidence to prove that the election of such person was undue, pursuant to the 15th section of the Act, sub-section 9, such respondent shall, six days before the day appointed for trial, deliver to the Master, and also at the address, if any, given by the petitioner, a list of the objections to the election upon which he intends to rely, and the Master shall allow inspection and office copies of such lists to all parties concerned; and no evidence shall be given by a respondent of any objection to the election not specified in the list, except by leave of the Court of Common Pleas or a judge at chambers, upon such terms as to amendments of the list, postponement of the inquiry, and payment of costs, as may be ordered.

9. With the petition petitioners shall leave at the office of the Master a writing, signed by them or on their behalf, giving the name of some person entitled to practise as an attorney in the Court of Common Pleas, whom they authorise to act as their agent, or stating that they act for themselves, as the case may be, and in either case giving an address, within three miles from the General Post Office, at which notices addressed

to them may be left; and if no such writing be left or address given, then notice of objection to the recognizances and all other notices and proceedings, may be given by sticking up the same at the Master's office.

10. Any person elected to any municipal office may at any time after he is elected send or leave at the office of the Master a writing, signed by him or on his behalf, appointing a person entitled to practise as an attorney in the Court of Common Pleas to act as his agent in case there should be a petition against him, or stating that he intends to act for himself, and in either case giving an address within ·three miles from the General Post Office at which notices may be left, and in default of such writing being left in a week after service of the petition, notices and proceedings may be given and served respectively by sticking up the same at the Master's office.

11. The Master shall keep a book or books at his office in which he shall enter all addresses and the names of agents given under either of the preceding rules, which book shall be open to inspection by any person during office hours.

12. The Master shall, upon the presentation of the petition, forthwith send a copy of the petition to the town clerk, pursuant to section 13 of the Act, subsection (1), and shall therewith send the name of the petitioner's agent, if any, and of the address, if any, given as prescribed, and also of the name of the respondent's agent, and the address, if any, given as prescribed, and the town clerk shall forthwith publish those particulars along with the petition.

The cost of publication of this and any other matter required to be published by the town clerk shall be paid by the petitioner or person moving in the matter, and shall form part of the general costs of the petition.

13. The time for giving notice of the presentation of a petition and of the nature of the proposed security shall be five days, exclusive of the day of presentation.

14. Where the respondent has named an agent or given an address, the service of a municipal election petition may be by delivery of it to the agent or by posting it in a registered letter to the address given at such time, that in the ordinary course of post it would be delivered within the prescribed time.

In other cases the service must be personal on the respondent, unless a judge at chambers on an application made to him not later than five days after the petition is presented on affidavit, showing what has been done, shall be satisfied that all reasonable effort has been made to effect personal service and cause the matter to come to the knowledge of the respondent, in which case the judge may order that what has been done shall be considered sufficient service, subject to such conditions as he may think reasonable.

15. In case of evasion of service the sticking up a notice in the office of the Master of the petition having been presented, stating the petitioner, the prayer, and the nature of the proposed security, shall be deemed equivalent to personal service if so ordered by a judge.

16. The deposit of money by way of security for payment of costs, charges, and expenses payable by the petitioner, shall be made by payment into the Bank of England to an account to be opened there by the description of "The Corrupt Practices Municipal Elections Act, 1872, Security Fund," which shall be vested in and drawn upon from time to time by the Chief Justice of the Common Pleas for the time being, for the purposes for which security is required by the said Act, and a bank receipt or certificate for the same shall be forthwith left at the Master's office.

17. The Master shall file such receipt or certificate, and keep a book open to inspection of all parties concerned, in which shall be entered from time to time the amount and the petition to which it is applicable.

18. The recognizance as security for costs may be acknowledged before a judge at chambers or the Master in town, or a justice of the peace in the country.

There may be one recognizance acknowledged by all the sureties, or separate recognizances by one or more, as may be convenient.

19. The recognizance shall contain the name and usual place of abode of each surety, with such sufficient description as shall enable him to be found or ascertained, and may be as follows : —

Be it remembered that on the   day of   , in the year of our Lord 18   , before me [*name and description*] came *A. B.*, of [*name and description as above prescribed*], and acknowledged himself [*or* severally acknowledged themselves] to owe to our Sovereign Lady the Queen the sum of five hundred pounds [*or* the following sums], (that is to say) the said *C.D.* the sum of £   , the said *E. F.* the sum of £   , the said *G.H.* the sum of £   , and the said *J. K.* the sum of £   , to be levied on his [*or* their respective] goods and chattels, land and tenements, to the use of our said Sovereign Lady the Queen, her heirs and successors.

The condition of this recognizance is that if [*here insert the names of all the petitioners, and if more than one, add*, or any of them] shall well and truly pay all costs, charges, and expenses in respect of the election petition signed by him [*or* them] relating to the [*here insert the name of the borough*] which shall become payable by the petitioner [*or* petitioners, or any of them] under the Corrupt Practices Municipal Elections Act, 1872, to any person or persons, then this recognizance to be void, otherwise to stand in full force.

(Signed)

[*Signature of sureties.*]

Taken and acknowledged by the above-named [*name of sureties*] on the   day of at   .   , before me,

C.D.

A justice of the peace [*or as the case may be*].

20. The recognizance or recognizances shall be left at the Master's office, by or on behalf of the petitioners, in like manner as before prescribed for the leaving of a petition forthwith after being acknowledged.

21. The time for giving notice of any objection to a recognizance under the 13th section of the Act, sub-section (4) shall, be within five days from the date of service of the notice of the petition and of the nature of the security, exclusive of the day of service.

22. An objection to the recognizance must state the ground or grounds thereof, as that the sureties, or any and which of them, are insufficient, or that a surety is dead, or that he cannot be found, or that a person named in the recognizance has not duly acknowledged the same.

23. Any objection made to the security shall be heard and decided by the Master, subject to appeal within five days to a Judge, upon summons taken out by either party to declare the security sufficient or insufficient.

24. Such hearing and decision may be either upon affidavit or personal examination of witnesses, or both, as the Master or Judge may think fit.

25. If by order made upon such summons the security be declared sufficient, its sufficiency shall be deemed to be established within the meaning of the 13th section of the said Act, and the petition shall be at issue

26. If by order made upon such summons an objection be allowed and the security be declared insufficient, the Master or judge shall in such order state what amount he deems requisite to make the security sufficient, and the further prescribed time to remove the objection by deposit shall be within five days from the date of the order, not including the day of the date, and such deposit shall be made in the manner already prescribed.

27. The costs of hearing and deciding the objections made to the security given shall be paid as ordered by the Master or judge, and in default of such order shall form part of the general costs of the petition.

28. The costs of hearing and deciding an objection upon the ground of insufficiency of a surety or sureties shall be paid by the petitioner, and a clause to that effect shall be inserted in the order declaring its sufficiency or insufficiency, unless at the time of leaving the recognizance with the Master there be also left with the Master an affidavit of the sufficiency of the surety or sureties sworn by each surety before a justice of the peace, which affidavit any justice of the peace is hereby authorised to take, or before some person authorised to take affidavits in the Court of Common Pleas, that he is seised or possessed of real or personal estate, or both, above what will satisfy his debts, of the clear value of the sum for which he is bound by his recognizance, which affidavit may be as follows :

In the Common Pleas.

Corrupt Practices Municipal Elections Act, 1872.

I, *A.B.* [*as in recognizance*], make oath and say that I am seised or possessed of real [*or* personal estate] above what will satisfy my debts, of the clear value of £.

Sworn, &c.

29. The order of the Master for payment of costs shall have the same force as an order made by a judge, and may be made a rule of the Court of Common Pleas and enforced in like manner as a judge's order.

30. The Master shall make out the municipal election list. In it he shall insert the name of the agents of the petitioners and respondent, and the addresses to which notices may be sent, if any. The list may be inspected at the Master's office at any time during office hours, and shall be put up for that purpose upon a notice board appropriated to proceedings under the said Act, and headed "Municipal Election List."

31. The time of the trial of each municipal election petition shall be fixed by the election judges on the rota, or any one of them, who shall signify the same to the Master, and notice thereof shall be given in writing by the Master by sticking notice up in his office, sending one copy by post to the address given by the petitioner, another to the address given by the respondent, if any, and a copy by the post to the town clerk of the borough to which the petition relates, fifteen days before the day appointed for the trial.

The town clerk shall forthwith publish the same in the borough.

32. The sticking up of the notice of trial at the office of the Master shall be deemed and taken to be notice in the prescribed manner within the meaning of the Act, and such notice shall not be vitiated by any miscarriage of or relating to the copy or copies thereof to be sent as already directed.

33. The notice of trial may be in the following form :—

Corrupt Practices Municipal Election Act, 1872.
    Election petition of
      Borough of
    Take notice that the above petition [*or* petitions] will be tried at   on the   day of   and on such other subsequent days as may be needful.

    Dated the   day of

        Signed, by order,
          A.B.,
    The Master appointed under the above Act.

34. A judge may from time to time, by order made upon the application of a party to the petition, or by notice in such form as the judge may direct to be sent to the town clerk, postpone the beginning of the trial to such day as he may name, and such notice when received shall be forthwith made public by the town clerk.

35. In the event of the barrister to whom the trial of the petition is assigned not having arrived at the time appointed for the trial, or to which the trial is postponed, the commencement of the trial shall *ipso facto* stand adjourned to the ensuing day, and so from day to day.

36. No formal adjournment of the court for the trial of a municipal election petition shall be necessary, but the trial is to be deemed adjourned, and may be continued from day to day until the inquiry is concluded.

37. The application to state a special case may be made by rule in the Court of Common Pleas when sitting, or by a summons before a Judge at chambers, upon hearing the parties.

38. The title of the court held for the trial of a municipal election petition may be as follows:—

> " Court for the trial of a municipal election
>   petition for the borough of [*or*
>   *as may be*] between
>   petitioner and
>   respondent,"

and it shall be sufficient so to entitle all proceedings in that court.

39. An officer shall be appointed for each court for the trial of a municipal election petition by the election judges, at the time that they assign the petition to the barrister; such officer shall attend at the trial in like manner as the clerks of assize and of arraigns attend at the assizes.

Such officer may be called the registrar of that court. He, by himself. or, in case of need, his sufficient deputy, shall perform all the functions incident to the officer of a court of record, and also such duties as may be prescribed to him.

40. The reasonable costs of any witness shall be ascertained by the registrar of the court, and the certificate allowing them shall be under his hand, unless the court shall otherwise order.

41. The order of the court to compel the attendance of a person as a witness may be in the following form :

> Court for the trial of a municipal election petition
>   for [*complete the title of the court*] the
>   day of   . To *A.B.* [*describe the person*].
>   You are hereby required to attend before the
>   above court at [*place*] on   day of
>   at the hour of [*or* forthwith, *as the case
>   may be*], to be examined as a witness in the matter
> of the said petition, and to attend the said court
> until your examination shall have been completed.

> As witness my hand, *A.B.*,
>   The barrister to whom the trial of the
>   said petition is assigned.

42. In the event of its being necessary to commit any person for contempt, the warrant may be as follows:

At a court holden on　　　　　　　at
　　for the　trial of a municipal election petition for
　　the borough of　　　　　　　before *A.B.*,
　　one of the barristers appointed for the trial of
　　municipal election petitions, pursuant to "The
　　Corrupt Practices Municipal Elections Act,
　　1872."

Whereas *C.D.*, has this day been guilty, and is by
the said court adjudged to be guilty, of a contempt
thereof. The said court does therefore sentence the
said *C. D.* for his said contempt to be imprisoned in
the　　　　　　　　gaol for　　　　calendar
months [*or as may be*], and to pay to our Lady the
Queen £ fine of　　, and to be further imprisoned in
the said gaol until the said fine be paid, and the court
further orders that the sheriff of the borough [*if any,
or as the case may be*], and all constables and officers
of the peace of any county, borough, or place where
the said *C.D.*, may be found, shall take the said
C.D., or into custody and convey him to the said gaol,
and there deliver him into the custody of the gaoler
thereof, to undergo his said sentence; and the court
further orders the said gaoler to receive the said *C.D.*,
into his custody, and that he shall be detained in the
said gaol in pursuance of the said sentence.

　　　　　　　　　　　　　　　A.B.
　　　　Signed the　　　　　day of
　　　　　　　　　　　　　　　A.B.

43. Such warrant may be made out and directed to
the sheriff or other person having the execution of
process of the superior courts, as the　case may be,
and to all constables and officers of the peace of the
county, borough, or place where the person adjudged
guilty of contempt may be found, and such warrant
shall be sufficient without further particularity, and
shall and may be executed by the persons to whom it
is directed or any or either of them.

44. All interlocutory questions and matters, except
as to the sufficiency of the security, shall be heard and
disposed of before a judge, who shall have the same
control over the proceedings under the Corrupt
Practices Municipal Elections Act, 1872, as a judge at
chambers in the ordinary proceedings of the superior
courts, and such questions and matters shall be heard
and disposed of then by any judge at chambers.

45. Notice of an application for leave to withdraw a
petition shall be in writing and signed by the petitioners or their agent.

It shall state the ground on which the application is intended to be supported.

The following form shall be sufficient :—

Corrupt Practices Municipal Elections Act, 1872.

Borough of   Petition of [*state petitioners*]
    presented   day of   .

The petitioner proposes to apply to withdraw his petition upon the following ground [*here state the ground*], and prays that a day may be appointed for hearing his application.   Dated this day of

(Signed)

46.   The notice of application for leave to withdraw shall be left at the Master's office.

47.   A copy of such notice of the intention of the petitioner to apply for leave to withdraw his petition shall be given by the petitioner to the respondent, and to the town clerk, who shall make it public in the borough to which it relates, and shall be forthwith published by the petitioner in at least one newspaper circulating in the place.

The following may be the form of such notice :—

Corrupt Practices Municipal Elections Act, 1872.

In the Election Petition for   in which
          is petitioner and
    respondent.

Notice is hereby given, that the above petitioner has on the   day of
lodged at the Master's office notice of an application to withdraw the petition, of which notice the following is a copy [*set it out*].

And take notice that by the rule made by the judges, any person who might have been a petitioner in respect of the said election may, within five days after publication by the town clerk of this notice, give notice in writing of his intention on the hearing to apply for leave to be substituted as a petitioner

(Signed)

48.   Any person who might have been a petitioner in respect of the election to which the petition relates, may, within five days after such notice is published by the returning officer, give notice, in writing, signed by him or on his behalf, to the Master of his intention to

210

apply at the hearing to be substituted for the petitioner, but the want of such notice shall not defeat such application if in fact made at the hearing.

49. The time and place for hearing the application shall be fixed by a judge, and whether before the Court of Common Pleas, or before a judge, as he may deem advisable, but shall not be less than a week after the notice of the intention to apply has been given to the Master as hereinbefore provided, and notice of the time and place appointed for the hearing shall be given to such person or persons, if any, as shall have given notice to the Master of an intention to apply to be substituted as petitioners, and otherwise in such manner and at such time as the judge directs.

50. Notice of abatement of a petition, by death of the petitioner or surviving petitioner, under section 17, sub-section 5, of the said Act, shall be given by the party or person interested in the same manner as a notice of an application to withdraw a petition, and the time within which application may be made to the Court of Common Pleas or a judge at chambers by motion or summons at chambers, to be substituted as a petitioner, shall be one calendar month, or such further time as upon consideration of any special circumstances the Court of Common Pleas or a judge at chambers may allow.

51. If the respondent dies, any person entitled to be a petitioner under the Act in respect of the election to which the petition relates, may give notice of the fact in the borough by causing such notice to be published in at least one newspaper circulating therein, if any, and by leaving a copy of such notice signed by him or on his behalf with the town clerk, and a like copy with the Master.

52. The manner and time of the respondent's giving notice that he does not intend to oppose the petition, shall be by leaving notice thereof in writing at the office of the Master signed by the respondents six days before the day appointed for trial exclusive of the day of leaving such notice.

53. Upon such notice being left at the Master's office, the Master shall forthwith send a copy thereof by the post to the petitioner or his agent, and to the town clerk, who shall cause the same to be published in the borough.

54. The time for applying to be admitted as a respondent in either of the events mentioned in the 18th section of the Act shall be within ten days after such

notice is given as hereinbefore directed, or such further time as the Court of Common Pleas or a judge at chambers may allow.

55. Costs shall be taxed by the Master, or at his request by any Master of a superior court, upon the rule of court or judge's order by which the costs are payable, and costs when taxed may be recovered by execution issued upon the rule of court ordering them to be paid; or, if payable by the order of a judge, then by making such order a rule of court in the ordinary way and issuing execution upon such rule against the person by whom the costs are ordered to be paid, or in case there be money in the bank available for the purpose, then to the extent of such money by order of the Chief Justice of the Common Pleas for the time being upon a duplicate of the rule of court.

The office fees payable for inspection, office copies, enrolment, and other proceedings under the Act and these rules, shall be the same as those payable, if any, for like proceedings according to the present practice of the Court of Common Pleas.

56. An agent employed for the petitioner or respondent shall forthwith leave written notice at the office of the Master, of his appointment to act as such agent, and service of notices and proceedings upon such agent shall be sufficient for all purposes.

57. No proceeding under the Corrupt Practices Municipal Elections Act, 1872, shall be defeated by any formal objection.

58. Any rule made or to be made in pursuance of the Act, if made in term time shall be published by being read by the Master in the Court of Common Pleas, and if made out of term by a copy thereof being put up at the master's office.

Additional General Rules made 10th day of December, 1872.

59. All claims at law or in equity to money deposited or to be deposited in the Bank of England for payment of costs, charges and expenses payable by the Petitioners pursuant to the 16th General Rule, made the 20th day of November, 1872, by the Judges for the trial of Election Petitions in England, shall be disposed of by the Court of Common Pleas or a Judge at Chambers.

60. Money so deposited shall, if, and when the same is no longer needed for securing payment of such costs, charges and expenses, be returned or otherwise

disposed of as justice may require, by Rule of the Court of Common Pleas or Order of a Judge at Chambers.

61. Such Rule or Order may be made after such notice of intention to apply, and proof that all just claims have been satisfied or otherwise sufficiently provided for, as the Court of Common Pleas or Judge at Chambers may require.

62. The Rule or Order may direct payment either to the party in whose name the same is deposited, or to any person entitled to receive the same.

63. Upon such Rule or Order being made, the amount may be drawn for by the Chief Justice of the Common Pleas for the time being.

64. The draft of the Chief Justice of the Common Pleas for the time being shall in all cases be a sufficient warrant to the Bank of England for all payments made thereunder.

65. The Barrister engaged may appoint a proper person to act as Crier and Officer of the Court.

66. The Shorthand writer to attend at the trial of a Petition shall be the Shorthand writer to the House of Commons for the time being or his deputy, and the Master shall send a copy of the Notice of Trial to the said Shorthand writer to the House of Commons.

Additional General Rules made the 27th day of January, 1875.

67. A copy of every order (other than an order giving further time for delivering particulars, or for costs only), or, if the Master shall so direct, the order itself or a duplicate thereof, also a copy of every particular delivered, shall be forthwith filed with the Master, and the same shall be produced at the trial by the Registrar, stamped with the official seal. Such order and particular respectively shall be filed by the party obtaining the same.

68. The Petitioner or his agent shall, immediately after notice of the presentation of a Petition and of the nature of the proposed security shall have been served, file with the Master an affidavit of the time and manner of service thereof.

69. The days mentioned in rules 7 and 8, and in any rule of court or Judge's order, whereby particulars are ordered to be delivered, or any act is directed to be done, so many days before the day appointed for trial, shall be reckoned exclusively of the day of delivery, or of doing the act ordered and the day appointed for

trial, and exclusively also of Sunday, Christmas Day, Good Friday, and any day set apart for a public fast or public thanksgiving.

70. When the last day for presenting petitions or filing lists of votes or objections, under rules 7 and 8, or recognizances, or any other matter required to be filed within a given time, shall happen to fall on a holiday, the petition or other matter shall be deemed duly filed if put into the letter box at the Master's office at any time during such day; but an affidavit, stating with reasonable precision the time when such delivery was made, shall be filed on the first day after the expiration of the holidays.

71. Rule 40 is hereby revoked, and in lieu thereof it is ordered that the amount to be paid to any witness whose expenses shall be allowed by the Barrister trying the petition shall be ascertained and certified by the Registrar; or in the event of his becoming incapacitated from giving such certificate, by the Barrister.

72. After receiving notice of the petitioner's intention to apply for leave to withdraw, or of the respondent's intention not to oppose, or of the abatement of the petition by death, or of the happening of any of the events mentioned in the 18th section of the Act, if such notice be received after notice of trial shall have been given, and before the trial has commenced, the Master shall forthwith countermand the notice of trial. The countermand shall be given in the same manner, as near as may be, as the notice of trial.

73. If all the respondents shall give notice of their intention not to oppose the petition, and no other person shall be admitted as a respondent, the Court of Common Pleas or a Judge may either declare the election void or direct the trial to proceed. Notice of such order shall be forthwith given by the Master to the town clerk, and if the election be declared void the office shall be deemed to be vacant fom the first day (not been a dies non) after the date of such order.

The Court or Judge may also make such order as to costs as may be just.

REGISTRATION FORMS,

No. 2.

Notice to be given by the Overseers to (Property) Claimants.

We hereby give notice, that all persons entitled to vote in the election of a knight or knights of the shire for the county (or for the riding, division, &c.) of   , in respect of any property situate wholly or in part within this parish (or township) who are not upon the register of voters now in force, or who, being upon the register, shall not retain the same qualification cr continue in the same place of abode as described in such register, and who are desirous to have their names inserted in the register of voters about to be made for the said county (or riding, &c.), are hereby required to give or send to us, or any of us, on or before the twentieth day of July in this year, a notice in writing by them signed, in which their name and surname at full length, their place of abode, and the particulars of their qualification, must be legibly written, according to the form hereunder set forth. Any person who is upon the present register may also make his claim, if he thinks fit; but it is not necessary that he should do s) if he has the same qualification and place of abode now described in the register

Dated this   day of June in the year   .

(Signed)   A.B. ⎫ Overseers of the Parish
              C.D. ⎬ (or Township) of
              E.F. ⎭

No. 3.

Form of Notice of Claim to be given to the Overseers

To the Overseers of the Parish of   [or Township
              of   ].
I hereby give you notice that I claim to be inserted in the List of Voters for the county of   [or for the
division of the county of   ], and that the particulars of my place of abode and qualification are stated in the columns below.

Dated the   day of   in the year

(Signed)
215

Christian Name and Surname of the Claimant at full length.	Place of Abode.	Nature of Qualification.	Street, lane, or other like place in this parish [or township] and number of house (if any) where the property is situate, or name of the property (if known by any), or name of the occupying tenant; or if the qualification consist of a rent charge, then the names of the owners of the property out of which such rent is issuing, or some of them, and the situation of the property

No. 4.

Notice of Claim to be given to the Overseers by £12 Occupier, omitted from the separate List, before 25th August.

6 Vic. c. 18, s. 15.   31 & 32 Vic. c. 58, s. 17.

To the Overseers of the Parish of   [or Township of   ].

I hereby give you notice that I claim to have my name inserted in the List of Voters for the county of   (or for the riding or division of the county of   ), and that the particulars of my place of abode and qualification are stated in the columns below.

Dated this   day of   in the year One Thousand Eight Hundred and

(Signed)

Christian Name and Surname of the Claimant at full length.	Place of Abode.	Nature of Qualification.	Street, lane, or other like place in this parish [or township] and number of house (if any) where the property is situate, or name of the property, if known by any.*

* If for successive occupation, a description of all the premises occupied during the twelve months preceding 31st July should be given.

216

No. 6.

List of Property Claimants.

County of   to wit,) The List of Persons claiming to be
or riding parts or division (entitled to Vote in the Election of a
of the county of   { Knight (or Knights) of the Shire for
as the case may be.   ) the county of   (or for
the riding parts or divisions of the county of   , as the
case may be) in respect of property situate in whole or in part
within the parish of   (or Township, as the case may be).

Margin for entering Overseers' Objections.	Christian Name and Surname of each voter at full length.	Place of Abode.	Nature of Qualification.	Street, lane, or other place in this parish [or township] and number of house (if any) where the property is situate, or name of the property and the name of the tenant; or if the qualification consist of a rent charge, then the names of the owners of the property out of which such rent is issuing, or some of them, and the situation of the property.

(Signed)   *A. B.* } Overseers of the said
       C. D. } Parish (or Township).
       E. F.

6 Vict. c. 18, Sch. A., Form 3.

No. 7..

List of £12 Occupiers.

County of   ) The List of Persons entitled to Vote in the
(or division, &c. of } Election of a Knight (or Knights of the
county of   )) Shire for the county (or division, &c., of the
county) of   in respect of the occupation as owner or
tenant of lands and tenements within the Parish (or Township) of
the rateable value of twelve pounds or upwards.

Christian Name and Surname at full length.	Place of Abode.	Nature of Qualification.	Street, lane, or other like place in this parish [or township] and number of house (if any) where the property is situate.

Dated this   day .of   One Thousand
Eight Hundred and
                    (Signed)   A. B. } Overseers of the Parish
                                     C. D. } (or Township) of

---

No. 8.

Notice of Objection to be given to the Overseers.

To the Overseers of the Parish (*or* Township) of
I hereby give you notice that I object to the name of the person mentioned and described below being retained in the List of Voters for the county (*or* for the division, &c., of the county) of

Christian Name and Surname at full length.	Place of Abode.	Nature of Qualification.	Street, lane, or other like place and number of house (if any) where the property is situate.

Dated this   day of   One Thousand
Eight Hundred and
                    (Signed)   A. B. [*place of abode, &c.*]

No. 10.

List of Persons objected to, to be published by the Overseers.

The following persons have been objected to, as not being entitled to have their names retained in the List of Voters for the

county of   (or for the   riding, parts, or division
of the county of   ).

(Signed)   A.B. ⎫ Overseers of the Parish
           C.D. ⎬ of   (or Town-
           E.F. ⎭ ship, as the case may be).

Christian Name and Surname of each Person objected to.	Place of Abode.	Nature of the supposed Qualification.	Street, lane, or other like place in this parish [or township] and number of house (if any) where the property is situate, or name of the property and name of the tenant; or if the qualification consist of a rent charge, then the names of the owners of the property out of which such rent is issuing, or some of them, and the situation of the property.

ADDITIONAL FORMS,
To be used in Boroughs where the boundaries are coextensive.
PARLIAMENTARY AND MUNICIPAL.
No. I1.
NOTICE OF CLAIM—PARLIAMENTARY.

No.   or   *Ward.*
Division One.

To the Overseers of the Township of   .

I claim to have my name inserted in the List made by you of persons entitled to Vote in the Election of Members to serve in Parliament, for the Parliamentary Borough of   , in respect of the qualification named below.
    Dated the   day of   .

Name of Claimant in full, Surname being first.	Place of Abode.	Nature of Qualification.	Name and Situation of Qualifying Property.

(Signed)

Reg. Forms.

No. 12

NOTICE OF CLAIM—MUNICIPAL.

No. or *Ward.*

Division One Three.

To the Overseers of the Township of .

I claim to have my name inserted in the List made by you of Burgesses of the Municipal Borough of , in respect of the qualification named below.

Dated the day of .

Name of Claimant in full, Surname being first.	Place of Abode.	Nature of Qualification.	Name and Situation of Qualifying Property.

(Signed)

No. 13.

NOTICE OF OBJECTION—PARLIAMENTARY.

No. or *Ward.*

Division One.

To the Overseers of the Township of .

I hereby give you notice that I object to the name of
being retained on the List of Persons entitled to Vote at the Election of Members to serve in Parliament for the Parliamentary Borough of .

Dated this day of .

(Signed) [*place of abode*], on the List of Parliamentary Voters for the Township of , No. , or Ward. Division One.

No. 14.

NOTICE OF OBJECTION—MUNICIPAL.

No.   or   *Ward.*

Division One Three.

To the Overseers of the Township of   .

I hereby give you notice that I object to the name of
being retained on the List of Burgesses of the
Municipal Borough of   .

Dated this   day of   .

(Signed)   [*place of abode*], on
the List of Burgesses for the Town-
ship of   , No.   , or
Ward.   Division One Three.

No. 15.

NOTICE OF OBJECTION—PARLIAMENTARY.

No.   or   *Ward.*

Division One,

To Mr.   ,   *Street,*   .

I hereby give you notice that I object to your name being
retained on the Lists of Persons entitled to Vote at the Election
of Members to serve in Parliament for the Parliamentary Borough
of   , on the following grounds:—

1. That you have not occupied for twelve months to July
   15th, 188 .
2. . . . .
3. . . . .
4. . . . .
5. . . . .
6. . . . .
7. . . . .
8. . . . .
9. . . . .

Dated this   day of   .

(Signed)   [*place of abode*], on
the List of Parliamentary Voters for
the Township of   , No. , or
Ward.   Division One.

No. 16.

NOTICE OF OBJECTION—MUNICIPAL.

No.   or   *Ward.*

Division One Three.

To Mr.   ,   *Street,*   .

I hereby give you notice that I object to your name being retained on the Lists of Burgesses of the Municipal Borough of , on the following grounds, viz. :—

1. That you have not occupied for twelve months to July 15th, 188 .
2. ....
3. ....
4. ....
5. ....
6. ....
7. ....
8. ....
9. ....

Date l this   day of   1879.

(Signed)   [*place of abode*], on the List of Burgesses for the Township of   , No.   , or Ward. Division One Three.

No. 17.

Notice of Objection to Parties inserted in the List of the Livery.

To Mr.

I hereby give you notice that I object to your name being retained in the List of Persons entitled to Vote as Freemen of the City of London and Liverymen of the Company of   in the election of members for the said City.

Dated the   day of   .

(Signed)   *A. B.* of [*place of abode*], on the List of Voters.

Note.—See 41 and 42 Vic. c. 26, s. 26.

6 Vic. c. 18, Sched. (C), No. 4.

No. 18.

Notice of Objection to be given to the Secondaries of the City of London, and to the Clerks of the respective Livery Companies.

To the Secondaries of the City of London [or to the Clerk] of the Company of .

I hereby give you notice that I object to the name of being retained in the List of Persons entitled to Vote as Freemen of the City of London and Liverymen of the Company of in the election of members for the said City.

Dated this day of .

(Signed) *A.B.* of [*place of abode*], on the List of Voters.

Note.—If the List contains two or more persons of the same name, the notice should distinguish the person intended to be objected to.

6 Vic. c. 18, Sched. (C), No. 5.

No. 19.

List of Freemen, being Liverymen, objected to, to be published by the Secondaries.

The following persons have been objected to as not entitled to have their names retained on the List of persons entitled to vote as Freeman of the City of London and Liverymen of the several Companies, &c.

Christian and Surname of each person objected to.	Place of his abode.	Name of the Company.

Dated, &c. (Signed) *A.B.* *C.D.* { Secondaries of the City of London.

LIST OF
MUNICIPAL AND PARLIAMENTARY
BOROUGHS.

M.—Under the Municipal Corporation Acts.
P.—Parliamentary.
Bound. Coext.—Municipal and Parliamentary, Boundaries co-extensive.
Scot and Lot.—Scot and Lot Voters.
Freem.—Freemen-rights reserved by the Reform Act.
Anc. rig. res.—Ancient rights reserved by the Reform Act.

NOTE.—There are many customs and usages which are observed in different Boroughs with regard to *servitude* which need not be noticed here; but it may be observed that many Tradesmen having reduced the years of apprenticeship from 7 to 5—notably in Liverpool—fewer admissions will take place now than formerly, the Charter of Liverpool and most other towns requiring a servitude of 7 years.

ABERAVON, M. & P.—Contributory — (Swansea district) *Res. Freem., and eldest sons at their death.*

ABERYSTWITH, M. & P.— Contributory — (Cardigan district)— Bound. coext.

ABINGDON, M. & P.—*Scot and lot.*

ACCRINGTON, M.

ADPAR, P.—Contributory—(Cardigan district).

AMLWCH, P. — Contributory — (Beaumaris district).

ANDOVER, M. & P.—*Freem. A few only surviving in 1866, from passing of Reform Act.*

ARUNDEL, M. & P.—Bound. coext.

ASHTON-UNDER-LYNE, M. & P.

AYLESBURY, P.—*Scot and lot.*

BANGOR, P.—Contributory—(Carnarvon district).

BANBURY, M. & P.

BARNSLEY, M.

BARNSTAPLE, M. & P.—*Freem. by serv. and all sons at 21.*

BARROW-IN-FURNESS, M.

BASINGSTOKE, M.—*One Freem. only surviving in 1866, from passing of Reform Act.*

BATH, M. & P.—*Anc. rig. res.*

BATLEY, M. & P.—Contributory with Dewsbury.

BEAUMARIS, M. & P.—Contributory — (Beaumaris district) — Bound. coext. *Two Freem. only surviving in 1866 from passing of Municipal Corporation Act.*

BECCLES, M.

BEDFORD, M. & P.—Bound. coext. *Anc. rig. res. Freem. by serv. and eldest son at 21.*

BERWICK-ON-TWEED, M. & P.— Bound. coext. *Freem. by serv. and all sons at 21.*

BEVERLEY, M. & P.—*Freem. by serv. and all sons at 21.*

BEWDLEY, M. & P.—*Anc. rig. res.*

BIDEFORD, M.

BIRKENHEAD, M. & P.—Bound. coext.

BIRMINGHAM, M. & P.

BLACKBURN, M. & P.

BLACKPOOL, M.

BLANDFORD, M.

BODMIN, M. & P.—*Anc. rig. res.*

BOLTON, M. & P.

BOSTON, M. & P.—*Freem. by serv.*

BOOTLE-*cum*-LINACRE, M.

224

BRADFORD, M. & P.—Bound. coext.
BRECON OR BRECKNOCK, M. & P.
BRIDGNORTH, M. & P.—*Freem. by serv. and all sons at 21.*
BRIDGEWATER, M. & P. Bound. coext. *Scot and lot.*
BRIDPORT, M. & P.—Bound. coext. *Scot and lot.*
BRIGHTON, M. & P.
BRISTOL, M. & P.—*Anc. riy. res. Freem. by serv. and all sons of freem. at 21.*
BUCKINGHAM, M. & P.—*Freem. Two only surviving in 1866, from the passing of the Reform Act.*
BURNLEY, M. & P.
BURSLEM, M, & P.—Contributory with Stoke
BURTON-UPON-TRENT, M.
BURY (Lanc.), M. & P.
BURY ST. EDMUNDS, M. & P.—Bound. coext.
CAERWYS, P. — Contributory — (Flint district).
CAERGWYLE, P.—Contributory—(Flint district).
CALNE, M.—*Anc. riy. res. Three survivors only of the old " Guild Stewards" in 1866.*
CAMBRIDGE, M. & P.—*Freem. by serv. and eldest sons of freem. at 21.*
CANTERBURY, M. & P.—*Freem. by serv. and all sons of freem. at 21.*
CARDIFF, M. & P.—Contributory—(Cardiff district) *Freem. No return made in 1866, a few of the old burgesses surviving.*
CARDIGAN, M. & P.—Contributory—(Cardigan district). *A few old burgesses surviving in 1866, from passing of Reform Act.*
CARLISLE, M. & P.—Bound. coext. *Freem. and all sons of freem. at 21.*
CARMARTHEN, M. & P.—Contributory—(Carmarthen district)—Bound. coext.
CARNARVON, M. & P,—Contributory — (Carnarvon district — Bound. coext.
CEFNLLYS, P. — Contributory — (New Radnor district).
CHARD, M.
CHATHAM, P.
CHELSEA P.

CHELTENHAM, M. & P.
CHESTER, M. & P.—*Freem. by serv. and sons and grandsons of freem. at 21.*
CHESTERFIELD, M.
CHICHESTER, M. & P.—*Two Freem. and eight burgesses only surviving in 1866, from passing of Reform Act. Scot and lot.*
CHIPPENHAM, M. & P.
CHIPPING NORTON, M.
CHIPPING WYCOMBE, M. & P.—*One Freem. only surviving in 1866, from passing of Reform Act.*
CHRISTCHURCH, P.
CIRENCESTER, P.—*Anc. riy. res.*
CLITHEROE, M. & P.—*Anc. riy. res.*
COCKERMOUTH, P.
COLCHESTER, M. & P.—Bound. coext. *Freem. by serv. and sons and grandsons of freem. at 21.*
CONGLETON, M.
CONWAY, M. & P.—Contributory—(Carnarvon district).
COVENTRY, M. & P.—*Freem. by serv.; not necessarily to freem.*
COWBRIDGE, P.—Contributory—(Cardiff district).
CREWE, M.
CRICCIETH, P. — Contributory — (Carnarvon district).
CRICKDALE, P.—*Anc. riy. res.*

DARLINGTON, M. & P.—Bound. coext.
DARTMOUTH, M. & P.—Bound. coext. *One surviving Freem. only in 1866.*
DAVENTRY, M.
DEAL, M. & P.—Contributory with Sandwich—Bound. coext.
DENBIGH, M.& P.—Contributory—(Denbigh district).
DERBY, M. & P.—*Freem. by serv. and all sons of freem. at 21.*
DEVIZES, M. & P.—Bound coext. *Anc. riy. res.*
DEVONPORT, M. & P.
DEWSBURY, M. & P.—Contributory with Batley.
DONCASTER, M.
DORCHESTER, M. & P.—Bound. coext.
DOVER, M. & P.—Bound. coext. *Freem. by serv. and all sons of freem. born in borough, at 21.*

LEAMINGTON, M.

LEEDS, M. & P.—Bound. coext.

LEICESTER, M. & P.—Bound coext. Scot and lot. Freem. by serv. to freem. and all sons of freem. born after admission of father.

LEOMINSTER, M. & P.—Bound. coext. Anc. rig. res. Scot and lot.

LEWES, P.—Scot and lot.

LICHFIELD, M.& P.—Bound. coext. Anc. rig. res. Burgage owners. Freeholders—Freem. by serv. to freem. of one of the 7 companies and eldest or eldest surviving son at 21.

LINCOLN, M. & P.—Bound. coext. Freem. by serv. and all sons born after admission of father.

LISKEARD, M. & P.

LIVERPOOL, M. & P.—Freem. by serv. to freem. and all sons of freem. who were entitled before 1st March, 1831, by serv. or birth—sons of freem. admitted since then by serv.

LLANDOVERY, M. & P.—Contributory with Carmarthen.

LLANELLY, P. — Contributory — (Carmarthen district).

LLANFYLLEN, M. & P.—Contributory—(Montgomery district).

LLANIDLOES, P.—Contributory—(Montgomery district).

LLANTRISSAINT, P. — Contributory—(Cardiff district). ¹

LLANGEFNI, P. — Contributory—(Beaumaris district).

LONDON, CITY, M. & P.—Freem., being also Liverymen.

LONGTON, M. & P.—Contributory with Stoke.

LOUTH, M.

LOUGHOR, P.— Contributory — (Swansea district).

LUDLOW, M. & P.—Freem., being sons of a "sworn burgess."

LUTON, M.

LYME REGIS, M. & P.—Survivors of Freem. admitted prior to 1st March, 1831.

LYMINGTON, M. & P.

MACCLESFIELD, M. & P.

MACHYNLLETH, P. — Contributory—(Montgomery district).

MAIDENHEAD, M.

MAIDSTONE, M. & P.—Freem. by serv. and all sons of freem., born after father's admission, at 21.

MALDON, M. & P.—Freem. by birth or serv.

MALMESBURY, P.

MALTON, P.—Scot and lot.

MANCHESTER, M. & P.

MARGATE, M.

MARLBOROUGH, M. & P.

MARLOW, Gt., P.—Scot and lot.

MARYLEBONE, P.

MELCOME REGIS, P.—Contributory with Weymouth.

MERTHYR TYDVIL, P.

MIDDLESBOROUGH, M. & P.

MILFORD, P. — Contributory — (Pembroke district).

MIDHURST, P.

MOLD, P. — Contributory — (Flint district).

MONMOUTH, M. & P.—Contributory—(Monmouth dist.)—Bound. coext.

MONTGOMERY, P. — Contributory—(Montgomery district).

MORPETH, M. & P.—Freem. by serv. to freem. or freebrother of a Company, and elected freem. by the Company.

NARBERTH, P. — Contributory — (Pembroke district).

NEATH, M. & P.—Contributory—Bound. coext.—(Swansea district).

NEVIN, P. — Contributory —(Carnarvon district).

NEWARK, M. & P.—Bound. coext. Scot and lot.

NEW RADNOR, P.

NEWBURY, M.

NEWCASTLE-UNDER-LYME, M. & P.—Bound. coext. Freem. by serv. to inhabitant trader and sons and grandsons at 21

NEWCASTLE-UPON-TYNE, M. & P:—Bound coext. Freem. by serv. and all sons at 20 and mariners are allowed to serve at sea.

NEWPORT (I. of W.), M. & P.

NEWPORT (MON.), M. & P.—Contributory with Monmouth and Usk. (Monmouth district)

NEWTOWN, P. — Contributory — (Montgomery district)

NORTHALLERTON, P.—Anc. rig. res.

227

Q 2

NORTHAMPTON, M. & P.—*Scot and lot.*

NORWICH. M, & P.—Bound. coext. *Anc. riy. res. Freeholders—Freem. by serv. and all sons born after father's admission.*

NOTTINGHAM, M. & P.—*Anc. riy. res. Freeholders—Freem. by serv., first-born son of freem. after father's admission, at 21—other sons by serv. whether in Borough or not—sons of other person by serv. in Borough.*

OLDHAM, M. & P.

OSWESTRY, M.

OVER DARWIN, M.

OVERTON, P. — Contributory — (Flint district)

OXFORD, M. & P.—*Freem. by serv. to freem. and all sons of freem. born in the city—unless father has put "a Bond in the Chest," i. e. for payment of Rates, and in that case born elsewhere.*

PEMBROKE, M. & P.—*Freem. by serv. with freem, or descendants and all sons of freem.*

PENRYN M. & P. — Contributory with Falmouth. *Scot and lot.*

PENZANCE, M.

PETERBOROUGH, M. & P.—*Scot and lot.*

PETERSFIELD, P.

PLYMOUTH, M. & P.—*Freem. the first apprentice to a freem. and eldest sons living at father's death.*

PONTEFRACT. M. & P.—*Anc. riy. res. Scot and lot.*

POOLE, M. & P.—Bound. coext.

PORTSMOUTH, M. & P.—Bound. coext. *Freem., only one surviving in 1866, from passing of Reform Act.*

PRESTON, M. & P.—Bound. coext. *Anc. riy. res. Scot and lot.*

PRESTEIGNE, P.—Contributory— (New Radnor district).

PWLLHELI, M. & P.—Contributory—(Carnarvon dist.)—Bound. coext.

RADNOR, P.

READING, M. & P.—Bound coext. *Scot and lot.*

REIGATE, M.

RHUDDLAN, P. — Contributory — (Flint district).

RHAYADER, P. — Contributory — (New Radnor district).

RICHMOND, YORK, M. & P.—*Anc. riy. res. Burgaye owners.*

RIPON, M. & ,P—Bound. coext. *Anc. riy. res. Burgaye owners.*

ROCHDALE, M. & P.

ROCHESTER, M. & P. — Bound. coext. *Freem. by serv. to freem. and eldest sons of freem. born in the city.*

ROMSEY, M.

ROTHERHAM, M.

RUTHIN, M. & P.—Contributory—Bound. coext.—(Denbigh district.)

RYE, M. & P.—*Freem. four only surviving in 1866.*

RYDE, M.

St. ALBAN'S, M.

St. ASAPH, P. — Contributory — (Flint district).

St. IVES (Cornwall), M. & P.—*Scot and lot.*

St. IVES (Huntingdonshire), M.

St. HELENS, M.

SAFFRON WALDEN, M.

SALFORD, M. & P.—Bound coext.

SALISBURY, P.—*Anc. riy. res.*

SANDWICH, M. & P.—Contributory with Deal—Bound. coext. *Freem. by serv. to freem. and all sons of freem. born in borough.*

SARUM (New),,M. & P.—Contributory.

SCARBOROUGH, M. & P.—Bound. coext.

SHAFTESBURY, M.&P.—*Scot and lot*

SHEFFIELD, M. & P.—Bound. coext.

SHOREHAM, (New), P.—*Scot and lot.*

SHREWSBURY, M. & P.—Bound. coext. *Freem. by serv. to a trade of which there is an incorporated Company.*

SOUTH SHIELDS, M. & P.—Bound. coext.

SOUTHAMPTON, M. & P.—Bound. coext. *Freem., a few surviving only from passing of Reform Act. Scot and Lot.*

SOUTHPORT, M.

SOUTH MOLTON, M.

SOUTHWARK, P.—*Scot and lot.*

SOUTHWOLD, M.

STAFFORD, M. & P.—*Freem. by serv. to a resident trader and sons and grandsons of freem. admitted 9th Sept., 1835.*

STALYBRIDGE, M. & P.
STAMFORD, M. & P.—*Scot and lot.*
STOCKPORT, M. & P.—Bound. coext.
STOCKTON-ON-TEES, M, & P.
STOKE-UPON-TRENT, M. & P.—Contributory with Burslem, Hanley, and Longton.
STRATFORD-UPON-AVON, M.
STROUD, P.
SUNDERLAND, M. & P.
SUDBURY, M. & P.—*Freem. by serv. to freem. and all sons of freem. at 21.*
SWANSEA, M. & P.—Contributory—(Swansea district). *Freem. by serv. to freem., and by marriage to freem's. daughter.—See Parliament return,* 1866.
TAMWORTH, M. & P.—*Scot and lot.*
TAUNTON, M. & P.—*Anc. rig. res.*
TAVISTOCK, P.—*Anc. rig. res.*
TENBY, M. & P.—Contributory—(Pembroke district). *Freem., a few surviving only from passing of Reform Act.*
TENTERDEN, M.
TEWKESBURY, M. & P.—Bound. coext. *Anc. rig. res. Freeholders and Burgage owners. Freem. and eldest sons of freem. on roll in* 1866.
THIRSK, P.
THETFORD, M.
TIVERTON, M. & P.—Bound. coext. *Freem., a few survivors only from passing of Municipal Corporation Act.*
TOWER HAMLETS, P.
TORRINGTON (Great), M.
TOTNES.
TRURO, M. & P.—Bound. coext. *Freem., only one survivor in* 1866.
TYNEMOUTH, M. & P.
USK, P.—Contributory—(Monmouth district).
WAKEFIELD, M. & P.—Bound. coext.

WALLINGFORD, M. & P.—*Scot and lot.*
WALSALL, M. & P.
WAREHAM, P.—*Scot and lot.*
WARRINGTON, M. & P.
WARWICK, M. & P.—*Scot and lot.*
WELLS, M.
WELSHPOOL, M. (under Ancient Charter) & P — Contributory — (Montgomery district).
WEDNESBURY, P.
WENLOCK, M. & P.—Bound. coext. *Freem. and sons of freem.*
WESTBURY, P.
WESTMINSTER, P.—*Scot and lot.*
WEYMOUTH, M. & P.—Contributory with Melcombe Regis—Bound. coext. *Scot and lot.*
WISTON, P.—Contributory—(Pembroke district)
WHITBY, P.
WHITEHAVEN, P.
WIGAN, M. & P.—Bound. coext *Freem. elected before the passing of the Reform Act; since then none elected. None now on list.*
WILTON, P.
WINCHESTER, M. & P.—Bound. coext. *Freem., two only surviving in* 1866, *from passing of Reform Act.*
WINDSOR, M. & P.—*Scot and lot.*
WISBEACH. M.
WISTON, P.—Contributory—(Pembroke district).
WOLVERHAMPTON, M. & P.
WOODSTOCK, P.
WORCESTER, M. & P.—*Freem. by serv. to freem. and eldest sons of freem. admitted before 1st March,* 1831, *and since then eldest sons of freem. who have been admitted by serv.*
WREXHAM, M. & P.—Contributory—(Denbigh district).
WYCOMBE (see CHIPPING WYCOMBE.)

www.ingramcontent.com/pod-product-compliance
Lightning Source LLC
Chambersburg PA
CBHW030858270326
41929CB00008B/480